£4.39
.8 5.0

CHB8525475

TAROT

Didier Colin

TAROT

READING THE FUTURE

5,000 responses
for effective readings

HACHETTE
Illustrated

Layout by Michel Méline and Jean-Claude Marguerite
English edition designed by Chris Bell
Cover by Graph'M

© Hachette 1990
This edition © Hachette Pratique 2001
This edition published by
Hachette Illustrated UK, Octopus Publishing Group,
2–4 Heron Quays, London E14 4JP

English translation produced by JMS Books LLP
Translation © Octopus Publishing Group

A CIP catalogue for this book is available from the British Library

ISBN: 1 84202 185 0

Printed in China

'... nothing is unique, because everything can be seen and recounted in as many different ways as there have been, there are, or there will, be people to tell it.'

Carlos Fuentes, *Terra Nostra*

Contents

Introduction

There are as many possible interpretations of reality as there are people on Earth. Consequently, it might seem foolish, presumptuous or even arrogant to put forward one's own interpretation of reality. After all, we can only see what is given to us to see.

Yet, blinded as we are by our fantasies and illusions, we no longer know how to see what is under our very noses. And when we want to see – that is when we have a pressing need to see, to know, to understand – and are effectively given the ability to do so, we are so impatient, so sure of finding answers anywhere but within ourselves, that we no longer even recognize the limits of our capacity to see and understand because we have lost touch with our spiritual selves.

The intensity and acuity of our vision is proportionate to our level of consciousness. We are fascinated by the apparent ability of 'clairvoyants' to see and interpret past, present and future events with varying degrees of accuracy. Since we ourselves have only a very hazy notion of the space-time continuum, we are easily impressed by their revelations and pronouncements, which seem to echo our own grasp of the facts of our existence.

Personally, I believe that our wonder at the power of the 'clairvoyant' is a retrograde feeling that drags us down, takes us back, outside of ourselves. It evokes faculties now largely dormant in modern man, which have no doubt been beneficial at some stage in our evolution, but are no longer needed. It is likely that, as these faculties waned, our intellectual and individuated capacities have evolved, locking us into a subjective interpretation of reality, forcing us to project our own vision of the world and to become aware of our own individuality.

Consequently, we are trapped in the labyrinth of our thoughts and ideas. The intellect is the tool that helps us to see and to abandon the illusory world in which we lived. It situates us at the centre of things. 'Seeing' or 'clairvoyance' is simply an external scrutiny of the past, present and future events that are nuanced in our lives, that react to – but do not originate – the movement of our lives.

This nuance is important if one wishes to understand that intellect and self-knowledge bring responsibility. We are able to exercise free will as conscious and creative beings, to act with a complete sense of 'being' from the moment we are born and set off on life's path. By contrast, the pronouncements of 'clairvoyants' render us mere bystanders, passive spectators as our lives play out, bearing no responsibility for what happens to us.

Life is an obstacle race. The events we experience and the circumstances of our lives help us, indeed, force us to become fully aware of our handicaps, although if we act only in accordance with these handicaps, we will never overcome them.

There is an alternative: either we can adopt a passive and meek attitude, surrendering to fate, a divine being or some other form of support, or we can opt for awareness and responsibility, by looking inwards and seeking within ourselves for the means of overcoming our limitations.

The things that happen to us, the situations in which we find ourselves, and the circumstances we encounter throughout our life are fundamental to us. They force us to confront our true natures, to take account of our conditioned reflexes and habitual reactions to events.

Because of them – or thanks to them – we can understand what is happening within us and can assess the consequences of our actions. Just as with history, the events that delineate the history of a life will be repeated so long as we fail to become the architects of our own destiny. We can modify the course of events, influence the evolution of a situation or transform the circumstances of our lives if we approach them from a different perspective, seeking and identifying the moment when we acted or reacted erroneously. Armed with this awareness, we need no longer blame inappropriate behaviour but can recognize how we have adopted one attitude rather than another at a particular time.

Generally, this inappropriate attitude is a reflex that we fail to master simply because we are not aware of it. We can always try to untangle the unconscious mechanisms that drive us to act or react in a particular way but, while this may be interesting and temporarily therapeutic, it also leads to a certain amount of complacency. It offers too many excuses to blame things we feel are beyond our control – such as events and circumstances in our past, or the behaviour of those with whom we have been involved – for the causes of our present faulty behaviour.

This interrogation of one's self – this quest for self – should arise spontaneously from a painful, stressful situation or difficult circumstances as they occur, rather than in hindsight. These are the real indicators of the current state of our consciousness. To look for a way out by seeking in our past for solutions or justifications for our problems resolves nothing in our present and leaves us uncertain as to our future. It is therefore here and now, in the present, that we must learn to think and act differently, making use of qualities, resources and skills at our disposal, which we may have neglected or failed to appreciate. Dismantling a faulty or negative state of mind can be very damaging, leading to a great emptiness out of which we feel powerless to drag ourselves.

Furthermore, by acting in this way, we are torn between what we should consider either in a positive or negative light. This in itself makes our psychological, emotional and moral situation even more complex and confusing, aggravating a lack of clear-sightedness and spontaneity. However, if we can find in ourselves a spark of intuition and creativity to set in motion a new mechanism – better adapted to our present state, and that we are potentially capable of assuming – then the reflexive behavioural patterns will disappear spontaneously, leaving a new state of mind that allows us to act or react in a more appropriate manner.

This 'magical transformation' – which is in some ways an echo of the fairy story of the frog turned into a prince by a kiss – is something that we can all achieve. There is no need for extraordinary circumstances or particular rituals in order for this revolution to take place within us. For each individual, it represents a fundamental discovery and a new approach to relationships, money, society, culture and religion – all those areas where creativity, fairness and humanity are so little favoured or valued.

Our distrust of the esoteric arts is reinforced by the blind faith that people often place in their practitioners, particularly when the latter are not always worthy of this trust. It is exacerbated by the way these arts are often presented by the media, which has created an outdated and artificial image that detracts from the importance of their role in the evolution of self-knowledge, while leaving us ignorant of their history.

Everything related to the basic tenets of the esoteric arts – whether we are talking about magic, alchemy, astrology, divination or religious and initiatory rituals – can be learned. And, since the esoteric arts are such an integral part of our culture, they could even be taught in schools alongside mathematics or human sciences. However, everything related to our interpretation of these arts must be learned through initiation. Esotericism diverges from modern science in that the latter is taught according to relatively immutable rules that are universally applicable. We simply learn these rules and put them into practice in order to acquire a basic expertise in the subject. On the other hand, simply learning the fundamental rules of esotericism is not sufficient to enable you to practise a divinatory art.

Just as knowing how to read music is not sufficient to allow us to interpret the melody, there is no point in learning the symbolic language of esotericism if one does not become proficient in interpreting it and applying it to one's life.

Practitioners of esotericism have not escaped the specialization that seems to be the golden rule of our age. But the language of symbols and myths – which forms the basis of all esoteric practices – does not favour one practice more than another. Astrology, geomancy, numerology, oneiromancy (the interpretation of dreams), Tarot, all start from the same principle. To consider that one or the other of these divinatory arts is more significant than another indicates a lack of clear-sightedness and humility. Too many practitioners of the divinatory arts tend to claim that only astrology, Tarot or numerology, for example, is the true art.

1 'The preoccupation with moral questions is entirely to be created; one discusses the politics that stir up general interest, one discusses private interests, and people become passionate in attacking or defending personalities; systems have their partisans and their detractors; but moral truths, those that are the bread of the soul, the bread of life, are left lying in the dust of centuries. All improvements are useful in the eyes of the masses, except that of the soul; its education, its elevation are pleasant dreams at the most to occupy the leisure of priests, poets and women, dependant on fashion or teaching.' (Jean-Jacques Rousseau, *Reveries of the Solitary Walker*, published by Hackett, 1992)

Thus, when presenting an 'interpretation' of their chosen art, they take care to conceal their sources and the keys of their 'interpretation'. In this way, they maintain the confusion in the minds of those who know, intuitively, that esotericism must surely contain the beginnings of responses to the questions that they are asking, but to which no one will give any simple, commonsensical answers. Esoteric practices and the divinatory arts involve a certain moral vigilance and self-discipline,[1] as well as an almost permanent awareness of those longings and desires which can never be completely satisfied in any one person.

Despite the wealth of information at our disposal we often make use of only a fraction of our knowledge or of our cultural riches. We fail to recognize the body of knowledge and experience that has been acquired over the course of our history and which could help us to understand the human condition. There are those who, through nostalgia or an idealistic view of the past, tend to consider that only ancient civilizations, such as those of the Sumerians, the Egyptians, the Celts or the Greeks, were truly possessed of a noble and authentic sense of the divine. I do not believe that the weaknesses or problems of our ancestors were so very different from those that we experience today. The same worries, the same concerns, the same questions arise eternally, whatever the era, culture or civilization. We always act in the same way to seek the answers that we need. Our fears and basic anxieties with regard to life and death, our difficulties in accepting our human condition are just the same as they ever were.

For many of us today, the esoteric arts are nothing more than superstitious and irrational practices that should be relegated to the past once and for all. Those who consider themselves realistic and rational tend to scorn those who seek their help to bring meaning to their lives. In reality, there is an historical basis to show that everything related to religion, self-knowledge, initiation and faith springs from the esoteric arts. They provided the foundation for astrology, alchemy and the divinatory arts. Even today's sciences have their roots in esotericism[2]. Therefore it is surely not a sign of progress to have lost sight of something that could help bring some meaning to our lives.

It is possible to find in esotericism the evolution and destiny of all things and all beings here on earth. Through esotericism, everything finds its place in a logic that is of the heart, the soul and of inspiration. When we lose our sense of our natural place in the scheme of things, everything falls apart around us and we become prey to perverse and contradictory influences, to isolated and unconnected verities that we cannot trust. Yet this is only because we have been tempted to believe that the truth, the answers to our questions and the solutions to our problems, is to be found outside ourselves, in a reality that we have created to reflect our idea of life and of humanity.

2 Read on this subject *Les Origines sacrées des sciences modernes*, Charles Moraé, published by Éditions Fayard, 1986.

Thus, we live in a veritable mirage of social, material and psychological realities, to which there is no alternative, other than marginality, delinquency, illness or madness. Consequently, it has become more important to be materially successful than to lead a good life and find success on a personal level. In order to dispel the worrying questions that hover at the back of our minds, we fall back on social, ideological, religious or humanitarian practices and ideas that have become the panacea for the modern mind. The threat of unemployment, failure, poverty, illness, death and war, constantly hang over us, haunting our dehumanized and media-led environment that panders to our baser emotions by showing us the full catalogue of nightmares and horrors of which we are still capable.

How have we managed to find ourselves marooned in this vast, complex and pitiless blind alley without any points of reference to anchor us, and no one to talk to?

The esoteric arts are by no means a negligible choice and recourse alongside any of the modern, technological and rational sciences. However, it is still vital that their practitioners do not give in to the temptation to reduce their arts and instruments to current socio-cultural and scientific models, simply to prove themselves and to convince rationalists and sceptics that they have reason to believe that 'it works'.

The Tarot – one of these esoteric arts – is an initiatory and divinatory game, a kind of grammar of the soul that helps us to communicate with ourselves, assists our understanding of the world and facilitates a clear-sighted and intuitive approach to reality.

The earliest known set of Tarot cards was the Indian *Desavatara*, consisting of 120 circular cards, illustrated with symbols inherent in Indian culture, but also common to other cultures – the tortoise, the fish, the lotus, the battle-axe, the bow, the sabre, the knife, the elephant, monkey, cow, tiger, etc. Gypsies and Bohemians, descendants of a caste of untouchables who were driven out of India around the 10th century AD, spread throughout Europe, some to Germany and

Italy, others via North Africa to Spain, later following the silk route that crossed the whole of the Orient, from Samarkand to Venice. They carried with them their *Desavatara* – also known as the *Ganjifa* to the Persians – a divinatory game and art. In this way, the game of Tarot as we know it today, appeared in Renaissance Europe, charged with a symbolism that had been endowed and enhanced by all the different cultures with which it had come in contact.

Divinatory Tarot is both an instrument of meditation and a kind of living reference book. By using the cards in your daily life you are simply engaging in a dialogue with your inner self. The cards themselves provide you with a very rich symbolic language, the fruit of the collective memory, applicable to all situations, all thoughts and desires, and all conditions of the heart and soul.

You may meet people who, despite the fact that they use the Tarot on a daily basis, or make a living from it, say they cannot use and interpret it for themselves. You would be wise not to approach them for a personal reading. After all, if they cannot conceive of having the means to be clairvoyant for themselves, how can they do so for others? Clairvoyance – 'clear seeing' – is not a supernatural state, but rather a spiritual one that takes into account moral, psychological as well as emotional behaviour, and it is easy to understand that some people may be unaware of their natural talents in this direction. By using the divinatory Tarot, you can enter into a new relationship with yourself and learn to understand your inner being, becoming aware of ways in which your conscious self may be at odds with your unconscious self. In order to enjoy the benefits of divinatory Tarot, you must obey certain rules and be prepared to spend some time in study. Finally, correct motivation is also essential to your understanding and mastery of the Tarot. Initially, you will no doubt encounter some natural obstacles and resistance. Some Arcana (Tarot cards) will 'speak' to you, while others will seem impenetrable, disquieting and strange.

Apprenticeship into the Tarot is a journey of initiation that will compel you to become more conscious of yourself and your behaviour, and thus to see the world of illusions in which we live with new clarity. When you have mastered its language and practised it for yourself and for others around you, you will gradually become aware of the conditioned reflexes that drive us, that determine our whole existence, and also of the active part we can play in what happens to us, in the events of our lives. You will then begin to understand that destiny does not depend on fate but on free will, and that it is entirely up to us alone to abandon outdated reactions and behavioural patterns, to become finally, purely and simply what we really are.

However, do not forget that divinatory Tarot is a game, and that it is by playing this game that we become freer and more aware. The apprenticeship to Tarot and the journey towards self-knowledge are games of the soul.

My method of interpretation

My own method of interpretation relies less on actual technique than upon a state of mind.

From a practical point of view, I would advise you to write down your various Tarot card readings in a notebook that you keep for this purpose (some blank pages are also provided at the back of this book). The notes should take the following form:

1 Date of your reading.

2 Write down your question.

3 Make your draw: shuffle the 22 cards of the Major Arcana in your Tarot set, while concentrating hard on your question. Choose four cards at random and arrange them in the order in which you pick them at the four points of an imaginary cross (*see page 41*).

4 Write down the names and numbers of the four cards that you have picked out, then choose a fifth card, by adding together the sum of the numbers of the four cards that you drew initially. If the resulting total is greater than 22, then add together the two digits of the result to give a number equal to or less than 22. This card should be placed in the centre of your cross.

If the number of the fifth card corresponds to one of those you have already drawn, you cannot actually place the card in the centre of your spread, as it already has another position as part of the cross. All the same, you should consider this card to be in the centre, and that this card therefore appears twice in your layout.

Note: The 22nd card, which is known as The Fool, must be counted as zero in adding the sum of the four cards that you have drawn to find the number of the fifth card. Consequently, for example, if you drew the following cards:

First card: I – The Magician

Second card: XVII – The Star

Third card: III – The Empress

Fourth card: XXII – The Fool

the sum of the four numbers of the four Arcana would be:

1 + 17 + 3 + 0 (and not 22) = 21

It is therefore card XXI, The World, which you should place in the centre of your cross-shaped draw, and not card number VII, The Chariot, which would result from the following incorrect calculation:

1 + 17 + 3 + 22 = 43

then add the two digits of this result together:

4 + 3 = 7

5 Following the instructions in this book, interpret your spread, and enter it in your notebook. At first, you will proceed by trial and error but, little by little, you will refine your interpretation, following the advice and information contained in this book.

I would emphasize the fact that you must find 'your' interpretation, using the interpretations presented in this book, drawn from the 22 cards of the Major Arcana, as inspiration.

By writing down the date and composition of your draws and making a note of your questions and interpretations, you can easily review your past concerns and questions. Thus, over time, you will be able to reflect on the nature of your interpretations in relation to what has actually happened in your life. You will be able to draw some useful conclusions from this, and as a result your interpretations will gradually become clearer and more accurate.

The cross-shaped spread

1 The Crucial Moment

'The cross is a symbol that dates from antiquity – it was used in Egypt, China, Knossos in Crete, where a marble cross dating from the 9th century BC was found. The cross is the third of the four basic symbols (according to Chas) along with the centre, the circle and the square.' [1]

The cross can be considered the primary and the ultimate symbol, since the square, the circle and the centre are all demarcated by it. However, its essence lies at the point where the vertical and horizontal lines of the symbol cross each other. This point is the centre where the old and the new come together. On the astral plane, there are forces that pull matter in a certain direction, upwards (Zenith), downwards (Nadir), backwards (Descendant) and forwards (Ascendant). These axes are a symbolic representation of the Christian salutation, the Sign of the Cross, in which a person traces a cross by

1 Jean Chevalier and Alain Gheerbrant, *Dictionnaire des Symboles*, published by Robert Laffont, 1969.

making contact with his centre, i.e., by touching his forehead, breast and left and right shoulders: In the Name of the Father (Zenith), the Son (Nadir) and the Holy Spirit (Descendant), Amen (Ascendant). The 'Amen/Ascendant' connection underlines the importance of self-knowledge and free will, as well as the awareness of one's destiny.

A reading based on an astral spread makes it possible to assess what brings someone closer to, or takes them away from, the centre of themselves. Its elements can indicate the intensity of a person's receptivity or openness to their centre, the place where all energies are concentrated, intensified and directed towards a supra-reality that contains all the realities of this world.

Involuntarily or otherwise, consciously or unconsciously, the centre exerts a powerful attraction. Sooner or later, everything that gravitates around it comes together within it. The doorway may be narrow, but the energy that passes through it is irresistible.

Thus one can understand the importance and the utility of the symbol of the cross in the Tarot layout. It focuses on a crucial moment in our consciousness, defining in symbolic language the state of our soul and mind at a precise moment in our lives. The interpretation of a cross-shaped layout, or spread, goes right to the core reality of a situation that we experience or a concern that we have. In the cross-shaped draw, past, present and future are brought together in a crucial moment of realization and awareness.

2 Meditation

Divinatory Tarot is, above all, an instrument of meditation. By using it we are able to 'divine' the self. In order to do so, we must be free of all worries of a social, material or emotional nature. In our modern world, we are constantly caught up in all sorts of concerns that have a permanent effect on our state of mind. We seem to feel the need to be doing something all the time, be it physically or intellectually, because doing nothing worries us. At the same time, unconsciously, we know that we must, and that we can, solve our problems. This is why we seek answers, solutions or support that we believe can help us in this task.

However, it should not be forgotten that our desire to know is nearly always matched by our fear of knowing. Whether we want to or not and whether we are aware of it or not, we often cling to our problems and worries. They give us a reason to live (or more precisely to exist), and to hope for a better future. This is why it is not sufficient just to see ourselves clearly, or to seek solutions to our problems. We also need to make ourselves capable of acting differently and to be determined to put an end to the problems and worries that seem to pepper our existence.

The cross-shaped draw can help us in this, by bringing together all the factors inherent in a current problem or situation. The spread of cards then becomes the support or prop that leads us towards the conclusions that will help us to resolve the problem or situation that concerns us. If we act positively on the basis of the lessons learned from the interpretation of the cards, sooner or later we will enjoy the relief that comes from being able to concentrate upon ourselves, having resolved our problems.

By using the Tarot cards according to this principle, they become a genuine instrument of meditation, which allows us to interpret the cards fully ourselves without having recourse to a third person.

3 Keeping a record of your spreads

As we have seen, the cross-shaped spread is ideal for finding solutions to day-to-day problems. The four cards laid out in the shape of the cross, plus the single card that appears in the centre of the spread, should generally suffice to give a clear picture. To add any further cards to the spread might complicate or confuse the interpretation, rather than make it any more tangible or clearer.

Concentrate on the four cards plus the central card before you, and then make your interpretation, while bearing in mind the question that concerns you and also the fact that this spread contains a key – perhaps even *the* key – to your problem or concern.

You must not over-extend yourself by making other draws, or by carrying out several readings at once. This is why I advise you to note your questions and the corresponding readings in a notebook so you can keep a regular diary of your readings. In this way, if you do not arrive at a correct interpretation on a particular occasion, you can revisit the spread at a later date.

Sometimes a problem or concern may absorb you so completely that you are incapable of seeing it clearly, effectively blinded by your emotions. Or you may be desperate to obtain a particular answer at all costs. In such cases simply wait for this inner turbulence to pass. Later, when the tension has eased, you can seriously reconsider the problem that was worrying you and go back over the reading that you carried out at the time. You can then be sure of having worked the problem through. It remains to discover the meaning of the key that you have been given – or, to be more precise, the key that you have given yourself – through the medium of the Tarot. It is impossible to draw clear conclusions at a later date if you have not made a note of the question and reading made at the time you were focussing on the problem. This is why it is so important and useful to keep a journal or diary record.

4 The Instantaneous Impression

By interpreting a five-card draw of the Tarot you gain an overview or an impression of the whole situation. This overview does not depend upon any pre-learned technique.

However, you can learn how to prepare yourself to grasp this overview instantaneously. To do this, if you are carrying out a reading for yourself, you need to be in tune with your inner self at the very moment that you choose the four cards; if you are doing a reading for someone else, you need to be able to capture the fleeting impression or feeling that you have when you first turn over the five cards of their draw.

Just as the only truth is that of the moment (nothing is more liable to change than the truth!), our thoughts flit here and there, moving constantly from one subject to another, rendering us incapable of conveying them in their entirety, or pinning them down. This is why artists – particularly painters and musicians – convey their thoughts in symbolic rather than realistic terms, in order to inspire similar thoughts and feelings in the viewer or listener. It is therefore important, when interpreting the Tarot cards that you learn to grasp the fleeting impression or thought that arises:

• at the moment when you turn over the cards picked by a person who is consulting you;

• at the moment you choose four cards, when carrying out a reading for yourself.

This instantaneous 'impression', this flash of intuition, gives you an insight into the totality of the situation. It offers an immediate overview that will be useful in your interpretation.

However, this impression or overview is not the same as an interpretation of the spread. It is here where most interpreters fall down. They prove themselves to be either good 'receivers' or good 'transmitters', but they are rarely good 'mediums'; in other words, they are rarely good transmitter-receivers[2], skilled at both. The instantaneous impression is what the 'receiver' picks up, while the interpretation is carried out through the 'transmitter'. You cannot have one without the other, which is why the majority of Tarot readings by 'clairvoyants' resemble a headless body or a disembodied head. They may be receptive, the 'radio' may be live and capable of receiving broadcasts, but the transmission is scrambled. Conversely, while the signal may be strong, the reception may be weak, and so the transmission does not come through very clearly.

2 In his treaty *De Divinatione*, Cicero, a Roman writer born in 106 BC, distinguished two means of prediction: natural intuitive divination, demonstrated occasionally in certain privileged beings – priests, clairvoyants or prophets; and reasoned or inductive divination, resulting from the interpretation of sacred signs appearing in the sky or on the earth, by the action of the divine. (Quoted by Robert Linssen, in his 'Histoire de la parapsychologie' in *Univers de la parapsychologie et de l'ésotérisme*, published by Martinsat, 1975.)

This certainly does not mean that you must concentrate on what is going on inside you at all times and at all costs. In fact, this would indicate over-intervention with the process, a fault that can be laid at the door of a number of modern therapies. You must simply take a 'snapshot' of the fleeting impression or thought passing through your mind at the moment when you select the cards (when performing a reading for yourself), or when you turn them over (if reading for someone else). Do not worry about 'developing' this photograph. If you have been attentive, that is to say 'receptive', it will be imprinted within you. All you have to do is interpret the spread of cards before you, by analysing each card in the chronological order suggested in this book, 'focussing' your interpretation along the lines suggested by the 'snapshot'. To continue the camera analogy, you can then lay your instantaneous snapshot over your interpretation of the whole, focussing the two together until you have a clear single image.

In this way, your instantaneous impression will meld and merge with your interpretation, and the latter will reveal and amplify the former.

5 Intuition or the memory-effect

There is no single, definitive conclusion that can be drawn from the interpretation of a spread of cards. On the contrary, each reading has its own logic, where a certain situation revealed by a particular card (the first card in your spread) leads 'logically' to certain consequences or results. This logic is good sense, or pure intuition. According to Carl Gustav Jung, 'intuition is the result of things seen or learnt that come back to us later in our memory, shifted in time'.[3] This memory is both individual and collective. We know a lot more than we realize. Our knowledge is often limited to what we learn through our habitual behaviour and our environment. It sometimes takes a new and strange situation to make us realize just how much we do know, being able to deal with these new circumstances almost without a second thought. Likewise, we sometimes have a feeling that a situation will develop or that

3 Carl Gustav Jung, 'Approaching the Unconscious', in *Man and his Symbols*, published by Aldus Books, 1964.

a problem will be resolved in one way rather than another. This presentiment is, as its name suggests, something intuitive that precedes feeling.

It is the state of mind in the split-second before a particular feeling takes hold. Feelings can often skew our judgement, preventing us from acting appropriately, by placing too much emphasis on emotional, intellectual or moral considerations. However, an instantaneous impression implies a state of receptivity and openness to something that springs neither from thought nor feeling.

Thus we may say that 'seeing', as it is generally practised, is in fact an uncontrolled leap into the unconscious and the collective memory. However, just as it is not enough to be able to read in order to understand what we read, there is no point in seeing what we are unable to understand or interpret in relation to our lives.

In each of us, therefore, there is a conscious (individual) and unconscious (collective) memory. But in all cases, intuition does seem to be a 'memory-effect' and not a supernatural state. In the Chinese I Ching or the Jewish Torah, it is possible to find all the solutions inherent in human problems[4]. The information compiled in these sacred books over the course of the centuries has benefited people of all eras. It was assembled through the observation of age-old human behaviour and the circumstances that this behaviour habitually generates. That is why these books have stood the test of time and still excite interest among people who 'intuitively' know that their pages contain much to reflect upon, as well as keys to their problems and concerns. Their content is both access code for and interpretation of our unconscious memory. Consulting these books is similar to consulting our own memory, or in other words, ourselves. They provide the prompts that we need to revive our memory and thus enrich our consciousness.

4 Read the series of 'Rabbi' novels by Harry Kemelman, featuring the rabbi sleuth David Small, who solves police riddles with the help of inspiration from the Torah.

It can therefore be said, that in the same way the divinatory Tarot enables us to see into our inner souls and to read ourselves like an open book.

6 The Fifth Arcanum

YOUR CURRENT SITUATION OR PROBLEM

The first card that should be interpreted is the fifth card drawn – the card that is in the centre of your spread, which you picked after having added together the numbers of the four cards that you chose (*see page 18*). If this figure is the same as one of the cards that you have already selected and placed elsewhere, you obviously cannot actually place it in the centre of your spread as well; but you must consider it to be there all the same.

The fifth card takes you to the heart of your situation or your concern and tells you about its nature. This is why your interpretation will be clearest and most useful if your question relates directly to the origin or causes of this situation.

This card is also known as the 'synthesis' and will therefore help you to understand the nature of whatever concerns you while providing you with information on how you perceive – or fail to perceive – your situation or matters at the heart of your concern.

In interpreting this card and, therefore, the situation, you can clarify the meaning of your question, developing or focussing it more clearly.

This approach to divinatory Tarot rests on a little known or ignored aspect of its practice, which favours analysis, self-analysis, reflection and meditation. It prompts us to question our desire and need to know. Too many who make use of the divinatory arts tend to do so with the sole aim of providing themselves with reassurance or comfort in the interpretation of their reality. Unfortunately, they are concerned solely with their own limited desires and expectations of seeing circumstances develop only as they wish.

A serious interpretation of a spread of cards in relation to a specific question must force us to see things as they really are. It is only by so doing that we can become aware of our errors, illusions, weaknesses and limitations.

Thus, those who use the divinatory Tarot to discover something about a current or future event, or the development of a particular situation, must first ask themselves if they are genuinely open to self-knowledge and to seeing themselves as they truly are; whether they are really ready to accept the true reality of a situation rather than what they simply imagine it to be.

The fifth card will give you clear guidance on this subject. This is why, in your interpretation of a spread of cards, it is, above all, to the fifth card that you should devote all your attention. It will allow you to orient the overall direction of your interpretation, and to involve either yourself or the person who is consulting you fully. It will provide you with information on the positive or negative influence that you exercise or that you could exercise over the probable evolution or outcome of the situation, which will be revealed to you by the fourth card of your spread.

7 The First Arcanum

YOUR BEHAVIOUR, YOUR DESIRES, YOUR ACTIONS

The second card to consider is the first card that you picked out and laid to the left of your spread. This card indicates your position or attitude within the situation in which you are currently interested.

As we have seen above, it is the card in the centre (the fifth Arcanum) that locates you psychologically in the situation concerned. It reveals your perception and understanding of the situation, as well as the actual nature of the situation.

The second card that you interpret allows you to understand how you are now behaving in this situation. In other words, are you the victim of this situation, succumbing to it, or is it of your making and are you in control of it?

Briefly, it is this card that brings you into the picture, taking you to the heart of the matter. This card will provide you with an understanding of what you are really doing. It is up to you to determine whether this behaviour or attitude is appropriate or not and whether the mode of action that you have chosen is suitable or not.

8 The Second Arcanum

CIRCUMSTANCES, EVENTS AND EXTERNAL FACTORS

The third card in your spread to consider is the second that you picked out and then placed to the right in your cross.

This card tells you about the prevailing climate that either favours or hinders the development of the situation in question. Alternatively, it will tell you about external elements and factors that may assist or impede you, by favouring or opposing the implementation of your initiatives, desires and plans.

Remember: there are no fundamentally beneficial or fundamentally malevolent cards. The cards present in a spread are each part of the whole that they form. In a cross-shaped spread there is no 'answer' *per se*. So it is pointless to expect to find one. In fact, by looking for such an answer, you are depriving yourself of the interpretation that you could draw from your spread. It can and must provide you with much more than just an answer, but rather an immediate and panoramic knowledge of all the essential factors and influences inherent in the given situation, including those of which you are unaware. Moreover, the very fact of seeking an 'answer' implies that you are not ready to see a situation as it really is and that you are not giving yourself every chance to understand and draw lessons from the information that is contained in your spread.

Initially, therefore, you should proceed in a methodical and analytical manner, giving careful consideration to each of the five cards of your cross-shaped spread, while ignoring any thoughts of the response that you may, despite yourself, be hoping for. Study the five cards, one by one, to discover the information they contain regarding the favourable or unfavourable factors inherent in your situation and your behaviour within it; next, you can synthesize all this information to give yourself an overview of the situation. It is only when you obtain this view of the whole that you become a 'seer'.

Remember that you had an intuition of this overview when you picked your cards. At this stage of your interpretation, you have at your disposal a symbolic language that allows you to see and understand the past, the present and the probable outcome of the situation, namely:

- the causes or origins of the situation;

- the situation at the time when you are carrying out your reading;

- the logical consequences of the situation or its probable outcome.[5]

It is a question of logical consequences, which need not be irrevocable. This means that, in all probability, if you do not intervene in the 'normal' course of events, if you leave things as they are and do not change the behaviour or state of mind that lie at the heart of the situation, you can expect it to develop according to the logical consequences revealed by the cards. It remains up to you to decide whether or not you consider these consequences and the probable outcome satisfactory.

To sum up, the overview of your spread – which gives you your 'seer' status – does not, therefore, provide you with an 'answer'. Nevertheless, it allows you to draw lessons from the information now at your disposal. Further, armed with a full realization of the cause of the situation or concern, you can decide whether to take action in order to make things evolve in the way that you wish. On the other hand, still armed with the same knowledge, you may decide simply to leave things as they are if the probable outcome indicated in your spread seems acceptable to you.

It is therefore easy to understand how Tarot can be a support in your life, since it gives you the choice to take action or not in the development of events that concern you. A Tarot reading does not give you an 'answer', but it helps you to find

5 See my book, *L'Astrologie et Votre Avenir*, published by Hachette.

solutions to your problems. In this way, it becomes an instrument of free will and the very opposite of any notion of an inescapable destiny.

9 The Third Arcanum

THE RESULTS OF YOUR ACTS

The fourth card to consider is the third card that you picked, which you placed at the top of the cross, between the first card and the second.

The third card provides the link between the trends revealed by the first card (your behaviour, desires and actions) and those revealed by the second card (external factors relating to your situation or problem). Depending on the nature of this card, you will know what forces flow between you and the external factors, and whether you are tackling matters well, or if, by contrast, your attitude and actions are actually inhibiting your situation's development.

The third card provides information on the consequences of your actions in the face of this situation. It also shows the practical meaning of whatever concerns you, or how the situation appears to others.

The information this card contains is therefore of some considerable importance. It is by our actions that we can judge an outcome, be it progress or otherwise. If there is any correlation between the actual result and the one that you were expecting, you will not be surprised by the information revealed to you by the fourth card. Indeed, it will give you an insight into the 'probable' development of this situation.

If this is not the case, it is because there is a discrepancy between the results that you were hoping for and those that are about to take place. You should consider whether your behaviour or actions are inappropriate to this situation (see the first and second cards), or whether circumstances are working against the outcome you desire (see the second, third and fourth cards).

10 The Fourth Arcanum

THE PROBABLE OUTCOME OF THE SITUATION OR PROBLEM THAT CONCERNS YOU

The final card for interpretation in your spread is the fourth card drawn, which you placed at the bottom of your cross.

This card will tell you how the situation that concerns you will develop in the near future – if you do not intervene.

It is up to you to decide whether you should take action or not, depending on whether the outcome revealed by this card seems positive or negative to you. However, do not interpret this card in isolation from the other cards that form your spread. The full significance of the fourth card is only to be appreciated in the light of the information revealed to you by the three other cards that you selected, together with the one that is in the centre of your cross. You should consider your spread as a cohesive whole, where each symbol has its own importance.

To remind you of the process, here again is the significance of each of the cards forming your spread in the shape of a cross.

- First card drawn: your behaviour, your wishes and your actions.

- Second card drawn: circumstances, events and external elements.

- Third card drawn: the results of your actions.

- Fourth card drawn: the probable outcome of the situation or the problem that concerns you.

- Fifth card drawn: the nature of the situation or the problem concerning you, and the way in which you are tackling it.

The Overall Picture

You must now synthesize the information that has been revealed to you by the combination of these five cards. The conclusions that you draw from it will help you take stock of the situation. Within the situation or problem you are asking about, your mind acts as a camera lens. If there is too great a discrepancy between the information revealed to you by the fifth card and the fourth card, it is because your thinking is blurred, out of focus. You now need to refocus your thoughts and actions so that the content of the two symbolic images is brought together, thereby bringing your external self and your internal self in sharp, harmonious focus.

In order to act or react effectively and correctly, the image needs to be clear. To this end, you must try to retrieve the instantaneous impression that I referred to earlier (*see page 25*). This will give you a clearer picture of yourself and your situation, and you will know what you must do. In this way, you can rekindle the innate good sense that lies within each of us, and which, as with all forms of life on earth, does what must be done.

Who asks the earth to spin? Nevertheless, it spins. Like the earth, do what you have to do!

Notes on Arcanum XIII (Death)
The image of Death represented by Arcanum XIII – a skeleton scything heads in the field of earthly life – is intended to make a deep impression on the person consulting the cards. This powerful image may provoke serious concern or even terror, but never indifference – as death never leaves indifference in its wake.

Who can truly boast that they are not afraid of death, their own in particular? Intellectually, we can find good reasons to ignore the reality that one day this is sure to confront us. Whatever our differences, we are all equal in the eyes of death. Ignoring this certainty does not allow us to escape the immutable principle of all life here on earth – everything begins and ends; everything that is born, lives and dies.

'One day you laugh, another you cry. One day you live, another you die', says a 12th-century French proverb. Therefore it is best to come to terms as soon as possible with such an unavoidable reality. Nothing in our education or upbringing gives us the ability to envisage the perspective of death in a healthy but serious way; it remains, in fact, the most tenacious taboo of present-day society.

We must not forget that apprenticeship in the use of the Tarot is a voyage of discovery initiated by the 22 symbolic cards of the Major Arcana. These indicate the psychological, moral and spiritual stages through which each of us must pass to find self-fulfilment – the individuation so dear to Jung that may otherwise be described as the fullness of being.

One of these essential stages is the acceptance that death is present right at the heart of life. But it is a regenerative death that is necessary for the constant renewal of life, without which life would or could not be. Integrating death – and not just the idea or concept of death – into our lives helps us to absorb the concepts of change, transformation and metamorphosis that are essential to life. According to the Upanishads 'Transformation is the immutable'. This is the reality to which the 'nameless Arcanum', as card XIII is sometimes called, alerts us. Without death, an immutable aspect of the reality of this world, no life or evolution would be possible. In order to be regenerated and give life, energy must forever cease to be repeatedly, folding into itself. If it did not do so, it would disappear, annihilating life with it.

Arcanum XIII teaches us that death lives at the heart of life, and life at the heart of death by stimulating our awareness of the words of the Gospel according to Thomas: 'For where the beginning is, there will the end be. Blessed is he who will take his place in the beginning; he will know the end and will not experience death'.

Using this book
– in brief

This book contains a pre-cut set of the 22 cards that make up the Major Arcana of the Tarot deck. Its practical format means that it can be carried with you quite easily, allowing you to consult the oracle of the Tarot at any time. Moreover, the following pages provide nearly 5,000 responses, enabling you to make a rapid interpretation of the reduced draw, which consists of four cards laid out in the shape of a cross plus a fifth card known as the synthesis.

Each of these responses – which can be combined with other cards in over 351,000 different ways – are divided into five themes:

1   Health
2   Love
3   Family
4   Work
5   Money

For each question that you ask, you will obtain a three-part response:

1 Overview of the situation
2 You in this situation
3 Probable evolution or outcome

Or, to make it easier, another way of looking at the above thee-part response is as follows. When you ask a question and deal 4 + 1 cards from your Tarot deck, this book will provide you with the means of understanding:

• your perception of the problem which preoccupies you;

• your situation in relation to the problem, at the time you consult the Tarot;

• the way in which the situation will most probably evolve.

With this book and the cards, you can learn how to act as your own interpreter and, if you wish, you can also interpret the Tarot for others.

To do so, carefully study the procedure set out in the next chapter and follow the steps required to find the three-part response to the question you wish to ask.

The procedure is very simple. You just need to make sure that you concentrate as hard as you can on your problem or question. This should not prove too difficult. After all, if a specific problem or a personal question is truly on your mind, you will feel a real need to understand the situation, or to know what might happen in the future – especially when the answers are within arm's reach.

Finally, it is important to make sure that you focus all your thoughts on the question posed whilst you are drawing the cards. The more you concentrate, the more accurate the cards' response will be.

How to use
this book

All the interpretations contained in this book have been made from combinations of the 22 symbolic cards that compose the Major Arcana of the Tarot, which are:

Card No. 1 – The Magician

Card No. 2 – The High Priestess

Card No. 3 – The Empress

Card No. 4 – The Emperor

Card No. 5 – The High Priest

Card No. 6 – The Lovers

Card No. 7 – The Chariot

Card No. 8 – Justice

Card No. 9 – The Hermit

Card No. 10 – The Wheel of Fortune

Card No. 11 – Strength

Card No. 12 – The Hanged Man

Card No. 13 – Death

Card No. 14 – Temperance

Card No. 15 – The Devil

Card No. 16 – The Tower

Card No. 17 – The Star

Card No. 18 – The Moon

Card No. 19 – The Sun

Card No. 20 – Judgement

Card No. 21 – The World

Card No. 22 – The Fool

1

7

13

These cards are all that you need to gain some immediate food for thought with regard to your current concerns.

Follow steps 1-15

19

II THE HIGH PRIESTESS	III THE EMPRESS	IV THE EMPEROR	V THE HIGH PRIEST	VI THE LOVERS
2	3	4	5	6
VIII JUSTICE	IX THE HERMIT	X THE WHEEL OF FORTUNE	XI STRENGTH	XII THE HANGED MAN
8	9	10	11	12
XIV TEMPERANCE	XV THE DEVIL	XVI THE TOWER	XVII THE STAR	XVIII THE MOON
14	15	16	17	18
XX JUDGEMENT	XXI THE WORLD	THE FOOL		
20	21	22		

1   Think hard about the problem or situation that concerns you, and choose the theme of your question which must be one of the following:

1   Health
2   Love
3   Family
4   Work
5   Money

2   Write your question on a sheet of paper, or enter it in the blank pages provided at the back of this book. (*See page 554*).

3   While reading your question again and concentrating hard on it, shuffle the 22 cards, face down.

4   Having shuffled the cards, divide the pack in two, place the top half face down on the table and the bottom half on top, making a single pack once more.

5   Spread the 22 cards out in front of you, being sure that they are still face down.

6   Read your question once more, and check that it really does set out the problem that currently concerns you.

If you have the slightest doubt, do not hesitate to reword your question. The more precise and well formulated it is, the more accurate and pertinent will be the response.

If you decide to re-write your question, you must start again from step 1:

1   Choose the theme of your question.

2   Write down your question.

3   Shuffle the cards.

4   Cut the pack in two.

5   Spread the pack out, face down, in front of you.

7   Choose four of the 22 cards in front of you, one after the other and at random, still concentrating on your question. They should still be face down.

Line up the four chosen cards in front of you in the order in which they were picked, from left to right.

8   Still without turning them over, lay the cards out to form the four arms of a cross, in the following order:

- place the first card you picked in front of you to the left;

- place the second card to the right of the first, leaving a space the width of a card between the two;

- place the third above and between the first two cards;

- finally, place the fourth card below and between the first two cards.

7

17

19

11

9   Now turn over the four cards, in the order in which you drew them, replacing them face up in their positions as the arms of the cross.

10   Note the number that appears at the top of each card and add them together.

Example:
first card drawn, The Star, number 17
second card drawn, The Sun, number 19
third card drawn, The Chariot, number 7
fourth card drawn, Strength, number 11

Thus: 17 + 19 + 7 + 11 = 54

Note: Of the 22 cards of the Major Arcana of the Tarot, only The Fool is unnumbered. However, it is accorded the value of 22, so when you deal a spread that includes The Fool, it should be regarded as number 22 when reading the responses in this book.

11   Now add together the two digits of this total. Then search through the 18 remaining cards to find the one corresponding to the new number provided by this method. Staying with our example above:

Total 54, so 5 + 4 = 9

The card that corresponds to number 9 is The Hermit. Find it in the remaining cards.

12   Place this new card in the centre of the cross that is formed by your four initial cards.

Note: (a) If the sum of the four cards comes to 22 or less, there is no need to add together the two figures making up this number. As the Major Arcana contains 22 symbolic cards, any number less than 23 will lead directly to one of the cards, making it unnecessary to add the two digits together.

> Example:
> first card drawn, The High Priest, number 5
> second card drawn, The Empress, number 3
> third card drawn, The Wheel of Fortune, number 10
> fourth card drawn, The Magician, number 1
>
> This gives: 5 + 3 + 10 + 1 =19

In this case, locate card number 19, The Sun, and place it in the centre of the cross formed by your four initial cards.

(b) Should the total correspond to the number of a card that has already been drawn, leave it in place, but consider this card also to be in the centre of the spread, and take it into consideration when obtaining the first part of your response (*see step 13*).

> If you have followed these twelve steps with care, you are now ready to find the response to your question.

13 First, note the number of the card that is in the centre of your spread.

> Next, refer to *You in this situation* (*page 75*) and read the response that relates to this number.

> This is the first part of the answer to your question.

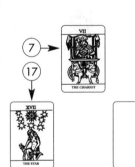

14 Next, note the numbers of the first and third cards you drew (the ones to the left and at the top) of your spread. Write these two numbers down next to each other in the order in which they were drawn.

Example:
first card drawn, laid to the left, number 17
third card drawn, set at the top, number 7

Note down: 17 and 7

Then refer to *Your Current Situation* (*page 85*) and read the response that you will find on the page where the two numbers corresponding to those you have drawn appear, after first selecting the symbol (health, love, family, work or money) which you have designated as the theme of your question. In our example, numbers 17 and 7 appear on page 258.

This is the second part of the response to your question.

15 Next, note the numbers of the fourth and the second cards (the ones to the right and at the bottom) of your spread.

Write down these two numbers next to each other, in the order in which they were drawn.

Example:
fourth card drawn, laid below, number 11
second card drawn, set at the right, number 19

Note down: 11 and 19

Refer to *Probable Outcome* (*page 319*) and read the response on the page where the numbers corresponding to the two you have drawn appear, having first selected the symbol (health, love, family, work or money) designated as the subject of your question. In our example, numbers 11 and 19 appear on page 434.

This gives you the third and final part of the answer to your question.

The 22 cards of the Major Arcana

THE MAGICIAN

1 The Magician

THE MAGICIAN IS INITIATIVE

With The Magician, everything begins and everything is possible. The Magician has all the abilities and qualities to tackle anything in his path, to take action and to succeed.

He is an artist, with all the tools he needs to succeed in his work. He is a magician with the ability to transform reality by producing or revealing new elements. Artist, artisan, juggler or conjurer, he is master of illusions, appearances and realities, in a world that he forges in his image, according to his desires and ideas.

Sometimes he is the harlequin who treats life as a game and wastes his talents, a person lacking stability and aware-ness, a joker who plays tricks, practises deceit and makes up stories. The Magician is endowed with energy, imagination and power of conviction, but no one can predict how he will use these qualities.

Whatever else he may be, The Magician is never inactive. He scours the land, eager for action. He is a builder, actor, entertainer, as well as helpful genie, medicine man, gossip and charlatan. He carries the magical initiatory staff, the magician's wand.

Appearing in your draw, The Magician might represent a child or a young, inexperienced man but one for whom great possibilities lie ahead. If concerning your particular problem or question, The Magician reveals that an initiative or action is being taken, or that it is there for the taking.

THE MAGICIAN: KEY WORDS

POSITIVE ATTRIBUTES: initiative – enterprise – action – empowerment – originality – gifts and talents – creativity – new beginnings – apprenticeship.

NEGATIVE ATTRIBUTES: over-diversification – irresponsibility – falsehoods – deception – gossip.

II

THE HIGH PRIESTESS

2 The High Priestess

THE HIGH PRIESTESS IS WISDOM

The High Priestess sees everything, hears everything and knows everything, but says nothing. She waits patiently for exactly the right moment, considers everything deeply and knows the beginning and the end of all things. She is intuitive, lucid, clear-sighted, inquiring, organized, ordered, reserved, sensitive and cultured.

An attentive and principled woman, she nurtures growth and development in others, and watches over them unerringly. She is a midwife facilitating birth and creation, whose knowledge is based on good sense and experience.

She is a wise woman who holds the keys to the doors of knowledge, light and life. Consequently, she is the guardian of the secrets of the soul, of birth and death, and of the past and future. In her and through her, birth and knowledge come together, as to acquire knowledge is to be repeatedly reborn. She never trusts appearances and is never prey to delusion or illusion. With The High Priestess, there is no dissimulation or pretence; everything is true, just, simple and genuine.

Anyone can acquire The High Priestess's wisdom. You must simply follow the path that leads to understanding and knowledge of the world. You must have a taste for life and know the value of the things around you.

In your draw, The High Priestess indicates a mature and responsible woman, someone who is trustworthy and wise but whose character is secretive and reserved – or who behaves in this way. As to your question or problem, The High Priestess indicates the serious nature of the situation – one in which not everything may have been fully revealed to you as yet.

This card is also sometimes known as The Lady or Female Pope, or The Papess in Latin-based languages.

THE HIGH PRIESTESS: KEY WORDS

POSITIVE ATTRIBUTES: wisdom – learning – the ability to wait – reflection – foresight – experience – serenity – lucidity – reserve – a serious, secretive and discreet nature – understanding of life.

NEGATIVE ATTRIBUTES: dissimulation – passivity – conservatism – protectionism – inability to communicate.

THE EMPRESS

3 The Empress

THE EMPRESS IS CREATION

The Empress's watchwords are creation, production, development, accomplishment, exploitation and fecundity. Clearly, this card takes one to the very heart of practical and everyday material life.

With The Empress, nothing is lost and everything is created. She is the fecund and fertile Mother Earth, fount of all life, generous, bountiful Mother Nature, producing and reproducing to infinity. She is the Virgin Mother who prolongs life by giving life, and who thus transmits the seed of eternal life.

The power of The Empress is that of feelings. Her force is emotional and her understanding of people and circumstances is instinctive, natural and spontaneous. She is a woman with an active, emotional and sensitive heart. Love, emotion and motivation are the three realms of the empire over which she reigns with her practical intelligence.

When interpreting the Tarot, The Empress indicates the involvement of a loving or amorous woman – a mother, a sister or a wife.

Concerning the question you are asking or the problem that is worrying you, The Empress reveals the material richness and potential productivity of the situation. In addition, she can sometimes provide clues as to personal motivations, generally those of a woman. She may also represent a woman who allows herself to be guided by her feelings.

Finally, The Empress heralds news. This may be good or bad, depending on the surrounding cards.

THE EMPRESS: KEY WORDS

POSITIVE ATTRIBUTES: abundance – productivity
– good feeling – generosity – practical intelligence
– the ability to communicate – an affectionate,
spontaneous, understanding nature – new.

NEGATIVE ATTRIBUTES: sectarianism – greed –
dependence – intransigence – possessiveness –
swayed by emotion rather than reason.

THE EMPEROR

4 The Emperor

THE EMPEROR IS ACHIEVEMENT

The Emperor is an authoritarian, rock-solid,
realistic character, sure of himself and his
prerogatives. He knows what he wants and
how to obtain it.

The Emperor reigns over the physical
and material world by sheer force of character and his
knowledge of life. He is a father with a protective and domineering personality – a family head who is well aware of his
responsibilities, which he treats seriously. He is a supervisor
or overseer, the conductor of an orchestra. Keen to create
order and harmony, he is an ambitious and objective
manager.

The Emperor imposes his commands and orders, creates
action and does so with mastery, certainty, sovereignty and
authority. He rules his empire.

Appearing in a spread, The Emperor indicates a serious,
stable, efficient and realistic man, a father, brother or husband.

In respect of a particular concern, the appearance of The
Emperor reveals that you are dealing with a concrete, solid,
durable situation or achievement, over which it is necessary to

exercise continual control, imposing your influence and making it yours. Finally, The Emperor confirms and bears witness to a fact, a particular truth, reality or a feeling.

THE EMPEROR: KEY WORDS

POSITIVE ATTRIBUTES: achievement – realization – certainty – conviction – power exercised in the physical and material world – domination of events and circumstances.

NEGATIVE ATTRIBUTES: fixed ideas – moral severity – intolerance – despotism – egocentricity – rigidity.

THE HIGH PRIEST

5 The High Priest

THE HIGH PRIEST IS DUTY

The High Priest embodies moral and spiritual power, from which he derives responsibility, authority and sovereignty, which form his destiny and his duty.

This is why The High Priest card represents a serious, experienced man, one who has wisdom and vast knowledge, but who is also worthy of respect and who is respected. His firm authority is always benevolent.

The High Priest is someone whom you can count on and trust and in whom you may confide; he will always know what should be done. In essence, he is the unifier, a joiner of souls, a man of religion.

He is a judge and advocate, a skilled, wise and reliable counsellor. He is an enlightened man who knows the rules of the game of life. He applies them well, ensuring that they are respected. He is sometimes a man of considerable importance

– a dignitary who exercises moral, intellectual or political influence. Or, more simply, he may be a mature man who has acquired a certain experience of life and a successful philosophy.

When you draw The High Priest card, it represents someone with whom you have a relationship, whom you should ask for advice or who is close to you.

In the context of your problem or enquiry, The High Priest indicates that it is time to face up to your responsibilities, to do your duty and accept your obligations. He also shows that you have the vocation to accomplish a particular task, assignment or course of action.

This card is sometimes also known as The Pope or The Hierophant, a term for someone, notably a priest, who interprets esoteric mysteries, or explains sacred doctrines.

THE HIGH PRIEST: KEY WORDS

POSITIVE ATTRIBUTES: sense of responsibility and duty – mission to accomplish – experience – moral sense – material and spiritual power – intellectual influence – superior authority – the desire to bring together and unite – a responsible and stable situation.

NEGATIVE ATTRIBUTES: sterile and critical intellect – partial judgement – unbending high moral tone – an influential character with dubious intentions or beliefs.

6 The Lovers

THE LOVERS SIGNIFY A CHOICE

This card underlines the importance of choice and free will. Temptation leads to indecision, over-diversification and a confusion of feelings and ideas. Without choice, without limit or without aim, an individual lives a life of doubt and uncertainty, pulled this way and that by good or bad, depending on the prevailing circumstances.

Making a choice involves setting out one's differences from others – one's personal style and originality – and affirming your personality.

Those who make a choice are resisting the temptation to let themselves be tugged upwards or downwards; they are refusing to be tossed between Good and Evil under the influence of other people or events, or to become victims of circumstance. The worst of all fates is to be left stranded on the crest of a wave of indecision and uncertainty.

How can you discover your real self? How can you learn to know yourself? Only by expressing your will, your desires, ideas, convictions, sentiments, motivations and limits, and by imposing your choices. This is the answer, since those who can take control of their choices in life become masters of their own destiny.

In a spread, The Lovers card indicates that you are in the position of being able to choose, even if the situation does not actually oblige you to make a choice or take a decision. Of course, this choice is sometimes related to your love life. Nevertheless, always bear in mind that to choose or not to choose means mastering or becoming a victim of your own self, your emotions, feelings and motivations.

POSITIVE ATTRIBUTES: choice – agreement – union – decision – determination – commitment.

NEGATIVE ATTRIBUTES: indecision – frivolity – easily influenced – emotional instability – vacillation – intellectual dissipation.

THE CHARIOT

7 The Chariot

THE CHARIOT IS WILL

Once a choice had been made, will can emerge and assert itself. It is then up to the individual to concentrate on his objective and, as the lone sailor of a yacht, to steer the course that has been plotted, despite wind and tides.

The warrior prince and conqueror grasping the reins of his chariot of victory guides his two fiery steeds towards the goal he has vowed to attain, surmounting all obstacles along the way, never relaxing his efforts.

The Lovers symbolize the need to make a choice and have an aim but The Chariot allows individuals to express their will and give of their best in order to achieve their aims and obtain what they want, what they deserve and all that is rightfully theirs.

The person revealed by The Chariot has a plan, a purpose, energy and persistence that promise success.

Appearing in your spread, The Chariot encourages you to look to the future, to explore your choices, decisions, undertakings and objectives fully, audacious, daring or ambitious as they may be, and to sustain the pressure until you have achieved your goal.

Sometimes the appearance of The Chariot heralds the imminent arrival of some news, a trip or journey that will lead you to act or to express or demonstrate your determination.

THE CHARIOT: KEY WORDS

POSITIVE ATTRIBUTES: will to succeed – courage – obstinacy – success via the strength of one's own efforts – energetic actions or undertakings.

NEGATIVE ATTRIBUTES: blind obstinacy – lack of discernment – unconsidered enthusiasm – faltering will.

8 Justice

JUSTICE IS EQUILIBRIUM

To attempt to realize your vocation, to explore your choices to the limit, to achieve your objectives or to obtain or accomplish your desires is useless without equilibrium.

Everything in the universe is governed by the equilibrium of the elements, forces and energies. Heaven and Earth, male and female, all that is above and all that is below, the visible and invisible (the known and the unknown) are held in balance. In order to maintain this equilibrium, we must understand the laws that govern Heaven and Earth, and act in accordance with them. As a Chinese proverb says:

'A millimetre to the right, or a millimetre to the left,
And the world would topple into the void.'

Justice is the guardian of these laws. It reveals and dictates what is right. Unrelenting, rigorous, incontestable, inescapable, Justice commands, clarifies and resolves. In accordance with primitive and instinctive nature, Justice does what has to be done, without concession and without emotion.

The appearance of Justice in your spread signals that you must find, or return to, equilibrium or balance. You must prove your integrity, your equity and impartiality, your ability to impose order and discipline or to submit to it yourself. This card sometimes heralds the appearance or intervention of worldly justice in your life, whether you appeal for this, or whether you are judged by it.

JUSTICE: KEY WORDS

POSITIVE ATTRIBUTES: equilibrium – serenity – moral rigour – integrity – order – law – discipline – selective and idealistic mind.

NEGATIVE ATTRIBUTES: injustice – a rigidity that inhibits or isolates – intolerance – arbitrary or partial judgement.

IX

THE HERMIT

9 The Hermit

THE HERMIT IS CLEAR-SIGHTEDNESS

Be prepared, everything is out there!

Alone in the night, lighting his way by the glimmer of a lantern, leaning on a stick that he rests on the hard ground, at the heart of the realities of life The Hermit advances through the darkness. He is dependent on none but himself and only sees what is given to him to see. His night is the night of the soul – ignorance.

His lantern is his spirit and clear-sightedness and his stick represents his direct awareness of this world.

Unlike The Magician – the Tarot's storyteller, who forges the world in his own image – The Hermit probes and extracts the truth from this world. He destroys illusions and sees things as they are, relying solely upon his lucid mind and profound judgement.

As The Hermit learns more and more about the world, with the aid of his staff and his lantern, so he understands more about himself. Thus his solitude is neither isolating nor reclusive, but a state that is strong, regenerative and radiant.

This is the solitude of a person who seeks and reflects, who advances cautiously step by step along the path of knowledge. It is somebody who calls things into question, who grows in spirit and then follows a chosen path with patience and tenacity.

If The Hermit appears in your draw, it indicates awareness or realization, a personal discovery; it can mean solitude, the need to spend some time on your own or to take a step back. It shows the desire to take long-term action backed by all the precautions required in order to achieve a clear and precise objective – all expressed through patience and a long-term perspective.

THE HERMIT: KEY WORDS

POSITIVE ATTRIBUTES: clear-sightedness – superior intelligence – tenacity – fertile solitude – voluntary retreat – maturing – research and discovery – awareness – consolidation of ideas, feelings or relationships – long-term enterprise – deep conviction – intuition.

NEGATIVE ATTRIBUTES: isolation, retreat or solitude imposed by circumstance –withdrawal into self – fantasy, illusion, false belief – fatalism – pessimism – avarice – persecution mania.

THE WHEEL OF FORTUNE

10 The Wheel of Fortune

THE WHEEL OF FORTUNE IS EVOLUTION

The wheel turns. Everything around us and within us is perpetually in motion. Evolution and revolution – an eternal return to the beginning, a perpetual new start. All life on Earth is subject to the immutable cycle of the seasons, to the sequence of days and nights, to the rotation of our planet round its own axis, and to the real and visible movement of the Sun and the Moon. What we enjoy today, may well come back to hurt us tomorrow or vice versa. Such is the way of fortune, chance, destiny and luck. 'Luck', said Albert Einstein, 'is the formula that God uses when he wants to remain anonymous'. [1]

While we may consider ourselves to be blessed by good luck, and impoverished by bad, both kinds put us to the test. So The Wheel of Fortune is also the wheel of the destiny that leads us along the path of life.

However, this wheel does not turn alone or roll freely. No, it turns on an axis and needs an impetus to set it in motion. Thus an action, initiative, thought or desire is required for The Wheel of Fortune to turn. As a result, whoever provides the impetus and starts the wheel turning also sets in motion their own destiny.

The appearance of The Wheel of Fortune in a spread always indicates a person or situation that is evolving – well or badly, depending on circumstances. If you leave the wheel to turn by itself, you will experience its highs and lows without being in control of events. However, if you turn the wheel yourself, you will control the development of your own situation and circumstances.

The wheel turns. Nothing is fixed or stays the same. Everything is in motion.

1 'Chance is the pseudonym God uses when He'd rather not sign His own name.'
Anatole France (1844–1924).

POSITIVE ATTRIBUTES: luck – change – evolution – progress – favourable circumstances – possibility of acting or intervening in the course of events.

NEGATIVE ATTRIBUTES: regression – loss – setbacks – difficult circumstances – the victim of events.

BOTH POSITIVE AND NEGATIVE ATTRIBUTES: unstable, developing, transitory and uncertain situations in which you do not feel secure.

11 Strength

STRENGTH IS THE MASTERY OF SELF

Through mastery of oneself, one can achieve control over circumstance and exercise ascendancy and power over events. Only inner strength allows us to escape from falling victim to the wide range of daily circumstances in which we find ourselves.

Real strength has nothing to do with violence. Strength is not imposed, nor does it make demands. Inner strength is peaceable, patient, firm and courageous, never violent or aggressive. If The Chariot reveals a will that exerts an exterior influence, Strength in turn reveals concentrated will. It is a gentle, internalized determination, a calm assurance of the mastery of self.

Those who are aware of their inner strength have found their own core. They are perfectly calm and serene. They have suceeded in taming their instincts, being able to express them without losing control.

Such people make use of the world but without exploitation. They have simply renounced their self and, as a result, are very much what they should be – fulfilled individuals who are strong in themselves.

The appearance of Strength in your spread indicates a stable, solid, unchanging situation. Alternatively, it may reveal the courage and will of which you are capable and the efforts that you must make in order to control a special situation or the circumstances of your life.

THE HANGED MAN

12 The Hanged Man

THE HANGED MAN IS ABANDONMENT

This can mean abandoning yourself, letting go, or it can signify abandoning something, giving it up or sacrificing it. Either way, The Hanged Man always involves a clear and relative submission – the suspension of an activity or attitude, the conclusion of some-thing or a perpetual balance.

Murderers and robbers used to be punished by being hanged by the neck until dead. Thus, anyone who was hung was seen to be suffering the consequences of their actions.

The Hanged Man tells us that there is no more time, that it is too late to act. It is indeed the hour of reckoning and one must now suffer or assume the consequences of previous deeds and activities – whether good or bad.

Whatever the circumstances, you can do nothing but wait and see what happens. If you accept the role and significance of The Hanged Man – namely that of living in a state of suspense – then the time will surely come when you can recover the situation. On the card, The Hanged Man is hung by one foot, between two trees. However, if you turn it upside down, you will see that the trees are also inverted so that their branches point downwards, while their roots point upwards.

The Hanged Man is the world in reverse. Re-establishment is necessary and inevitable, sometimes fatal. Nevertheless, a change must take place. After all, Death, which follows, is already close by! If change, renewal and adaptation are not possible, then everything about you and your life will remain in suspense.

THE HANGED MAN: KEY WORDS

POSITIVE ATTRIBUTES: abandonment – confidence – faith – receptivity – sense of paradox (reversal of values) – letting go – the ability to wait.

NEGATIVE ATTRIBUTES: unconsciousness – victim of one's actions, errors or circumstances – irresponsibility – passivity – laziness – not letting go – situations that go nowhere – lack of self-control.

13 Death

DEATH IS CHANGE

Here on earth, nothing is eternal, yet nothing dies. Rather, everything is transformed. This is the exact meaning of this thirteenth card that is to be found right in the heart of the Tarot pack.

Although it is sometimes referred to as the nameless card, in fact, quite wrongly, we dare not pronounce its name. As a word, death often carries a social taboo. But in not talking about death, we express, to some degree, a lack of faith, maybe even a lack of love. This is an indication of impoverishment of the soul or spirit and of an excessive attachment to the material things of life. Death is not an end in itself, but a stage through which we must pass to be transformed from one state to another.

What comes from the earth will return to the earth; what comes from above will return there. Each according to its own.

Death, in the Tarot, indicates a symbolic death rather than actual death. The old gives place to the new. We reap what we have sown. We abandon that which no longer has reason to exist. A page is turned, a line is drawn and we move on to other things. Such is the way of life – and such is also the true meaning of death.

When you deal the Death card, it heralds a radical change or a turning point in your life. It is the consequence or the result of your previous actions and the sudden end to a situation or attitude that had to change.

Yet there is also a positive side to this. Sometimes, turning up Death can indicate something profitable or beneficial; it could be something advantageous that has been obtained thanks to your own merits, a reward that is the fruit of your labour and efforts.

DEATH: KEY WORDS

POSITIVE ATTRIBUTES: radical, imminent, inevitable, necessary change – profit, gain, benefit – a turning point in your existence – the logical conclusion of a situation – the end of a period in your life.

NEGATIVE ATTRIBUTES: halt – rupture – radical change imposed by circumstances – loss – the inevitable end of a situation.

XIV

TEMPERANCE

14 Temperance

TEMPERANCE IS REGENERATION

Relentlessly and unceasingly, life must be generated and reborn, otherwise it will disappear. It is like the water cycle: from underground springs to streams, from streams to rivers, from rivers to the sea, from the ocean to the skies, where the water evaporates and becomes clouds, from clouds to the rain that enters the earth and feeds the underground reserves and springs. The water of life is unfailingly regenerated following the movement of the Earth and the Heavens.

This cycle of regeneration applies equally to the currents of our thoughts, which circulate within us and through us. As they too are regenerated, so do they regenerate us.

Yet time also trickles away. With time, our character often becomes softer and more temperate as we gradually perceive the true measure and real meaning of life.

When you deal the cards, Temperance indicates a situation that appears like a new day. It is a constructive and positive change, a sign of new and happy circumstances. Equally, it may mean a great opportunity or the possibility of making use of all the assets and means at your disposal.

Temperance provides you with the measure, the rhythm and the tempo but it is up to you to make the music!

Temperance provides a means of understanding and makes us more communicative, ready to initiate dialogue and open to new exchanges. It is up to us to express ourselves, because Temperance is the bearer of great news. Always listen to it very carefully, as it is an angel that passes through your life, providing some special opportunity. Seize it while you may.

TEMPERANCE: KEY WORDS

POSITIVE ATTRIBUTES: opportunity – privileged relationships – beneficial circumstances – journeys, discovery, new relationships – constructive interactions – revelation – good news – study, reflection, appraisal, research – negotiation.

NEGATIVE ATTRIBUTES: hesitation – tendency to re-examine repeatedly – easily influenced nature – stagnation – poor reflexes – impulsive, unconsidered reactions – perfectionism.

XV

THE DEVIL

15 The Devil

THE DEVIL IS DESIRE

Humankind is said to stem from a fallen angel. Believing himself the equal of the divine power, this angel spurned this power and turned from the light, only to be plunged into night, darkness, and chaos.

So, closing our eyes brings darkness and obscurity, not light. The images that we project in this 'night of the soul' are nothing but fantasy, projections of our desires that mask the light of reality.

The fallen angel lies dormant inside each of us and keeps watch. The angel within is a mixture of good and evil, making sure that we are always torn between these two poles. This is why we must not deny, ignore or conceal the good and the evil that battle for control inside ourselves.

The Devil is the one that divides. In reality, good and evil are aspects of the same perception or concept. But we live our lives in a state of division, the dichotomy that is the internal or external opposition of good and evil. We become aware of the nature of the good and evil of which every one of us is capable by the expression and manifestation of our needs and wishes.

To desire something is to seek, to aspire, to wish for something. Tell me what you desire, what you are looking for and to what you aspire, and I will tell you who you are. We are, or we become, our own desires. Consequently, The Devil shows us chained to our desires as surely as death is chained to life, in an immutable and fatal cycle.

Turning up this card is not necessarily a sign of either good or ill. Its appearance should simply warn you that you are susceptible to an impulse, an irrepressible desire to do or obtain something, whatever the cost may be.

It is up to you to take stock, to determine whether this is good or bad and to evaluate the inevitable consequences.

The Devil is always related to the physical and material aspects of life. The principle of physical science, according to which 'for each action there is an equal and opposite reaction', can also be attributed to The Devil.

Finally, The Devil may sometimes reveal an advantageous financial situation – or equally, it can be the expression of a passion, specific anger, crisis or excess.

THE DEVIL: KEY WORDS

POSITIVE ATTRIBUTES: sound instinct – constructive passion – advantages, benefits, profits – flourishing material or financial situation – ambition – amorous passion – sensuality – intense creativity.

NEGATIVE ATTRIBUTES: blind desire – moral or material confusion – irrepressible, destructive or self-destructive urges – domineering or manipulative nature – violence – excess – anger – conservatism – greed – exaggerated sensuality – selfishness.

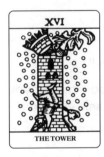

THE TOWER

16 The Tower

THE TOWER IS DELIVERANCE

When there is too much tension in the atmosphere, a storm is inevitable. So in life, the storm is the equivalent of the crisis that is necessary to release the tensions and passions that lead to disorder, chaos and destruction.

The sequence is often described as involving upheaval, disruption and purification. He who seeks to be the equal of God, who sins by presumption and pride, or who lives by the sword, perishes by God's rod of lighting. He will be struck down. But to him may also be revealed the power of truth and the transience of worldly objects and values.

In other words, after the storm, peace and order reign once again – it is this disruption that validates them.

The Tower heralds an inevitable upheaval, an unforeseen event that is taking place or will take place in your life, which will lift a great weight from you.

The Tower leads to deliverance, relief and liberation. It is like childbirth. You can do nothing to stop it, and it always results in something new.

THE TOWER: KEY WORDS

POSITIVE ATTRIBUTES: deliverance – clarification – liberation – purification.

NEGATIVE ATTRIBUTES: inevitable upheaval – sudden calling into question – rupture – destabilisation – state of shock.

17 The Star

THE STAR IS INSPIRATION AND HOPE

We are all born under a good star, but you will have to look inside yourself in order to seek and find it.

Once found, you must follow your star, as it will guide and protect you. It will also help you to act correctly, will purify and strengthen you and will be a continual source of regeneration by allowing the currents and cycles of life to flow through you.

It will also be a key factor in inspiring you to create and shape your own destiny throughout life.

The Star indicates creation, birth or a happy event. It allows you to hope, to believe and to have faith in life and yourself. It is a benign muse, the inspiration for the happiness that lies within each of us.

THE STAR: KEY WORDS

POSITIVE ATTRIBUTES: luck – hope – inspiration – creation – birth.

NEGATIVE ATTRIBUTES: this card is never negative – but its receptive character makes it easy to neutralize and it is susceptible to influence by the characteristics of the adjacent cards in the draw.

18 The Moon

THE MOON IS SENSITIVITY

The five senses are our connection with the physical world. If the eyes are the windows of the soul, all five senses are the pathways through which we identify and discover the world around us. They are the instruments of our feelings and sensitivity and The Moon is their symbolic representation.

The Moon, light of the night, holds sway over the rhythm of the tides. In the same way, it exerts an influence over our senses, moods and thoughts. It enhances our feelings and sensations, making us imaginative, receptive and occasionally anxious. Yet it also fascinates and bewitches, which is why 'moonstruck' is another way of saying that someone is unable to act in a normal manner, often because they are in love.

When you deal the cards and come up with The Moon, it can represent your family life, your parents, your origins, your roots or the very bedrock of your life. But it can also mean a confused, difficult or unsatisfactory situation – some illusion, falsehood or an illness – or even your most intimate and private thoughts.

THE MOON: KEY WORDS

POSITIVE ATTRIBUTES: creative imagination – gentleness – family life – popularity – intuition – nostalgia.

NEGATIVE ATTRIBUTES: disillusion – confusion of ideas and feelings – illness – injurious relationships – anxiety, fear of the unknown – situations causing pain or conflict – lack of autonomy – a hold over someone – exerting pressure on another.

19 The Sun

THE SUN IS CLARIFICATION

Let there be light, and let it illuminate the truth, such is the purpose of The Sun.

The Sun is the ultimate illumination, clarification and revelation – even the shadows are revealed by the light of The Sun. It shows up and illuminates pure, simple, sincere, reciprocal feelings and affinities. The Sun brings people together and warms the soul, the heart and the body. It promises success, joy and the happiness of being, living and giving to those who abandon themselves to its rays.

Idyllically expressed, The Sun entreats us to live like carefree children, playing in the garden of Eden, growing up in the paradise of the soul, happy and content with our feet in the water of innocence, our naked bodies caressed by The Sun's beneficial rays.

However, we must never look The Sun in the face, because its light can blind. Too much sunlight is akin to night. Remember what happened to Icarus in Greek myth, who flew too close to The Sun: his wings melted and he fell to his death. The Sun cannot be reached and it can never be extinguished. It is an endless state of being and regeneration. It takes nothing and needs no one, yet is capable of giving all.

THE SUN: KEY WORDS

POSITIVE ATTRIBUTES: pure, sincere sentiments – shared feelings – complicity – affinities – success – joy in living – clarification.

NEGATIVE ATTRIBUTES: deceptive appearances – superficial behaviour – false happiness – blind ambition.

20 Judgement

JUDGEMENT IS RENEWAL

When all the light is done, when all is said and done, when illusions and lies no longer have reason to exist, then renewal knocks at the door. It is the dawn of a new day. Each of us must reveal our true selves, without mask or disguise and without pretence.

At the hour of Judgement, sickness will be healed and man will emerge from his dreaming. Truth shall reign supreme and all shall be pardoned.

Unlike Justice, whose laws are dictated by Man, the Judgement of God does not condemn. It confronts the very soul, evaluating it purely on the basis of our sense of right and wrong, our conscience. In so doing, it gives us the opportunity to return to that very state of innocence that was our primordial, original and eternal nature.

To draw Judgement indicates healing, reconciliation, a call, a proposition, a vocation, rebirth or renewal.

Judgement allows you to see and judge yourself as you really are. You can be entirely honest with yourself, being quite simply and absolutely what you are. This, in truth, is all that is asked of us in the final analysis. Everything else is given to us, however ill equipped we are to receive it.

JUDGEMENT: KEY WORDS

POSITIVE ATTRIBUTES: renewal, reconciliation, healing – proposition – promotion – consecration – recognition of merits.

NEGATIVE ATTRIBUTES: an event or situation that is the consequence of your acts, from which you cannot escape.

21 The World

THE WORLD IS COMPLETENESS

To our eyes, the world seems infinitely vast, unlimited except by the horizon. In reality, the boundaries and true essence of the world are set by the four elements: air, fire, earth and water.

These four are essential to the order and harmony of the world. Without them, it would sink into disorder and chaos. Within the parameters defined by the four elements, the world is organized and everything has its place and form.

The soul of the world, central to life itself, is symbolized by a naked woman standing upright on her right foot. She is the converse of The Hanged Man, who hangs in the void by his left foot.

She rules over the four elements and maintains harmony within the visible world. She is the guardian of the door through which flow all the currents of life, from birth until death. She represents the individual and collective consciousness. Consequently, she is the living mirror of our thoughts, our desires and our acts, whether good or evil.

If you draw The World card, it reflects very precisely the state of your soul. It could indicate the fulfilment of your wishes, a moral, sentimental, spiritual or material abundance and the realization of your aspirations and ideas, possibly even the need to escape.

It also reveals your potential riches and talents, a desire to gather together all the elements at your disposal, a thirst for the absolute and for harmony.

Yet whatever the case, never forget that this card represents your consciousness – the world is in you, because you are composed of the same elements as the world itself.

THE WORLD: KEY WORDS

POSITIVE ATTRIBUTES: satisfaction – joy – plenitude – happiness – success – accomplishment – broad perspectives – new possibilities – potential material, intellectual or spiritual riches – fertile imagination – expansion – opening up to the exterior world – relations abroad – idealism.

NEGATIVE ATTRIBUTES: vague desires – a sacrifice necessary to fulfil wishes (particularly in conjunction with the Hanged Man) – lack of common sense – Utopia – unrealistic ambitions.

THE FOOL

22 or 0 The Fool

THE FOOL IS THE TRAVELLER

At any given point in our lives, we are all travelling. These may be physical journeys, from one place to another. Equally, they may be evolutionary, as we pass from one stage of life to another; or spiritual, changing from one state of mind to another, moving from one thought, emotion or feeling to another.

To some extent, every one of us is always in a state of departure or motion, moving on in life, whether mentally or physically. As The Fool carries the world – his world – in his pack, so each and every one of us carries in ourselves the sum of what we are: our past, present and seeds of our future.

The Fool is a vagabond, tramp or hobo, a wanderer who seeks a new place to hang his hat. He walks, he advances and seeks, but he cannot settle in any one place – because the true object of his quest is himself.

This is why, when you turn over the card and see The Fool, it indicates a sudden impulse that is driving you to move on, to live differently or to seek inspiration elsewhere.

This is the card of travel, adventure and forward motion. However, it is also the indication of heedlessness, restlessness, a touch of folly; it is the dreamer or solitary seeker.

The Fool provides the link between The Magician of all beginnings and all possibilities and The World of self-fulfilment. He embodies the evolved person, symbolized by The World, and the newborn, symbolized by The Magician.

The Fool thereby represents the eternal and immutable cycle of life, death and rebirth. Indeed, it is by having no place to settle that we are renewed – dying at each stage so we can be better reborn as ourselves. 'Be passers-by', said Jesus in the Gospel according to Thomas. 'This world is a bridge, cross it, but do not set up home here', says an Indian proverb. The Fool reminds us that we are just passing through this world. He shows us that life is nothing but a stage in our journey and that the end of the line is just a frontier to crossed, somewhere beyond the horizon, in order to rejoin our country of origin – the Universe itself.

THE FOOL: KEY WORDS

POSITIVE ATTRIBUTES: departure – journey – movement – a move – seeking – forward motion – meeting – a person coming towards you and you towards them.

NEGATIVE ATTRIBUTES: unconsidered impulses – error – heedlessness – instability – a character that is easily influenced – restlessness – incoherence – flight.

YOU IN THIS SITUATION

THE MAGICIAN

1

1 The Magician

In this situation you believe that you are able to act of your own free will, that you must be enterprising and constructive but that everything still remains to be done.

Your question may be related to a person who is immature or young in years, or to someone who is potentially rich in good qualities and possibilities but lacking in experience; it may concern a new position that might offer attractive prospects, if you can demonstrate initiative and imagination.

THE HIGH PRIESTESS

2

2 The High Priestess

You are cautious, reserved and in a state of uncertainty in this situation. You find it difficult to open up to others. You are not telling everything that you know, but this does not mean that you are not thinking about it.

Your question may concern a more mature person – either in terms of years or experience – (most probably a woman) or someone who is dedicated to study or research and who possesses a degree of wisdom. On the other hand, it may reveal an important situation that is not totally fulfilling, as its possibilities are not readily apparent.

THE EMPRESS

3

3 The Empress

Here, you are bringing generous and positive feelings into play while at the same time remaining realistic and aware of your capabilities, of what you want and what you are.

Your question may relate to an excellent and upright person (most likely a woman) who is full of goodwill and good feeling. It may reveal a situation that is good in the material sense and from which you can certainly profit even more.

4 | The Emperor

THE EMPEROR

4

Here you are demonstrating authority in either a positive or negative way, depending on the circumstances. Sure of yourself and of your prerogatives, you seize the initiative with confidence. You have the power. It is up to you to make good use of it.

Your question may relate to a decision-maker, someone (generally a man) who may well be very sure of himself, uncompromising, down-to-earth and who may support or oppose you with equal zeal. Alternatively, it may reveal a position that is solid and long lasting, so long as constant pressure is maintained, along with constant monitoring of all related aspects.

5 | The High Priest

THE HIGH PRIEST

5

In this situation you demonstrate your seriousness, tenacity and wisdom. You are doing your best to ensure that all the elements involved are clarified in order to reach a harmonious conclusion.

Your question may concern a mature or experienced person (generally a man), who is able to provide moral and/or material support when the need arises. It may relate to an intelligent, cultured person or a stable, significant situation, one where moral, social and material responsibilities are always at the fore.

6 | The Lovers

THE LOVERS

6

This is a situation with two interpretations: either you are faced with a choice or it is simply a matter of your love life.

Your question may be related to a person who is definitely looking for a relationship or improved communication. Alternatively, it may be someone who has some difficulty in finding their way in life, in making choices, in settling down and in finding stability, particularly on the emotional front. It can also reveal a situation where a choice is needed, one where you must take a decision or reach an agreement.

7

7 The Chariot

Here, you are forging ahead, determined to make every conceivable effort to ensure that you achieve your aims as quickly as possible.

Your question may be related to a headstrong, dynamic, daring person, who remains undaunted by any obstacle, or it may reveal a situation where you must not relax your grip or let your attention slip if you want to be successful. It may also, quite simply, concern a move, a journey or an adventure that will be by no means relaxing.

8

8 Justice

In this situation you maintain an honest, upright attitude. If need be, you are capable of bringing things to a firm conclusion or simply of demonstrating your balanced approach to both material and moral issues.

Your question may be connected to a relationship with a person linked, closely or distantly, with the legal world (lawyer, judge, etc.), or with a person who is well-balanced, but more guided by rules and principle than feelings. It may also reveal a situation where elements of justice are brought into play, or simply a good, stable, risk-free situation.

9

9 The Hermit

Without any doubt, you are feeling alone and isolated – as if you have no one to rely upon except yourself. Alternatively, you may be looking quite seriously for solutions to your problems and answers to your questions.

Your question may relate to a single or elderly person, or someone who is involved in study or research. It may be someone who is very withdrawn, or not very generous. Alternatively, it may be a cautious, concentrated, ambitious and secretive person – someone who is advancing step by step towards the goal they have established for themselves. It may also reveal an austere, difficult situation that is developing slowly and in which you need to act with extreme caution.

10 The Wheel of Fortune

THE WHEEL OF FORTUNE

10

Here, it looks as if you are allowing yourself to be carried along by events, enjoying the highs and enduring the lows, but basically trusting in yourself and your future.

Your question may be related to a person who is currently touched by luck of some sort, be it good or bad. It could be about someone who is failing to keep a grip on his destiny, allowing himself to be carried along by the tide of events. Alternatively, it may reveal an unstable situation (but one that is not without riches) that is, most certainly, evolving – whether negatively or positively.

11 Strength

STRENGTH

11

Clearly, you have the situation well in hand. You are maintaining gentle pressure, and whatever happens you will get what you want as a result of the calm power of your will.

Your question may be related to a strong-willed, brave, understanding and determined person, one who does not fear difficulty or responsibility and knows how to control the situation. It could also reveal a solid, unchanging situation that can provide reliable and tangible support, whatever the circumstances.

12 The Hanged Man

THE HANGED MAN

12

You are not in full control in this situation and you must accept this state of affairs for the moment; you can do nothing – or you are doing nothing – to change things.

Your question may be related to someone who is denied free choice in some way or is in a situation of dependency. Equally, it may be someone who is suffering the consequences of their past errors, finding themselves in a dead-end, from which there is apparently no way out for the moment, or in which nothing constructive can be done. Alternatively – and more simply – it may be a situation where you simply need to wait and accept what is happening, grinning and bearing it patiently as you do so.

13

13 Death

In this situation you are the person responsible for – or possibly the victim of – a radical, unexpected change that will certainly lead to something new in your life.

Your question may deal with someone who is looking for change, who is currently undergoing change or who will experience a change in their way of life or in things that are important to them. It could also concern the end of something: an abrupt halt to an established situation or of a material or moral advantage you may have.

14

14 Temperance

In this situation, you are weighing up the pros and cons and assessing all aspects before deciding to act. You are keen to ensure that relations between the people or parties concerned should be good.

Your question may be related to a conciliatory person. It may be someone gifted at communication, who is open to new and unusual ideas and who is always ready to exercise influence to ensure harmony. It may also reveal an unforeseen situation, one offering opportunities and new chances, whether they are intellectual, emotional or business-related.

15

15 The Devil

Undoubtedly, here you are behaving in a rather excessive or passionate way, or maybe you simply believe that all means are acceptable and good in order to achieve your ends.

Your question may be related to someone who is tortured by their passions or desires, or who is greedy, self-absorbed, very attached to material goods and doubtless lacking in scruples. It may also reveal a situation that is disorderly, disconcerting, elating, intense, troubling and troubled, but which may nevertheless turn out to be very profitable when it is related to the material world or your finances.

16 | **The Tower**

THE TOWER

16

You are feeling destabilized and are influenced by feelings of anger in this situation. Or maybe you have just suffered an unavoidable moral or physical shock – one that may turn out to be an unpleasant blow dealt by fate or, on the contrary, a real liberation.

Your question may concern a person who, similarly, has just suffered a shock or who has initiated or suffered a sudden but necessary upheaval in their existence, liberating them from all constraints. Alternatively, it may reveal an unstable situation, an inevitable upheaval, or a sudden, unforeseeable event that calls everything into question and which you may even consider to be a deliverance or relief.

17 | **The Star**

THE STAR

17

In this situation you feel fine and in perfect harmony with your environment and the people around you. You are confident in yourself and in the opportunities that are available to you.

Your question may relate to someone who is attentive, receptive, inspired and creative, or to a person who is full of hope and good will. It may also reveal an easy, relaxed, happy and trustworthy situation or one that has to do with creation or something new, unexpected and positive.

18 | **The Moon**

THE MOON

18

Isolation and feelings of nervousness are apparent in this situation. You are prey to terrible confusion and trouble, due to misunderstandings and differences of opinion, and are suffering physical or moral malaise. All in all, things are none too good!

Your question may be related to a person whose intentions or behaviour is not clear, or to someone who is morally or physically ill or caught up in an intense, unpleasant relationship. It may have to do with someone who is too dependent upon, and smothered by, their family environment. It could also concern a difficult situation that must be resolved as a matter of urgency.

19

19 The Sun

Here, like the sign itself, you radiate ease and happiness. You can see things clearly and your physical and mental aptitudes are at a peak. Ready and willing to share your happiness and ideas, you are all set to be swept away by the attraction of affinities.

Your question may be related to an open, warm, communicative person who carries with them a certain success, or someone who is in a happy relationship, or who sincerely hopes to be in one. It may also reveal a situation that will most certainly be the springboard for success or a useful and necessary clarification that identifies various elements favourable to the success of projects and undertakings.

20

20 Judgement

In this situation, a proposition is put to you, you are being called upon, or you are undergoing change and renewal.

Your question may concern a relationship with someone who is currently undergoing major change or getting back on their feet after a difficult period in their lives. It may reveal a situation that is recovering or changing for the better, starting afresh on a sound, healthy footing.

21

21 The World

In this situation, for you everything is possible. You have plenty of trump cards up your sleeve and circumstances are favourable. In short, you have all that you could wish for.

Your question may be related to someone who is far away, of whom you are thinking or who is thinking of you. It may have to do with someone who is happy and totally fulfilled, who knows how best to use their talents and gifts. Yet again, it could relate to someone who is achieving the fulfilment of all their wishes. It may also indicate a fertile situation that is expanding towards new horizons.

22 The Fool

THE FOOL

22

Here, you are acting impulsively and quickly but nothing seems able to hold you back; it is useless to try and make you see reason.

Your question may be related to someone who is very restless, who is on a journey or travelling, someone who is continually on the move, never stopping to take stock of what is going on around them. Equally, it could be someone who is leaving their past behind them once and for all, who is turning the page, or who arrives or leaves suddenly. It may also reveal a situation in which events are taking place at break-neck speed, and are impossible to rein back – in a positive or a negative sense.

YOUR CURRENT
SITUATION

' If I knew how a tree contracts to a seed,
I could also predict how the tree grows from
this seed. If we know the core of the situation,
we can predict its consequences. '

Marie-Louise Von Franz
La psychologie de la divination ou le Hasard significant
Éditions Poiesis-Payot

➕ You are currently enjoying high levels of energy, have sound instincts and are receiving excellent advice from those around you. All this guarantees stable and healthy vitality and real freedom of choice.

❤ You conduct your emotional life with a certain amount of reserve, but you are sincere and unambiguous. The initiatives you take on the romantic front are both sound and constructive.

👪 You can exert influence within your family circle through your enthusiasm and generous initiatives, and also by anticipating the wishes of your nearest and dearest.

📋 A professional initiative enables you to put into practice a carefully constructed plan, even if you need to keep it under wraps and demonstrate a certain amount of caution.

🏦 You are in a position to implement constructive, stabilizing initiatives on the financial front. You will look after your assets in a skilful way.

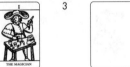

➕ Your high levels of physical and intellectual energy guarantee you freedom of choice and enable you to benefit fully from your health and well-being.

❤ You are in a position to take constructive, practical, intelligent initiatives in your love life. You can act freely, confident that you will achieve your emotional goals.

👪 By acting constructively and intelligently and with the support of those close to you, you will introduce your initiatives successfully or achieve your goals.

📋 Your professional initiatives will help you firm up your plans and act in a skilful and constructive way to impose your wishes and exploit your skills and energy.

🏦 Sound and healthy circumstances help you to introduce useful and smart initiatives that will guarantee profit and the solidity of your finances.

| 1 | 4 |

4

1

You are taking reasonable initiatives or following the shrewd advice of experts. As a result, you will be assured of stable vitality and healthy levels of energy.

You have the determination to make your wishes come true or to affirm your feelings, thereby demonstrating just how serious you are about your commitments.

You are fully responsible for the determined initiatives that will meet with the approval and encouragement of your family circle, ensuring that they become reality.

Your practical, serious initiatives and plans may find approval among influential or informed people, who will then be able to support and help implement them.

Make some concrete, determined moves on the financial front and carry out some projects, but do not exceed the guidelines imposed by your obligations and responsibilities.

| 1 | 5 |

5

1

You are faced with an important choice or need to ask the advice of an informed person or consult a doctor. This should provide you with the reassurance you require and allow you to focus your energies more effectively.

You are taking an initiative or making an important choice in your love life. The consequence will certainly be a union or a much more stable relationship.

Someone close to you or a member of your family will give you the approval, support or advice you need to make an important choice or implement a decisive initiative.

You are using all your skills, energy and spirit of initiative to ensure that an agreement is put in place or a contract is concluded that has every chance of succeeding.

It is time for you to make key choices and implement decisive initiatives as dictated by your sense of duty. They will also prove useful to the stability of your finances.

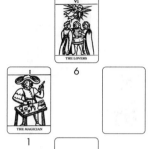

You are full of vitality, energy and enthusiasm and have everything you need to ensure stability and balance.

If you demonstrate initiative, determination and goodwill, you will achieve all your romantic hopes and dreams.

It is time to act decisively and determinedly to make choices, put your enthusiastic initiatives into practice and behave in an astute and positive manner on the domestic front.

Take the initiative and use all your energy, professional skill and goodwill to make choices and agreements that will help your current situation.

Resolve to make dynamic choices and take astute initiatives that will be useful to your financial situation.

You can achieve a healthy balance in your life and put your dynamism and energy levels to constructive use by acting with determination to make the best of the opportunities open to you.

You are keen to act as honestly and fairly as possible to achieve what you want in your love life.

Be strict and determined in your domestic initiatives. The combination of your efforts, straightforwardness and honesty should enable you to achieve what you have in mind.

Act with discipline and rigour when preparing your initiatives and plans at work. Don't relax your efforts or will to succeed. You will get there in the end.

Be tough and disciplined in preparing your financial plans or initiatives. Don't relax your efforts to achieve a degree of balance in your monetary affairs.

1 8

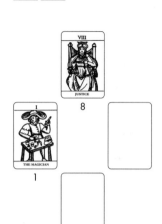

8

1

Be cautious, sensible and prudent when it comes to establishing balance and maintaining your energy levels.

You are full of goodwill towards people, but you are also realistic about your close relationships. The search for balance in your life sometimes threatens to override other concerns. This makes you rather demanding if not entirely uncompromising.

Your own stability is your highest priority. As a result you take prudent, considered initiatives and are guided by your determination to be just and fair.

The long-term plans that are currently being drawn up with thoroughness and rigour will certainly consolidate the stability of your professional position.

Take prudent and carefully considered initiatives or implement long-term plans to help bring balance to your financial affairs.

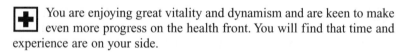

1 9

9

1

You are enjoying great vitality and dynamism and are keen to make even more progress on the health front. You will find that time and experience are on your side.

You can focus freely and actively on precise emotional goals and can assess their importance with clarity and realism.

You will soon come to understand to what extent your current plans and future ideas are both useful and essential to the development of your domestic environment.

Your dynamic initiatives and projects are making speedy progress. As long as you leave nothing to chance, you will be in a position to assess their long-term consequences.

It is time to make moves to help your finances make speedy progress. Nevertheless, you should remain cautious and realistic and leave nothing to chance.

✚ You are enjoying excellent levels of energy and vigour, and your morale is high. As a result, you feel completely in control of your personal development.

♥ You are free to do as you choose and can help your love life develop according to your wishes, secure in the knowledge that there will be a successful conclusion.

Your willingness, initiative, skill and courage will allow you to exercise influence in your domestic environment. The situation will develop along the lines you were anticipating.

You are taking constructive, if somewhat bold, initiatives to achieve full control over your professional development. They have every chance of success.

You have everything you need to bring about the constructive and balanced development of your financial affairs. You can therefore act with complete confidence.

✚ Your health situation is static. A rest would do you some good, so make some plans to achieve this.

♥ You will be obliged to make unbiased, unselfish moves. Alternatively, even though you act with the best of intentions, you will not achieve your emotional goals.

You feel constrained by, or over-dependent on, your family circle. You, however, are the only one who can make an appropriate response or take the unselfish and courageous steps that are needed to regain control over your domestic circumstances.

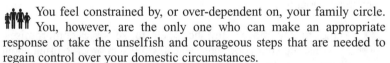
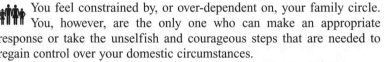

You may not be able to execute a plan or act on your own initiative, but by tackling the task at hand and making clear your own professional ability and good intentions, you will succeed in redressing the situation.

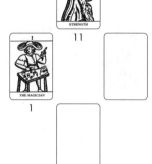

It is not easy for you to achieve financial independence, but it should be within your grasp if you demonstrate your spirit of initiative and goodwill.

1 12

It is time to take some radical steps to recover from the physical and mental fatigue you have been experiencing. It has been preventing you from pursuing your wishes and desired course of action.

Radical action is needed if you are to overcome a limiting, unsatisfactory or dead-end situation in your love life.

Now is the time to take radical action to get your situation back on track and eliminate the constraints or obstacles that are jeopardizing its development, or simply to acquire independence.

You must take some radical steps to ensure that you acquire or regain greater freedom of action, which will probably also be the catalyst for an important change in your situation.

Decisive action is needed to overturn a limiting financial situation or monetary impasse.

1 13

It is time to make a careful assessment of your true potential. Take the appropriate action and initiatives, find the right compromises and avoid any factors potentially harmful to your health.

Make sure that your initiatives are both well-timed and skilful and that you demonstrate your diplomacy and empathy. If you feel that radical change is required in your love life, however, now is the time to do something about it.

Make timely moves and be open to sensible compromises. Demonstrate your good sense and flexibility in order to bring about a basic change in your domestic environment.

Try to demonstrate flexibility and diplomacy. Make the appropriate arrangements and agreements needed to carry out your plans for change. You will be able to resolve a certain professional matter if you impose your will with care.

You have the upper hand in a profitable transaction or business arrangement, which will prove useful in bringing about an important change or the conclusion of some financial business.

You expend your extremely high levels of energy almost without thinking, sometimes in an intemperate or chaotic way. It is time for a little moderation.

You are open to compromise only if it brings your emotional targets closer or helps you to reach your goals or impose your wishes. At heart, you are still independent and nonconformist.

You are making moves on the domestic front to pursue your own goals and are taking advantage of various opportunities that will allow you to satisfy your own desires.

You are working hard at negotiations and are imposing compromises and agreements to ensure that your plans succeed and your professional targets have every chance of being met.

It is time to show some initiative and to take advantage of events or circumstances that will bring success on the financial front.

Your apparently highly excitable condition puts you at risk, and there is a danger that you will act prematurely or in error unless you adopt strict measures and provoke a health crisis that will ultimately prove beneficial.

You risk bringing disruption to your love life by your sudden, impulsive actions or your wish to satisfy your desires at all costs and achieve your ends by whatever means.

You will take sudden steps to achieve your aims and satisfy your wishes as quickly as possible and with little regard for the methods.

You will make disruptive moves to achieve your professional targets or execute your plans with all possible speed. You don't mind what risks you take or what means you use.

You are prepared to use all possible means to achieve your financial ambitions. Take care, you will reap what you sow.

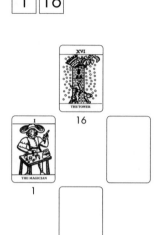

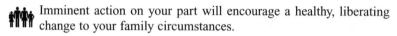 Take action to detoxify your body. Eliminate stress and any other potentially damaging factors that could diminish your enthusiasm and adversely affect your open, receptive nature.

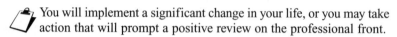 You are taking positive steps towards declaring your feelings or bringing about changes to your love life. These changes are inevitable but will prove beneficial.

Imminent action on your part will encourage a healthy, liberating change to your family circumstances.

You will implement a significant change in your life, or you may take action that will prompt a positive review on the professional front.

Your financial skills and flair will prompt a reappraisal of your situation and assets and instigate new and positive initiatives.

A health problem or general feeling of fatigue and lassitude will prevent you from taking maximum advantage of your natural resources and will have a negative impact on your energy.

You never quite manage to express your feelings fully. You are scared that your hopes and plans will fail, and, rightly or wrongly, you feel insecure and disappointed as a result.

Your initiatives and plans will be difficult to bring to fruition, but if you persevere and act intelligently, you can improve conditions and pave the way to success.

You need to demonstrate a spirit of initiative and prove your skilfulness in order to introduce a new venture and create favourable conditions at work.

Your own capacity for hard work and a financial initiative will help you improve your resources, and although progress may be slow, it will be completely above board.

1 18

➕ You can find positive, dynamic ways to clear up health issues and at the same time banish any doubts and worries on this score.

♥ Take the initiative to clear up any confusion, including the misunderstandings and subterfuges that so often accumulate in your emotional life.

It is up to you to shed light on domestic affairs. Alternatively, your own dynamism and enthusiasm will clear up delicate or difficult issues that may arise and introduce bad feeling at home.

Despite the delays and the obstacles in your path, you will be able to carry out your plans for a partnership or association. Your initiatives and undertakings will be met with approval.

You can take positive steps to clarify your situation and execute your plans on the financial front, even if there are problems to resolve and obstacles to overcome on the way.

18

1

1 19

➕ Your goodwill and dynamism will prompt a return to top form and your former high levels of energy.

♥ You are using your initiative to change your attitude or to be more appreciative and understanding. As a result, your love life will become clearer, different and happier.

Action is required. Use your goodwill and skill to introduce something new on the domestic front that will clear the air and leave the way open for you to carry out your plans successfully.

You will make moves to show your plans or activities in a new light. Alternatively, you will reconsider a possible partnership carefully.

You will take steps towards achieving the successful re-floatation of your finances.

19

1

1	20

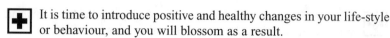 It is time to introduce positive and healthy changes in your life-style or behaviour, and you will blossom as a result.

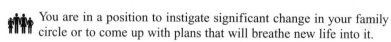 You are trying to inject new energy into your love life or assemble all your emotional resources. This will result in a real transformation on the emotional front.

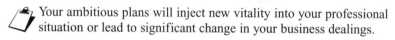 You are in a position to instigate significant change in your family circle or to come up with plans that will breathe new life into it.

Your ambitious plans will inject new vitality into your professional situation or lead to significant change in your business dealings.

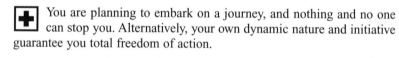 You are making some bold plans or gathering together all available assets in order to implement change or produce a revival in your financial affairs.

1	21

 You are planning to embark on a journey, and nothing and no one can stop you. Alternatively, your own dynamic nature and initiative guarantee you total freedom of action.

You want everything, you want it now, and nothing is going to stand in your way. Although your intentions may be sincere, watch out for mistakes that could lead to impulsive and extravagant behaviour.

You are making plans for a journey or move that will bring you all you desire on the domestic front.

You are planning a sudden departure. This will lead to a much more interesting situation all round. Alternatively, you are searching for the assistance you need to execute an important project.

If you are in need of help or support on the financial front to carry out your plans, try to secure it soon, because success will follow hot on its heels.

➕ You are brimming with vitality and dynamism, but have a tendency to waste your energy. If you have the chance, get away for a while and relax.

❤️ You are adventurous and impetuous and are easily carried away, finding self-control difficult. There is no real harm in this, unless you confuse dreams with reality.

👪 You will make a sudden decision to set off on a journey, to move house or to distance yourself from your family circle in order to find your independence.

📋 You are enterprising and full of enthusiasm and initiative. Fortified by these qualities you can look for a way to carry out your plans or find a job.

🔳 Look for help or support when you are carrying out your plans. Ultimately, however, you should rely only on your own efforts to answer your needs.

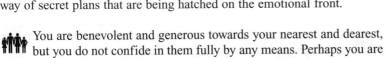

➕ Your reserve and caution guarantee the liberal but not excessive use of your natural enthusiasm and energy.

❤️ You are expressing your feelings with a certain reserve and propriety, perhaps even with a degree of timidity, but this will not stand in the way of secret plans that are being hatched on the emotional front.

👪 You are benevolent and generous towards your nearest and dearest, but you do not confide in them fully by any means. Perhaps you are being a little secretive in order to keep your current plans under wraps.

📋 Demonstrate caution, discretion and patience when you conceive and carry out a potentially profitable plan in which you have the initiative.

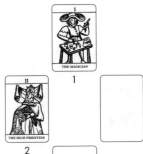

🔳 Be careful with your money and cautious in the management of your affairs. You can then take generous initiatives or be confident of their success.

2 3

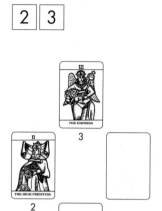

➕ Your cautious, serious nature and sense of responsibility assure you of high but measured levels of energy and vitality.

❤ Although you do not overtly show your feelings, they are deep, serious and genuine. All the efforts you make to bring stability to your love life will be fully rewarded.

👨‍👩‍👧 Your discretion, serious nature and sense of responsibility enable you to be confident of the moral and material support of your family.

📋 Your cautious, serious and responsible behaviour at work will ensure that you have all the support you need to take action or carry out your plans.

🎲 Examine your current situation in a methodical manner, taking into account your assets and liabilities and act with caution, but don't lose sight of your generosity.

2 4

➕ With your reserve and prudence, you are confident that you are balanced and have made the appropriate health-related choices.

❤ Although you are naturally reserved and inclined to conceal your feelings, you will soon come to appreciate their value and importance and make a decisive emotional choice.

👨‍👩‍👧 A decisive choice lies before you, but you must demonstrate caution and discretion before revealing or imposing it.

📋 You are demonstrating prudence and caution in the hope of making the best choice or reaching the right agreement, either discreetly or even secretly.

🎲 Do not rush into decisions and be selective in your choices. You will then be assured of stable finances.

✚ Your measured enthusiasm and controlled energy guarantee stable health and a calm but assured maturing, both physical and mental.

♥ Your caution and natural reserve will enable you to fulfil your secret hopes for your love life.

👪 Your family's circumstances are based on stable, sincere values and are focused on a particular couple. Alternatively, you are employing caution and discretion in your efforts to execute your plans and gradually introduce stability into your domestic circle.

✎ Tackle your plans with prudence and discretion, but don't relax your efforts to secure the support you need for success.

▦ No matter what obligations and responsibilities you have to assume, you are secretly making efforts to progressively stabilize and improve your financial position.

✚ Your natural reserve and caution are based on your desire to maintain your balance at all costs and to be consistently able to make the best choices.

♥ You are undeniably honest and loyal on the emotional front, but this also makes you demanding, even intolerant on occasion, and highly selective in your choice of partner.

👪 Be cautious and selective in your choices and decisions, but don't be too fussy or uncompromising with your loved ones.

✎ You are making choices and decisions or reaching agreements with caution and discretion, opting for the solution you feel is the fairest and the best.

 It is time to be prudent and discreet, bringing all your experience to bear when making financial choices.

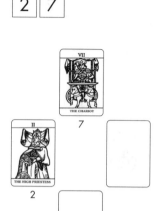

2	7

➕ Be cautious and reasonable and you will succeed in controlling your energy and dynamism and make the best practical and positive use of it.

❤️ You will have a premonition that will turn out to be true. Alternatively, you may experience a personal revelation or a discovery that will prompt you to overcome your natural reserve and achieve your emotional goals.

👪 You will discover or divulge a fact that until now has been kept secret or has been obscure. Without doubt this will encourage you to find ways to achieve your domestic goals.

📋 You are methodically searching for the best ways to achieve your aims or bring your plans to fruition. You may have kept these secret until now, but the time has come to reveal them.

💰 Be careful and realistic with money and you will, in time, succeed in improving your financial position.

2	8

➕ You exhibit caution and balance in issues relating to your personal development or in changes that you might experience. You will make sure that you do not do anything that might jeopardize your equilibrium.

❤️ Your natural reserve and instinctive caution don't appear to be inhibiting progress in your love life, but they do set the boundaries of your romantic experience according to your own need for emotional stability and security.

👪 Despite apparent inertia or a constant concern to maintain domestic stability and balance, your family's circumstances continue to develop at their own pace, making slow but sure progress.

📋 Your professional position can develop only if it remains within the framework imposed on it by a need for balance and stability.

💰 Be careful with money. Wait for the right moment or favourable circumstances, in order to take stock of your situation, its stability and your resources.

You are enjoying high levels of concentrated, focused energy, as a result of which you are wise, resilient and, more important, aware of the precautions you must take to protect your stability.

You are discreet, trusting and emotionally aware, and you know that, with time, your relationships and ties are becoming deeper and more stable.

Your discretion, good sense and strength of character will eventually allow you to achieve a stable domestic situation and achieve your domestic goals.

Your powers of conviction are effective yet unobtrusive and your ability to concentrate is intense. Coupled with your perceptiveness, these qualities enable you to find practical, realistic solutions to issues at work.

You are assessing your current resources with realism and caution. This will allow you to take a long-term view of your finances.

You are succumbing to physical weakness and low morale as a result of negligence rather than intent. Currently it is difficult to say how your health will develop.

You may be showing signs of self-sacrifice and self-denial or a tendency to be influenced by events around you. No matter what the circumstances, you are not following your chosen path emotionally and are beginning to see that this is the case.

You are devoted to your nearest and dearest, but your family circumstances leave you little freedom of choice and action. All the same, you can expect changes to take place.

You lack autonomy at work. Alternatively your professional situation is well and truly blocked, but perhaps you are aware, without revealing it, that change is on the horizon.

Although you may, to some extent, be aware of the fact, you are currently being restricted by a feeling of lethargy. You need to rely on particular developments in your circumstances to effect a reversal in your financial fortunes.

2 | 11

Caution and temporary lethargy will prompt you to implement radical changes in your behaviour or lifestyle and help you make the most of your well-being.

You are able to introduce major changes in your emotional behaviour or your relationship in a quiet, cautious way. You will take the situation in hand and achieve your aims.

An unassuming, confident and perceptive attitude will help you reap the rewards of domestic opportunities or encourage an important, vital change.

You are aware that you can truly benefit from a professional situation that is completely under control. You can act confidently but cautiously to introduce dramatic and ambitious changes aimed at reinforcing your position.

Take care to be cautious, vigilant and moderate in your financial dealings and you will keep a firm grip on monetary issues.

2 | 12

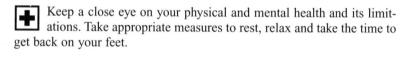

Keep a close eye on your physical and mental health and its limitations. Take appropriate measures to rest, relax and take the time to get back on your feet.

You are secretly making moves to find compromises or well-timed agreements. However, your love life is unlikely to make much progress as a direct result of these changes.

Your domestic circumstances are not easy, even if you don't admit it. You are making real efforts to be more understanding and to find appropriate, intelligent compromises that will put things right.

Be discreet, diplomatic and accommodating if you want to set a situation to rights, resolve a problem or become more independent. If necessary, bring to light any information that might be appropriate.

An honest and timely assessment of your funds will help you face up to your financial obligations and constraints. Your subsequent moves will be measured but effective.

2 13

  Your inertia, passivity and carelessness may well jeopardize your health rather seriously, or confront you with a major problem that will require an energetic and radical solution.

Your hidden passions are sure to be the catalyst for imminent, inevitable and profound changes in your emotional life.

Wisdom and passion, stability and disorder are all confused in your family life at the moment, and you are finding it hard to rein in your desire for radical change.

Despite your apparent stability and good sense, in reality you are impatient to profit with all speed from developments at work that could prove to be to your advantage.

You are studying the possibility of a radical change or the significant profit that you could achieve from the conclusion of a particular deal. You are impatient for this event to take place and are secretly trying to speed up the process.

13

2

2 14

You have a tendency to accept misfortune and upheaval passively, without expressing your true feelings. Your instinctive reactions, together with your accommodating, flexible nature, will help you adapt to the most disruptive of circumstances and minimize their impact.

You are doing everything in your power to redress a delicate situation that is hanging by a thread or to prevent upheaval or rupture in your love life, a crisis you are anticipating in silence.

You are doing everything possible to set a difficult situation to rights or to prevent, or minimize, upheavals that will threaten your domestic stability.

After a period of anticipation and preparation, professional negotiations will suddenly get back on track. You will find yourself in a position to reach agreements that you had already foreseen or envisaged.

A sudden and well-timed exit or solution on the financial front will surface, although it will almost certainly disrupt your plans and forecasts.

14

2

2 15

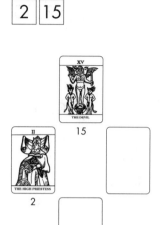

XV

THE DEVIL

15

II

THE HIGH PRIESTESS

2

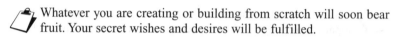 You enjoy excellent powers of recovery and are aware of how to make the best, measured use of your reserves of energy.

Your apparent reserve, stability and good sense belie your deep, passionate feelings, and in spite of yourself, you encourage similar passion in others.

Your calm, reserved attitude conceals a demanding, passionate temperament. You have ambitious dreams and will not rest until they come true.

Whatever you are creating or building from scratch will soon bear fruit. Your secret wishes and desires will be fulfilled.

If you are cautious, vigilant and imaginative your finances will no doubt flourish.

2 16

XVI

THE TOWER

16

II

THE HIGH PRIESTESS

2

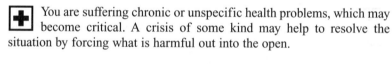 You are suffering chronic or unspecific health problems, which may become critical. A crisis of some kind may help to resolve the situation by forcing what is harmful out into the open.

You will suffer a shock or an upheaval in your emotional life that will free you from the misunderstandings, disappointments and irritations that have been bubbling under for far too long.

Unspoken facts, misunderstandings and hypocrisy are creating a negative atmosphere in your domestic environment. The disruption that will occur will prove to be beneficial.

Even if you are unwilling to admit or express it, you really believe that an upheaval or crisis is vital if the problems, disagreements and feelings of insecurity currently threatening your professional status are to be resolved.

The results of an on-going assessment of your finances are not looking good, leaving you feeling insecure and certain that a crisis or upheaval is imminent.

104

✚ You have a radiant, healthy glow and a physical and mental stability that never leaves you short of energy.

♥ Despite your emotional purity and reserve, you don't doubt for a moment the sincerity and depth of your emotional relationships.

👪 You are looking forward to a happy event, which will bring a great deal of joy to your family.

📋 If you demonstrate discretion, caution and wisdom, you will be able to create a new partnership or achieve great success in any new and innovative undertakings.

💰 Your caution and good sense in relation to financial matters are fully rewarded. As a result you can enjoy your assets and resources to the full.

2 17

✚ Take a close look at your behaviour and lifestyle. You are too careless or passive, which are tendencies that could jeopardize your health. Take matters in hand, however, and you can avoid this.

♥ In theory, you are trying to change your behaviour and resolve emotional issues with appropriate discretion. In practice, however, your situation is getting worse, and if you allow things to continue as they are, nothing will be resolved.

👪 Despite the signs of change that you have been quietly noting, you cannot prevent a deterioration of domestic matters. You are at least aware of this situation, no matter how powerless you may be to change it.

📋 Expect to encounter difficulties when you are bailing out a professional situation or solving a problem, particularly since you cannot control all the elements involved. It could be that you are not being told the full story.

💰 If you are unable to discuss financial issues or even admit them to yourself, you will never succeed in re-floating your business. Your finances may deteriorate further.

2 18

2	19

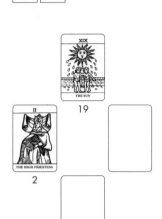

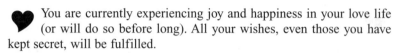 Your calm, unruffled character and quiet, cautious nature bring you inner harmony and great vitality.

You are currently experiencing joy and happiness in your love life (or will do so before long). All your wishes, even those you have kept secret, will be fulfilled.

You will experience joy and happiness with your nearest and dearest. Alternatively, the harmony that reigns in your family is due mostly to one particular member, who is both generous and wise.

You are carefully assembling all the factors necessary for the formation of an alliance of some kind or the realization of a personal and professional goal. You are throwing yourself wholeheartedly into this exercise and can be assured of its complete success.

Your financial position is stable and clear, allowing you to bring together all the resources at your disposal and benefit from them in a useful and constructive way.

2	20

As long as you steer clear of any ill-considered or hasty behaviour you can start anticipating a return to normality on the health front.

By acting sensibly and shrewdly and making steady progress, avoiding thoughtless or hasty behaviour, you will discover the solution to or revival needed in your love life, or find the way to make the necessary changes.

You are secretly looking at the prospect of a change, a house move or a new lease of life that will occur on the domestic front.

You are giving serious thought to a proposal before giving your response and becoming involved in a new development, change or reappraisal of your current status.

A mixture of cautious and bold action, of lethargy and energetic movement will assist in the re-floating of your finances.

Your steady, cautious nature means you have no problems fulfilling your obligations and responsibilities, confident of your physical and mental well-being.

♥ A union with a solid basis or a serious, stable emotional relationship has every chance of flourishing.

Your steady, cautious nature allows you to assume your obligations and responsibilities freely, leading to a stable, flourishing family life.

The approval or unobtrusive but genuine support of an influential person will provide you with the opportunity to achieve the progress on which you were counting.

If you remain cautious and aware of your material and moral responsibilities, you will succeed in bringing all your resources together and accomplishing the expansion on which you were counting.

21

2

A combination of caution, impatience and ill-timed impulsiveness leaves you with fluctuating energy levels. Your best option is to take a break and relax a little, especially as you are under no illusions about your health.

♥ You are concealing or restraining your affectionate feelings or generally showing caution on the emotional front. However, the arrival of a person close to your heart or an unexpected meeting threatens to disrupt matters.

Your natural steadiness makes you cautious when faced with the prospect of change, a house move or travel plan.

The anticipated arrival of someone or an event you have been expecting could have a significant impact on your professional situation.

Be cautious when moving your money around, or put some to one side for a journey or to help bring about a change of some kind.

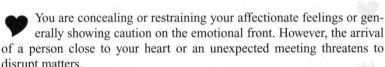
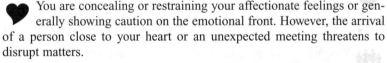
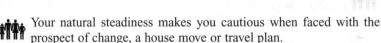

22

2

3 1

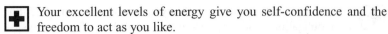 Your excellent levels of energy give you self-confidence and the freedom to act as you like.

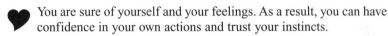 You are sure of yourself and your feelings. As a result, you can have confidence in your own actions and trust your instincts.

Be generous, understanding and determined and you will achieve what you want in your domestic situation.

You can achieve your professional ambitions if you are proactive, enterprising and determined.

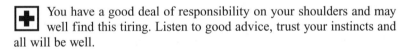 Your financial situation is sound at present. As a result you can act as you see fit.

3 2

 You have a good deal of responsibility on your shoulders and may well find this tiring. Listen to good advice, trust your instincts and all will be well.

You are sure of your feelings and are remaining faithful to your promises, but there is perhaps something that you do not know, a secret in your life that is preventing you from acting freely.

You are aware of your responsibilities and obligations on the domestic front.

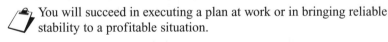 You will succeed in executing a plan at work or in bringing reliable stability to a profitable situation.

Your situation is sound, but you must not forget your material and moral obligations.

➕ Your energy levels are excellent and you are feeling dynamic. It is time to take action and forge ahead.

♥ Follow your feelings and instincts. You are in a good position to achieve your emotional goals.

👪 You seem active and sure of yourself and your feelings, and you have every reason to be so. Everything is looking rosy, and your family life is developing well.

📝 Courage and hard work never hurt anyone. Forge ahead and you will certainly succeed.

💠 Your financial situation is sound, but you can make sure it progresses still further.

3 4

4

3

➕ Your energy levels are strong and steady, giving you the ability to tackle your responsibilities.

♥ You are currently in a stable, harmonious relationship or you are taking action to put your emotional life on a more secure and balanced footing.

👪 Your family life is enjoying a certain harmony, so don't be too strict with the people around you.

📝 The realization of a particular goal and its stability will require a certain degree of strictness and rigour in your professional behaviour.

💠 Your financial situation is good, but is subject to several constraints and obligations.

3 5

5

3

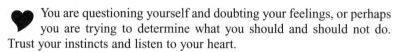

3 6

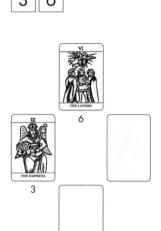

 You have great vitality, but you are still seeking to achieve a balance. Keep a close eye on your health.

 You are questioning yourself and doubting your feelings, or perhaps you are trying to determine what you should and should not do. Trust your instincts and listen to your heart.

You might feel rather alone, but in reality you are loved and appreciated as indeed you should be. Don't allow clear-sightedness to stifle your spontaneity.

You are in an interesting situation, but you must ask yourself where it is leading. An alternative will no doubt present itself. Think hard before taking action.

You must consider your options and make some important choices. Be sensible.

3 7

 Your energy levels are on the increase. You are making a good recovery and things are going well for you.

Your current situation is developing fast and you are in a good position to achieve what you want.

You hold all the winning cards and can manoeuvre your situation in the direction of your choice.

Your current situation is developing fast and profitably. You hold all the trump cards to suceed.

Your financial position is progressing. You can trust in current developments.

You are currently brimming with energy and vitality. What more could you ask?

You are sure of the genuine nature of your feelings and are sure of yourself. This is where your strength lies.

You have your present situation perfectly in hand, leaving you free to act as you see fit.

As things currently stand, your situation can only improve and achieve greater equilibrium. This will strengthen your position, if it still needs it.

 The growth of your finances depends on you alone, on the way you handle things and on the way you respond to current circumstances.

You are not in the peak of health. Take a rest if you feel the need and find ways to recover your natural energy and form.

You are in an uncomfortable situation. Dissatisfied, you doubt yourself and everything around you. When you react, trust in your instincts. You are up to the task in hand.

Your current situation is not totally satisfactory, but for the moment you have no alternative but to wait and investigate the problem in a thorough manner.

You must examine your position carefully. It appears that the promises it offered may not be realized even though it remains potentially advantageous.

Hazardous circumstances and constraints may currently be limiting your finances. Careful consideration should, however, enable you to put things right.

3 10

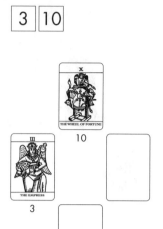

| + | Your good health depends on you alone, on your understanding and your natural instinct for self-preservation. |

Now is the time to take some positive action in order to achieve your emotional objectives.

Your situation is developing just as you hoped. Enjoy the change to the full, since you were no doubt its catalyst.

Your working situation should soon begin to develop profitably. Alternatively, a positive change is in the air.

You will reap what you have sown. You can therefore count on excellent profits that follow an upward curve.

3 11

Your measured dynamism, calm, intelligent nature and finely tuned instinct for self-preservation guarantee excellent health.

You are reaching a compromise or seizing an opportunity that will allow you to control the situation or achieve what you want on the emotional front.

Be understanding and open to compromise. You will achieve your domestic goals almost effortlessly.

Diplomatic behaviour will lead to profitable arrangements that will favour and consolidate your professional status.

You are in a position to do some good deals. Alternatively, a series of compromises is required to maintain your current position.

You are full of intense but poorly managed levels of energy. You seem excitable, irritable and impatient. Calm down or risk the unfortunate consequences of your own excesses.

You seem to be a victim of your own feelings and desires, following your instinct rather than reason. It is up to you to determine when this is an appropriate response to changing circumstances.

Continued dependence on satisfying your material desires will not bring the independence you claim to want but do little to achieve.

You are in a position that offers undeniable advantages but little freedom of action.

You may have ambitions that are beyond your means. Be cautious and try to contain your ambitions. Alternatively, you will achieve financial independence.

You are in a state of shock. It is likely that your current situation is undergoing major disruption. Take care of yourself in order to be able to face up to it.

You have just suffered a shock and are undergoing the radical changes that result.

It is time to implement key changes on the domestic front and rid yourself of any limiting factors.

You should be able to introduce a significant work-related change, the consequences of which will prove both useful and profitable.

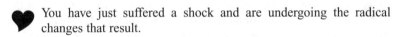

You have the power to find the way out of your current financial impasse and introduce profitable change.

3 | 14

You are physically healthy and normally calm. Everything is going well, and you can get on with your plans without fear.

You may be feeling romantic and inspired, or you may be in love. You are certainly enjoying a phase in your emotional life that is full of hope and promise.

A number of happy events seem to be occurring within your current domestic circle. You would be unwise not to relax and enjoy them.

You are in a good position to create a new situation or introduce innovations that prove to be profitable.

All your hopes should be encouraged. This is a time of good luck and opportunity for you.

3 | 15

There are some serious problems on the horizon. It would be unwise to play games with your health, so don't treat problems too lightly but at the same time avoid dramatizing them. You are well aware that your state of mind is also important.

You are in the middle of a crisis in your love life, or you are the victim of a relationship overwhelmed by passion. Beware of violent reactions, selfish desires or feelings that could cloud your judgement.

Your family life does not seem to be harmonious at the moment. No matter what your problems (illness, conflicts in your relationships, disappointments, delays, ups and downs of any kind) it is time for a forceful response if you want to avoid a crisis.

Your current professional environment is not particularly satisfactory, but you could take steps to turn it to your advantage. Expect to suffer a few delays, however, and to be confronted by a wide range of problems. Alternatively, there may quite simply be an error or a mistaken opinion at the root of your current situation.

Delays, mistakes and disappointments are the key words in your current situation. Accept the fact, don't dramatize it and don't make yourself ill over it.

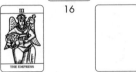

 You are in a perfectly good position to resolve any problems you may have or to face changes or upheavals in your life. Alternatively, you might find that a great weight has been lifted from your shoulders.

Your feelings are obvious, your behaviour is transparent and your relationships are healthy. Whether intentionally or not, you are the catalyst for a rather puzzling upheaval that brings you much joy.

You can shed light on your domestic circumstances and thereby avoid being surprised by any upheavals in the future.

Your professional position is so clear that you should have no fear of disruptions or sudden challenges that it may involve. You will always know how and when to withdraw if necessary.

You certainly have the means at your disposal to get things moving on the financial front or to find a satisfactory solution to your problems. What are you waiting for?

3 17

You are currently enjoying a new lease of life, recuperating or making a voyage of self-discovery. In case of illness, you should make a full recovery.

Circumstances should encourage action, or the achievement of your goals, or your love life could well experience a real revival.

You could be the one to get things back on track. Don't be afraid to ask for what you need. Your honesty, spontaneity and generosity will ensure that you get it.

Your constructive energy and intelligence should certainly help you achieve professional targets. Make suggestions and be proactive because conditions are encouraging.

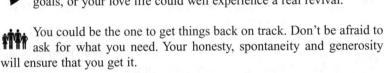

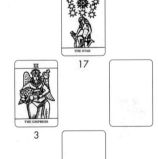

You are in a favourable position to emerge from any financial difficulties or get back on your feet.

| 3 | 18 |

XVIII

THE MOON

| III | 18 |

THE EMPRESS

3

✚ You may be tired, worried and restless, but you have nothing much to worry about in relation to your health. You might not be feeling on top form but your body is healthy enough.

♥ There will certainly be a few obstacles or delays before your wishes can come true, but rest assured that you will eventually get everything you want.

👪 Circumstances do not look particularly encouraging on the domestic front at the moment. However, this state of affairs will not last.

📋 Despite a few problems or delays, for which you are not responsible, you will see all your efforts fully rewarded and achieve your goals at work.

🁢 Despite a few last-minute obstacles, problems or delays, you will meet your financial targets in the end.

| 3 | 19 |

XIX

THE SUN

| III | 19 |

THE EMPRESS

3

✚ You are on top form and can act as you see fit. Be proactive, get things done, travel and trust your instincts.

♥ It is time to express your feelings and succumb to your impulses of affection. The person in your thoughts feels the same way. If you have yet to meet, it will not be long.

👪 Do just what you want to. You will derive much happiness and satisfaction from all your domestic ventures.

📋 Give free rein to your spirit of enterprise and take the opportunity to be proactive and get results. You are certain to achieve success.

🁢 You will put into effect a transaction that will prove universally profitable. What are you waiting for?

You are sufficiently aware of your duties and responsibilities not to let things slide. You have nothing to fear on the health front.

Although your current situation is stable, change and renewal are on the horizon.

 Be open to all options. If you continue to be kind and understanding you will resolve family issues and find the answer to any questions that may arise.

 You should be well placed to implement a profitable agreement or lucrative deal, and you enjoy greater prestige as a result.

Your financial position is healthy even if it is subject to a number of obligations and responsibilities.

You appear to have a passionate and sentimental nature. Your emotional state is, therefore, the key to your health and vitality, and if affairs of the heart are going well, then so is your health.

You are in such a good mood, your feelings are so transparent and your heart and mind are in such harmony, that there is no reason why you should not reach all your goals.

You can take steps to unite and gather all your loved ones around you. It is your generous, sincere and spontaneous attitude that entitles you to do this.

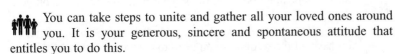 The time is right to go into partnership or association with friends or people close to you. A potential agreement is looking extremely auspicious.

You are ideally placed from a material point of view and apparently open to all options. Profitable results are inevitable.

3 | 22

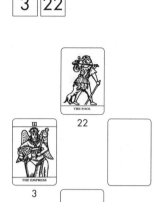

 Avoid stress and unnecessary haste and all will be well.

You are acting spontaneously, following your impulses and your instincts. It is up to you to decide whether you are right to depart, take action or rush into such things.

You might have to act in haste or leave suddenly, or you may be faced with a sudden event.

Your current situation is in a state of flux, and this seems to be a good thing. Take speedy action, forge ahead and don't forget the trump cards up your sleeve.

You are in a good position to secure what you need at the moment. It's time to get out and look for it.

4 | 1

You have high levels of energy and a keen awareness of your responsibilities, leaving you with nothing to fear on the health front. Even so, try to avoid overworking.

You are determined and sure of your rights. You can, therefore, act with assurance and in full confidence of a positive outcome.

You are imposing your own rules, your will and initiatives on your family. Be firm but understanding.

You have all the resources you need to ensure professional stability and support. As a result, you are in a strong position to take any necessary initiatives or decisions.

You have things well in hand, and there is no danger that you will relax your grip.

✚ You have a contradictory nature but are aware of the fact. You are, therefore, able to maintain a well-balanced state of health.

❤ You are more emotional than your apparent assurance and conviction would suggest. There is certainly someone or something close to your heart.

👪 Others currently expect you to be determined and to assume the role of decision-maker. Don't disappoint those around you.

📋 You will have to take a decision or make an important choice, taking on a decisive role, in order to bring a current plan to fruition.

▨ If you are firm in your choices and sure of your decisions, you will maintain your current balanced position.

✚ You are definitely not lacking in willpower, energy or intelligence. Matters are progressing well at the moment and you should have nothing to worry about.

❤ You are making plans and enjoying the company of someone with whom you are in complete agreement. Everything seems to be going as you would hope. Press on confidently.

👪 You are almost certainly acting as head of the family, and those around you are reaping the rewards of this, just as they had hoped. They know that no matter what happens, they can count on you.

📋 You have the courage, willpower and determination needed to ensure that your professional status develops. If you act decisively and with focus, you will almost certainly achieve your aims.

▨ It seems that nothing can stop you. You have a firm grip on the situation and the desire to make satisfactory progress.

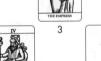

4 5

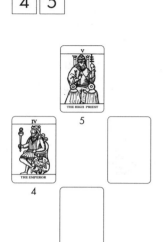

5

4

✚ Be careful. Don't do anything rash on the health front. Your current responsibilities won't allow you to cope with it.

♥ You are undergoing a maturing process and learning from your experiences. Your behaviour reflects this development and your actions are considered and sensible. There is no danger that you will be involved in anything by chance.

👪 You certainly have a number of moral obligations and responsibilities on your shoulders, but you accept them and bear the burden with confidence.

📋 If you are practical and realistic, you will go far without too much difficulty. As a result, things will settle down, and any doubts on the professional front will be dispelled. Trust no one but yourself, continue at your own pace and act with tenacity and determination.

🁢 You are practical, realistic, lucid and vigilant. Your finances will progress as planned, uninterrupted by chance mishaps.

4 6

6

4

✚ Everything is going well. Your self-control and practical intelligence keep instability and uncertainty at bay and protect you from the ups and downs most people experience at some time or other.

♥ You are ideally placed to ensure that things develop on the emotional front as planned. Sooner or later, however, you will have to make an important choice.

👪 No matter what immediate decisions or choices you may face, stay on track, be realistic and constructive and things will go as planned.

📋 Professional issues are developing nicely, and you have sufficient determination, conviction and common sense to make the right decision or form an agreement or association if necessary.

🁢 Only you are now able to judge if a certain change is possible or not. Be realistic, but if an opportunity presents itself, don't let it pass you by.

➕ What more could you want? You are energetic, active and confident and in full control of your life.

❤️ Current relationships seem to be stable and reliable. Whatever you are looking for on the emotional front will come your way if you continue to maintain control and act both intelligently and energetically.

👪 You have the power to ensure that your family life develops in the way you would like. As a strong head of the family, you are sure of yourself and firm in your decisions. Do not abuse this authority, however.

📋 You have what it takes to build on and expand your business or to ensure the satisfactory progress of your current position. Your determination and strength of character allow you to direct operations and take control of events.

💰 Your finances are reliable, particularly as you have them fully under control. You are not work-shy and are prepared to make the effort needed to secure further progress.

➕ Keep a close eye on your health. Be self-disciplined and determined if you want to remain well-balanced, and don't let things slide.

❤️ You may be rather too sure of yourself and your ability to run the whole show. Be aware of your own weaknesses and any constraints you may face. Be strict with yourself.

👪 You hold the domestic reins but yet you feel somewhat constrained. No matter what happens, your balance and stabilty and that of your family are not in question. Keep a cool head on your shoulders.

📋 You want to keep your professional environment well-balanced. Alternatively, you may feel obliged to maintain the status quo. If you are firm, practical, realistic and diplomatic you will achieve your aims.

💰 Don't give way to your weaknesses and keep your current financial position under control. Unfortunately, for the time being at least, you cannot expect much more.

121

4	9

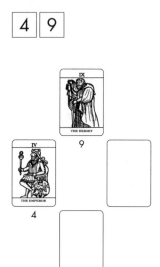

✚ Don't be misled into thinking you don't need to take precautions, and at least be vigilant about your health. Although you can have a degree of confidence in yourself at the moment, you need to ask yourself if this will always be the case.

♥ It is sometimes necessary to banish doubts and throw caution to the wind. If you find yourself forced to start a new chapter in your life or be the instigator of major change, make sure you are ready to take full responsibility for your actions.

👪 You are right to leave some room for doubt, as long as you do not question yourself or your decisions. People will then appreciate how determined you are, even if you are obliged to implement major change, break things up or bring issues to a close.

📋 The changes you plan will be achieved only in the long term. Be patient and strict and prove your staying power. You will then achieve your aims, reaping what you have sown.

🎲 Think hard and don't loosen your grip. You will then be able to direct your financial affairs, confident that you will enjoy real profits.

4	10

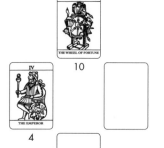

✚ You are firm but adaptable, capable of acting with certainty and discipline when necessary. Such behaviour helps protect you from health risks.

♥ Weigh up the pros and the cons and make a thorough assessment of your chances. You are free to make matters develop as you wish, which is both an opportunity but also a responsibility.

👪 You can act as you please regarding domestic matters. If you are firm, determined and diplomatic, you will make sure that things will work out for the best.

📋 It is up to you to confirm your position and your ability to take control and lead. You must know when to seize or create opportunities, by putting useful compromises and agreements in place and negotiating in a flexible but assured way.

🎲 Weigh up your chances well and act as you see fit. You have the situation well in hand.

➕ You give the impression of doing too much and wearing yourself out. Yet, in reality, despite your energetic and rather intemperate nature, you know your limits and how far to push yourself. All the same, try to demonstrate a little caution.

❤ You have an energetic but disciplined nature, which currently puts you in a good position to gain the upper hand. You are, however, no longer able to hide the passionate and demanding side of your temperament.

👪 Although you are managing your domestic environment with skill, you may be rather demanding, a little too authoritarian or even slightly selfish. It is worth stopping to think.

✍ You are ambitious, realistic and sure of yourself, and you have good reason to be so, since your present position is assured and you seem to be able to achieve all your goals at work. If you are concerned about a particular problem, rest assured that it will be resolved in a profitable way.

🔲 The will to succeed, direct and control never hurt anyone, as long as it is founded in realism and moderation. You appear to possess all the right qualities, and now is the time to take advantage of them.

4 11

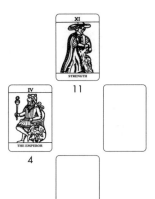

➕ No matter how sure you are of yourself, it is important to remember that we are all potential victims of chance or accidents. Be a little less presumptuous and more attentive to what is going on around you. In this way, you will avoid finding yourself in an unpleasant situation.

❤ If you have decided to be the catalyst for an emotional disruption, rest assured that it is vital but will not imperil your position. Tackling problems from an intellectual point of view simply will not suffice.

👪 You are planning some kind of upheaval or significant change. Make sure that you are in a strong enough position to accept the consequences of this action. Don't impose this disruption on those close to you without serious thought.

✍ You are the instigator of a crisis or fundamental upheaval that appears to be the only solution to your current problems. You are certainly acting with conviction and hopefully are right to do so.

🔲 You will take a sudden decision to review, reappraise or destabilize your current financial standing. Alternatively, you may decide to distance yourself, once and for all, from risky or dangerous enterprises.

4 12

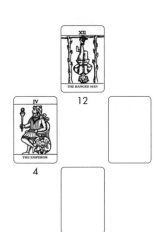

13

4

You are sufficiently intelligent to make more time for yourself if you need to. As a result, you are also aware of how you can return to peak form.

When you are self-confident, sure of your feelings and hopeful yet realistic and practical, and when circumstances are propitious, you feel rejuvenated and ready to tackle life's changes and challenges.

It is time to implement longed-for changes. You have plenty of imagination but still remain realistic and practical.

You will be able to realize your hopes and dreams, which will lead to a radical and advantageous change.

You have good ideas and seem in an excellent position to put them into practice and derive maximum profit. They are likely to be extremely advantageous.

4 14

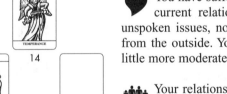

14

4

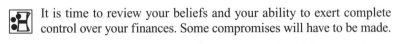

You are feeling permanently tired, or something always seems to be nagging at you. Make sure that things don't get any worse, and don't make the excuse that you haven't got the time to focus on yourself.

You have suffered, or will suffer, a disappointment. Alternatively, a current relationship may be plagued by misunderstandings and unspoken issues, not to mention complicated and negative interference from the outside. Your attitude may be a little inflexible, so try to be a little more moderate if you want to find common ground.

Your relations with your loved ones are currently not at their best, or matters don't seem to be going as you would like. If you are prepared to be intelligent, flexible and understanding, however, everything will be resolved.

It seems that you will have to make concessions or find intelligent and timely compromises for things to develop constructively. Your attitude was certainly not ideal or things were less stable than they appeared. No matter what the case, you can easily get matters back on an even keel.

It is time to review your beliefs and your ability to exert complete control over your finances. Some compromises will have to be made.

Your initiative and energy will shed light on what is good and what is bad for you. You have an expansive nature, and nothing seems capable of restraining it at the moment. All the same, don't over do it.

You know what you want, and your actions appear to be in line with your thoughts, words or feelings. There is no reason you should not achieve all your emotional goals.

You are in control of an apparently harmonious situation. Persist with your assured yet liberal attitudes, and everything will work out.

You seem to focus all your energies on your ambitious plans for development. You are confident and have the makings of an achiever. At present, you are in an enviable position on that score, and you seem certain to succeed.

You have a good grasp of the resources at your disposal and seem to have a knack for turning them into profit. Your current position appears sound and encouraging.

Although you are convinced you are in tip-top condition and feel fully in control of your health, perhaps you should review this before testing circumstances force a reappraisal on you. If you are currently experiencing problems with your health, they will probably soon be over.

If, for some reason, your recent behaviour has not been very fair, it is always possible to change your attitude, to make amends or to forgive. This will considerably improve your current emotional life.

You will either make a specific suggestion that will probably lead to a significant change in your current position, or you will make amends, revise your judgement and return to favour. Either way, this would certainly help to lessen the tension in the atmosphere.

Following an upheaval or reappraisal, of which you were either the instigator or the victim, you will have to review your current position with care and determination. Alternatively, your current position may mean that you must make specific proposals if you want to get things moving again.

Recognize whether you have made any mistakes and, if possible, make amends with speed. This action can only help matters. Alternatively, consider anything new that will get your current position moving again.

4 17

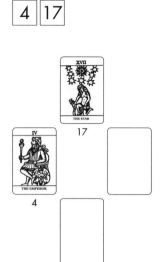

17

4

✚ All is well at present. You seem perfectly well-balanced and are fully in control.

♥ You are in a strong position to achieve your dearest wishes and desires, to make your dreams a reality and to enjoy a degree of fulfilment in your emotional life.

👪 Your desire to bring people together and your sense of community put you in a privileged position at the heart of your family. It is time to be proactive and introduce changes that will easily succeed.

📋 Your ability to bring things together or achieve expansion and your imagination and sound common sense allow you to achieve your professional goals or vocation or create a new and promising situation.

💼 Your financial situation looks promising. As a result, you are in an ideal position to consider many new angles. You must, however, remain realistic and practical.

4 18

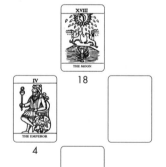

18

4

✚ If you persist with your current attitude, it won't be long before you run into health problems. You must take a firm stance and admit the need for more responsible behaviour.

♥ You seem sure of yourself and certain of success on the emotional front, but if your conviction rests on shallow foundations or false reasoning you will most certainly experience disappointment. Give your actions and future more thought.

👪 If you have plans to leave, you will be disappointed by your journey. Otherwise, irritating events or difficulties will hold you back. No matter what the case, mistrust sudden impulses or actions that have not been given due consideration.

📋 You are in danger of making a mistake. You will be disappointed if you throw yourself into the fray or try to resolve a particular situation prematurely. Be prepared for delays, difficulties and problems of all sorts. Think things through carefully.

💼 You are in the process of making a mistake, or you can't seem to find the help you need. Be realistic, don't be in too much of a hurry and don't continue your wrong-headed behaviour.

126

Everything is going well. You are much too aware of your weak spots to take any risks in relation to your health. You are steering a sensible course.

4 | 19

No matter what you wish for your love life, success is assured. Consequently, you can have every confidence in your actions.

You are acting as head of your household and squaring up fully to your responsibilities. This brings plenty of joy, satisfaction and recognition. If you are proposing any specific plans in relation to your domestic environment, they have every chance of success.

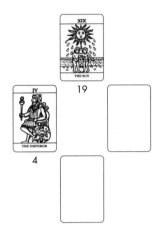

You are certain to achieve real success in your personal undertakings or in your job and will doubtless be aided in this by an important or influential person. Alternatively, this is the best time to make an agreement or form an association.

If you have a contract in your sights or are set to reach an agreement in the near future, rest assured that your plans will be realized with the best possible outcome.

You are free to act as you wish and, despite temptations, it seems you opt to behave in a reasonable way. This attitude helps to protect you from any potential health problems.

4 | 20

You are free to develop your love life in whatever direction you choose. Perhaps you are waiting for something new to happen. Alternatively, you may be inclined to meet new people and reconsider your feelings and even decide to live in a different way. No matter what you choose, you are aware of what you are doing and that the decision is yours alone.

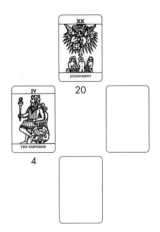

It is time to make an important choice or come to a vital decision. This will prompt desirable and positive change, which will bring to an end any difficulties and uncertainties you have been experiencing.

Give a firm response to any proposals put to you or make your own specific suggestions. These may well result in business being put back on a firm footing or a situation enjoying a new lease of life. No matter what happens, it is up to you to decide.

Be firm and practical in your decisions, especially if you have to respond to proposals or take action to recover your financial position.

127

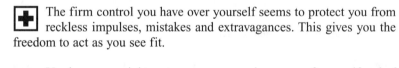

You are full of good intentions and resolutions and capable of sticking to them. Bearing this in mind, nothing too negative should befall you on the health front. Forge ahead with confidence because it seems that nothing will stand in your way.

It appears that nothing can rein in your feelings of affection or prevent you from achieving whatever you hold most dear. You will experience great happiness.

If you are planning a journey or a move, rest assured that it will live up to your expectations completely. You have the power to be proactive and to achieve anything you want in relation to your family circle.

It is time to forge ahead. You are active, combative and determined to win, and you should enjoy success and achievement in your professional plans or ventures. You have the wind in your sails and the winning line approaches.

You may surprise yourself or everyone around you with your energy and ability to make real progress in your financial position. It will, in turn, allow you to raise your standard of living.

The firm control you have over yourself seems to protect you from reckless impulses, mistakes and extravagances. This gives you the freedom to act as you see fit.

You have your sights set on someone and are sure of yourself and of success. Alternatively, you may be keen to meet someone or have decided to depart, turn a page in your love life and leave the past behind you. No matter what the case, it is up to you to make the decision.

It is not always easy to leave the past behind and take the decision to leave. You seem thoroughly determined, however, and nothing can prevent your speedy and decisive actions.

The current situation is certainly only temporary, and you have the willpower and necessary abilities to navigate your way quickly round this obstacle. You may need to count on the involvement of a third party or take some action yourself.

Your restraint and good sense will protect you from extravagances or reckless behaviour. It is better this way.

➕ Your sense of duty and intellectual strength ensure that you are always aware of your balance, and can put your energy to the best use.

❤️ No matter what choices and decisions you make or advice you can offer, your attitude to others is sound and you do not enter into things lightly.

👨‍👩‍👧 You are skilful when it comes to mixing business with pleasure. While you take the decisions, you manage to be both reasonable about new plans and perspectives and open to suggestions from those around you.

📋 No matter what choices, initiatives, plans or agreements you face in the future, you have both the power and the means to bring things to a rapid conclusion.

💼 Your current position seems stable, sound and reliable. It is up to you to assess the opportunities before you and to take the appropriate initiative. The ball is in your court.

5

➕ Disciplined, responsible and willing behaviour should guarantee that you are safe from most risks to your health.

❤️ You are reasonably determined to throw off your inhibitions, get out of a rut or consolidate the relationship with someone close to you.

👨‍👩‍👧 Your good sense and efficiency mean you are never wrong-footed by unexpected events. As a result, the stability of your family situation is assured.

📋 You are in a good position to impose your wishes and demands, to clear up doubts and get things moving. This will ensure that your situation begins to develop.

💼 Your current financial position is reliable and fairly well-established but in need of a shake-up. It is time to move forward.

5

5	3

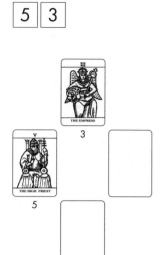

➕ There are two options on the health front: either you are behaving in a reasonable and balanced way that ensures you are full of vitality, or you need to submit yourself to a rigorous regime in order to maintain your health.

♥ Your love life seems to be stable, although perhaps you are not committing to it as fully as you would really like.

👪 Your domestic life seems secure and on an even keel. If you have to take serious or important decisions, be firm but fair.

📋 Your position is currently subject to certain strict and rigorous procedures. Nevertheless, they should make it more productive and advantageous.

🏠 Your finances are well organized and strictly controlled, or you are awaiting a legal decision. Whichever is the case, be extra vigilant about your immediate duties and responsibilities.

5	4

➕ By remaining cautious, attentive and concious of your responsibilities and moral power, you should enjoy excellent health.

♥ Your behaviour suggests that you are solitary, celibate and even anti-social. It is time to sort out where your feelings fit into this.

👪 Your acute sense of responsibility and firm moral fibre urge you to assume family responsibilities with both wisdom and insight. This will help you find clear solutions to any problems that may arise.

📋 You have the skills and qualities required to assume all your responsibilities and undertakings, which in turn will ensure that you can encourage your position to develop slowly but surely.

🏠 Your financial position is constantly improving, albeit at a rather slow pace.

➕ You have the necessary strength of character, self-confidence and self-control to maintain excellent balance and stability.

❤️ Your emotional relationships are strong and serious and guarantee a stable, happy love life.

👪 If you have a family decision to make, you are in a strong position to carry it out in the way you think is appropriate, with a clear conscience and complete confidence.

📝 Consider the alternatives on offer carefully and seriously. Make wise choices, seek profitable agreements, put the necessary positive alliances in place and come to bold decisions. You have all the resources needed to carry out these plans.

📇 Your reliable financial position encourages positive agreements, associations or choices.

➕ You are the victim of your own responsibilities and obligations, which leave you below par, both physically and mentally. Remember, however, that you hold all the trump cards to rectify this debilitating situation.

❤️ You do not feel comfortable in your current love life, but you are equipped emotionally with the means to find your way out of this temporary malaise.

👪 Your family circle is weighing you down by its restrictions and obligations. Perhaps you are not finding it entirely satisfactory. You have nothing to reproach yourself with, but perhaps you should impose your point of view a little more firmly.

📝 The time to wait and see what happens is over. Press ahead and fight your way out of current difficulties. You will make progress and overcome obstacles in your path.

📇 Your finances are sound but restricted by the duties you are obliged to assume. You will, however, succeed in eliminating these constraints and making progress.

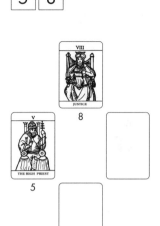

| 5 | 8 |

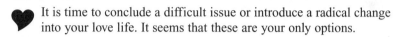 Your good sense protects your health from serious risk. If the need does arise, however, be self-disciplined and keep a watchful eye on your stability and balance.

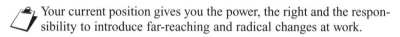 It is time to conclude a difficult issue or introduce a radical change into your love life. It seems that these are your only options.

If the stability and balance of your family circumstances depend on it, you must make a radical change or eliminate potentially harmful factors. You must behave with rigour, discipline and determination.

Your current position gives you the power, the right and the responsibility to introduce far-reaching and radical changes at work.

Your financial stability and dependability bring great profits, provided that you stay within the law.

| 5 | 9 |

 It is time to calm down, be sensible and make do. If you keep a careful eye on things, nothing too serious can happen.

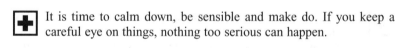 Your honest, accommodating attitude, firm principles and experience will help you adopt the appropriate attitude to ensure that you cope on the emotional front.

 Your current domestic arrangements give you the authority to implement useful, timely agreements.

A serious, in-depth debate is taking place in relation to your current circumstances. Weigh up the pros and cons carefully and remain cautious, realistic and responsible. Make sure that you are prepared to be flexible and make reasonable concessions.

It is always a good idea to take stock of your position, weighing up all possible opportunities and assessing your potential. Give yourself a pat on the back if you are already doing this.

5 | 10

You are responsible for your own actions and their consequences, whether positive or negative. If you are currently experiencing health problems, now is the time to take firm steps to rectify the situation.

You are well aware of your passionate, intemperate, demanding behaviour. This is undoubtedly the cause of the many ups and downs in your somewhat unstable love life.

You are rather demanding and ambitious within your family circle. Nevertheless, you are quite right to be so, as circumstances are particularly encouraging.

Everything seems to be moving in the right direction. Your hopes and ambitions will be realized.

If you have not already done so, you are in a good position to see your financial ambitions bear fruit. Do not abuse the resources at your disposal, but take advantage of your privileged situation to make further progress.

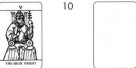

10

5

5 | 11

From time to time it does no harm to feel a little off-balance and out of kilter or to have one's convictions challenged or environment disturbed. This is a good way of testing your resistance and your physical and mental energy.

Any adventurous or reckless intentions on your part will have been quashed by your sense of duty and caring attitude. In the end, it is all for the best.

You will have to take responsibility for an upheaval or sudden change in your current domestic circumstances, but this will only serve to strengthen the family's stability and potential for success.

It is your responsibility under the current circumstances to initiate a major change or much-needed reassessment. This will strengthen your position and your confidence.

Avoid adventurous or reckless enterprises at all costs. They are likely to destabilize your financial position. Alternatively, if you are currently undergoing a crisis, it will prove to be temporary, and you will soon be back on your feet.

11

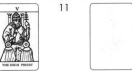

5

5 12

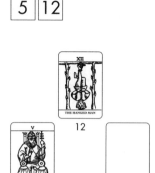

12

5

➕ It is time to relax. You would be unwise not to enjoy this feeling of well-being, especially as it will not prevent you from shouldering your responsibilities or from fulfilling your commitments.

❤ If you are experiencing a degree of peace and plenitude in your love life, don't imagine it is a sign of weakness or lack of awareness. Enjoy the hope and confidence it brings.

👪 You are aware of the realities of life and are receptive to the people around you. In some ways, you would like to do something new in relation to your family life, but the moment is not yet right. Bide your time and look forward with confidence to the future.

📋 Show some imagination and be receptive to what is going on around you. You could be an innovator, implementing new, creative elements to revive a rather stagnant professional position.

🎛 You are looking for new horizons, but for the moment just content yourself with returning to a healthy and realistic financial position based on actual assets. Anything else will have to come later.

5 13

13

5

➕ Take health issues seriously, and you may well have to give up some of your current activities. There is no need for drama, however, but take matters in hand and sort out the problems.

❤ Things aren't going too well in your love life. In any case, a radical change is needed.

👪 A significant development is taking place in your domestic circumstances, but there is no point being despondent and fatalistic about it. Get a grip and don't lose sight of your responsibilities.

📋 A number of problems and difficulties are currently challenging your everyday life. However, radical changes, which will be implemented at work, will provide the best solution.

🎛 You have made some mistakes or inaccurate calculations, or you have counted on the support of something or someone unreliable. A fundamental change is needed in your financial position.

5 14

You seem to be at ease with yourself and particularly well suited to your surroundings and environment. As a result, you can enjoy a great sense of well-being.

Your sensible, reasonable and accommodating behaviour does nothing but good for your love life, allowing you considerable satisfaction and emotional happiness.

The positive influence you bring to bear on your family combined with your moral and emotional strength enable you to make the arrangements and agreements that are necessary under the circumstances.

Your current position endows you with the authority or responsibility of reaching positive agreements or forming associations in which you have the initiative or hold the key.

Your financial position is clear and stable. What is more, you are currently enjoying success concluding some profitable deals and advantageous transactions.

5 15

If you feel inclined to change your lifestyle and behave in a more reasonable, self-possessed manner, you are moving in the right direction. This is really your only way to achieve good physical and mental shape and the key to unlock your energy reserves.

Give your current situation or your emotional responses serious reconsideration. You will then be able to avoid traps set by passion or resist potential harmful and disruptive influences.

You will have to approve, support or encourage a domestic development or a review of your family circumstances. This should avert or eliminate any material or moral confusion in your relationships.

You can support or prompt a positive development at work that should bring your professional targets closer.

Your financial position is returning to a degree of normality or undergoing a change for the better, enabling you to enjoy it in a more reasonable way.

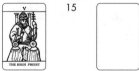

135

5	16

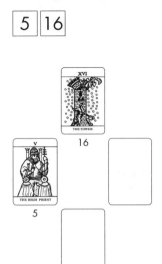

16

5

 You have a sufficiently long-term view to know how to avert any potential health risks or to protect yourself from anything that may disrupt your sense of well-being. If you do have a serious health problem, however, rest assured that it will be only temporary.

If you are not already doing so, you will start to enjoy a sense of fulfilment in your emotional life. The consequence of this will be a major change and reassessment of your lifestyle. No matter what form this takes, it is auspicious.

You can support the blossoming or expansion of your family affairs, even if this involves some major upheavals or the sudden need for reappraisal.

You are on the point of achieving great things and seeing your wishes and ambitions come to fruition. This will lead to a major development or sudden reappraisal of your professional life.

Stable, positive circumstances will give you the freedom to provoke or implement necessary changes or a review.

5	17

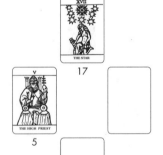

17

5

You will accept your responsibilities more easily if you know you can loosen your grip from time to time. Take a holiday or short break, it will do you the world of good.

You are forging ahead, conscious of your duties and responsibilities but receptive to what is going on around you. It is typical of you to try to lend fate a helping hand, and this positive attitude could well occasion a happy event in your love life.

Don't hesitate if you are intending to do something new in relation to your family. You have the power and the means to succeed.

Forge ahead and be innovative, shaping circumstances to your requirements. Be imaginative and original, and your professional boldness will pay dividends. The field is open for you to achieve your hopes or to attain a personal goal.

It may be that you are on the lookout for new financial options. You may well gain some useful assets as a result.

136

You seem to have many burdens and responsibilities to bear, which are not beyond you but do leave you vulnerable to certain health problems and a debilitating physical and mental fatigue. You need to take yourself in hand and see a doctor if necessary.

5 18

A serious, responsible attitude enables you to anticipate or head off emotional problems and difficulties before they occur.

Despite an apparent stability, there is a certain amount of confusion in your domestic environment at the moment. Your strong moral sense and conscientious behaviour should allow you to smooth it over, even if you cannot fend it off all together.

A surfeit of concerns and responsibilities is making you unhappy, but remember that you have the moral strength and the reserves to face up to and overcome these challenges.

Your debts, liabilities and responsibilities do not leave you with much of a financial margin. Be thankful, at least, that you are in a position to take on and carry this heavy load.

 You are enjoying excellent health at the moment and are reaping the rewards from it.

5 19

Everything is coming together to forge a deep and happy union, if it has not already occurred. Alternatively, you may find yourself making rational decisions that will bring joy and happiness in your love life.

Your family is united, and everything is going well. This background of affection and happiness forms an excellent basis for sound judgement and sensible decisions in which everyone will feel involved.

You may have an agreement or contract in mind or perhaps you are intending to go into partnership or take an important decision in relation to your job. You are guaranteed total success. What are you waiting for?

Your current financial position allows you to finalize a deal or a contract, to make choices or take decisions with complete freedom and confident of success.

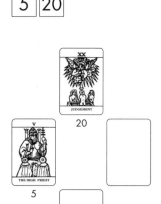

Your goodwill combined with your courageous and profound sense of duty should protect you from potential health risks. Alternatively, if you have suffered a period of poor health, you will enjoy a recovery and all will be well.

It is up to you to take action to implement change, renewal or reconciliation in your love life. Only you can bring about rapid and complete success on this front.

You can lend your approval or dynamic support in the event of a potential development in your domestic circumstances or in the resolution of a recent problem.

It is time for action to prompt successful and effective progress at work, to bring about a fresh start or to raise or respond to interesting proposals. You will earn the esteem of those around you or perhaps even obtain a promotion.

You have all the qualities and resources that are needed to ensure that your finances make progress or a fresh start. You should respond actively to an interesting proposition that you will receive.

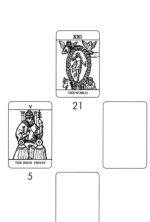

Since you are well-balanced physically and mentally, health issues will not affect your personal development.

Your behaviour may be strict and demanding, but it is also shrewd. It encourages positive developments in your love life and ensures that your relationships are healthy and sound, thus contributing enormously to your sense of balance and stability.

Your family life forms the basis of your personal stability, allowing you to shoulder your responsibilities calmly and to expand your professional horizons. It also makes you demanding on the domestic front.

Your circumstances seem solid and well-balanced, encouraging and on course to flourish or develop significantly. If you are expecting a legal decision, you can be sure that it will be to your advantage.

Financial matters are safe and reassuring. Seek the support of a professional or respect the rules of the game if you want to achieve your ambitions.

Your sense of duty and responsibilities limit your behaviour in an appropriate way and keep you from excess. In the event of any unexpected changes in your health, however, you should not hesitate to consult a doctor.

Your conscience is telling you not to give in to sudden outbursts of affection and rash impulses. Nevertheless, a little spontaneity and a touch of impulsiveness from time to time never do anyone any harm, particularly when they come from the heart.

Your family circle, although stable and dependable, will go through a period of transition, to which you lend your full approval and support.

Your situation is steady and sound. It will undergo a period of transformation, if it has not done so already, or you may be obliged to make a move or implement a change of some kind.

Your finances are sound. You just need to treat with caution any sudden impulses, or you may make mistakes as a result of your impatience or thoughtlessness. Otherwise, everything is going well.

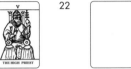

Do all you can to establish and maintain your equilibrium, making the best use of your energy levels to be ready for any eventuality. Don't try to do too many different things at once.

You have a choice to make in your emotional life and you are free to act as you see fit. Take the initiative, be enterprising and any doubts will soon vanish.

You have affectionate relationships with your family. You will hear some good news, make a fortunate choice or take action that will ensure that a project or initiative, such as a family holiday, comes to fruition.

After hesitating for a while, you will make an important choice, stop being indecisive and grasp the initiative. Alternatively, you may be hoping to reach an agreement that will give you more freedom of choice and encourage your enterprising spirit.

You are still more or less unclear about your financial position, and you are wondering what choices to make and what options you have in order to profit to the maximum from your assets and personal qualities. Be determined and focused, and you will find yourself in a good position to demonstrate to others what you are capable of achieving.

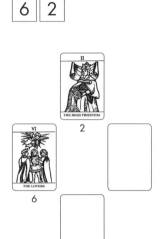

6 2

2

6

➕ Your energy may be at a bit of a low ebb but you are able to compensate with your balanced behaviour. You know your limitations, how to look after yourself and how to safeguard your equilibrium.

❤ You will make a decisive, precise and carefully considered choice on the emotional front, although you may keep it secret for a while. Alternatively, you are in search of balance in your private life. Sometimes, however, you are too indecisive or too inflexible. Find the middle ground or accept the advice of someone who is more experienced than you are.

👪 You are faced with a choice that will affect your domestic arrangements or a person close to you. You must give equal consideration to your feelings and your well-being when weighing up the options. You feel obliged to make this decision, even if people are waiting to see you trip up.

📋 An imminent and important choice awaits you. Alternatively, you should reach a fair and reasonable agreement that will make your situation more stable. It is time to prove your determination.

⌛ If you have a financial choice or decision to make, take the option that seems the most reasonable and safe. Otherwise, be patient and your financial position will find its own balance.

6 3

3

6

➕ If you are facing a choice, you must take the sensible option. Try to trust your instincts, which are well-honed enough to ensure that you know what must be done, and be cautious in your search for balance.

❤ It is up to you to make the choice with which you are faced. Alternatively, you are engaged in scrutinizing a fruitful relationship. Or your current feelings are forcing you to think again about a person you hold dear and the possibility of a relationship with them.

👪 If you have a decision or a choice to make, you will opt for the solution that is most realistic and most profitable to your family. Alternatively, you may have engaged on a long drawn-out search for an agreement or a better balance within family relationships. You are quite right to do so, and you should achieve your aim in the end.

📋 You have a serious choice or agreement to make before your position can become more profitable materially. Alternatively, consider the options open to you before adopting the one that will prove most profitable.

⌛ Make informed, cautious choices and realistic, profitable agreements. Act sensibly and your financial position will reap the rewards.

➕ You are free to make decisions and act as you wish, but make sure you always accept responsibility for what happens to you, whether good or bad. Avoid indecision and ambivalent behaviour. Instead, get in tune with your body and let yourself be carried along by your energy. This can only give you more self-confidence.

❤ Do not prevaricate about choices in your love life or about forming a serious, secure relationship. On the other hand, if you are feeling emotionally uncertain, rest assured that things will change in the near future.

👪 After a slight hesitation, you will come to a decision that encourages a more practical, steady development in your family circle. You will soon receive the confirmation that this is the right choice.

📋 If an agreement, contract or association is on offer, grasp it with both hands. Such opportunities will ensure your situation becomes altogether more solid. Be firm and determined in your choices. Circumstances are in your favour, so take advantage before things start to change.

💰 If several alternatives are open to you at the moment, welcome them all because they are sure to consolidate your financial position. Alternatively, expect to experience a few more fluctuations in your finances.

4

6

➕ Your ambivalent nature, which can lean both towards strife and towards peace and stability, is well under control. You are sure of your choices. Confident in yourself, you enjoy a sense of well-being that makes you sociable and receptive.

❤ You are sure of your choices, decisions and feelings. Your control over emotional issues is both relaxed and happy. Alternatively, you are free to take confident steps towards a partnership or union.

👪 Shared feelings and unfailing emotional ties mean your domestic circle is stable, secure and happy. Whatever your decisions, you have total freedom of choice and the full approval of those around you.

📋 You can make important choices in all confidence and take calm, constructive decisions or make sound agreements or associations in relation to the stability and development of your situation. In this way, you will find your position further strengthened.

💰 Possible choices, agreements or contracts will confirm or strengthen your financial position. You have freedom of choice and action, and the support or advice you need will come your way.

5

6

6 7

7

6

➕ If you choose wisely, take firm and radical decisions and change your attitude or behaviour, you will shake off any health concerns. If you fail to do this, you will at least regain control over your equilibrium.

❤ It is time to end your indecision and implement wise choices that bring your targets within reach. It is up to you to forge ahead and overcome any problems that you may have in your love life.

👪 You have an important decision or choice to make that could bring personal success within your family or triumph over uncertainty. Be firm and you will make the changes that you want.

📋 You will make a profitable agreement or an advantageous decision that will be a determining factor in the development of your position. Professional matters will then be free to develop and you will triumph over any uncertainties or problems you may have.

🎴 Be steadfast and determined when making important choices that could help your financial position. If a potential agreement or partnership is in your sights, it will turn out to be profitable.

6 8

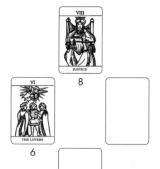

8

6

➕ You are adaptable and your accommodating, flexible nature is the basis of your balance and stability. In the event of uncertainty or indecision, opt for the solution that is the most normal, logical and simple.

❤ If you are feeling indecisive and your emotions are ambivalent, uncertain and prone to change, impose a degree of discipline on yourself. If you do not, you will find yourself swept along by the tide without being able to resist or take your bearings. A flexible attitude is not incompatible with self-discipline.

👪 The dynamics and relationships within your domestic environment seem calm and well-balanced, making it adaptable and open to new possibilities. If you face a difficult decision, opt for the solution that is right for everyone.

📋 Learn to adapt to circumstances and maintain your relationships without letting yourself be swept along by events. To maintain equilibrium at work, learn how to make resolutions and compromises and show flexibility without losing sight of discipline and justice.

🎴 You need to be more adaptable, flexible and understanding, while remaining resolute and firm in your choices and decisions. In this way, you will have no difficulty in resolving financial issues.

142

If you are aware of your tendency to be indecisive or weak when faced with temptation, so much the better. If not, it is time you gave these character traits some serious thought and took the appropriate action.

You will begin to appreciate just how passionate are your feelings, how intemperate is your behaviour and how wild are your desires. Given the current situation, it is up to you to judge how appropriate your conduct is. If it is simply your nature, it is not a question of changing yourself but rather, or at least, not being duped.

You will no doubt discover that there are some troubled feelings, bad influences and passionate relationships at work within your domestic circle. Alternatively, you will have cause to question yourself over an opportunity, the grounds for a rather excessive choice or a hasty and contrary decision that you have made.

It is possible, even essential, to make some urgent decisions that will help you at work. Alternatively, you may find an interesting agreement or advantageous contract regarding a long-term opportunity.

You seem to be aware of your liking for risk-taking, of your inability to resist temptation and your unstable conduct in money matters. Become aware of your limits to avoid living beyond your means.

It is time to shake off any health problems or to avoid risky or fool-hardy ventures that might destabilize you or upset your balance.

The development of your emotional relationships in the immediate future depends on you and your role as a catalyst for the change or reappraisal, which could free you of uncertainty. Take care that you do not fall in love on impulse and learn to say no to dangerous adventures.

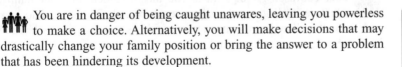

You are in danger of being caught unawares, leaving you powerless to make a choice. Alternatively, you will make decisions that may drastically change your family position or bring the answer to a problem that has been hindering its development.

Whether you encounter agreement or disagreement at work, the outcome will encourage professional development. Be resolute and determined in your choices and decisions.

Make well-timed resolutions to be sure of the positive development of your financial position and guard against dangerous temptation and indecision, which could endanger your assets.

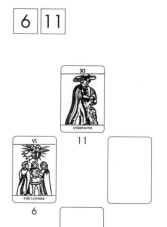

6 11

➕ You appear to be in control of your emotions and your receptive nature, assuring you of greater autonomy, balance and energy.

❤️ Whether your feelings have only just been revealed or whether they are the fruit of an established relationship, you are enjoying a happy and emotional situation. There is no reason to doubt what you are feeling. A choice or decision will help make your dreams come true.

👪 Excellent emotional relationships ensure that your domestic environment is calm and happy. The positive atmosphere at home makes new decisions or wise choices easier to implement. You can turn your hopes and wishes into reality, slowly but surely.

📋 You are in a position to make prudent choices. You can also come to a decision or agreement in relation to a new business or concept. Trust in the privileged relationships you enjoy with those around you.

💰 Your inspired financial choices and decisions allow you to exert total control over your position as it expands and becomes more solid.

6 12

➕ You feel weak or in need of a rest. You should ask yourself whether this is the result of your indecision and apathy combined with your concern about being ill. Rather than dramatizing it, you should treat this testing time as a learning experience and be spurred on to take action.

❤️ You feel confused or have just experienced a disappointment or made a mistake. Even if you think there is no longer any hope, get a grip on yourself, don't be influenced in your choices and avoid making a drama out of the situation.

👪 Your confused feelings make you too dependent on your family, which is itself going through a rocky period. Face up to bad luck and, no matter what disappointments or problems you experience, learn to be firmer in future decisions and choices.

📋 You have acted in error, but you were unsure how to make the right choice at the right time. Alternatively, you may have just suffered a disappointment or setback. Whatever the case, don't lose heart. Learn from this experience, and do not compound your error.

💰 You did not make a good choice or you have made an error in your finances and, for the moment, your position seems at a standstill. Don't let things continue in this way and learn a lesson for the future.

6 | 13

➕ You are at one with yourself and your environment. This may be the result of your self-knowledge and emotional intuitiveness, but you need to be continually aware of anything that could prove harmful to your health in order for you to be able to eliminate it.

❤ Your feelings, current relationships and much-hoped for (or exist-ing) union form the basis of a radical and happy change in your existence, which is something you should enjoy to the full.

👪 A clear choice or decision will lead to a radical, profitable and happy change in your family's circumstances, in which relationships already seem to be harmonious.

📋 You will make a positive decision, reach an agreement or form an ideal partnership. This will prove to be profitable all round, bring-ing about change for the better and leading to further progress and success.

▣ Your financial position is extremely good at the moment and may even undergo a radical change for the better. Take positive, wide-ranging and ambitious resolutions, arrange positive alliances or contracts or, simply, profit from your position to reach any targets you have set yourself.

13

6

6 | 14

➕ Reconsider your choices and decisions. Learn how to question yourself, as and when necessary. Aim for more flexible and appro-priate resolutions, and you will soon feel well-balanced again.

❤ Re-examine your options and review your decisions, making amends if required. You need to be more flexible and understanding in your emotional relationships. If necessary, reconsider the nature of your feelings, which are undergoing a rebirth to a certain degree. Be firm and take full advantage of this opportunity to make a fresh start.

👪 Look again at your choices. Make sure that you are open to change and that you welcome any discussions that could help promote agreement or set in motion a revival within your family. You may find the solution to a problem that you are currently facing.

📋 The decisions, resolutions or agreements that you are to make will be aimed at revitalizing your position or getting it back on a firm footing. To do this, remain open to suggestions and discussions.

▣ You will make decisions, resolutions or agreements that are aimed at setting your affairs to rights, adapting yourself to current circum-stances or getting your financial position back on a firm footing.

14

6

145

6 15

15

6

➕ You are currently flourishing both physically and mentally. This makes you keen to make the most of your resources and the possibilities open to you, but don't abuse your energy or give in to excess.

❤ Great passion is on the horizon (if it has not already arrived), and it will open up your emotional horizons. Be prepared to express your feelings freely.

👪 The emotional relationships within your family circle are intense. You can make wide-ranging decisions with regard to your family or your home, and you should certainly enjoy substantial rewards.

📝 You can make resolutions, agreements or alliances that will enhance your position and provide you with the possibility of putting your professional and financial ambitions into action.

💼 Your financial position is undergoing a period of expansion, leaving you in a strong position to make necessary decisions and form vital agreements. Be bold and resolute in your choices.

6 16

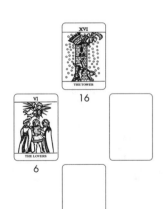

16

6

➕ You are sometimes indecisive and sometimes extravagant and impulsive. You certainly have an emotional temperament, which can be destabilizing. Make sure that your hasty actions and instinctive, uncontrolled decisions do not result in reckless behaviour.

❤ A meeting or sudden decision will turn your emotional life on its head. You will need to decide if the upheaval in question is beneficial and liberating or if, on the contrary, it casts doubts on your current relationship and leaves you unsure of your ground. No matter what the answer, avoid making any sort of premature decision.

👪 Thoughtless choices and impulsive actions are incompatible with your current family circumstances and will bring more discord than harmony. Unless you are planning to leave or to be the catalyst for major change, be cautious in your decisions.

📝 Unless it is your intention to cause inevitable but necessary upheaval or instigate a sudden but liberating turn of events, it is important to avoid premature decisions or hasty action or agreements.

💼 If you do not try to contain your rash impulses and ill-considered decisions, your situation will flounder. Alternatively, you may have to make a choice quickly and take prompt but resolute decisions in order to get your financial affairs moving again.

Make sensible choices and prudent decisions on the health front and you should be able to draw on your inner strength and enjoy a new lease of life or find a new image.

The stability of your emotional relationships encourages birth and creation or the fulfilment of your deepest wishes and dreams.

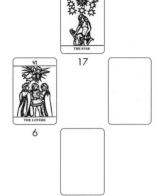

You are making decisions that are aimed at achieving something new in your family circle or home life. You will obtain the approval that you need and appreciate just how encouraging current circumstances are. In short, everything is going as you would wish.

You will reach an agreement, set up an alliance or association or make some confident resolutions that are aimed at bringing about a new development or important stability. An original, creative idea or innovation could help you achieve your ambitions.

Make sensible, practical choices to consolidate your financial position or use your assets to their best advantage.

Be careful when making choices. You can be too indecisive, too easily influenced and prone to emotional instability. This may cause you problems or lead you to make mistakes related to your health.

Your emotional position appears confused. You are either making the wrong decisions in your choice of companions or you are the victim of your own vulnerable, anxious nature, which encourages mistaken judgements and a tendency to stand by as things around you deteriorate. You need to react and learn to take a hold of yourself.

This is a confused and uncertain situation that does not encourage wise decisions. Alternatively, you may be facing troubled, conflicting relationships within your family but are too indecisive or too easily influenced emotionally to be able to act with determination. If this is the case, get a grip on yourself.

You seem to find it difficult to make sound and constructive decisions. It could be that you have not managed to come to a reliable agreement, leaving you vulnerable to problems, disappointment or delays in your professional life.

You appear to be unable to decide what course of action to adopt on the financial front. No matter what your current problems or difficulties, be firm in your choices and resolutions.

6	19

19

6

➕ Be determined, make an effort and shake off your natural indecisiveness and ambivalence. You will achieve success when it is reinforced by your balance and stability.

♥ Act as you see fit to form a union or find emotional fulfilment. There are no shadows on the horizon. You have all the trump cards, and the time has come to play your hand.

👪 You are free to make choices and do what is necessary to form sincere, affectionate relationships and make sure that things progress or, quite simply, see your family united, happy and fulfilled. If you decide to take a journey, it will turn out favourably.

📋 Make wide-ranging choices and take some bold decisions, and act with courage and determination to make agreements. You will soon find that your efforts reap dividends in the form of an all-out success and a total clarification of your situation.

💰 Act with courage and determination in your decision-making and introduce clarity into your financial affairs. You will overcome your concerns and achieve considerable growth of your finances.

6	20

20

6

➕ If you make sensible decisions and subject yourself to a little discipline, you will easily achieve balance. This, in turn, will revive and rejuvenate you and place you in a position either to review your health or make a swift recovery if you are ill.

♥ A well-balanced emotional situation or a steady, healthy relationship encourages a revival or reconciliation. Alternatively, you may be making some harsh but fair resolutions in order to regain a degree of equilibrium in your love life.

👪 You must be resolute and strict but fair when making decisions and submitting to a regime of self-discipline in your relationships. Your family circumstances will undergo a revival or get back on an even keel.

📋 Subject yourself to a little discipline if you want to make the right decisions. Don't hesitate to act as a trouble-shooter, you are fully entitled to do so. If an agreement depends on a legal decision, rest assured that the verdict will ensure that your situation is set back on its feet.

💰 Subject yourself to some discipline before making decisions aimed at re-floating your finances. Sometimes you just have to submit to harsh but fair decisions.

6 21

➕ You are considering the best way of regaining your balance and, slowly but surely, will begin to thrive once more, making the best use of your resources.

❤ Your feelings clearly bear the stamp of good sense and reliability, and you are seeking certain emotional fulfilment. Demand the best, but don't ruin your chances on the basis of an idealistic vision of love.

👪 You are making wise choices and realistic, mature decisions in order to gather your world around you and allow your family circle to blossom fully.

📋 You have some clear and realistic decisions to make. Alternatively, you may be hoping to reach an agreement, establish an alliance or set up links that will help widen your professional horizons.

21

💰 Make clear choices and realistic decisions in order to achieve your financial targets, albeit slowly but surely.

6

6 22

➕ On the whole, you are fairly indecisive, but it must be said that you are willing to search for equilibrium in your life, even if it depends to a large extent on your emotional temperament and a tendency to act impulsively and thoughtlessly.

❤ Despite your indecisiveness or timidity, you find it difficult to contain your feelings of affection. You would be wrong to do so, especially if such feelings are deep and sincere. Alternatively, if you have not already met someone special, you will do so soon.

22

👪 You may be wondering whether you should embark on a journey or a move that will affect the whole family. The decision lies with you.

📋 You will need to make a move, go on a journey, take action to reach an agreement or make important choices about your circumstances. The arrival or departure of a particular person may not favour this.

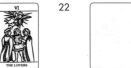

6

💰 You will have to make the decision to move, go on a journey in order to reach an agreement, make choices or take measures that will be useful to your financial position. If you are wondering whether you will have the means to make a journey that is close to your heart, rest assured that you need have no worries on this front.

149

7 1

1

7

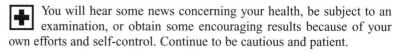

Thanks to your courage and self-control, you are able to achieve a healthy balance in your life. You are disciplined and adopt a regime that allows you to make progress and demonstrate your initiative and approachability.

In your search for justice and balance, you try to conquer uncertainty in your relationships and achieve your emotional goals, while leading as near a normal life as possible.

Make an effort, be strict but fair in your actions and attitude and you will succeed in overcoming any potential difficulties. Take your much hoped-for initiatives and stay in control of domestic events.

You are behaving in a determined and disciplined way and acting with precision and efficiency. You are quick to take courageous, progressive initiatives, and as a result you will achieve your aims. Stick to your guns, and you will see your plans come to fruition.

Make an effort to stay on the path that you have marked out for yourself, and you should have no problem on the financial front.

7 2

2

7

You will hear some news concerning your health, be subject to an examination, or obtain some encouraging results because of your own efforts and self-control. Continue to be cautious and patient.

Your efforts and self-control will bring new discoveries or revelations, casting doubts and uncertainties in your love life to one side. It is time to put an end to your solitary lifestyle and reserve.

You will learn something new, discover a family secret or undertake a task that will bring to an end something that has been preoccupying you. It may also bring to fruition some plan that you have been thinking about for a long time.

Your efforts will enable you to cast aside all the doubts and uncertainties that have assailed you for some time. You can then make cautious but persistent moves to complete a project, undertake a plan close to your own heart or finally achieve something for which you have long been striving.

You will hear news about your financial position that will eliminate many of the doubts and uncertainties that have plagued you for some time. This will confirm that you were right to be so cautious and discreet but persistent in your attempts to attain your objectives.

You are enterprising, active, dynamic and spirited. Your efforts mean you can tip the balance in your favour, making you receptive, understanding and open to all possibilities.

Exercise your will or take action to make things develop in the same way as they have for someone who has been in your thoughts. Alternatively, rest assured of success in your emotional life, as long as you make a determined effort and demonstrate both understanding and generosity.

You can follow your desires and undertake what you want on the domestic front. If you show courage and generosity in your actions, you will find luck is on your side and success is within reach.

Give your position the boost it needs by taking action to attain higher productivity or make a worthwhile achievement. Anything that you tackle now will have every chance of rapid success.

You are right to concentrate all your efforts on boosting your finances. If you continue to demonstrate such enthusiasm in everything you do, you will certainly achieve your aims rapidly.

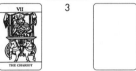

You are dynamic, enthusiastic and full of goodwill. You have confidence in yourself and in your resources and qualities. This makes it a good time to travel, undertake new activities and generally to act as you see fit.

You are asserting your will with subtlety and strength, affecting both your actions and your feelings. You inspire great confidence.

You are currently the person in charge of your family circle. You can act as you wish, confident of your abilities and potential to achieve success.

What are you waiting for? You are a fighter and an entrepreneur, sure of yourself and your abilities and determined to attain your objectives. No matter what the cost, you may well succeed where others have failed.

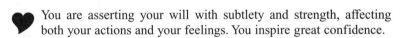

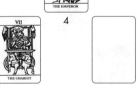

You appear sure of yourself and your abilities, and apparently nothing can stop you in your eagerness to attain your objectives. With so much confidence, things are bound to go as you would like.

7	5

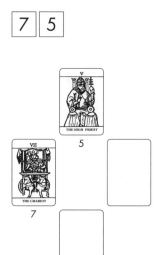

✚ If you make an effort and demonstrate your goodwill and courage, you will triumph over adversity. Alternatively, you will simply regain your stability and peace of mind.

♥ Use your drive and determination to make changes to a stale, limiting and unsatisfactory situation on the emotional front.

👪 Your obligations and sense of duty will help you make determined efforts to extricate yourself from a constraining domestic situation. You will be able to speak freely once more.

🖋 If you are determined to conclude things and act positively, you should easily overcome your difficulties. You will succeed in your undertakings and find that your position has made progress and stabilized.

⊞ You are in an impasse or working under severe limitations. You must make an effort to assume your obligations, overcome your difficulties and work towards progress on the financial front.

7	6

✚ Take positive steps to bring your uncertainties and indecision to an end, and to eliminate any temptations that could harm your health and general equilibrium.

♥ You will make a radical but arbitrary resolution or a definitive emotional choice, take action to end your indecision and banish temptation, or wave goodbye to any potentially harmful relationships.

👪 Act with enthusiasm and determination to bid farewell to indecision and unstable relationships as well as to any disagreements that might have a negative impact on your domestic circumstances. You must rid yourself of such problems before you can reap the rewards of your efforts.

🖋 Do whatever is necessary to finalize an agreement, make an important choice, bring a disagreement to a conclusion or resolve some uncertainty or unfinished business. You will soon reap the rewards.

⊞ No matter what the nature of your current efforts and their objectives, they will soon be rewarded. You will then be in a good position to make useful choices and take radical decisions that could prove profitable.

✚ You are keen to achieve balance at all costs and to impose your will on others. This is all well and good, but make sure that this desire to succeed does not lead you to overdo things and take pointless risks. You have enormous energy, but don't abuse it.

♥ It is your aim to achieve your emotional goals with all possible speed. You know you have the means to achieve them but you must exercise self-discipline or risk becoming the victim of your own impatience, over-excitement and impulsive actions.

👪 You are managing to contain your violence, anger, excitability and impatience, no matter how difficult you find it. You are quite right to do so, since this is the best way to get what want.

✎ Sometimes you need to know how to lay down the law with a degree of severity and intransigence, particularly when stability or the benefits of a situation are at risk. Equally, it is important to recognize your own need to submit yourself to the rigour of the same rules or law.

🎴 If you want matters to improve, be proactive and put your affairs in order with all speed. Remain strictly within the letter of the law in any actions you take to achieve your aims.

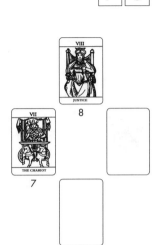

✚ Your endeavours will ensure that you avoid risky, dangerous undertakings and make rapid progress. Alternatively, you may become ill or suffer some small accident that will alert you to the precautions that you will need to take in future.

♥ Your actions lead to some sort of liberation or a reassessment of your emotional situation. You will soon realize that this is the only attitude to adopt in these circumstances, and it will encourage you to continue in the same vein.

👪 You need to provoke an upheaval or vital review of domestic matters to ensure the slow but sure development of your family's circumstances. Make sure not to push your luck too far or get out of your depth.

✎ Despite an upheaval or disconcerting work-related reappraisal, you will realize that it was necessary in the long term to secure satisfactory progress. Your efforts will free up your professional position.

🎴 Having acted recklessly or carried out a somewhat brutal but vital reassessment of your finances, it is time to learn the lessons of this difficult experience and take precautions to ensure a trouble-free future.

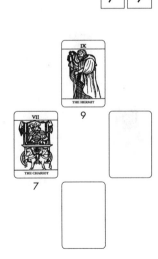

153

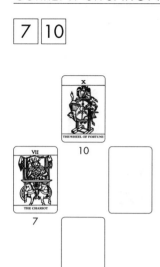

You know how to draw on personal resources to revitalize yourself and exercise your will, while at the same time remaining aware of everything that is going on around you. In this way, you can keep forging ahead.

It is time to take action to bring something new to your situation. You have the self-confidence to encourage positive developments and a successful outcome in your love life.

You want to bring about something new in your domestic situation that will help it to develop. Circumstances are encouraging.

You are so active and inspired that you will introduce something new into your professional situation, or have innovative ideas that will make matters progress and achieve speedy success.

Events are encouraging your chosen financial path, which will lead successfully and naturally to the achievement of all your hopes.

No matter what your worries, weaknesses or health problems, your efforts will certainly be rewarded, and you will overcome these difficulties and get back on track.

You have the necessary strength of character to resolve emotional concerns or problems and show initiative and courage. Alternatively, you will overcome your disappointment and disillusion and be able to rectify earlier mistakes.

Your courage and goodwill allow you to face up to any problems you might encounter and smooth out any difficulties in your path. Despite domestic ups and downs and delays, you will still be able to achieve what you want.

You are currently experiencing difficulties, delays and changes of all kinds in your professional life. Nonetheless, you have the necessary courage and willpower to surmount these obstacles and resolve the problems that you face.

Disappointment, delays and errors seem to be dogging you on the financial front at the moment, but you have sufficient strength to overcome these difficulties and get back on your feet.

➕ Your will, readiness and control of your energy and natural vitality enable you to live in harmony with your true nature. Feel free to follow your impulses.

♥ Feel free to abandon yourself entirely to your relationship. Rest assured that your acts and desires are untainted and that, as a consequence, everything you do will be a source of joy and success.

👪 You can do what you like or embark on anything you want that might make you more independent, certain that all will be well.

📋 Your resolve and efforts are rewarded in a logical and natural way. Be assured that you will be successful in your undertakings or that you will obtain complete satisfaction in your work.

🗃 If circumstance dictate, you can take steps to clarify your present financial position and ensure that it makes progress. This action will free you from its constraints or enable you to reach an agreement that will prove profitable.

7 12

12

7

➕ You can give yourself a new lease of life, achieve a prompt and total recovery or bring about a complete change in your behaviour or in your situation. This will give rise to a complete revitalization in your current circumstances.

♥ Your efforts and common sense enable you to alter your behaviour, implement change on the emotional front and make good your mistakes. In other words, things will change for the better.

👪 It is time to revitalize your domestic circumstances. Alternatively you are ready to put an end to a situation, implement a change, an alteration in attitude, or an appraisal of your current efforts and their effectiveness.

📋 You can respond actively to the positive proposals on offer. They will, however, lead to a complete change in your position or bring about a total revival of your work situation.

🗃 You are making an effort to put your situation back on a more advantageous and prosperous footing, or you are aiming to make radical changes that could revitalize your resources and get your business back on track.

7 13

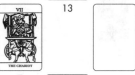

13

7

7 14

14

7

➕ Your efforts and character will allow you to thrive and adapt to any circumstances and opportunities that may arise. If you are thinking of embarking on a journey, don't hesitate. It will be entirely fulfilling.

❤ Your love life is about to blossom. No matter what happens, you have all the right qualities and know how to be flexible enough to adapt to the most diverse circumstances and situations.

👪 Your efforts and wish to succeed will be rewarded fully. Your flourishing, well-balanced family circle allows you to establish happy and timely relationships, make sensible arrangements and show adaptability to, and understanding of, new circumstances.

📋 You can be confident of any steps taken to achieve your wishes or carry out any beneficial development of your circumstances. You will have highly satisfactory business dealings and so see all your efforts largely rewarded.

📇 Expand your business, reach new agreements or make the necessary compromises to help your finances make progress and flourish.

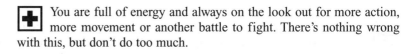

7 15

15

7

➕ You are full of energy and always on the look out for more action, more movement or another battle to fight. There's nothing wrong with this, but don't do too much.

❤ You have such a strong will and you make so much effort and expend so much energy in achieving your desires that nothing and no one seems able to stand in your way. Only you can know whether or not you are right to act like this.

👪 You will suddenly depart, forcefully impose your will or do everything within your power to achieve your wishes. Nothing and no one will be able to stop you. Only you can know, depending on circumstance, whether or not this sort of behaviour is justified.

📋 You could take action or leave in order to bring about immediate progress in your position. No matter what your wishes or the advantages that you would gain by this, however, keep events under control and don't lose sight of your goals. Success depends on your resolve alone.

📇 Steer clear of reckless acts and your desire to satisfy your wishes at all costs, particularly if you have the means to do so. Apart from this, you can take action to get what you want done quickly or to allow your financial affairs to progress.

✚ You have the strength of mind to protect yourself from any physical risks or to act bravely and responsibly in your effort to triumph over adversity and leave your health problems behind.

♥ Despite your efforts, you will not necessarily manage to achieve the agreement or reconciliation that you seek. Expect to experience an upheaval or disruption in your love life.

👪 Should unpredictable events occur, take the opportunity to instigate major change or upheaval. In fact, this will provide a valuable boost to your personal standing and allow real progress to be made.

📋 Take concerted action to ensure that a static situation gets moving again, but make sure that rules are respected and that you do not lose sight of your duties and responsibilities. You are sure to overcome your difficulties and, if necessary, turn the situation to your advantage.

🔲 Be on your guard against any destabilization of your financial position. Take action to inject new vitality into a stalemate, but allow yourself to be guided only by your keen sense of duty and responsibility.

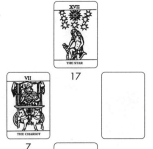

✚ You can easily overcome your contradictory nature by adapting your choices and decisions to circumstances, by mixing business with pleasure and remaining open and approachable in everything you do. Look for a happy medium.

♥ Your will and resolve will allow you to start new relationships and to enjoy deep and genuine ties that form spontaneously and naturally, based as they are on real affinity.

👪 It is up to you to decide whether to take action to obtain something new in your personal or family relationships. What are you waiting for? You have every chance of success.

📋 A happy coincidence or sequence of events is favouring the progress and evolution of your professional relationships. Alternatively, it may be that you need to reach some agreement or make a deliberate choice in order to achieve something new for yourself.

🔲 Take action to hurry along decisions or choices that will be financially favourable to you. You will not be disappointed, and your efforts will be fully rewarded.

7 18

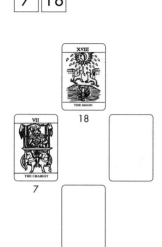

➕ If you make an effort and show courage and determination, you will overcome your worries, weaknesses or health problems.

❤ Despite your efforts and willingness to do so, you don't seem to be able to shake off your worries or to overcome the disappointments, problems and conflicts that are currently dominating your love life.

👪 You will make a move or go on a journey in order to resolve a family problem. Alternatively, you may be showing courage and dedication in overcoming your current difficulties. No matter what happens, your efforts will certainly be rewarded.

📋 Your courage and desire to succeed in whatever you do mean that you are in a good position to overcome the difficulties and obstacles in your path. Don't worry, your efforts are not in vain.

🗄 Pre-emptive action is essential in order to offset probable delays and money difficulties and any other obstacles you may encounter. In spite of everything, you should then be able to achieve your goals.

7 19

➕ You are brave, disciplined and willing. Your dynamism allows you to sparkle, and you feel in complete harmony with your surroundings and those around you.

❤ If you haven't already done so, you will succeed in forming a relationship with someone who will prove sincere, well-balanced and straightforward. You have every reason to congratulate yourself on this state of affairs.

👪 If need be, you can take rigorous but impartial steps to clarify your situation. Alternatively, any actions aimed at maintaining equilibrium and harmony in your family life are open to you and are heartily recommended.

📋 You know that you are within your rights but don't abuse this state of affairs. Your efforts to attain a clear, well-balanced situation are largely rewarded, and you will succeed in reaching agreements and making the progress for which you hope.

🗄 Take rigorous but strictly legal steps to clarify or make progress with money matters or come to some agreements that will prove equally profitable.

➕ You will receive some good news regarding your health. Alternatively, if you are ill, your resolve and tenacious, patient efforts will ensure recovery and get you back on form.

❤ You will have news that leads you to reconsider your personal life. Alternatively, you may take cautious but effective action to inject new vitality into your love life.

👪 You will receive an invitation. Alternatively, you may be acting with caution and realism in order to bring a project to an end or to instigate an action that could bring about a change or revival in your situation.

📋 You have some news, someone makes a proposal that allows you to reconsider matters, or you look seriously at the possibility of change or something new. The waiting has not been in vain.

🁢 New information is made available, or there is a proposal that allows you to take more precise, effective action in bringing about a change or a progressive reassessment of your situation.

➕ You enjoy hard work or even a struggle, allowing you to take on any challenge. Act as you see fit and you will achieve your targets through sheer willpower.

❤ The field is clear and you have all the aces up your sleeve to achieve your goals or to take your love life to the next level by dint of your own willpower.

👪 Take action and use all your energy and skill to help your family circumstances flourish. No matter what your wishes, your strength of character will help them come true.

📋 No matter what efforts you are making or battles you are engaged in, you have the resolve and skill to bring about a successful conclusion. With the forecast looking so good, it's full steam ahead.

🁢 Your endeavours and resolve will ensure positive developments. All you need to do is nudge financial matters along a little, and success will be yours.

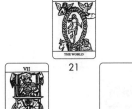

7 22

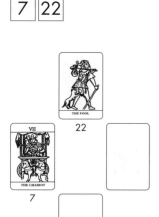

VII   22

7

➕ At present, you are dynamic, energetic and enterprising, and it seems that nothing can stand in your way. Follow your instincts in everything you do.

♥ You are forging ahead and have the absolute will to succeed in your love life. Come what may, however, keep a rein on your impulses and desires.

👪 You want to leave or speed up a transitional phase. It looks likely that you will succeed.

📋 You are eager for professional matters to make speedy progress. Nothing seems able to hold you back, and success depends on no one but yourself. Launch yourself into action, focusing on your desired changes, including possible journeys.

🂠 You are successfully negotiating a period of transition or change that will speed up financial growth. You should not, however, relax your efforts for a second and avoid premature action.

8 1

VIII   1

8

➕ You are well-balanced and expend energy carefully. It is this that makes you cautious when taking decisions and initiatives or when imposing your point of view.

♥ You have a natural tendency to be precise but fair when expressing your wishes. On the emotional front, this can make you seem fussy and demanding, even perhaps a little cold, distant or severe.

👪 The stability of your family life relies on your caution and experience, and the fact that you know how to take reliable, realistic decisions. Don't be too harsh in your judgement, however.

📋 Give any legal decision you have to make careful, prior thought and rely on your experience, sense of fairness and realism. Alternatively, your stable situation allows you to take or welcome new risk-free initiatives.

🂠 Your naturally balanced and cautious character means that you rely on no one but yourself on the financial front. As a result, you tackle projects or initiatives with extreme caution

You are well-balanced and self-disciplined and control events in your life by following your own path with calm determination, while keeping a cautious eye on events around you.

Your balanced nature means you can allow your relationships to develop simply and naturally. All the same, do not confuse patience with apathy and inertia, and do not become too demanding, selective or restrictive where your true feelings are concerned.

Your natural stability and ability to observe impartially allows you to have a calm, reserved control over the steady development of your family situation.

If your position depends on the delivery of a judgement, which you are currently awaiting, it will be to your advantage. Even if you can do nothing for the moment, it will lead to something positive. Otherwise, your balanced situation develops normally, assuring even greater stability.

Your sense of economy means that you generally act in a cautious, reserved manner in matters of finance.

You have total control over yourself and your health. Your stability relies on your energy, good instincts, understanding and intelligence. What more can you ask for?

Your natural steadiness, strength of character and clarity of judgement ensure you are in control and always sure of your feelings and consequent actions.

Your family situation seems solid, well-balanced and perfectly controlled by your own stable, understanding, generous behaviour or that of a woman who is close to you.

You are in a stable, sound and well-balanced situation over which nothing seems able to cast doubt for the moment. You control the ins and outs of what happens through a capacity for hard work and intelligence.

The stability of your situation indicates that your resources are carefully controlled, and also allows you the intelligent acquisition of other assets without too much worry.

8 4

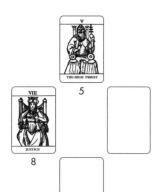

➕ Your equilibrium is dependent on the absolute necessity to subject yourself to self-discipline and stick to it rigorously.

♥ You have no choice but to demonstrate strength and self-discipline in your current emotional situation. Alternatively, you may be in a stable, well-balanced relationship, but you lack freedom of choice.

👪 Your family situation will not achieve harmony and settle down by itself. It is up to you to decide whether authoritarian control of the situation is a good thing or not, and whether it might be worth making a few concessions.

📋 Your situation obliges you to make serious and definitive judgements. Impose order and self-discipline to ensure that your business develops well – and to demonstrate authority and determination in relation to your obligations and duties.

🁢 Your current situation forces you to maintain a precarious or uncomfortable state of affairs. A good deal of self-discipline is needed if you are to meet your obligations.

8 5

➕ You must be rigorous and determined to eradicate anything that might prove harmful to your equilibrium.

♥ Something will be brought to a definite and final conclusion. The time for going back over old ground has gone. You must turn the page and do what your conscience and duty dictate.

👪 Your conscience is telling you to bring a situation to a close, and to be impartial and inflexible in your decisions and judgements when doing so. The stability of your family situation depends on it. Otherwise, it is you who will be judged.

📋 Things are breaking down, or a legal decision will bring an end to an established situation. This will allow you to reach an agreement or receive the approval of an influential person on whom your current position depends.

🁢 An exacting legal decision or a very strict financial regime can only prove profitable to the stability of your situation.

➕ Your accommodating nature and ability to adapt to circumstances and the most diverse of relationships is based on your steadiness and natural self-discipline.

8 6

❤️ Adopt a balanced and self-disciplined attitude when making the decisions or choices that lie before you. Consider all the aspects, finding the best possible arrangements and drawing maximum advantage from your privileged relationships.

👪 Be accommodating and fair in your choices, decisions and judgements. Well-timed agreements and open, frank discussions will benefit your relationships and enhance the stability of your situation.

📋 The steadiness of your situation means that you are ideally placed to make wise decisions, correct choices and fair compromises – and to reach the agreements that will make everyone happy.

▥ A stable financial situation makes you receptive to any opportunities that may be offered, and allows you to make choices and decisions and reach the necessary agreements.

➕ Subject yourself to some serious self-discipline in order to control your intense energy. You should channel your tendency towards over-excitement and use your dynamism and taste for action and conflict to the best advantage.

8 7

❤️ You must decide on a strict code of conduct for yourself. If not, you will succumb to the temptation of satisfying your desires at any cost, or become prey to potentially harmful influences. Don't be too hard or too rigid in your judgements.

👪 Inflexibility and your wish to impose your will at all costs is evident in your judgements and your concern to follow pre-established rules, come what may.

📋 Staying true to your principles offers a very solid foundation. You can be rigorous in your judgements and redouble your efforts to ensure that your situation progresses profitably. This will accelerate a process that is set to bring you success.

▥ Ensure that your situation progresses on a sound footing. Don't hesitate to demonstrate a degree of daring, but ensure that everything you do is strictly legal, particularly if you are in a hurry to succeed.

8 9

+ You are well-balanced, attentive and receptive. As a result, there is nothing to stop you continuing at your own pace, demonstrating your customary level of caution and tenacity.

♥ You always seem to demonstrate caution in your judgements, and the care you take to preserve the stability of your emotional situation makes you very receptive and attentive to the depth and true nature of your feelings.

👪 You seem extremely demanding and fussy in the concern that you show in preserving the stability of your family situation; but you also realize that stability is not incompatible with the introduction of something new. It is all a matter of striking the right balance.

✎ A well-balanced, healthy, reliable situation means you can begin the search for long-term innovative trends, original ideas and creative undertakings, and perhaps make some interesting discoveries along the way.

▦ You seem well aware of the state of your resources. Consequently, you are not at risk of receiving any unpleasant surprises on the financial front.

8 10

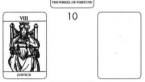

+ Through self-discipline, clean living or a strict life-style, you will succeed in protecting yourself and overcoming or eradicating any health problems.

♥ Strict and firm behaviour will ensure you can shake off anything that may hinder your love life or hold back its development. Do not resort to being unfair.

👪 The stability of your situation is threatened by your worries and fears, or by certain confusing factors. You will soon see, however, that all these problems are of little importance and will sort themselves out.

✎ The stability of your working situation allows you to solve any problems, or to overcome delays and any obstacles that may arise. They will disappear as quickly as they came.

▦ It is in your interests to put your affairs or finances in order. Your current problems will be resolved as a result.

➕ Stability and balance give you full control over your situation and your mental and physical powers.

❤ Your happy, healthy and well-balanced emotional life gives you total freedom of action when expressing your feelings. This brings with it clarity of judgement and the possibility of perfect harmony.

👪 Your family situation seems perfectly happy, healthy and well-balanced. As a result, you can let it develop naturally.

📋 You are in the process of reaching the perfect agreement that will aid the expansion and stability of your situation. Alternatively, your clarity of judgement and your situation's healthy stability will allow you to consolidate your position.

💰 Your healthy, well-ordered finances put you in a solid position and allow you to achieve a degree of expansion successfully.

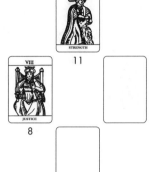

➕ It is vital that you subject yourself to a degree of self-discipline and a number of constraints. Only this will ensure your recovery from any illness or restore your equilibrium.

❤ To ensure a revival in your love life, or a favourable outcome, apply some restraint and make tough decisions. You must also ensure that your relationship gets back on an even keel.

👪 A judgement, or your stringent, balanced attitude, will release you from certain constraints and allow you to witness a natural revival in your circumstances – even though you may not feel as if you have any choice in the matter.

📋 A verdict has just been reached, and this gives you freedom of action once again. It allows you to enjoy a certain revival in your fortunes and to feel free of some previous restrictions.

💰 If you want to see your finances revive and be free from constraints, ensure that any judgements you make in relation to your money are fair and impartial

8 13

13

8

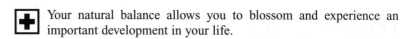

➕ Your natural balance allows you to blossom and experience an important development in your life.

❤ Your love life will flourish, allowing you to make an important change or radical transformation.

👪 Don't worry about being too demanding or having ambitious ideas when bringing a situation to a conclusion or effecting a major transformation on the domestic front. You have the power and moral strength needed to achieve this.

📝 No matter what decision is made about you or your circumstances, rest assured that it will be entirely favourable and bring about profitable change.

▨ A stable and potentially advantageous situation should provide you with the means to make a significant profit or a radical change.

CURRENT SITUATION

8 14

14

8

➕ Your natural balance allows you to resist any tempting reckless impulses, while at the same time allowing you to respond actively to the opportunities on offer – to leave, to enjoy a new lease of life or to adapt to circumstances.

❤ If you suddenly decide to administer some form of justice, ensure you are fair, understanding and tolerant. You must adapt to circumstances. Be accommodating and if nothing too grave has occurred, be prepared to forgive.

👪 Don't hesitate to exchange your rather stern, rigid, brusque but impartial attitude for rather more diplomatic and accommodating behaviour. In the current circumstances, you need to know how to make this transition with care.

📝 Even if you are sure of your rights and prerogatives, learn to adapt to circumstances and listen to other people's points of view, making, if necessary, appropriate arrangements and agreements that will be useful to your situation.

▨ Even if you are sure of your rights and decisions, be less rigid and more flexible in the way you handle your assets and more receptive to potential transactions, exchanges and opportunities.

166

➕ You need to subject yourself to some stern self-discipline to avoid the risks of excess. If you are ill, you won't get off lightly – some serious treatment, a strict diet or even surgery will be required.

♥ You demonstrate a certain moral severity in your emotional relationships, but are you as pure in your intentions and honourable in your behaviour as you would have everyone believe? If the answer is yes, you must now do what your conscience dictates.

👪 If you feel you demonstrate too much moral probity, tell yourself that it is this very attitude that is currently keeping things stable. The exercise of power, even within one's family, relies on rules and principles.

📋 Be fair but impartial in the exercise of your responsibilities; and be scrupulously honest if you want to enter into an agreement or contract that will prove useful in terms of furthering your ambitions. It could all turn out to be very profitable.

🗐 Your money matters currently depend on the law, legal advisers and officialdom. This might be because you are entering into an important and advantageous contract, or it might mean you are paying for a mistake.

8 | 15

15

8

➕ Resolve to eradicate anything likely to throw you off course or destabilize you and you will manage to retain your well-being, come what may.

♥ Resolve to cut things short, make some important but salutary decisions and take a look at anything that needs reassessing. Bring things to an end if no other course of action seems open to you.

👪 Make some wise resolutions and sensible choices and be selective and unyielding in your decisions. This conduct will ensure you are in a good position to face up to any upheavals that might take place, or even go as far as breaking point if need be.

📋 Be demanding and uncompromising in your resolutions and in any difficult choices you might be making. This will ensure you will succeed in putting your situation back on its feet or freeing it from any hindrances. If you don't manage to avoid a crisis, then at least you will be controlling and containing it.

🗐 Maintain the stability of your situation by ensuring that your choices are wise yet liberating, and your decisions restrictive but beneficial.

8 | 16

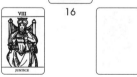

16

8

8 17

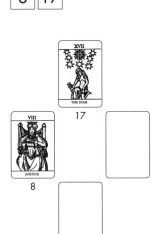

XVII
THE STAR

17

VIII
JUSTICE

8

➕ You are currently well-balanced, resourceful and active. You have the ability to achieve whatever you like.

❤ By demonstrating fairness, honesty and a balanced attitude combined with sheer willpower, you can achieve what you want and see your wishes and aspirations become reality.

👪 Your resolve and efforts to achieve your hopes and dreams depend upon your steady approach to things or on a reliable and stable situation. As a result, anything you do is likely to work out well.

✍ Be rigorous and determined in your endeavours to achieve something that plays a major part in your hopes and aspirations. If circumstances are on your side, such behaviour should help everything work out as you wish.

🗒 Impose a code of conduct on yourself and stick to it firmly. Providing circumstances are on your side, all your wishes should then be achieved.

8 18

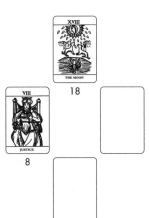

XVIII
THE MOON

18

VIII
JUSTICE

8

➕ Your balance, dependable nature and self-discipline allow you to resolve any health problems.

❤ If you have to face a situation of conflict and confusion, be as firm as possible. Act as if you yourself were on trial, in order to overcome any problems that may arise.

👪 Whatever the problems, conflicts and annoyances that you currently face on the domestic front, you have sufficient stability and control to deal with them and resolve them as necessary.

✍ If no other choice presents itself, take the strong measures needed to resolve your problems and defend your corner and your rights. Alternatively, your upright character and scrupulous integrity allow you to face up to the difficulty and confusion of your situation.

🗒 Be scrupulously honest and strict on the financial front. You will then be in a good position to resolve any monetary problems.

Your natural stability and balance make you cautious but fair in your behaviour. This allows you to live in harmony with yourself and those around you, and take full advantage of your well-being.

By relying on your natural stability and caution, you will eventually find harmony in your relationships and love life, as well as the sincere partnership that you are seeking.

Your judgements are fair, accurate and considered. They shed a positive light on your domestic situation and help your family ties to flourish.

By ensuring that you behave with scrupulous honesty, remaining rigorously faithful to your word and consistent in your judgements and behaviour, you will find the agreement you are looking for and obtain the success you deserve.

Be cautious, fair, precise and consistent in your judgements and you will have all the clarification and agreement you need for success.

8 19

Your natural stability favours your personal development and allows you to enjoy a new lease of life or make a quick recovery after an illness.

Your upright nature, honesty and fidelity can only benefit the way in which your situation develops, allowing you to experience a genuine revival in your love-life.

Your situation is developing in a stable, well-balanced way, with circumstances that encourage renewal and positive change, or a totally justified reconsideration.

Thanks to a fair but strict decision your situation is moving rapidly towards a revival or a very positive change.

Your situation seems stable and well-balanced. This will help it become revitalized, or allow you to respond favourably to any proposals that you may receive in relation to a profitable change.

8 20

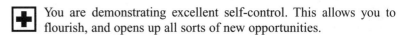

8	21

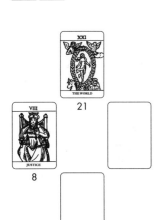

✚ You are demonstrating excellent self-control. This allows you to flourish, and opens up all sorts of new opportunities.

❤ Your fundamental loyalty, strong principles and the genuine nature of your feelings mean that you will experience total fulfilment in your love life.

👪 Your loyalty and integrity allow you to control your family situation with a gentle but assured hand and to experience a degree of satisfaction and fulfilment.

📋 Your integrity, strength of character and calm confidence in yourself and your situation mean that you are able to carry out a significant expansion of your area of responsibility or even in the range of your activities.

🁢 Your stable, healthy financial situation gives you the opportunity to rally all your assets and resources and take careful, practical steps towards expansion.

8	22

✚ Your balance and stability make it possible for you to make a journey, or set off in search of adventure without the risk of falling from the straight and narrow.

❤ Reason tells you to avoid behaving impulsively or recklessly. Depending on the circumstances, ask yourself if you are right or wrong to protect yourself so rigorously – particularly since there is a risk that an outside event will suddenly upset things.

👪 Sure of your rights and good faith, you may be tempted to leave on a whim, in the hope of dispensing justice or finding your own peace of mind. Alternatively, the arrival or departure of someone close to you may upset matters without actually calling them into question.

📋 The stability of your situation encourages a departure or move, taking action to assert your rights, or the outcome of arbitration. Alternatively, it may allow you to change work place or career.

🁢 Secure in the knowledge that your financial situation is balanced and sure of your own honesty, don't hesitate to assert your rights or make a rapid and desirable transition.

Your caution, tenacity and reliability allow you to make steady, calm progress, demonstrating initiative and skill if the need arises.

A sudden realization or withdrawal into yourself enables you to take your relationship to a new stage and take some useful initiatives.

 You discover, or become aware of, something new that provides a boost to your family situation and enables it to develop slowly but surely, making progress towards new initiatives and plans.

Patience, time, caution and tenacity enable you to advance your plans, or to discover the best way of using your talents, while assessing carefully how best to achieve your ambitions.

Be cautious and realistic on the financial front. Even if new possibilities arise, do nothing without prior consideration.

 You are cautious but confident in yourself and your abilities. You know when it is possible to move ahead, and when it is better to hold back and reflect more deeply. Such good sense can only be beneficial, and guarantee you enjoy excellent stability and good health.

You need to be careful and considerate but firm when telling others what they need to know. You are the only one who knows what will come to the surface when things become clear.

 Your research and investigations are rewarded but if you want to ensure your situation remains stable, be careful how you use what you have discovered.

You are taking plenty of precautions and considering the question that interests you carefully. You are still at the research stage and not quite ready to put your plans into action. However, in the circumstances, you are quite right to want to look into things more closely and take your time.

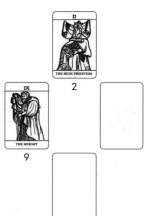 Take a good hard, realistic look at your financial situation. Be clear how you should maintain its present state, while working with patience and seriousness to take it further.

9 3

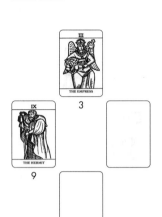

The Empress
3
The Hermit
9

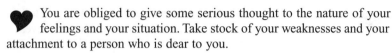
Only you can understand and do what is necessary to escape this difficult, isolating situation with all its constraints.

You are obliged to give some serious thought to the nature of your feelings and your situation. Take stock of your weaknesses and your attachment to a person who is dear to you.

You are looking for the means to escape your situation or to be more independent, but you feel isolated and without support. You must rely only on yourself.

Circumstances require some precision, patience and hard work, but although this may seem rather restricting, it is the only way you will achieve your goals.

Although your situation may be sound, you are still obliged to act with caution in order to look after your responsibilities.

9 4

The Emperor
4
The Hermit
9

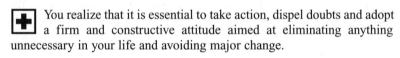
You realize that it is essential to take action, dispel doubts and adopt a firm and constructive attitude aimed at eliminating anything unnecessary in your life and avoiding major change.

You are becoming aware of the need to bring a particular situation to a close, put some distance between yourself and someone else, or make a radical and necessary change on the emotional front.

You do not make decisions lightly but take your time and reflect deeply. However, once you have made up your mind, you don't change it.

You realize that a change is indispensable if there are to be steady but constructive developments. Although this may be difficult, it will prove to be very profitable.

After a period of doubt and reflection, you will become aware of the need to make a change in your current situation, if you want to look beyond your usual horizons.

✚ After mature reflection and taking a wide range of precautions, do what your duty dictates. Being so sensible, what could you be scared of?

♥ You act with caution, flexibility and discretion to reach agreements and compromises that may prove useful with regard to your long-term stability.

👪 Before making the arrangements that are necessary to bring about the agreement or approval you need, you are very cautious and consider every aspect of the matter carefully.

📋 You are cautious but unremitting in your efforts to make the arrangements you need in order to reach an agreement, or to obtain the authorization required to reach a long-term objective.

🔳 Be clear about the direction you want your finances to take. Try to find appropriate solutions that will ensure their reliability and stability in the longer term.

✚ You are aware that you tend to be excitable and excessive, but you still find it difficult to resist temptation and hold back. Ultimately, only you have the power to decide what may or may not be an appropriate attitude in the present circumstances.

♥ You discover a passion, or become aware of strong feelings and emotions. Despite your self-awareness, you cannot restrain your impulses or your excessive and intolerant behaviour.

👪 You are are being scrupulous about facing up to ambitious choices or bold decisions. Despite your experience or maturity, you cannot control your passionate behaviour.

📋 You are displaying a mixture of caution, tenacity and earnestness in making some important choices, bringing one or a number of agreements to a successful conclusion or achieving some ambitious objectives.

🔳 You are concentrating all your efforts and physical and mental energy on finding the correct balance in your financial situation, which is currently rather chaotic, but rich in possibilities.

9 7

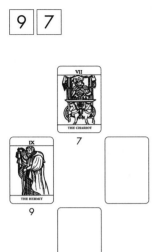

7

Caution and personal experience protect you from risks. Alternatively, a sudden realization enables you to act in an effective and constructive fashion.

You are aware of the need, or are looking for the means of creating a sudden but beneficial reassessment of your emotional involvement. Alternatively, despite your vigilance, you will be unable to avoid an upheaval or crisis that will provide the opportunity to move on to better things.

You learn or discover some overwhelming news. If it is negative, take care and do all that you can to contain its repercussions. If it is positive, it will provide you with the means to allow your situation to develop. In either case, the end result will be beneficial.

Your research and personal discoveries will allow you to make a sudden leap forward, or they will be the catalyst for a major but positive upheaval or crisis. In turn, this will provoke some real progress and open doors that will enable you to achieve your goal.

You are taking plenty of precautions and are realistic and cautious. You will have a sudden inspiration that will allow you to ensure your financial matters make progress.

9 8

8

You are going back to basics or becoming aware of some hitherto unrecognized aspects of life that are important to you. This will allow you to revitalize your physical and mental well-being at a deep level.

You become aware of the genuine nature of your emotions, or are on the look-out for new, sincere feelings, However, your needs and strict sense of morality, together with a tendency to keep a distance from others, prevent you from achieving full satisfaction in your love life.

You are alert for anything new that might bring balance to your position. You are certainly not lacking the inspiration to ensure this is achieved.

Be cautions and realistic in any inquiries that you make and concerning any subsequent discovery. Be careful also about how you are tempted to use the information you have and any new ideas that may be useful in revitalizing your position.

You are cautious and patient in seeking out new aspects of your financial situation and schemes that might be useful in ensuring the slow but sure development of your resources and stability.

174

➕ You are acting cautiously and sensibly to clarify health issues. You will discover all you need to know to feel at ease with yourself and your environment in the long term.

❤ You have become aware of the real value of your feelings and the happiness of your situation. This fortunate discovery leads to a positive evolution in your love life. If you are alone, you will not remain so for long.

👪 Revelations made at the heart of your family circle clarify the situation and lead to positive results. Consequently, do not hesitate to shed light on anything that requires clarification.

📋 Caution, experience and realism are needed to reach a perfect agreement or an ideal partnership that favours the continuing progress of your situation. Alternatively, it may be you alone, through your tenacity and clarity of judgement, who has power over the positive development of your situation.

🗄 You are aware of your resources and options. By leaving nothing to chance and never losing sight of your long-term aims, you can take cautious but clear steps to ensure financial progress.

➕ You are making conscientious efforts to return to form and enjoy increased levels of physical and mental energy. You will no doubt succeed in your aims.

❤ You feel the need for a revival in your love life, either in terms of feeling less alone, or regaining purity in your feelings. Alternatively, if a conflict arises with a loved one, you are seeking to forgive or be forgiven.

👪 Your situation seems to rely entirely on your own good sense and experience. If you have any revelations to make or if matters require further clarification – with a view to a renewal or reassessment – you can be fully confident of any action you take.

📋 Slowly but surely your work is becoming constructive and your situation more established, even if are you acting alone. There can be no doubt that you are searching for a renewal, or a change for the better.

🗄 Don't be concerned that you are taking too many precautions when it comes to getting your affairs back on a sound footing or positively reassessing your situation. This can only serve to provide you with additional assurance for the future.

9 12

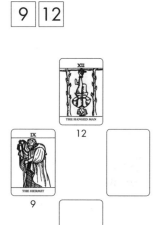

12

9

Search and you shall find: in this case you will find a way to free yourself from constraints or to escape from a stale situation, or to recover from physical and mental frailty.

Aim to use everything at your disposal to release your pent-up feelings and allow your emotions to blossom.

Find the perfect solution. Take the long view and expand your habitual horizons. In this way, you will, little by little, manage to satisfy your hopes and achieve your wishes.

You have some major, long-term plans and ambitious objectives in mind. You can achieve them by finding specific and realistic ways of making your situation more solid and less dependent.

You need to come to a thorough understanding of what is at the root of a current financial stalemate and make a careful assessment of it in order to find a realistic solution.

9 13

13

9

You act very quickly, moving from thought to deed to bring a situation to a conclusion or bring about a vital change.

You are aware of how a radical change in your emotional life is both essential and inevitable You are seeking the best and quickest way to achieve this.

You learn or perceive that a fundamental change is necessary in your current family situation. Do all that is needed to bring this about as soon as possible.

Fate dictates that there will be an important change in your work. You show that you are certainly aware of the need for this transformation by carrying out a serious and honest assessment of the most suitable and effective solutions.

The change currently taking place in your financial affairs may have two causes, the positive cause being the profitable outcome of something that you have long foreseen, the negative one being the loss or freezing of your assets or profits.

9 | 14

➕ Although you are very cautious and conscientious in terms of your approach to your duties and responsibilities, you are also physically adaptable and mentally flexible .

♥ Be punctillious about reaching agreements but adopt a flexible attitude which will be more appropriate in the current circumstances. Listen hard to what course of action your sense of duty advises you to take.

👪 Be aware of your duties and responsibilities, but also be clear in making reasonable concessions and reaching agreements that will make your situation dependable, peaceful and harmonious.

📋 Be conscientious and methodical in seeking profitable agreements that will prove useful and provide a better understanding of how you should adapt to the current situation.

⌗ Whatever happens, don't let your sense of duty and responsibilities slip. Remain open to any opportunities and agreements that may be put to you, and that will allow you to adapt your situation to current circumstances.

14

9

9 | 15

➕ You cannot be blind to your own failings and, despite your good intentions to be guided by caution and good sense, you know that you find it difficult to resist temptation and excess. Don't forget that you have total freedom of choice and are responsible for your actions.

♥ You are strongly tempted to plunge yourself into a troubled and passionate relationship. Only you can decide whether this is really what are you looking for.

👪 Despite your caution and wariness, you cannot seem to remove yourself from the climate of turmoil and over-excitement that reigns in your family circle. This is certainly not the ideal atmosphere in which to make the choices and decisions that are down to you alone.

📋 Don't let yourself be outflanked by the current climate of turmoil and disorder that exists around you. Try to find considered, mature and realistic solutions that will serve to make your situation more advantageous.

⌗ Be clear, realistic and vigilant in your decisions. Don't be tempted by extreme solutions or choices that are beyond your means.

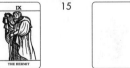

15

9

9 16

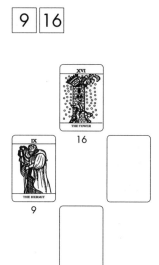

16

9

➕ You know exactly what you must do to avoid or eliminate anything that troubles you, holds you back or makes you ill at ease. Alternatively, although you are cautious, watch out for anything that could have a sudden, destabilizing effect or the risk of an accident.

♥ You realize that an upheaval in your love life is both inevitable and necessary, and you are currently putting all your efforts into bringing one about.

👪 You discover something or hear news that frees your situation, puts it back on track or turns things upside down. It might even be you who instigates this shake-up, through the revelations that you make or via a personal crisis of conscience.

📋 Find precise, realistic solutions to free things up and make every effort to get your situation back on track or instigate a major, beneficial change. This sudden shake-up will, ultimately, play a part in your progress

🎲 Don't turn a blind eye to any reassessments that might be useful to the long-term development of your financial situation. Be cautious and realistic and avoid dangerous undertakings.

9 17

17

9

➕ Your receptive nature brings you balance and also makes you cautious, attentive and acutely aware of the opportunities open to you but also of your limitations.

♥ If your cautious and demanding behaviour makes you quite solitary at heart, it does not prevent you from being receptive to what is going on around you or aware of the deep, genuine nature of your feelings.

👪 Your natural caution and good sense mean that, with time, you should find the stability to which you aspire. You can then go with the flow and surrender to an amicable and harmonious situation, even if you are not demonstrative within it.

📋 You make an interesting discovery. Alternatively, you concentrate all your attention on the study or invention of something new and creative.

🎲 You take lots of precautions and are preoccupied with leaving nothing to chance. This allows you to manage your finances wisely and remain aware of your assets, but it may also limit your situation to some extent.

9 18

You know very well what is not right, but it is not enough simply to recognize this. You must act or react accordingly, aware of what remains to be done if you want to solve your problems.

If you are alone, the thought of remaining so for ever fills you with despair. Alternatively, things are not going too well in your love life. In either case, it is not enough simply to accept the facts. It is time for you to undergo some real soul-searching.

You are aware of the problems in your domestic circle and are trying to find sensible, realistic solutions. However, given the confusion of the situation, perhaps you should behave a little more pro-actively or firmly before you are completely overwhelmed by events.

You are at risk of being disappointed in your work or of discovering something that displeases you. Only you can find the solutions to your problems.

You are almost certainly facing some difficulties at the moment, but you are the only one who has the power to resolve them. Self-reliance is the order of the day.

18

9

9 19

Slowly but surely you will begin to move towards real fulfilment and the removal of any obstacles that remain between you and your well-being.

You are quietly determined to improve matters in your emotional life. Equally, you are well aware of the value of a genuine or special relationship that casts a rosy glow over everything in your life.

You are seeking a total clarification of your family circumstances. Your own solitary and determined investigations are fully rewarded and you will achieve your aims with relative ease.

Take a careful look at the ways in which you might reach a useful agreement. Alternatively, cautiously and discretely instigate the development of your role or bring about a notable change in your position.

You are clarifying your financial situation by finding solutions that will encourage its development.

19

9

9 20

20

9

You are pragmatic, cautious and in full control of yourself. These qualities will help you to blossom or regain your well-being.

You are gradually finding the safest way to revitalize your love-life. Your quiet strength, tenacity and deeply held convictions mean you are sure to achieve your aims.

You discover something that is likely to lead to renewal or change. Remember to keep a controlling hand on the reins while exercising caution and forbearance.

The discovery of an essential factor or the exact solution to your problems will lead to a revitalization, change or development in your professional situation.

You are currently seeking the best way of responding, accurately and realistically, to a proposal. Alternatively, you may be trying to come to terms with some significant changes that will be useful to your financial situation.

9 21

21

9

You are receptive and benefit from an excellent instinct for self-preservation that ensures you maintain good energy levels and favours your personal development.

You realize just how close you have become to someone, if not physically, then at least in terms of thoughts and feelings. Alternatively, you may be very aware of the wealth of emotions that you are currently enjoying.

You succeed in finding the best way to achieve your long-term goals for your family circle.

Your attempts to bring about profitable circumstances are sure to be far more successful than you expected, and you will soon see an expansion of your professional horizons.

You are well aware of your resources and the possibilities open to you, but this does not stop you from being cautious or from relying on vigilance and realism to attain your long-term objectives.

9 22

➕ You may be right to wonder if you really are in a fit state to leave. The answer is that a little change won't do you any harm. Alternatively, take fast and positive steps to find solutions to your problems.

♥ A revelation, crisis of conscience or a discovery, may prompt you to leave suddenly. Whilst this is probably to enable you to talk to the other person involved, it will also ensure that you are not the only one to have grasped the situation.

👪 It is a slow process, but you will eventually find the way to leave, make a transition or move – or perhaps even reveal everything that you know or have discovered. In so doing, you will relieve yourself of the burden that has been weighing you down for some time.

📋 You are clear about what you want and the steps you will take to get it. Alternatively, unless you suddenly have to make a work-related journey, you may have the opportunity to make some revelations, or pass on your knowledge or experience to others.

🁢 You are very aware of the current state of play on the financial front, and your experience dictates exactly what you can achieve. Be very careful not to make any mistakes.

10 1

➕ You are approaching a positive phase in your life during which you will be in full control of yourself both mentally and physically. You can be active and energetic and make use of your spirit of initiative.

♥ Your current emotional situation is going through a period of change. Act as you see fit to achieve your plans and wishes, without allowing yourself to be swept along by events.

👪 Achieving calm control over current events and circumstances in your home life will help bring about useful projects and facilitate initiatives and decisions.

📋 You have every chance of seeing your situation develop quickly which cannot simply be put down to luck. As a result, you can exercise your talents, take new initiatives and make prompt decisions.

🁢 Your financial situation is evolving, and you have every chance of being able to put your skills and spirit of initiative into action and profit from these favourable circumstances to the full. Don't refrain from acting promptly and effectively.

181

10	2

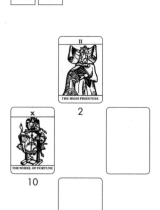

Find a natural way to shake off your current feelings of frailty, apathy or inertia and take the sensible precautions and decisions that are needed.

Your reserve, or the inactivity of someone close to you, is preventing matters from developing normally, making you susceptible to weakness and dependence.

Before your family circumstances can evolve appropriately, find a way to deal with all the factors that are currently preventing its natural development.

Take advantage of a slow-down in your progress to analyse its causes. Try to give serious consideration to the best way of shaking off this state of inertia.

For the moment the natural evolution of your financial affairs seems blocked. Take advantage of this state of affairs to analyse the cause of the problem and to reach some carefully considered conclusions.

10	3

Things are evolving in such a way that you will experience a radical change and achieve or regain true well-being.

You risk losing the affection of someone close to you. Alternatively, a third person will cause a sudden and radical change in your emotional life.

Circumstances allow you to make an important change in your family life and bring to an end a particular state of affairs or take some positive action.

Events are developing very profitably, providing you with the opportunity to benefit from, or be the catalyst for, a radical but potentially advantageous change.

Your financial situation is likely to develop in an extremely advantageous way, even if it must undergo a change to achieve this.

10 4

➕ Your flexible nature combined with your naturally abundant energy gives you the advantage of being able to adapt to circumstances while remaining fully in control. As a result you have complete freedom of choice.

❤️ Current circumstances and events will make you more flexible and accommodating and will lead you to make some definite decisions about your emotional life.

👪 You can be confident that you will reach all the agreements and make all the arrangements necessary to boost the current situation, in either the long or short term.

4

📋 You need to learn how to adapt to circumstances and reach sensible agreements without in any way diminishing your own standing. Such an attitude will strengthen your position.

10

▦ Current circumstances imply that you will be able to make arrangements that will obtain guarantees for your financial situation.

---

10 5

➕ If you continue to neglect your health, you will need to consult a doctor in the near future – unless you start imposing far stricter rules on yourself.

❤️ You want to see your love life progress quickly, but it is not certain that your obligations and responsibilities will allow this to happen.

👪 You are expecting a rapid and possibly somewhat unwarranted development to take place, but it will all turn out for the good.

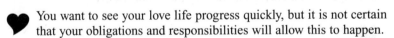

5

📋 Work-related matters will progress quickly and to your advantage, bringing security, consolidation or the support of an important person in their wake.

10

▦ By remaining faithful to your own rules and sense of duty, or the views of others, you will soon reach your financial targets and see useful developments.

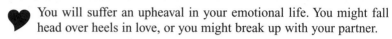

10 6

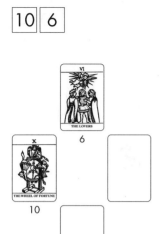

➕ You may well soon suffer an upheaval or shock that risks throwing you off balance.

❤ You will suffer an upheaval in your emotional life. You might fall head over heels in love, or you might break up with your partner.

A sudden upheaval within your family circle will dispel once and for all any uncertainties or indecisiveness.

Things are heading inexorably towards breaking point, a reassessment or a sudden but beneficial upheaval. If the latter should prove to be the case, it will be disconcerting nonetheless due to the choices that will appear rapidly in its wake.

Sort out the options currently open to you as soon as possible in an effort to get your financial situation moving again.

10 7

➕ You are currently charting a course of personal development. Circumstances are favourable, encouraging you to be active, so take advantage of your energy and demonstrate your resolve.

❤ Your love life will soon give you some satisfaction, so sit back and enjoy it. Alternatively, take advantage of these fortunate circumstances to achieve all that you wish.

Family matters are developing in a direction that will give you the freedom to act as you see fit to realize your ambitions. Take advantage of these very favourable circumstances.

Take advantage of the current highly favourable circumstances to be innovative or creative and bring a new sparkle to your life. You should succeed in your professional life and see your efforts rewarded.

It seems that luck (if there is such a thing) is on your side. Circumstances are certainly favourable to you at the moment, so take advantage of this to achieve your goals with comparative ease.

➕ Ensure that you are firm and self-disciplined to prevent your health from deteriorating, or avoid the hazards engendered by your unstable, turbulent lifestyle.

❤️ Circumstances may conspire to limit your freedom to express your feelings. You will have to be self-disciplined and firm to overcome the inevitable stumbling blocks, disappointments or conflicts.

👪 Avoid conflict, confusion and disappointment by imposing a certain amount of discipline and order within your family. Do not allow yourself to be drawn into being party to any injustices or into making any bad judgements.

📋 Order or discipline are now required in your professional life. You may even seek recourse to the law to prevent matters from developing in a confusing way or to make sure you do not fall prey to deception, traps or conflict.

💼 To avoid your situation dissolving into confusion, take determined and immediate steps to become more self-disciplined. If you have made a mistake, it looks as though you will have to face the consequences.

➕ You will obtain confirmation that your health is excellent and discover that everything is OK. Enjoy your vitality and well-being.

❤️ All will become clear in your love life, enabling you to immerse yourself confidently in this special, loving relationship.

👪 You will be able to bring a special quest to an end and find exactly what you have long been seeking. The object of your search will suddenly be revealed to you, but the fact that you have found it is certainly not down to luck.

📋 You will experience well-deserved joy or personal success. Alternatively, you will achieve complete satisfaction in your investigations or in a personal activity.

💼 Financial matters are developing very positively. Nevertheless, remain extremely cautious when faced with anything that seems too good to be true.

185

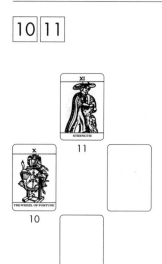

10 11

11

10

You are totally in control of yourself physically and mentally. You are therefore in an ideal position to thrive and enjoy your feelings of well-being.

Your love life is bringing both satisfaction and happiness. The time when you can be completely confident of your emotional situation and its future is almost within reach.

You family situation is in the process of experiencing very positive growth and development.

Act to improve your situation, increase the scope of your activities and broaden your horizons socially. You will still be able to retain a controlling hand.

You are in a strong position to take control and use every possibility that comes your way to advantage.

10 12

12

10

You are too easily influenced and lacking in stability, making you physically and mentally weak. You may want to change this aspect of your character, but you are too impulsive and spread yourself too thinly to be able to do so with any success.

You want action or movement or to leave on the spur of the moment, but you are prevented from doing so by the constraints and deadlock of your situation. It is this state of affairs that makes you feel so frustrated and long to rebel.

You will be held back or stopped in your tracks despite your eagerness to get things moving. There is no point in trying to press on when circumstances are against you. For the moment, simply let events take their course, even though you may have to postpone a journey that you had planned.

You will suddenly be brought up short or an inappropriate, poorly considered plan of action will prevent your situation from progressing. Do your best to avoid acting on impulse or too quickly; it is important to think things through before you act.

Avoid reckless or untimely actions, sudden impulses or excessive haste in your financial dealings. If not, you may find yourself making mistakes and being unable to make any further progress.

➕ You are aiming for greater stability, but to achieve this you need to make a change in the way you live or eliminate anything that threatens your well-being.

❤️ Your situation is making natural progress. This means that anything that ought to be changed, resolved or eradicated will be tackled once and for all.

👪 You should recognize that a radical change will benefit your situation, and that such a change will, in any case, form part of the logical course of current events.

📋 You obtain the authorization or support you need to make progress, but you must undergo a period of radical and advantageous change, or reject out of hand anything that does not form an integral part of your future progress.

🔲 You can profit from a change in your financial circumstances or from the completion of a financial transaction, but do remain aware of your duties and obligations.

10 13

➕ You can rely on your freedom of choice and natural flexibility, which will enable you to adapt to the most diverse of circumstances and situations with ease. However, be careful not to confuse relying on freedom of choice with being careless, or flexibility with instability.

❤️ You have a tendency to let yourself go with the flow of events and be passive, agreeing with what loved ones say rather than taking control. Re-examine your motives and the sincerity of your feelings and consider the importance of your decisions.

👪 Matters are developing in such a way that you should easily reach all the agreements and make all the arrangements that your situation requires in order to progress.

📋 An agreement can be reached that will help you to move forward, or make the decisions that are necessary by remaining open to discussion. Rest secure in the knowledge that whatever happens, you are able to adapt to circumstances.

🔲 Events are progressing rapidly, and your choices should be guided by their speedy development. You will find it easy to cope with the changes.

10 14

10 15

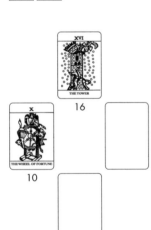

15

10

+ You are in full control, both physically and mentally, and are able to achieve your ideal level in terms of fitness and health.

♥ You can take steps to achieve what you want very quickly in your love life if you ensure that you are in the driving seat, even if the prevailing climate is rather emotional.

👪 You can exert your influence over current events and use practical means to achieve your goals rapidly.

📋 All that you want is within reach. You have the power to steer things in the right direction, to succeed and to reap significant rewards for your efforts rapidly.

💼 The wind is behind you and your destination is in sight. Your efforts should be rewarded on the whole, so sail ahead but stay in control and don't change course.

10 16

XVI

THE TOWER

x
16

THE WHEEL OF FORTUNE
10

+ Your steadiness and self-discipline should allow you to avoid any accidents, health related or otherwise, but nevertheless, remember to take care.

♥ You are aware of the impending break-up of a particular relationship, but it is useless to try and intervene.

👪 Your family situation will be subject to an upheaval or a sudden reassessment. This is a fairly predictable occurrence, since it is a logical step in a recent series of events. Whatever form it may take, face up to it with self-discipline and firmness.

📋 Your professional situation will undergo a sudden about-turn or a total change. It is useless to try to reverse the process as it seems there is no possibility for recourse.

💼 You are caught by a sudden and serious turnaround in your financial situation; unfortunately it proves to be a *fait accompli*.

As you are entering a phase of peace and tranquillity, both mental and physical, allow yourself to be guided by your receptive nature and creativity.

10 **17**

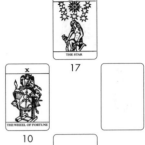

You are realizing the true value of your feelings slowly but surely. You will find what you have long been looking or hoping for.

You will soon discover new aspects of the situation or circumstances that are beneficial to the achievement of your goals.

Your patience, tenacity and realism will allow matters to progress peacefully. You know how to take advantage of this, but act with discretion to match the circumstances.

As long as you remain vigilant and realistic, you can profit greatly from new and potentially advantageous circumstances that will prove beneficial to your finances.

If you do not react with determination you may well experience some serious health problems that will leave you weakened, both physically and mentally.

10 **18**

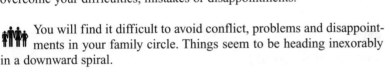

Unresolved problems prevent you from taking matters a stage further. The situation remains unclear and you will be unable to overcome your difficulties, mistakes or disappointments.

You will find it difficult to avoid conflict, problems and disappointments in your family circle. Things seem to be heading inexorably in a downward spiral.

You cannot avoid problems, ups and downs, delays and disappointments. This will limit your development at work or ensnare you in frustration and difficulties.

Your financial affairs may be constrained or even suffer a setback as a result of the disappointments that you will encounter, mistakes that you have made or a certain laxity on your part.

10 19

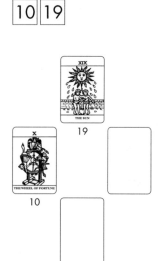

Your mental strength and physical energy allow you to flourish and be at one with yourself and your environment. You are in absolute control of your personal development.

A sincere partnership and a genuine, special relationship are the driving forces behind the positive change in your circumstances, which will also benefit from your self-confidence and emotional strength.

Your high principles will allow you to achieve everything you want and to control the favourable circumstances you are now enjoying.

Your working life is progressing in such a way that an agreement, or an association, is made or confirmed, bringing with it success, happiness and fulfilment.

Your financial situation is making positive progress. You simply need to keep a firm grasp on it.

10 20

If you rely on your intelligence and instincts you will soon recover from any illness. Alternatively, you will have no difficulty in adopting a healthy and positive change in your behaviour.

Your instincts tell you that a revival is in the air. Your understanding of events at an emotional and subconcious level may well help it on its way.

Rely on your natural understanding and receptivity to clear the way for a reassessment or revitalization of your domestic situation, or, at least, a return to normal.

Take practical, carefully thought-out steps to guide your situation towards an interesting new stage, or to make a quick response to any proposals for change.

Respond quickly to suggestions aimed at change or renewal as they could be useful in helping your situation progress and could turn out to be very profitable.

✚ You are certainly going through a remarkable period of personal growth. Enjoy it wholeheartedly.

♥ Rest assured that your love life is developing in a very positive way and that you are about to become fulfilled emotionally.

👪 Your constructive and intelligent approach together with your protective behaviour are beneficial to your family, and you should find that your domestic situation becomes completely fulfilled.

📋 Your intelligent and constructive professional approach combines with your natural authority to guarantee progress and allow you to reap deserved rewards.

▣ You control the development of your finances in a very intelligent and practical manner. As a result, you can rest assured that you will get everything that you want.

10 21

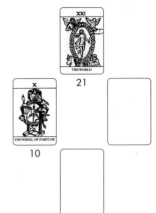

21

10

✚ Everything appears unstable, inconsistent and undisciplined, constantly swinging from high to low and back again. Calm down and find your natural equilibrium.

♥ Your love life may seem to be progressing apace, but this may just be because it is unstable. One thing is clear, however, you will decide to leave, willingly or not.

👪 Things around you are in a constant state of flux, leaving you unsure about everything. One day everything is fine, the next it is not. Suddenly, on a whim you may give in to an impulse to leave or you will carry on regardless.

📋 Things are moving fast at the moment, and this can sometimes make you a little insecure. You may suddenly decide to leave, to change your position, or to take the opportunity of an about-turn, to free yourself from the grip of these unpredictable circumstances.

▣ Undoubtedly, you have been enjoying some good fortune in your current financial situation, but it is rather unstable. Watch out for mistakes or any rash impulses to which you might be tempted to give in.

10 22

22

10

11 1

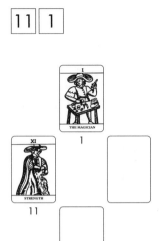

➕ Even if, for the moment, you feel rather limited in some ways, you are still in full control of yourself, physically and mentally. Sooner or later, you will be able to act more freely.

❤ Trust in yourself. Have faith and you will achieve more independence and succeed in taking the initiative in your love life.

👪 Your moral strength and calm control of circumstances help you to take the steps needed for greater independence, or to help someone close to you.

📋 You will be able to achieve more autonomy in your work situation, as long as you are first clear about how to maintain your position and take control of the current situation.

💰 Content yourself for now with being in charge of your finances. As a result, you may well be able to carry out certain projects or take some new initiatives.

11 2

➕ Your mental and physical strength, self-confidence and self-control make you aware of a need for change that will prove useful to helping you maintain your stability.

❤ You know that a change is needed in your love life, but you are giving yourself the time and the means necessary to control the situation and decide exactly when such a change should take place.

👪 Currently, you seem in control, but a radical change is likely to call into question the present stability of your family situation and force you out of yourself.

📋 Ensure that you are in control of your situation and aware of any changes that are needed to start things progressing again in a positive manner and achieve their potential.

💰 If you ensure you are in control of your present circumstances, and can analyse them in detail, you should be able to chase away all your doubts and perhaps even make progress towards dispelling the current state of inertia.

11 3

➕ You enjoy excellent physical health with lots of mental energy. Add to this very good instincts and a real ability to adapt and what more could you ask for?

❤️ You are taking control of your love life quietly but confidently. In doing so, you demonstrate generosity and emotional understanding.

👪 So-called 'feminine' qualities are currently characterizing your domestic situation – gentleness, understanding, instinctive intelligence and sincere and sensitive involvement in relationships. These will allow your situation to flourish.

📋 Your professional situation is progressing impressively. You find it easy to make the appropriate arrangements and agreements that will facilitate the achievement of your plans and ambitions.

💰 You are fully in control of your financial situation. You can be confident in carrying out any well-timed deals.

11 4

➕ You are blessed with great energy and vitality and know how to use it with assurance and to good effect.

❤️ A certain innocence and moral purity saves you from passionate excesses, but by no means prevents you from behaving possessively towards your loved one.

👪 You will get what you want through a combination of moral strength, quiet but unwavering determination, and a gentle attitude.

📋 You are in a good position as far as your professional situation is concerned and as long as your intentions are true and your determination unwavering. You will need to be constructive and act strategically in order to succeed.

💰 You have an intelligent and constructive take on your situation and can be assured of its solidity and future growth.

11	5

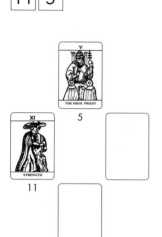

➕ Your quiet strength and confidence protect you and give you a natural inclination to avoid risk, and also to trust in your conscience and instinct.

♥ Your mental strength means you can contain or minimize shocks or upheavals in your emotional life and draw from them some constructive lessons.

👪 The upheavals taking place in your family life are a logical part of its evolution and growth. In reality, they serve to reinforce its dependability and stability.

📋 You are keeping a firm hold on your situation. As a result things are getting back on track, or are suddenly freed from whatever was holding them back. Events should prove that you were right to behave as you have been doing.

🎛 By keeping a steady hand on your affairs, you will avoid the risk of destabilizing your financial situation and what's more, be in a position to congratulate yourself on having resisted temptation!

11	6

➕ Your vitality, coupled with a receptive, generous nature ensure that you can maintain an all round feeling of well-being.

♥ Your emotional situation and your love life can only be described as excellent. As a result, your hopes and aspirations prove to be fully achievable.

👪 You have a gentle, but firm hold over your situation. It should allow you to fulfil your hopes, enjoy a close relationship with your nearest and dearest and take new decisions aimed at achieving your dreams and aspirations.

📋 Your quiet strength and self-confidence allow you to act with more independence, to gain real control over and make some innovations in your work situation.

🎛 You have matters well in hand and so can rely confidently on favourable circumstances that will allow you to achieve your wishes.

➕ Whatever your health concerns or problems, you will easily surmount them through your own efforts and great mental and physical energy.

❤️ Whatever the worries or obstacles that are currently springing up in your love life, you can act in complete confidence to overcome them and come out on top.

👪 You should not find it too hard to resolve or contain any current problems. Have confidence in yourself and your situation, and don't relax your efforts.

📋 By keeping your situation well in hand and maintaining a constant effort to achieve your aims, you will overcome the difficulties and obstacles confronting you and succeed in making real progress.

📇 Don't relax your efforts. Despite the delays, obstacles and difficulties that you are facing, your financial situation is set to progress.

➕ Your great physical and mental energy assure you of a very sound and satisfactory feeling of well-being.

❤️ You are quite right to be confident and satisfied with your emotional situation. At its heart lies a sincere and well-balanced union.

👪 Your family situation is making progress in a happy and well-adjusted manner, providing you with considerable satisfaction.

📋 You are in a position to make some real progress, enter into an ideal partnership or succeed in bringing a necessary stability to your situation. At the same time, you continue to respect the rules and conform to strict norms. If a legal judgement is pending, it will be to your advantage.

📇 You have your financial situation well in hand, and despite real success in this area, you still have enough self-discipline to preserve your assets.

195

11	9

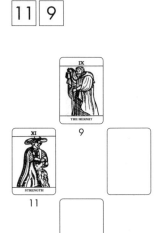

9

11

✚ Your self-control, reliability and experience give you the power to revitalize yourself and reassess your situation whenever this becomes necessary.

♥ You are becoming aware of the need to bring about a change or renewal in your love life. Feel free to take firm but cautious steps in this direction.

👪 You may realize that it would be wise – and perhaps even necessary – to make a few changes in your situation. Feel free to take such steps, ensuring that you adopt any necessary precautions along the way.

🖉 You are studying a proposal or the possibility of a change, but are taking your time and taking all the necessary precautions before making up your mind. Given the circumstances, you are quite right to behave in this way.

⌗ You are waiting until you can be sure that you are able to bring about a change in your finances; or you may be reconsidering your situation carefully in order to give yourself a bit more freedom and control over your resources.

11	10

10

11

✚ You are fully in control of yourself both mentally and physically, and your personal growth is progressing well. You should therefore make the most of this fortunate state of affairs.

♥ Your love life is very positive on all counts and is currently happy and fulfilled.

👪 You have your family situation well in hand and can provide it with the means to develop and flourish.

🖉 You are free to do as you wish and have everything you need to make excellent progress, or to broaden the scope of your activities and widen your professional and social horizons.

⌗ Having full control over all your financial resources and the options open to you, you can now move forward as you see fit.

✚ You enjoy high levels of physical and mental energy, but you only feel free to use it within the framework of your duties and obligations. If you want to stay in good shape, perhaps you should seek the advice of a doctor.

♥ You are hanging on to a situation that is less than ideal. It involves too much restriction and too many sacrifices to be really fulfilling.

👪 You certainly have a lot of obligations and responsibilities to assume within your family circle, but you are looking after the situation well.

📋 You have a good hold on your professional position, even if it leaves you with little freedom of choice and fails to provide you with sufficient openings. For the time being, it is in your best interests to maintain your position, without turning a blind eye to the constraints or limitations that are imposed on you.

⌛ Your moral and material obligations make it necessary for you to continue in a stable but rather impotent financial situation for the moment. But you can hope for more in the future.

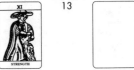

✚ Your self-possession makes you sure of your choices and decisions. It also enables you to eliminate anything that might present a threat to this state of affairs.

♥ The purity and sincerity of your feelings will be repaid when a radical change takes place in your love life, allowing you to overcome any associated hardships.

👪 You have to make a difficult, but wise choice or take a testing but necessary decision, the immediate consequence of which will be a radical change. Have confidence and be brave!

📋 You should not have any doubts as to your decisions or agreements, since these will certainly lead to a significant and advantageous change in your affairs.

⌛ You have matters well in hand and by taking the necessary decisions you are able to cope with any changes that may take place, but that should also prove profitable.

11 14

You enjoy high levels of energy and have an excellent ability to adapt to circumstances, all of which assures your vital well-being.

You know how to adapt to circumstances and are open, receptive and understanding, without renouncing your resolve or relaxing your efforts. In this way, you will manage to retain control over any emotional situation without appearing to do so, and are in a position to achieve anything you want.

You know how to adapt and maintain the control you have on the domestic front. Thanks to this, you will be able reach the compromises and make the arrangements that will allow you to succeed and achieve your aims.

You have the will to succeed. You will find the right moment to make compromises or the necessary arrangements that will help your professional situation to develop.

Ensure the progress of your financial situation by knowing how to adapt to circumstances, or, if need be, by making the necessary arrangements or compromises.

 11 15

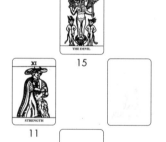

You are blessed with an energetic and determined temperament and an unshakeable will. As a result, you exercise excellent self-control and don't spare yourself from criticism.

Beneath that gentle exterior, you cling tenaciously to your rights. Consequently, when it comes to your feelings, you are very demanding, selective, critical and even sometimes uncompromising. But are you sure this is enough to protect you in the passionate climate that holds sway in your love life at the moment?

Your natural determination and self-discipline may still not prevent you from becoming embroiled in a situation of excess or turmoil. Maintain a firm hold on your situation and don't succumb to the temptation of taking arbitrary decisions.

You can achieve your plans for expansion or succeed in making your ambitions reality – but only as long as you play by the rules and ensure thoroughness and self-discipline are key strategies in your desire for success.

Your financial situation appears sound and well-balanced, allowing you to be ambitious or to make sure matters develop and progress.

➕ Your assurance, quiet strength and determination to leave nothing to chance, make you wise and cautious, whatever the circumstances.

❤️ Despite your tenacity and the confident control you exercise, you will soon realize that an upheaval is inevitable – and that the best thing to do is simply to submit to it.

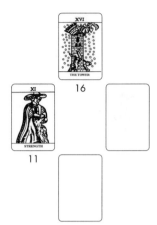

👪 You exercise confident and calm control over your situation. This gives you an awareness of the upheavals that are necessary for its natural development, or enables you to anticipate them and protect yourself from any destabilizing impact.

🖊️ You are sure of yourself and your position. Your experience gives you the right to protect yourself against inevitable upheavals, or to find a quick but possibly disconcerting solution that will nevertheless prove to be quite liberating.

▦ By relying on your experience and long-term views, make sure you foresee and take precautions against the upsets that might disrupt your affairs. Find an appropriate solution aimed at keeping your assets free from harm.

➕ You have lots of physical and mental energy and are full of self-confidence. You can therefore enjoy personal growth and fulfilment.

❤️ You exercise a gentle but tangible hold over your emotional situation and have the power to make it develop according to your wishes.

👪 Let yourself go with the flow of events in full confidence. You hold all the right cards to make your family happy and progress towards new and positive developments.

🖊️ Make fate your ally. Have confidence in yourself and take advantage of the fortunate circumstances that favour your personal development as well as new and original ideas.

▦ Take advantage of your current streak of luck and the fortunate circumstances you are enjoying to improve your financial situation.

11	18

✚ Thanks to your mental strength, energy and resourcefulness, you will finally succeed in overcoming your health-related concerns and worries, and will solve your problems.

♥ If you can be brave and morally strong, conflicts on the emotional front will not really harm you. In fact you will find that you don't have to resolve them as they will disappear by themselves.

👪 Your mental strength and the firm but gentle hold you exercise over your family circle allow you to overcome with ease any problems or difficulties that may arise.

✎ Maintain your stance firmly and despite the delays, arguments, obstacles or disappointments that may arise, you will succeed in retaining control over the situation.

▣ Remain in control financially speaking. Don't let yourself be beaten by any confusion, worries or disappointments that you may encounter, and everything should turn out fine.

11	19

✚ You radiate vitality and energy. Circumstances, together with your self-confidence and well-being ensure that you will thrive. Make the most of it.

♥ You are enjoying a wonderful love life, your relationship radiates depth and stability. As a result, you can take whatever steps you choose on the emotional front, confident of being able to achieve what you want.

👪 Your family situation is completely stable and happy. It gives you a great deal of satisfaction and favours the success of generous action and practical achievements on your part.

✎ The power to succeed lies entirely in your hands. You could set up an advantageous partnership or reach a profitable agreement that proves a key factor in your success.

▣ In addition to a level of stability, you are enjoying a privileged financial situation, which allows you complete freedom of action.

You are sure of yourself and confident of your resources and the options open to you. This gives you the power to revitalize yourself, which only goes to prove that a character combining flexibility with strength is the best protection you can have.

Act now, with plenty of assurance and conviction but also with flexibility and understanding with a view to making an appreciable change in your love life.

You are totally free to take action aimed at revitalization or making an appreciable change in your family situation. In order to succeed in this, you must show a combination of flexibility and steadfastness.

You have the freedom to take constructive and intelligent steps to bring about an appreciable change or instigate a renewal in your working situation.

You are free to take action in all confidence to effect a substantial change or revitalize your financial situation in a constructive way.

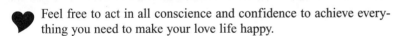

You are on good form and full of energy and can quite reasonably concentrate on personal growth and enjoy your current feelings of well-being.

Feel free to act in all conscience and confidence to achieve everything you need to make your love life happy.

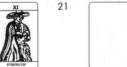

You can move ahead with full confidence and with integrity to make sure that your domestic situation develops and flourishes.

Be confident and assemble all the advantageous factors currently at your disposal, rally significant support and broaden your social or professional horizons. In so doing you will achieve your aims.

There are a great deal of financial possibilities currently at your disposal. You can act confidently to improve money matters still further.

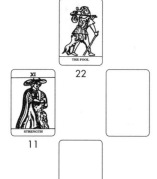

You are self-confident and fully in control, mentally and physically. This makes you free to forge head, make a move, travel and enjoy your well-being to the full.

You exercise a gentle but firm hold over your emotions. This allows you to act as you see fit and reassures you of the aptness of your impulses and the way you behave. If you are alone, you can look forward to an important, unexpected meeting.

Your situation seems well in hand. Make all the changes you are currently contemplating – such as travel or a move – and things should turn out well.

You have everything you need to succeed in anything that you do with a view to strengthening your position or bringing about a useful change.

The firm grip that you have on your financial situation allows you to make some headway towards a progression, or to employ your resources in a way that is both useful and profitable.

You can emerge from your current state of weakness, physical and mental fatigue, or get out of the constraints and limits that your unsatisfactory state of health is imposing on you and feel rejuvenated and ready to make a new start.

The only way out of your current constricting and unsatisfactory situation is to see it ended or radically transformed, so that you can make a fresh start and make some new arrangements.

You are in a situation that is limiting you or is not leaving you free to act. You are therefore looking for a way out that will permit you to be able to put an end to this current state of affairs and to take the initiative once more.

You are not free to act as you wish in your current situation. Therefore, if you want to seize or regain the initiative you must either make a sacrifice, or change the situation or activity completely.

Some fortunate initiatives can liberate your financial situation and permit you to start afresh from a new angle which, though it may still be uncertain will at least prove more profitable.

➕ You are not on top form at the moment, and you may feel inclined to let events simply take their course or to wallow in a state of inertia or endless anticipation. This inactivity can be justified only as a way of maintaining your general health and not overdoing things.

♥ You are demonstrating flexibility, adaptability and skill at finding ways to achieve peace of mind and emotional stability. However, you still feel dissatisfied and constrained.

👪 You are trying to find concessions and compromises to safeguard the stability of your domestic situation. However, since you are still constrained by your own reserved behaviour and a lack of freedom to act, little progress is being made.

📋 Given the current state of your professional affairs, you would be advised to be flexible and adaptable and open to agreements that will maintain the stability of your position. Do not confuse intelligent compromises with harmful concessions, however.

🔳 Your finances are not healthy and your funds are limited. Try to be adaptable and amenable to concessions and compromises that will help to maintain the status quo.

➕ Take care not to become over-excited or hyperactive. You may end up creating serious health problems for yourself.

♥ You are in thrall to your deepest feelings and your instinctive desire for satisfaction at all costs. These tendencies point to an emotional life that is both intense and dangerously chaotic.

👪 You want to extricate yourself from an awkward, restricting situation at all costs and are no longer able to control your anger or rebellious instinct. It is important to remain approachable and understanding, however.

📋 Regardless of consequences, you are seeking to fulfil desires and ambitions that could provide a way out of a restricting situation at work. As long as you behave intelligently and openly, you will succeed.

🔳 You will either enjoy your financial gains to the full or be dissatisfied with your resources and want to live beyond your means.

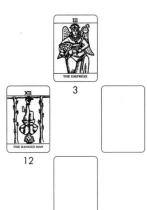

12 4

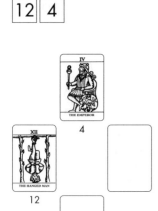

4

12

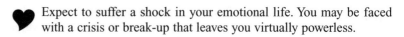 Expect to experience a blow to your health or a shock, which will either free you from a state of emotional and physical weakness or make you the victim of an accident. Be on your guard and take precautions against this sort of risk.

Expect to suffer a shock in your emotional life. You may be faced with a crisis or break-up that leaves you virtually powerless.

You are being forced to impose a challenge or beneficial shake-up on your family environment. Alternatively, you will have to break free, abruptly and positively, from a stalemate.

You will soon be able to liberate yourself, suddenly and completely, from all that is holding you back professionally. You can then re-assert yourself and take control of your affairs.

It is time to free yourself of debts, restrictions, obligations and financial dependency for good. Once you have cleared up your monetary affairs, you will be able to take over the helm again.

12 5

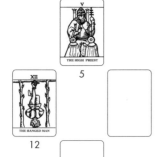

5

12

You are going through an uneventful phase. Enjoy your open and generous nature and your feeling of well-being. Trust your inner strength and resources but don't ignore your responsibilities.

You may well feel too exposed or vulnerable to make the necessary moves on the emotional front. Although you worry that things are not improving in your love life, you can rest assured that everything is on course and that your hopes will be realized quite naturally.

Trust your family and domestic circumstances. If you stay loyal your hopes will be fulfilled.

A degree of objectivity or a particular sacrifice may, paradoxically, allow you to gain ground or accomplish something new. This could provide the means to get back on your feet and enable you to move on.

Your financial situation is not hopeless, but your emotional and physical responsibilities leave you little room for autonomy.

➕ You are experiencing difficulties on both the emotional and physical fronts, but do still try to make choices and resolutions that will help you get over this awkward, frustrating period.

❤️ You are in a confused, difficult and disappointing situation, and you are failing to make choices when they present themselves. It looks as if this is no accident and may be the consequence of past mistakes.

👪 Disturbed, adversarial, unhealthy relationships dominate your family life. You are, naturally, dissatisfied, particularly as you are in no state to fight or confront such problems and are, therefore, suffering the consequences.

📋 You are failing to reach an agreement, make a choice or take steps that could help you out of a difficult and worrying professional stalemate. Don't let yourself be worried unduly by all this, or matters may deteriorate further.

📇 You have probably made mistakes and are now paying for them. Sadly, there is nothing else you can do about it at the moment. Be aware that it will be tricky, but not impossible, to extricate yourself from this situation.

12	6

➕ Your efforts have paid off handsomely, and you have restored your well-being and high levels of energy.

❤️ After a period of anticipation, you can at last make moves to get what you want from your love life. You will enjoy a period of emotional fulfilment and happiness.

👪 You will have to make an effort to reach a full understanding of your situation or make the moves needed for you to become totally open, happy and fulfilled.

📋 In spite of concessions you make or obstacles in your path, you are trying hard to rid yourself of professional limitations and to overcome restrictions.

📇 You are in a good position to improve your financial situation, even if it does not accurately reflect the resources that you currently have at your disposal.

12	7

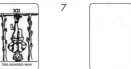

12	8

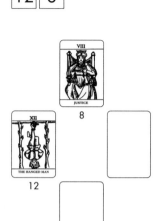

8

12

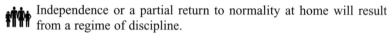 If you want to make a speedy recovery, regain your independence and balance and overcome a general feeling of frailty, you will have to embrace a strict regime of self-discipline.

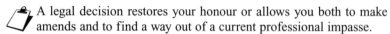 You need to regain your emotional equilibrium, and to do this, you must face up to a tough, logical and important decision that will focus the direction of your love life.

Independence or a partial return to normality at home will result from a regime of discipline.

A legal decision restores your honour or allows you both to make amends and to find a way out of a current professional impasse.

You need to review your finances and adopt a more rigorous regime of self-discipline. It may limit your lifestyle, but it will enable you to regain a measure of equilibrium.

12	9

9

12

The time has come for you to agree to make a number of sacrifices or embrace certain measures that will enable you to achieve your true potential.

Forget your current restrictions and feelings of dissatisfaction for a while and enjoy what you already possess, even if you don't fully appreciate it. You will then find what you are looking for.

Have faith, relax, be patient and remain alert. You will ultimately find what you seek.

Your losses and gains are currently more or less equal. Under the circumstances, it is certainly in your best interests simply to let events take their course. You may then discover that what is to come is infinitely better than what you have had.

If you agree to make a few sacrifices and remain both cautious and alert, you will have no financial problems.

12 10

You will soon recover from a sense of emotional and physical frailty and break free from current constraints.

Look forward to an imminent escape from your emotional stalemate. If, however, you do leave suddenly, be certain of your decision and take care that you do not repeat the same mistakes in the future.

If you decide to make an impulsive departure, make sure it is absolutely necessary and that no alternative action is possible. If it does not bring real benefit, it will be a mistake.

Circumstances will compel you to make a sudden departure, possibly on impulse, in order to escape a restricting and frustrating stalemate at work.

Avoid premature action and impulsive, ill-considered moves, even if current circumstances appear to be constraining or limiting your financial potential.

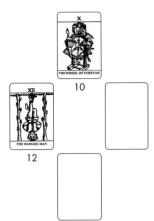

12 11

You are bound by rules, values or responsibilities that encourage you to make good use of your energy and keep a firm grip on your health, even under the most difficult or restricting of circumstances.

You are subjecting yourself to various responsibilities and commitments. At first these may appear limiting but they will prove to be emotionally empowering.

By shouldering your responsibilities and obligations you will find that you are able to exercise appropriate and moderate control over your family circle.

If you assume your professional responsibilities and obligations and devote yourself to an important cause, you will gain control and take the upper hand at work, not to mention a degree of psychological power.

It is time to take on responsibilities and financial obligations that compel you to honour your commitments. Make sure you remain in full control.

12 | 13

There is only one remedy for emotional and physical weakness and one way out of a limiting or stagnant situation. Your steadfast determination will put an end to these problems once and for all.

Make determined efforts to bring a current stalemate in your emotional life to an end. You will then be able to walk away, feeling free and triumphant.

You have to regain your autonomy or bring about a radical change in your domestic situation. Behave with determination and make the necessary efforts to break free of your constraints.

The only way you can achieve your aims, overcome limitations or escape a professional stalemate is to decide on a timeframe, eliminate all obstacles and implement radical, profitable change.

Your efforts are paying off, but don't relax them in the face of any obstacles you encounter. You are on the verge of experiencing a fundamental, profitable change in your finances.

12 | 14

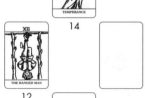

Despite weakness or emotional and physical constraints, your overall balance is not in danger. You need to be more flexible and adaptable to circumstances.

You should be less rigid and unbending. Being more flexible and prepared to make compromises will enable you to feel freer and calmer, and more confident of your love life.

Although you may not be in a comfortable situation and are not free to act as you wish, you need to show that you are flexible. In spite of everything, be conciliatory, accommodating and fair.

In light of the current professional circumstances, your only option is to come to fair compromises or appropriate understandings. You will be able to free your situation from whatever is undermining, restricting or slowing down its progress.

No matter what your current financial constraints or obligations are, you should try to remain flexible, accommodating and adaptable to circumstances.

➕ You feel rather weak or are placing limitations on yourself by adopting extreme and disproportionate precautions or measures.

12 15

❤ You may not be deceived by extreme and selfish feelings but you remain a slave to them or a victim of an intense relationship that leaves you feeling isolated and dissatisfied.

👪 You know exactly what is going wrong, stultifying your domestic situation or limiting your freedom of action. However, you will go to the other extreme, despite your lucidity and alertness. Beware: you may well not avoid the worst.

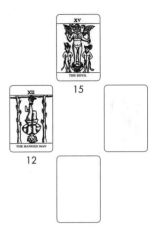

🗒 You are desperately seeking a way out of an impasse or a limiting situation. Take care that you do not give in to your desire to achieve your aims at all cost without considering the certainty of the outcome.

📇 You seek or find answers that lie beyond your actual means or you take measures that are disproportionate to your financial resources. It is time to stop and think. There is still time to be realistic and abandon your search.

➕ You will soon overcome emotional and physical weakness. Alternatively, your negligence, irresponsible attitude and fatalism may make you vulnerable to an accident and powerless to do anything about it. A word to the wise should suffice.

12 16

❤ You will soon overcome constraints on your normal emotional progress or indulge your dangerous tendency to carelessness to challenge or break up your love life.

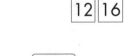

👪 An on-going stalemate will suddenly respond constructively to change. Alternatively, if you fail to respond to events, you can expect to experience a crisis, upheaval or even a major challenge in your domestic situation.

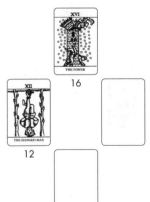

🗒 A situation that was failing to develop normally is resolving itself. Alternatively, you are being drawn unwillingly into a crisis that will challenge your professional status.

📇 Matters will resolve themselves abruptly, bringing you huge relief. Alternatively, your irresponsible and sloppy behaviour will lead you straight towards financial disaster.

| 12 | 17 |

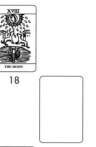

+ Feel confident enough to enjoy your high energy levels and general sense of well-being to the full.

♥ Feel free to give in to your genuine, sincere feelings and to embrace a relationship that will fulfil all your hopes and desires.

👪 Your domestic situation deserves the loyalty you show it. Your calm self-confidence will allow you to maintain easy control over emerging and positive changes at home.

✎ Although you seem to be sacrificing some factors or devoting yourself to a cause, you are still sure of your prerogatives. You are exercising subtle and confident control and can count on success.

⊞ Although your finances are currently limited, you remain strong and courageous enough to acquire new resources, thereby also remaining in control.

| 12 | 18 |

+ You are in a precarious state of health and unable to remedy it. Alternatively, your own carelessness and negligence jeopardize your emotional and physical health.

♥ You have taken a wrong turning on the emotional front and are about to trip up or experience disappointment. Trust in your instincts when they tell you it is time to abandon a false position or deceitful relationship.

👪 There appears to be someone in the family circle whose influence is upsetting your domestic harmony or who is ill. No matter what the cause, your domestic situation is currently suffering, and there is little you can do to change it.

✎ You are failing to make professional progress or to be as productive at work as you might wish. You are faced with all sorts of delays, problems and obstacles.

⊞ If you are looking forward to receiving funds or revenue, you will be disappointed and tempted to abandon hope of them. Alternatively, although you have made inroads into clearing up your financial situation, not all your problems have been solved.

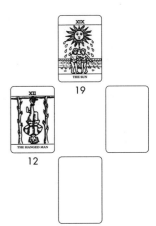

If you have had health problems or are still feeling weak, you will soon recover and feel on top form again.

A relationship based on mutual and sincere feelings is your best means of overcoming current obstacles to maintaining emotional control over the situation.

You are able to keep domestic issues under control and exercise your own authority by devoting yourself to your family. In return, they are united and happy and bring you great joy.

You have the authority, power or necessary support to overcome the restrictions or factors that are currently undermining your professional position. You are in a good position to establish a working partnership or agreement or, indeed, to implement major change.

If you want to release yourself from current financial constraints, make sure that you shed light on your monetary affairs and enlist serious advice and strong support to help you.

If you follow to the letter a course of treatment or piece of advice you have received concerning your health, you will make a speedy recovery and be able to move on.

A new emotional factor, change or sacrifice releases you from various constraints and responsibilities or completely revitalizes your love life.

You seem to be taking on a number of domestic commitments, but you also have a new development in mind that could relieve you of some of your current constraints.

A proposal or change will allow you to reinforce your professional situation and shoulder your responsibilities with fewer limitations.

You will have to review your finances. Alternatively, a new development will release you from current obligations.

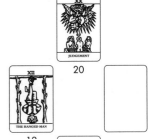

12 21

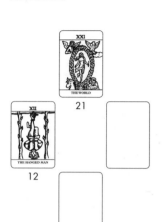

21

12

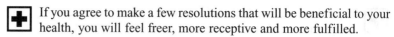

+ If you agree to make a few resolutions that will be beneficial to your health, you will feel freer, more receptive and more fulfilled.

♥ You will feel fulfilled in your love life only if you resign yourself to making some important choices and if you allow yourself to succumb to your emotions.

 If you devote yourself wholeheartedly to your family and agree to make certain choices, you will feel happy and in harmony with the current situation.

If you want your position at work to be able to achieve its full potential or widen its scope, both socially and professionally, you must embrace an important agreement or essential choice.

Do not give up your choices or agreements prematurely. Be confident that they could ultimately generate financial growth.

12 22

22

12

+ You are not at your best – far from it, in fact – and the only solution is to take time out and rest for a while.

♥ You will have no choice but to give up or to leave, because your relationship offers no other solution at the moment.

You are not in a position to change things at the moment nor to make a sudden, impulsive departure. Such a move would surely be a mistake.

You hope to be able to escape suddenly from a professional stalemate. Alternatively, you must depart, give up a position and leave everything without knowing what you will find or even what may await you elsewhere.

You may have no financial independence at the moment and no choice but to seek help and support from others or find an alternative source of funds with which to bail yourself out.

➕ Things are progressing well and to your advantage. You will soon be able to express your energy and initiative freely and positively.

❤️ You will soon bring a relationship to an end or be in a position to take the initiative and make positive moves towards success in love.

👪 A situation will come or be brought to an end, allowing you to take the initiative and use your skill and accommodating nature to reach the best compromises and understandings.

📋 Something will soon come to an end or there will be a radical change at work that prompts you to take new and more appropriate initiatives. Alternatively, you may at last be able to use your energy and skill to reach positive understandings or useful compromises.

⏳ It is time to profit from more appropriate transactions or decisions, which will bring you the financial wherewithal and the opportunity to use your initiative.

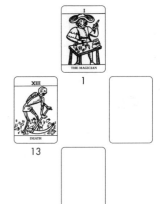

13 | 1

13 | 2

➕ If you want to maintain or regain your stability, you must eliminate any potentially harmful factors in your lifestyle, including a tendency to over-indulge. You need to change your attitude completely, even if it involves taking extreme measures.

❤️ You know, even if you don't actually express or admit it, that a radical change is inevitable in your emotional life. You need to face the fact that matters cannot stay as they are and that you must end the exploitation, excesses, chaos and damaging influences that currently prevail.

👪 A fundamental change is underway or a situation is coming to its natural conclusion. Sadly, you can do little but accept the obvious and recognize that, despite your reservations, it is all for the best.

📋 A complete change is taking place at work, or a situation is reaching its logical and final conclusion. If you can prepare for the new circumstances and accept them with a certain amount of common sense, you can turn the change to your advantage.

⏳ Take your time and behave with a degree of discretion before making a key change to your financial situation or before profiting significantly from a transaction, sale or business deal.

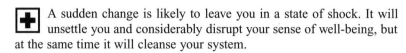

13	3

✚ A sudden change is likely to leave you in a state of shock. It will unsettle you and considerably disrupt your sense of well-being, but at the same time it will cleanse your system.

♥ You will experience a major transformation in your emotional life. It may be unsettling and cause you to feel out of your depth, challenging everything you know, but it will also prove to be liberating.

👪 A fundamental, overwhelming change will occur in your domestic situation, and there is little you can do to avoid it. It will mark the start of a new chapter in your family life.

📋 You are in danger of losing your job or of experiencing a major, upsetting change that will challenge many aspects of your life. Although the experience will be unsettling, it may at the same time prove truly liberating.

💰 If you don't take care, you may lose your money. A radical change or the logical, inevitable conclusion of an unsatisfactory, unstable arrangement hangs in the air.

13	4

✚ A radical change or turning point in your life will help you take control of your health concerns and protect your inner strength and natural resources.

♥ A key development could make you more emotionally confident and help you to embark on constructive, intelligent moves in your love life.

👪 You can exploit a key event or the conclusion of a situation to consolidate domestic issues, accomplish something new or make constructive changes within your family.

📋 A fundamental change or the logical conclusion of a situation will present you with the opportunity to bring about something new or make people accept your original ideas.

💰 An essential change or the conclusion of a deal, transaction or sale will bring you greater financial certainty and present you with the means to implement something new and original on the monetary front.

You need to resolve health problems and other issues, eliminating any potentially harmful factors in your lifestyle and listening carefully to the wise words of a doctor or specialist.

Trust the dictates of your conscience and sense of duty. Now is the time to bid farewell to any harmful or destabilizing influences in your emotional life.

A change will inevitably occur in your family life, eliminating all its troubles, concerns and conflicts and bringing events to their appropriate conclusions.

A professional issue is destined to resolve itself, removing potential obstacles. It could be that you lose a job or position, but because the atmosphere was so unpleasant, this should not cause you too much regret.

It is imperative that you sort out your finances, and any potentially damaging factors must be dealt with as a priority. You need to have a serious look at the stability of your monetary situation.

You will undergo a radical change or experience an important development that brings with it excellent health. You will be able to enjoy a real sense of balance and well-being.

An agreement will bring harmony to your emotional life or a choice will bring you great happiness. Alternatively, it could simply be that you will embark on a relationship that will transform your life to a considerable extent.

An essential, important and favourable change will take place in your family life and may well result in a positive, advantageous agreement or relationship.

You will be able to conclude a positive agreement under the most favourable conditions or to establish a partnership that is far-reaching and profitable.

You will reap the rewards of an agreement or partnership that could well transform your finances.

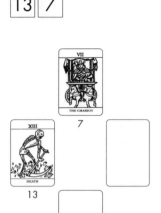

A radical change will produce a prompt and fundamental return to health, enabling you to recover your dynamism and energy and move forward without fear.

A radical change or the resolution of a problem will inject renewed vitality into your love life.

A major change or resolution will allow you to get closer to your domestic goals and even bring about a dramatic upturn in your family situation.

You will be able to make dynamic proposals and accomplish major innovations as a result of a radical change or the logical conclusion of a business deal.

A significant development or the conclusion of a transaction will prompt you to refocus your financial situation and make important, dynamic progress.

You will experience a radical, overall change in your life that will guarantee you a calmer, more harmonious feeling of balance and well-being.

There will be a major change or development in your emotional life. After that, there will be no going back.

An important and fundamental change will help you make your domestic situation more harmonious, just and stable from every point of view.

A key change with significant potential will help you regain your professional balance. Alternatively, the imminent resolution of an issue will offer a number of options from which you can benefit.

You may bring about major, profitable changes in your finances, enabling you to place your affairs on a firmer foundation.

13 9

➕ A significant development will prompt an awareness of your real state of health and encourage you to give up some extravagant habits and abandon your overtly impulsive behaviour. You will then find yourself in a position to adopt a wiser, more thoughtful and more measured lifestyle.

❤️ A fundamental change in your love life will prompt you to rein in your more thoughtless impulses, restrain your irrational responses and adopt a more cautious, thoughtful and pragmatic attitude towards emotional issues.

👪 You may be prompted to abandon plans to depart or to move house after a significant development or the conclusion of a particular issue. You will at least give the idea the cautious and pragmatic consideration it merits.

📋 You are perplexed and wary in the face of the seemingly inevitable end of a professional situation or a major development at work. You would be wise to be proactive in your search for pragmatic and constructive solutions.

🎴 A radical change or the conclusion of a business deal will prompt cautious and careful behaviour in the future.

13 10

➕ An essential change in your lifestyle will help you develop a more balanced and stable attitude, which will be combined with a much greater awareness of your responsibilities.

❤️ Thanks to a radical change in your emotional life or the end of a particular situation, you will come to have a much greater awareness of your duties and responsibilities.

👪 You will see a fundamental change in your domestic life that moves matters forward in a way that reflects your own ideas of duty and responsibility.

📋 Combined with your strength of mind and sense of responsibility, a major professional development will help you make determined and highly focused progress.

🎴 A radical change or deal will prompt you to make progressive, rational and profitable financial moves.

13 11

11

XIII

13

➕ A fundamental and important change will bring with it critical choices and decisions that will make you fully aware of your own potential and well-being.

❤️ You need to make decisive choices and implement radical change if you want to keep a grip on your emotions. Make sure your feelings are really genuine.

👪 Your domestic goals involve critical choices, important decisions and radical change.

📋 Significant developments at work will help you make important choices and reach firm agreements, and these may be the catalyst for a new and stable partnership that will consolidate your professional status and secure its successful progress.

🗳️ The happy conclusion of a business deal will give you control of the situation and guarantee the success of your financial deals, agreements and decisions.

13 12

12

XIII

13

➕ You may well fail to experience the relief you believed that radical change would bring. Your efforts and determination to extricate yourself will have to continue if you really want to break free of the factors that are limiting your energy levels.

❤️ Imminent and significant developments will affect your love life. You will be forced to read the writing on the wall and suffer the consequences. However, you can take comfort from the fact that they will help you to overcome current obstacles and allow you to enjoy the resulting freedom.

👪 Key changes on the domestic front will highlight the way out of an impasse and the route forward to success.

📋 Important developments at work should help you resolve any issues, overcome obstacles and surmount current problems. The way ahead is clear.

🗳️ A fundamental change or the conclusion of a transaction or business deal will bring release from financial constraints and help matters to progress.

Radical change will prompt a review of your health. Show both wisdom and courage and you will be able to adapt to circumstances and enjoy your inner strength. Flexibility is the key.

A critical change in your love life will encourage you to be flexible, understanding and accommodating.

Significant developments will encourage you to find more appropriate opportunities or answers, and you will be able to enjoy greater calm and harmony as a result.

Key developments will prompt you to review your professional status and help you find more appropriate solutions to your circumstances. You will come to intelligent, pragmatic compromises that will help you achieve your objectives.

Fundamental change or an excellent business deal will prompt you to think both intelligently and pragmatically about potentially useful transactions or compromises.

13 14

Things are moving ahead with speed, but you can be certain that an imminent development that will be both radical and liberating may well require extreme measures.

Sudden and significant developments may jeopardize your love life. Take care: you are heading towards a chaotic and passionate atmosphere in which you will focus on nothing but your own desires.

Major changes on the domestic front will prompt unforeseen but conclusive developments within your family.

Profound and remarkable changes at work are underway. Things are moving so fast and the measures that are taken are so extreme that it is too soon to say if the results will be profitable or not.

Major developments or the conclusion of a business transaction should bring considerable profit your way. Your finances should improve dramatically.

13 15

`13` `16`

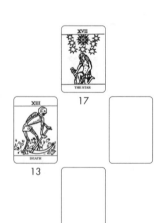

➕ Serious change will bring confidence in your emotional and physical strength. You need have no fear of upheavals or the difficult times you may experience.

❤️ You will experience radical and difficult developments in your emotional life and are unlikely to avoid the consequences that these involve. You may feel shaken, but you will lose neither control nor strength of character.

👨‍👩‍👧 You will need plenty of courage and self-confidence to avoid losing control or being affected by disruptive events on the home front that are both imminent and inevitable.

📋 You will have to maintain your self-control and demonstrate all your strength if you want to avoid falling prey to disruptive, disconcerting events and radical change.

💼 Essential changes and inevitable upheavals will challenge your financial affairs, and you will need to demonstrate courage and strength of character to save face and control events.

`13` `17`

➕ Radical change will bring with it confidence in your natural resources and the opportunity to enjoy your healthy state to the utmost.

❤️ A major upheaval in your love life will present you with the chance to experience a whole range of new emotions.

👨‍👩‍👧 A critical change that is currently taking place will soon present you with an opportunity to realize your hopes and aspirations. You will be able to introduce innovation into your domestic environment and benefit from encouraging circumstances.

📋 A radical change or positive and profound transformation will help you put into practice your hopes, aspirations and original ideas.

💼 You will reap the financial rewards of a fundamental change or the conclusion of a business deal. You will soon have the leisure in which to realize your hopes and aspirations.

➕ You will put an end to your health concerns. Alternatively, you will make a change in your lifestyle that encourages you to take better care of yourself.

❤️ A fundamental change in your emotional life or the end of relationship may well plunge you into a state of panic or highlight a wrong turning in your life.

👪 It is time to demonstrate your authority and eliminate tedious and negative domestic factors, even if they represent the catalyst for essential change.

📋 Use your authority and strength of purpose to combat any untoward factors at work. You may have to make important changes and should not hesitate to do so.

📇 Although you have forced yourself to change or have concluded a deal through sheer strength of character, inevitable delays or financial problems will result.

13 18

➕ You have a duty to yourself to implement essential changes that can shed light on your health and help you to be comfortable with yourself and your surroundings.

❤️ A new and strong relationship may well be triggered by an important change in your love life.

👪 Your sense of duty will instigate an important change that will bring your family closer together in joy and contentment.

📋 Triggered by key developments at work, you will come to a positive agreement, establish a profitable partnership or win the support and approval of an influential figure.

📇 A major change or successful business deal will be the catalyst for you to reap the rewards of your hard work and will guarantee that your finances are stable and trouble-free.

13 19

13 20

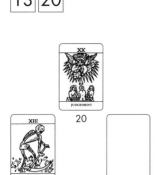

20

13

A radical change or complete recovery will prompt you to review your choices and lifestyle. You will experience an important revitalization.

Your emotional life will be completely transformed by significant developments, which will force you to review your emotional choices and put matters on a more permanent basis. You will pursue a healthier, more normal course of action.

There will be changes on the domestic front, and these will prompt a review and renewal of issues. You will make a radical decision.

Key professional developments prompt you to review your options and reconsider proposals with interest. Things will seem more attractive and tempting, but only you can decide which is the more profitable route.

Significant developments or the conclusion of a business deal will encourage you to make the essential financial choices that can revive your situation or respond to proposals made to you.

13 21

21

13

A significant change in your lifestyle or behaviour will bring a greater sense of freedom and fulfilment and perhaps the chance for a holiday.

Important developments in your love life will help you both to do as you please and to achieve what you want.

Your domestic situation is making excellent progress. Important changes will encourage you to expand your family's horizons and help it achieve its full potential.

You will eventually bring about the change you anticipate and make the progress you desire. You will push back your professional boundaries at the same time.

A key change or transaction has prompted the development of your finances. This is no accident, and you are merely reaping the rewards of your efforts.

Imminent and radical developments will help you to depart or reach a significant turning point in your life. Beware careless acts.

♥ A fundamental change will soon take place in your emotional life, prompting someone to leave or return.

🏠 Following an inevitable change in your domestic situation, someone close to you will depart or return. It is possible that you could also be moving house.

📋 Major developments or the conclusion of a deal will be the catalyst for someone's arrival or sudden departure, and this may force you to seek new opportunities or wider horizons at work.

💰 Your resources may suddenly dry up, or you may be compelled to seek new financial possibilities. A business deal may come to a logical and profitable conclusion, completely transforming your finances.

13 22

THE FOOL

22

XIII

DEATH

13

 You are remarkably adaptable and flexible, but you must remain aware of how important it is to resist the temptation to abuse your power or be too easily swayed by circumstances.

♥ Although you may reach compromises and come to understandings, these cannot protect you from either your insatiable desire to get what you want at all costs or the excessive and irrational behaviour of someone close.

🏠 You will have to reach some compromises or come to difficult but necessary agreements if you are to have any hope of achieving your domestic targets.

📋 Heated debate and negotiation will soon be necessary. You will need all your energy and dynamism together with your powers of persuasion if you are to make the right moves at work or reach your professional targets.

💰 Intense negotiations or difficult but necessary transactions will lead to agreements that will bring financial progress or success.

14 1

THE MAGICIAN

1

XIV

TEMPERANCE

14

14 2

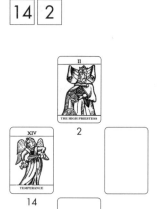

Your flexibility and adaptability will protect your from the risk of accident and help you steer clear of activities that could jeopardize your health. Heed these wise words.

Understandings and compromises will not prevent crises, break-ups or upheavals in your emotional life. You know in your heart of hearts that these are inevitable.

You know deep down that domestic upheaval is inevitable, despite all the discussions, agreements and compromises. What's more, you recognize that this is a positive if challenging and potentially disruptive development.

Negotiations, well-timed understandings and intelligent compromises will open up your professional circumstances or be the catalyst for a welcome release. You were expecting this to happen, but not just yet.

The circulation of your money, a transaction or the movement of funds will transform your finances without challenging their over-all stability or your economic sense.

14 3

You are flexible, intuitive and adaptable, and these attributes also guarantee excellent health and high levels of energy.

Your relationships seem blessed with good fortune, and you can be sure that events will conspire to help you realize your hopes or introduce a new and happy element into your love life.

Your ability to understand and adapt to circumstances and your generosity will promote intelligent arrangements and compromises. There will be developments on the domestic front.

You will go through a creative and productive phase at work. Positive and encouraging circumstances will help you fulfil your hopes and aspirations or implement new ideas or proposals.

You will be able to conclude new transactions or reach positive settlements that will reinforce both your status and your funds.

You are being overly passive, allowing yourself to be easily influenced. Instead, you should respond more proactively to resolve health issues or fight against any weakness.

Your compromises look more like concessions. Alternatively, your current relationship is marked by rows and misunderstanding. Expect to experience disappointments and to enter a difficult period in your love life.

Your domestic environment is characterized by arguments, futile discussions and struggles between members of the family. An unpleasant atmosphere prevails at home, and the only way to deal with it is to exercise your authority.

You will fail to reach agreements. Alternatively, you are at risk of making inadequate concessions in the face of inflexible and stubborn colleagues, who will do you no favours.

You will fail to reach agreement or come to satisfactory financial compromises, leaving you with no choice but to make concessions on this front.

You are naturally adaptable and feel at one both with yourself and with your environment. As a result, you enjoy good health and high energy levels.

You will embrace agreements that help you form a sincere and happy relationship based on mutual affection.

Well-timed, clear understandings help bring harmony to your family and your immediate circle. You will find the agreement or support that you need.

Your negotiations and transactions will be successful. You will reach key agreements or win the support or approval of an important and influential person, who may help you make professional progress.

Business transactions will introduce a degree of clarity into your situation and guarantee financial stability, reliability and expansion.

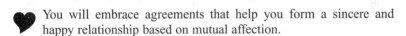

14 6

➕ Your accommodating nature and adaptability will help you make the right choices and guarantee a healthy balance and stability and high levels of energy.

❤ New understandings will inject vitality into your love life. Alternatively, your open nature will prompt a review of your choices and the best way to achieve a good relationship.

👪 Well-timed agreements will help revitalize things on the domestic front. You will review your options, decisions or agreements.

📋 Skilled negotiations, understandings and compromises will help bring fresh life to your professional situation and encourage favourable agreements or specific choices.

▦ Various transactions or negotiations will help you revive your finances and review future choices and agreements. The results could be interesting.

14 7

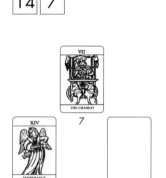

➕ Your calm, flexible nature is helping to ensure your vitality and enabling you to use your energy to achieve what you want.

❤ Your openness and natural flexibility allow you to make happy and positive changes and to achieve what you want from your love life.

👪 You need be quite certain about reaching the necessary understandings and concessions for positive developments at home.

📋 Negotiations, settlements and skilful compromises will help you win the day and achieve your goals. You will need to put up a good fight and apply all your mental powers and strength of character.

▦ Flexibility and concessions are the order of the day. They will help you succeed and give you the freedom to get what you want.

You are aware of what you must do to control your irrational impulses and make the appropriate concessions for a balanced lifestyle. In your case this is a key requirement.

You are quick to reach the understandings and compromises that will lead to a more balanced love life.

You will soon reach understandings and compromises that will help to maintain the stability of your domestic situation and get things back onto a normal footing.

Fortuitous understandings and profitable compromises are on the cards. Order and self-discipline will be vital and will dominate your professional environment once more.

 Make sure you can rely on the opportunities and resources that are at your disposal before launching into a venture. Respect the laws of economic good sense.

14 | 8

 Make the most of the options open to you to ensure that things go well and be ready to listen to any professional or expert advice.

You will easily reach the necessary understandings and find the agreement, help and support you currently need in your love life.

All the concessions that are needed to create a stable domestic life will be reached. You will come to understand that you were right to let the experts in these matters have their way.

Serious and lengthy negotiations will eventually produce the right agreements and compromises. Better still, you will find that someone with influence has faith in you.

 You will come to recognize that you have an obligation to carry out certain transactions or reach particular agreements and that these could bring greater stability and security to your finances.

14 | 9

14	10

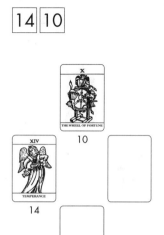

Despite your apparent indecision, useful and healthy compromises are within reach. You will identify the perfect moment to make appropriate choices or necessary moves.

Since you are being guided by your feelings, you leave yourself open to compromise and concession, which can help matters develop on the emotional front.

You are adapting well to choices, decisions or agreements that are currently improving domestic issues.

Negotiations and compromises will help you reach agreements or make choices that add weight to your professional status.

If you find decision-making difficult, be guided by those choices and agreements that will be of the greatest help in improving your financial position.

14	11

Your hard work and flexibility are the key ingredients in your excellent health and high energy levels. They guarantee you freedom of action.

Your efforts are rewarded by the positive agreements and compromises you have reached. As a result, you are in charge of your emotional life in a subtle but effective way.

The concessions and compromises that are currently in hand will enable you to take gentle but firm control of domestic issues. The outcome will be positive.

Your efforts and determination to reach agreements and make compromises will be rewarded. You will gain the upper hand in any negotiations, and your firmness and determination will enable you to maintain your professional position.

Transactions, negotiations, concessions and opportune, dynamic compromises will help improve your financial situation. You will have increased authority over events happening around you.

If you want to regain your physical and mental balance and stay in good condition or simply get better, you will have to become more self-disciplined, or follow a serious course of treatment or diet.

You are feeling under pressure and may well agree to certain compromises in order to maintain your emotional balance. Alternatively, you will agree to an unsatisfactory situation that leaves you with little freedom of action.

Just and fair compromises and understandings will either be reached or imposed, but they will not bring you greater freedom to make decisions on the domestic front.

You need to accept a number of rules and demonstrate a degree of self-discipline, even if you still feel frustrated and restricted in your actions and movements. At the moment you have no alternative but to agree to the compromises on offer.

You should accept the economic measures and financial restrictions imposed on you, accommodating them as effectively as you can. For the moment, you have no other choice.

You will find timely solutions and take sensible steps towards making a real change in your behaviour or lifestyle, bringing to an end an uncertain situation.

Not even the understandings, compromises and concessions that good sense dictates will save you from a radical change in your emotional life. You will come to see that they are absolutely necessary.

Despite your past search for concession and compromise, it will become apparent to you that only a radical change will solve your domestic problems.

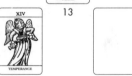

Current agreements, compromises and opportune solutions favour or at least do not rule out a major development at work. You would be wise to accept that this is vital.

Sensible compromises and appropriate solutions are within reach, helping you to bring about a major change or improvement in your financial situation.

14 15

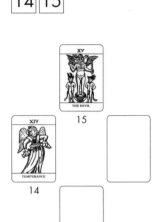

+ Your flexible and adaptable nature is a key factor in your ability to make the best use of your extraordinary vitality. As a result, you can enjoy a real sense of well-being.

♥ Your accommodating nature, adaptability and sense of timing will enable you to control your emotions and instincts, both of which are currently somewhat unsettled.

Agreements and compromises will be put in place at home that will help you achieve your domestic objectives and assert yourself with confidence while also remaining flexible.

You can be confident that your negotiations will succeed in bringing about profitable contracts and effective compromises. You will achieve your professional targets and at the same time maintain firm but flexible control at work.

You will reach well-timed agreements and compromises that will lead to financial success.

14 16

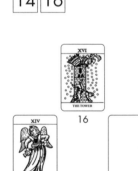

+ Your own flexibility and instinctive intelligence will bring release or even save you from potentially disruptive or destabilizing factors.

♥ Fortuitous and positive compromises will bring relief to your emotional life. They could have upsetting consequences, however.

Your accommodating nature and concern to preserve domestic peace will not allow you to avoid an upsetting challenge.

Intelligent and well-timed compromises will lead to a disruptive and fundamental challenge, which may actually prove beneficial. Don't worry unduly.

Although you have taken conciliatory, appropriate and sensible precautions, you will face a testing time, which may or may not be positive, depending on the current state of your finances.

➕ Your flexible, independent and reliable nature will guarantee a real sense of well-being, high levels of energy and untroubled health.

❤️ Although you have an independent nature, you remain unsure of your feelings. It could be that you are completely devoted to the person you love or that they are currently assuring you that their feelings for you are genuine.

👪 The imposition of constructive arrangements and compromises on the domestic front will make it easier to adapt to current circumstances or achieve something new.

📋 You can confidently negotiate a new position or business deal, secure in the knowledge that you will reach a useful compromise without having to make any important sacrifices.

💰 A healthy financial situation is making you independent and sure of your resources and your prerogatives. It will help you to take constructive and intelligent action.

➕ Instead of giving up or letting your health deteriorate, you would do better to follow the advice of a doctor.

❤️ Current compromises and understandings in your love life will not help much. If you are not careful, matters may deteriorate.

👪 Although you have an accommodating nature and are determined to resolve matters, you will fail to stop them deteriorating. Under the circumstances, you would probably be wrong to find compromises or make concessions.

📋 You are determined to reach useful agreements or reasonable compromises, but your negotiations will probably not succeed. You are in danger of being disappointed or seeing your situation go downhill.

💰 You will make important moves or find the right ways, through compromise and agreement, to resolve or at least limit your financial difficulties.

14 19

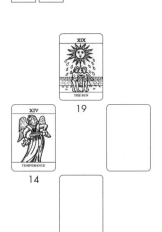

19

14

➕ Your accommodating nature and natural flexibility guarantee inner calm and a feeling of harmony both within yourself and with those around you. What's more, you also enjoy great vitality.

♥ Agreements and concessions will help you to maintain or develop a loving or genuine relationship. You will now be able to enjoy this union to the full.

👪 Calm, intelligent, understanding and loving relationships are all around you, guaranteeing domestic harmony, although you may yet have to come to certain understandings or compromises.

📋 Your negotiations are crowned with success. You will agree contracts or form partnerships that present you with even more opportunities for progress.

💰 You can now put in place agreements or compromises that will present you with potentially profitable choices and decisions, and, as a result, your financial position will be much more satisfying.

14 20

20

14

➕ Make an effort to find useful compromises on the health front. You can then recover your energy levels and find your inner dynamism once more.

♥ Try to find the best ways in which your emotional life can develop by making effective agreements or compromises. You could return to a former happier state or perhaps change for the better.

👪 You should make an effort to discuss and agree matters on the domestic front. This will help your situation to develop, expand or find a degree of peace.

📋 Concerted efforts are being made and constructive compromises are being reached. These will improve your position and lead to major and positive change.

💰 You need to make an effort and find a way, be it a timely compromise or by some other arrangement, to bring about a change or revival in your financial situation.

You can make the conciliatory moves to help maintain your balance and guarantee your personal growth and well-being.

There are many good reasons for you to demonstrate your generosity, tolerance and understanding. You will establish the foundations for a stable and flourishing love life.

Fair and just compromises will reinforce the stability and harmony of your family life.

Serious and tough negotiations will be brought to a conclusion by reasonable and flexible discussions. They will lead to a satisfying expansion of your professional position.

You must be prepared to be fair in discussions and agreements if you want to take full but measured advantage of your financial assets.

If you intend to leave or go on a journey, now is the time to do so. Alternatively, although you are accommodating and flexible by nature, you will not be able to resist an impulsive, even unsettling response.

You are anxious to find understandings and reach compromises, but you will fail to curb your zeal or restrain your impulsive, even thoughtless reactions.

A well-timed agreement will put you in a position to depart or move house. Alternatively, despite a compromise, someone in your family circle will leave and you will be unable to stand in their way.

Appropriate understandings and compromises encourage the arrival or departure of someone in your professional circle. The change may give you the go-ahead to embark on a journey, make a move or finally escape from your constraints.

Now is the time to make transactions or move funds. Do not give in to careless or excessive expenditure.

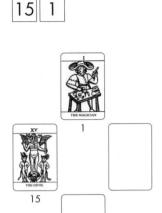

Take care, because your highly excited state may soon bring problems, encouraging you to take dangerous risks or make serious mistakes. If you are ill, you will have to take every available measure to recover.

The turbulence and passion dominating your emotional life, combined with extreme behaviour and a burning desire to satisfy your own needs at all costs, leave you vulnerable to both serious mistakes and their consequences.

An element of chaos exists in your domestic situation. Should your aim be to achieve your goals at all costs, it will be possible, but only at your own risk. Whatever the case, sudden upheavals are inescapable.

Impatience, over-excitement, lack of preparation and excessive ambition will leave you at risk of losing absolutely everything.

If you live above your means or if you are over-ambitious or untruthful, you are in imminent danger of suffering the consequences.

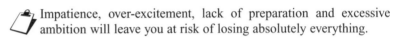

You are blessed with intense levels of energy, but you take advantage of it only when you feel the need to turn over a new leaf, reinforce your strength or accomplish a task close to your heart.

Although you are in control and in a stable emotional situation, you have a passionate nature, and once your feelings are engaged it is hard for you to hold yourself back.

You have been secretly hoping for new developments, and these are likely to occur, rewarding your patience and your expectations.

Even if matters are still under wraps, you should soon be able to achieve your professional goals, witness the successful outcome of ambitious projects or profit from a new product, invention or innovation.

Your financial hopes and ambitions are certain to be fulfilled. You will then be able to economize and stabilize your financial affairs without feeling that you must restrict your spending.

15 | 3

➕ You could well be the victim of an acute blow to your health, and all because of your over-indulgence, excesses, tension, over-excitement or generally unhealthy lifestyle.

❤ Conflicts of a passionate nature could well develop, leading to serious disappointments or bitter disillusionment.

👪 Conflicts, disappointments, health issues or other concerns may well plague your domestic life. You will have to draw on your generous and solicitous nature to confront these difficulties.

📋 You may encounter delays or problems, but you should be able to bring your ideas to fruition, achieve your ambitions and succeed in attaining a really outstanding level of productivity.

📠 Despite the difficulties and delays lying in your path, you should succeed in achieving your financial ambitions.

15 | 4

➕ You are lucky enough to have high levels of vitality which you seem to use intelligently, even when you are exposed to temptation or the opportunity to over-indulge.

❤ It seems that nothing can stand in the way of your determination to achieve your emotional aims. As a result, you are clearly in control of your love life.

👪 If a turbulent, extreme or tedious situation arises in your domestic life you will know how to deal with it and resume control of events. Alternatively, you are already clearly in command of domestic issues.

📋 In realising your desires and ambitions, you will use your talents, authority and constructive intelligence to achieve even more success.

📠 You can fulfil your financial aims and also clear up and take control of your monetary position.

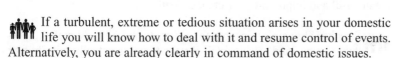
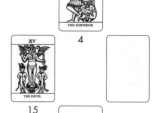

15 5

5

15

You may need to go to great lengths to curb your turbulent or over-excited state. Do all you can to recover and return to normal health as soon as possible.

Although it is your nature to be rather intense, circumstances are prompting you to change your behaviour, review your emotional life and pursue more sensible, normal relationships.

You would like to review and change things on the home front, returning to a more normal, serious and reliable situation.

If you want to achieve your aims and satisfy your desires or ambitions, you need to be above reproach legally. You should review, reappraise or change aspects of your professional life.

Your impressive financial results will help you to take positive action to re-float your business or review your position from a legal point of view.

15 6

6

15

You are lucky enough to have high levels of energy that encourage you to make instinctive, correct choices and give you an increased sense of well-being, but beware of excessive or careless behaviour.

You want to satisfy your desires and passions at all costs, and it seems that events have conspired to bring you a completely fulfilled love life. Under such circumstances, only you can determine just how meaningful and important your choices really are.

You have big ambitions, but to achieve them you must make important choices and ask yourself if your target is actually within your grasp. If it is, all will be well on the domestic front.

Your plans, desires and ambitious projects for major growth or an important partnership have every chance of success.

Your financial situation looks generally positive and is leaving the way open for judicious choices and correct decisions. You will come to agreements that will expand your finances.

➕ Be on your guard against acting on irrational whims or indulging your unstable and reckless nature. Try to get a grip on yourself, control your instincts and avoid mistakes.

❤️ Your desire to reach your aims at all costs is blinding you to reality, making you impatient, impulsive and careless. Although nothing seems able to thwart your outbursts, you need to recognise when you have gone too far.

👪 You may well want to leave in a hurry without so much as a backward glance, but you are wondering if this desire is justified. Although impulsive and possibly careless, such action should still prove to be positive.

📋 You will soon be making progress towards your professional goals and asserting your authority. It could be that you will depart and gain the upper hand by virtue of your own efforts.

🗄️ You will take hasty, even premature, steps on the financial front, but such moves will ultimately prove positive.

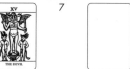

➕ You overcome weakness by resorting to strict measures, nipping in the bud any temptation to over-indulge by beginning a rigorous regime of self-discipline. This increases awareness of your physical and mental balance and underlines your responsibility for your own welfare.

❤️ If you are going through a rough patch in your love life or find yourself at the mercy of your weaknesses and passions, take comfort from the fact that order and justice will ultimately win the day.

👪 No matter what your desires or ambitions on the domestic front or the turbulence that prevails at home, order, stability and a sense of what is right will prevail in the long run.

📋 Your desires or ambitions can come to fruition only if you submit to rules, regulations and a strict regime. Alternatively, if you wish to put paid to the chaos and turmoil of a situation, you may have to have recourse to the law.

🗄️ Adhere to strict rules, adopt a regime of self-discipline and your finances will become more stable, reliable and balanced.

15 9

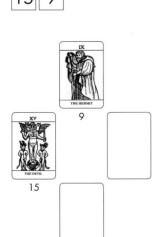

9

15

Despite your remarkable vitality and a tendency to waste your energy, it appears that you will have to show caution in decisions concerning your health.

You are too intense in your relationships. Whatever the outcome, you will know the true nature of your feelings.

If you really want to realize your desires at all costs, you need to make sensible choices and decisions and reflect carefully to avoid taking any extreme or careless action.

You are becoming increasingly aware that the main focus of your efforts and energy at the moment is directed towards reaching an agreement. However, you need to show that you can be deliberate and cautious in the choices you make. This is the only route to success.

Although your finances are looking positive, be cautious, systematic and careful in agreements, choices and decisions.

15 10

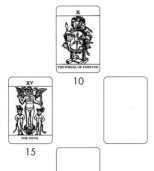

10

15

The intense levels of vital energy and unquestionable drive with which you are blessed give you the ability to forge ahead with ease and assert yourself both emotionally and physically.

You can assert yourself, satisfy your emotional desires and achieve whatever you want in love. Don't relax your efforts to stay in control of your feelings, however, because the consequences could be problematic for you otherwise.

Your domestic situation will soon develop along the lines you wish as long as you take the necessary initiative.

Nothing seems capable of undermining your determined efforts to achieve results. Nor can anything stand in the way of you and your rapid professional progress.

Everything is conspiring to bring your financial targets closer. You will be in a position to make impressive progress.

➕ Although you have high levels of energy, which can get out of hand, you do not lack self-discipline or courage. As a result, you are able to exercise self-control and maintain your essential equilibrium.

❤ You have your passions and impulses under control and you are maintaining a balance in your close relationships with great strength of character.

👪 The turmoil, extreme behaviour or arguments that appear to be besetting your domestic circumstances can be eliminated by positive, bold and tough action.

📋 If you want to satisfy work-related desires or ambitions, you should be tough and self-disciplined and aware of how to assert both yourself and your will to succeed.

💹 You have everything you need to achieve your financial ambitions and desires, giving your affairs a firmer foundation.

➕ You are becoming aware that you have been uncontrolled, weak and vulnerable to temptation and that this behaviour has compromised your health. Your only solution is to demonstrate caution and moderation.

❤ You are coming to see how over-dramatic, uncontrolled and self-indulgent your life is. You may now want to escape from this situation at all costs, but to do so you must understand fully to what extent you are a victim of your own impulses and desires.

👪 You appreciate that you have got yourself into a difficult, questionable position by trying to do too much or go too fast too soon. You now need to find a way out of the impasse.

📋 If you take extreme, illegal or dubious measures, you are in danger of finding yourself in a highly questionable position from which there is no escape. Fortunately, you have the means to recognize the difficulty in time and to think carefully before making moves or surrendering your position.

💹 Bear in mind that by yielding to the temptation to be reckless on the financial front, you risk getting caught up in a monetary impasse. You really must show caution.

13

15

Your over-indulgence and weaknesses will quickly lead you to change your behaviour completely. Alternatively, by taking extreme measures, you will be able to eliminate potentially harmful factors for good.

You want to make a radical change in your love life and are prepared to go to any lengths to succeed. You will then reap what you have sown, for good or ill.

You have a burning desire to introduce significant changes in your domestic situation. You may well soon succeed in doing so, regardless of the means you choose. If your action is justified, so much the better; otherwise, beware the consequences.

You want to make a major change in your situation, and you can do so soon. Alternatively, a change or profitable development will bring you benefits, even if the way it is carried out appears to be rather confused and over the top.

You are going to make a fundamental change to end your damaging rate of expenditure or re-appraise your unreasonable ambitions. Alternatively, you are soon going to be able to see some positive and advantageous financial changes.

15 14

14

15

You have intense, sometimes turbulent or uncontrolled levels of vital energy. These are now well under control, however, and you are finding the happy medium that you need for calm and continued self-assurance.

By controlling your passions and impulses and tempering your desires, you are able to reach agreements and compromises that encourage a peaceful and harmonious relationship.

You have a firm hold on the situation and are in a position to reach understandings and compromises that contribute to a peaceful and calm domestic environment.

You are well in control and are sure of your rights and goals. You can direct negotiations to bring professional success and reward.

You have your financial situation well under control and are therefore in a position to undertake profitable negotiations or carry out advantageous transactions.

15 16

 If your behaviour is uncontrolled or self-indulgent, you won't have to wait long for an upheaval, such as a health problem to occur.

Lack of restraint, excessive behaviour or the blind pursuit of your own goals will lead to an emotional crisis that could prove either beneficial or catastrophic, depending on the circumstances.

You are so keen to achieve your aims and assert your own desires or authority that it will not be long before the results become clear. Whether these will be for better or worse, will very much depend on the circumstances.

The desire to make a positive or destructive change at work is so great that nothing can stand in the way of an upheaval, which could prove either liberating or catastrophic, according to the circumstances.

Your finances will undergo a profitable change or your spendthrift behaviour or over-weening ambition will lead to serious losses.

15 17

You enjoy abundant amounts of energy but don't abuse it. Instead, you use it to help you shoulder your responsibilities and show your open, resourceful and imaginative nature.

You can curb your blind desires, intensely passionate relationships and impulsive outbursts. You must adopt a thoughtful attitude and behave responsibly, and only then will you be able to give full vent to your feelings.

You can win the support, help and approval you need in order to realize your desires, satisfy your hopes and aspirations or achieve something new in your domestic situation.

You are certain to win the approval or support of someone influential to help you realize your desires and fulfil your aspirations. It could be that you will bring about a new and innovative element on the professional front.

 Staying within the limits imposed by your sense of duty and your responsibilities will help you enjoy maximum profit from your resources and satisfy your financial desires and ambitions.

15 18

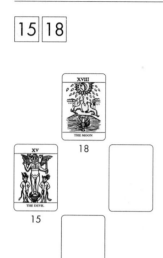

➕ Your weaknesses, over-indulgence, abuses and indecision are in danger of jeopardizing your health and making you ill.

❤ Intensely passionate relationships, a self-indulgent emotional life and blind ambition in love lead only to mistakes or disappointment.

👪 If you don't watch out you will be in danger of being guided solely by your desires or of falling victim to bad influences. As a result, you may experience disappointment and disillusion or even make mistakes you will later regret.

📋 Your overwhelming desire to come to a professional agreement leaves you vulnerable to mistakes and disappointment, or liable to make the wrong decisions.

🎲 Impatience, premature action or greed will harm agreements or decisions you make on the financial front, and serious mistakes may result.

15 19

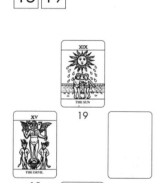

➕ You are in danger of wasting your abundant energy. You assert yourself both physically and emotionally quite freely and unquestioningly.

❤ Secure in the knowledge that you will be completely satisfied, you will enjoy a rewarding and successful emotional life.

👪 You will achieve all you wish to on the domestic front, seeing your family united and happy.

📋 Feel free to do as you wish and act assertively and confidently to tackle all professional hurdles successfully.

🎲 You have the means at your disposal to assert yourself and satisfy your financial ambitions.

15 20

 Self-discipline and a strict regime will help stabilize your health, curb your excitability and enable you to exercise self-control.

You are judging your own passionate or self-indulgent behaviour somewhat harshly. Alternatively, others are being hard on you. Whatever the case, it is time to review your emotional life, make amends and adopt a fairer, more normal and better balanced attitude.

If you adhere to the strict regime that guarantees your domestic stability, you will introduce both a new energy and a measure of normality to the situation. You will eliminate the turmoil, chaos and rows that currently prevail.

Dissension, disagreement and mistakes can only be resolved through impartial judgement. This will bring a sense of renewal and rehabilitation together with highly desirable, profitable change.

Curb your spending and adhere to strict and sensible rules. You will then have no trouble getting back on track.

15 21

You are fully aware of just how much energy you have and make cautious use of it in your quest for fulfilment and expansion. You wisely resist the temptation to over-indulge.

You know that you are behaving recklessly or that your relationship is much too intense. This clear thinking guarantees a fulfilling and successful love life.

You are all too aware of the current unsettling and reckless state of your domestic life. Ironically enough, this incoherent, chaotic situation will bring its own rewards.

You are aware of the potential of your professional situation, although it may seem incoherent and disorderly at the moment. However, it is in this chaos that the way ahead is to be found.

You are conscious of all the means at your disposal and aware that if you are cautious and careful, you will achieve your aims for financial expansion.

243

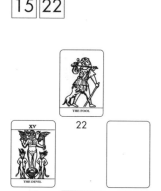

15 **22**

Excitability combined with the impulsive and careless misuse of your energy can only lead to mistakes. Sooner or later, you will have to suffer the consequences.

Your irrepressible behaviour is dictated by your overwhelming desires rather than genuine feelings. You are prepared to do anything to satisfy them. This attitude leaves you exposed to mistakes.

It seems that you have a single desire: to leave, move out and tear yourself away from your domestic circle on an irrepressible whim. Are you sure you know what you are doing?

Your incessant need to achieve your aims and satisfy your desires and ambitions leaves you impatient and impulsive. You are at risk of making mistakes you will regret or seeking extreme measures.

You seek to satisfy your financial ambitions at all costs. You have the means to do so but run the risk of making mistakes or indulging in thoughtless and premature action, with uncertain consequences.

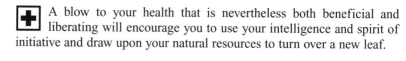

16 **1**

A blow to your health that is nevertheless both beneficial and liberating will encourage you to use your intelligence and spirit of initiative and draw upon your natural resources to turn over a new leaf.

You have fallen head over heels in love or are seriously affected by an emotional upheaval or crisis, and, as a result, you are having trouble controlling the situation, despite your attempts to do so.

A salutary crisis or liberating upheaval is taking place on the domestic front. It may well prompt new initiatives.

An upheaval, salutary crisis or sudden challenge at work enables you to be innovative, original and inventive along your path to success.

A financial crisis may suddenly cut off your resources. However, you are full of ideas and initiatives and will succeed in turning this upheaval to your advantage in the end.

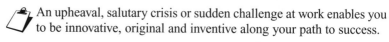

➕ A crisis or a sudden change in your condition will ultimately prove positive and help you recover from aches and pains, illness or a chronic health problem.

❤ An inevitable upheaval, sudden challenge or unavoidable crisis in your emotional life is forcing you to come out of your shell. It also relieves you of grievances, repressed feelings or hidden anxieties.

👪 A rather brutal but inevitable change looms in your domestic life. However, you were expecting it and can face it with equanimity and common sense as you know it will prove positive.

📋 A sudden challenge or crisis overcomes your natural reserve, improves your professional status and eliminates any limiting, destabilizing or immobilizing factors.

📋 A sudden crisis will help you put the finishing touches to your accounts, clean up your finances, correct any mistakes and eliminate harmful factors.

➕ An upheaval or alarm prompts you to take your health seriously so that you are able to make the most of your sense of well-being calmly and intelligently.

❤ An upheaval or volte-face prompts you to take sensible, rewarding steps towards the free expression of your feelings, which will help you build a genuine relationship.

👪 A sudden domestic upheaval brings you great joy and helps you achieve your goals intelligently, positively and constructively.

📋 Following a sudden disruption, you appreciate how best to proceed to establish a profitable partnership, act constructively or reap the maximum benefit from your professional situation.

📋 A sudden change of circumstances makes it possible for you to take clear, concrete steps to get the most out of your finances.

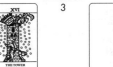

245

16 4

➕ If you are ill, you may make a spectacular recovery. In any case, you must reconsider your health and review every aspect of it.

❤ An upheaval or crisis in your emotional life prompts you to reappraise issues intelligently and constructively. You are in the process of reconsidering your position and forgiving or seeking forgiveness yourself, as the case may be.

👪 Sensible and constructive behaviour and your control of domestic issues enable you to channel events and transform an upheaval or crisis into positive rehabilitation or renewal.

📋 You need to embrace upheaval at work and to take charge of it in a constructive and positive way.

🏠 Upheavals or challenges are inevitable. Use them profitably to shed light on your finances, get them back on track and establish a solid financial foundation.

4

16

---

16 5

➕ You are in a state of shock or have experienced violent emotion, probably because of an upheaval in your life. You are resourceful, however, and can turn this to your advantage and move forward.

❤ A major upheaval or total and complete volte-face is enabling you to achieve your wishes on the emotional front. You are helped by the support and approval of an influential person.

👪 Your domestic situation is undergoing major upheavals or fundamental changes that will ultimately lead to new horizons.

📋 You are experiencing disruption and major but salutary changes at work. These are supported by an influential person but offer you enormous potential.

🏠 You could well have great possibilities already at your disposal or within reach, but a total change or about-turn in your finances is almost inevitable.

5

16

➕ A blow to your health or a sudden, overwhelming event will soon prompt you to take important decisions about your lifestyle.

♥ You may meet someone or you may already have fallen head over heels in love. Alternatively, you are involved in a break-up or emotional crisis of some kind. Whatever the case, you are having trouble controlling your emotions.

👪 An upheaval or challenge in your domestic life may force you to leave suddenly, take some major decisions or face challenging but positive choices.

📋 As a result of an upheaval or sudden challenge at work, you are obliged to leave abruptly, make major resolutions quickly or, alternatively, speed up a vital agreement.

💰 Following an upheaval or challenging financial situation, you will be forced to leave suddenly or make serious decisions to try to regain a measure of balance in your monetary affairs.

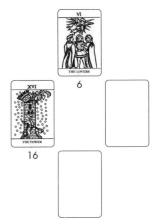

16 6

➕ If you are suffering a blow to your health, an upheaval in your life or an emotional shock, seek the help, advice or support you need. Alternatively, you will soon be relieved of a problem, and this will help you make psychological progress.

♥ An upheaval in your personal life is affecting you deeply. It is an emotional shock, but it is also shedding light on your situation, allowing you to overcome your problems or resolve conflicts.

👪 A sudden shock will help you to resolve a conflict or overcome some domestic problem. You can then forge ahead and achieve your aims under the most favourable conditions.

📋 A sudden upheaval will allow you to gain the emotional and material support of someone important. You can then overcome your problems and act freely to make professional progress.

💰 A major turn of events will free you from some of your material and emotional commitments, leaving you to pursue your financial goals.

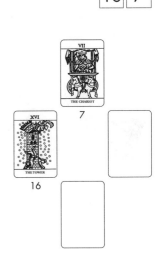

16 7

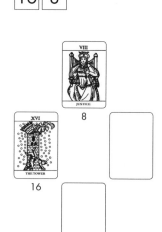

16	8

8

16

➕ An emotional shock, crisis or unforeseeable blow to your health is forcing you to make choices and think about the ways you can protect your balance and well-being.

♥ An upheaval or sudden challenge in your emotional life is putting paid to doubts and indecision. You are now able to face the reality of a disagreement, conflict or break-up.

👪 Disagreements or upsetting conflicts must be resolved through impartial, radical and beneficial measures so that justice and equilibrium can be re-established.

📋 Disruptive discord or conflict at work must be dealt with impartially and radically, in such a way that allows fairness and balance to be introduced into the situation once more.

💰 An upheaval or sudden review of, or challenge to your financial situation will prompt important and tough choices and decisions.

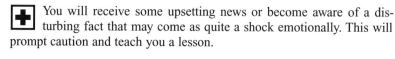

16	9

9

16

➕ You will receive some upsetting news or become aware of a disturbing fact that may come as quite a shock emotionally. This will prompt caution and teach you a lesson.

♥ You will hear bad news or discover something disturbing that will challenge certain aspects of your love life. It will prompt you to be more circumspect and think things over more seriously.

👪 Upsetting news will disrupt your domestic life. Alternatively, you will give careful, cautious consideration to an upheaval or sudden challenge that is currently taking place.

📋 Upsetting news may actually benefit your position. Alternatively, you may discover that the challenges or significant changes that are currently taking place will have long-term professional consequences.

💰 It looks as if you will hear something upsetting, but the news will actually come as a relief, answer questions or banish doubts. You will, however, remain cautious and circumspect.

➕ A blow to your health or an upheaval in your way of life could well allow you to develop in a more balanced, stable and rational manner.

❤️ You are being emotionally affected and worried by a disconcerting but salutary upheaval. It is also allowing you to see the wood for the trees at last and to move forward in a more balanced and reasonable way from an emotional point of view.

👪 The stability and balance of your domestic situation is supported by a beneficial upheaval or change.

📋 A reasonable and useful change is promoting stable and balanced progress at work and guaranteeing your rights.

🏦 Rational, fair developments will encourage financial progress and allow you to be sure of your rights and the control you have over monetary matters.

16 10

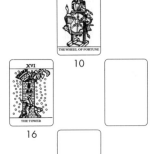

➕ A new awareness is proving somewhat disorienting but is shedding welcome light on your lifestyle, prompting you to be more cautious, confident and energetic.

❤️ You are going through a period of intense introspection, which is upsetting but essential and reveals things about yourself and your emotional life that will ultimately bring increased self-confidence and faith in your situation.

👪 You are aware that upheavals and challenges are occurring in your domestic situation. Even so, you are not losing self-possession or self-control but are confronting the reality with both circumspection and a degree of pragmatism.

📋 You are aware of the advantages you can glean from the upheavals taking place at work. They are necessary to your success, because they are giving you better control over essential elements.

🏦 Beneficial upheavals or challenges give you better control over your financial situation and make you more certain of your rights and privileges.

16 11

16 12

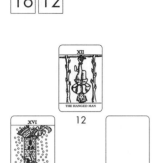

12

16

➕ An accident, emotional shock or blow to your health may well force you to take a rest. Alternatively, you will be able to make a spectacular recovery.

❤️ You are affected by an upheaval or sudden challenge that causes an emotional shock. It also creates a new awareness, enabling you eventually to free yourself from what was undermining or thwarting your love life.

👪 Your domestic situation is undergoing dramatic but inevitable upheavals. You can't do much about this, but it will gradually free you from what was undermining or restricting matters at home.

📋 An apparent stalemate is working out in a spectacular but liberating way, allowing you gradually to regain your independence or freedom to act.

📟 Your financial situation is suddenly resolving itself in a spectacular if somewhat disconcerting way, bringing greater autonomy and increased independence.

16 13

13

16

➕ Upsetting circumstances are giving you an opportunity to make a bold, determined and radical change in your behaviour or lifestyle or in health-related matters.

❤️ You will be able to exercise confident control over your relationships and start a new chapter in your love life.

👪 The domestic upheavals that are taking place will highlight your strength of character and remarkable courage, which will allow you to control the radical change you will have to introduce.

📋 You have the necessary strength of mind, courage and ability to cope with challenges at work and to implement both radical and positive change.

📟 A major financial disturbance will prove beneficial, helping you to face the resulting developments with confidence and courage.

➕ A warning or brief but possibly brutal blow to your health prompts you to be more cautious and flexible, to make concessions and adopt a healthier, calmer lifestyle.

♥ If you are flexible and accommodating you will find advantages in the challenges that your emotional life is currently undergoing.

👪 Everything can work out for the best as long as you show flexibility and understanding and take advantage of the positive aspects of any current domestic challenges.

✏ Changes that are taking place in your circumstances will give you the chance to start fruitful negotiations, find opportune compromises and turn what may appear to be a negative intervention into something wholly positive.

📠 Upheavals or sudden challenges are giving you the chance to enter into profitable negotiations or undertake advantageous transactions.

16 14

➕ A blow to your health or an accident will force you to go to great lengths to deal with it or to recover as quickly as possible.

♥ An inevitable emotional challenge is plunging you into turmoil and highlighting all the extreme and negative aspects of your love life.

👪 Expect major upheavals to take place. They will probably reflect your desires but may cause disruption in your domestic life and sow the seeds of doubt and disorder.

✏ The power or intervention of an influential person, whose ambitions and intentions coincide or correspond with your own, will abruptly and positively enhance your position at work.

📠 The upheavals that are currently taking place will make you even more confident of your rights and privileges and give you the ultimate power over your own finances.

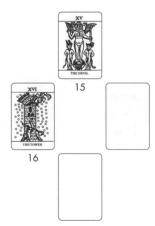

16 15

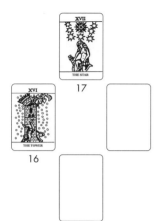

➕ An alarm on the health front will prompt sensible resolutions, a return to basics and judicious recourse to your inner resources and receptive nature.

❤ A passionate affair or an upheaval in your love life will lead you to discover new feelings and emotions and promise a real measure of fulfilment in love.

👪 Upheavals or challenges in your family life will prompt you to make sudden, new resolutions or sensible choices or to wipe the slate clean.

📋 An agreement will suddenly be reached, allowing you to achieve something new and to take innovative or inspired decisions that could generate definite progress.

🗄 A successful agreement, wise choice or the decision you are hoping for will bear fruit and enable you to take full advantage of the resources at your disposal.

16 18

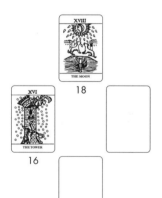

➕ A health problem or accident leaves you feeling negative and in a state of turmoil. Remember that you have what it takes to recover.

❤ Dramatic developments will banish conflict and uncertainty, dispersing the shadows that have been darkening your emotional life. The changes will, however, involve some disillusionment or deep disappointment.

👪 You can use an upheaval, challenge or crisis to sort out domestic problems and get a grip on the difficulties that currently prevail in your family life.

📋 You are experiencing some inevitable upheavals in your work situation, but as long as you do not shrink from the effort required you can overcome the problems or obstacles.

🗄 An inevitable upheaval or sudden challenge is prompting you to embark on a struggle to overcome your current financial difficulties.

An alarm, temporary illness or sudden but brief health scare is knocking you sideways, though not undermining your fundamental equilibrium. Indeed, it is providing you with an opportunity to purify your system and eliminate harmful or adverse factors.

A major change sheds new and positive light on your situation and guarantees that you will enjoy a well-balanced relationship.

An upheaval or sudden challenge is all for the good. It brings you both joy and satisfaction in your domestic situation, although it may disrupt matters within the family in the short term.

New developments will give you the green light to clarify your professional situation and achieve a profitable agreement or form a balanced and highly positive partnership.

A sudden, positive change is clarifying your financial situation, bringing you security and satisfaction.

16 19

An accident or blow to your health is making you more clear-sighted and cautious. You are seeking ways to make a full recovery on your own and to protect yourself from potential risks in the future.

Following a major upset, you are reviewing and questioning your own conduct, deciding to make amends or offer forgiveness where appropriate.

Upheavals or sudden challenges in your domestic life are prompting you to seek practical solutions that may bring genuine renewal.

Maintain your self-possession and clear-sightedness in the face of any upheavals you are currently experiencing. Learn lessons from them and be aware of the potentially positive results.

A sudden upheaval or reversal is prompting you to be cautious and find practical solutions to financial mistakes and new ways of making money.

16 20

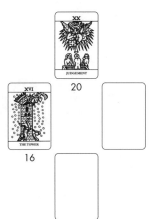

16 21

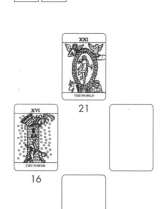

21

16

 You are experiencing a period of progress and rapid and significant change that will enable you to blossom and flourish.

 Sudden events are making your emotional life change rapidly and for the better, providing it with the means to achieve its full potential.

 Fundamental upheavals will promote progress on the domestic front, helping it reach its full potential.

Sudden, liberating events or salutary upheavals bring rapid progress and substantial growth at work.

Major but beneficial changes provide you with the means to expand your finances quite considerably.

16 22

22

16

Avoid whims, thoughtless and impulsive behaviour or unnecessary, irrational risks. Steer clear of making dangerous mistakes through carelessness or extreme acts. In short, avoid any hasty or impetuous action.

An upheaval, shock or sudden challenge will prompt you to leave abruptly on a whim and without much consideration. It seems that nothing and no one can hold you back.

An upheaval in your life encourages you to depart suddenly, to leave your family or to move home in haste.

An upheaval or sudden challenge in your work releases you from previous constraints and helps you forge ahead. Alternatively, the change will prompt you to leave, bid an abrupt farewell to the past and start a new chapter in your professional life.

No matter what new and upsetting, even bewildering, factors arise, you should avoid hasty responses, unless they involve extricating yourself with haste from a difficult situation.

✚ You are finding it hard to rely on your natural resources, leaving you feeling muddled, anxious and unwell. Channel your energy in a more useful way and act sensibly to make the most of your well-being.

♥ You are finding it difficult to accept and express your emotions and to cope with the consequences. This is causing you to feel upset and worried and making you unsure about how justified and well founded your feelings really are.

👪 The conditions may seem favourable, but the time is not yet right to undertake anything radically new with regard to your family situation unless you can devote yourself entirely and unstintingly to it.

✍ An original or creative idea, a business deal or a new company will materialize only if you devote all your talent, energy, skills and time to it.

▣ Sort out your financial resources and the use you make of them as a priority, channelling all your energy and skills to the task.

✚ Enjoy your good health and wealth of natural resources – but don't overdo it.

♥ Despite your reserve, discretion or modesty, it is hard to disguise the fact that you are feeling emotionally fulfilled, even blissfully so.

👪 Your hopes and dreams for your family are fulfilled. Your stability, wisdom and discretion are recognized.

✍ If you are considering a new business idea, partnership or company, there is every chance that your plans will come to fruition, turning out exactly as you wish.

▣ Take reasonable and discreet advantage of your financial resources. Life is full of new possibilities – all the more so because the circumstances are so auspicious.

17 3

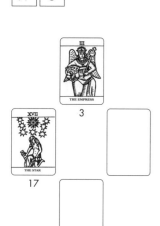

3

17

➕ You hold all the trump cards you need to enjoy a new lease of life. Seize the opportunity to draw on all your personal resources, including your good health, to create, develop or achieve anything you want.

♥ Thanks to a healthy and harmonious relationship, combined with your generosity of spirit, you will be able to achieve something new and happy in your love life.

👪 You have everything you need to introduce something new to your family life or to bring about a fresh start, with significant and beneficial changes.

📋 The creation of a company, a new idea or the re-floating of a business venture is about to put your work situation on a new footing, which will be both beneficial and profitable.

🗄 Thanks to your intelligence and inspiration, you are managing to revive your finances and enjoy the profits and benefits. Stay calm but enjoy them to the full.

4

17

➕ This is a period of total fulfilment, and you are enjoying the best of health. As a result, you are being constructive and intelligent and deriving the greatest possible benefit from your well-being.

♥ Your hopes and dreams are coming true, creating a sense of total fulfilment in any affairs of the heart.

👪 Now is the time to take constructive, intelligent action to bring your hopes and dreams to fruition and to bring harmony and fulfilment to your family life.

📋 Thanks to beneficial circumstances or solid support, you are sure to achieve your plans for expansion and innovation; these will widen the scope of your activities and open up new horizons.

🗄 Basing your actions on tangible values or reliable support from others, you can take steps to maximize the potential of your resources or dramatically improve your finances.

256

17 5

Your calm, receptive and highly resourceful nature is curbing your impulses – and with good reason. Things will improve slowly but surely, but do not lose sight of your duties and responsibilities.

As far as your love life is concerned, you are anxious to fulfil your hopes and dreams and are no longer concealing your spontaneity and emotions.

A house move, happy event or new venture is about to take place. Giving your full attention to the situation will put your family circumstances on a firmer, more secure footing.

An approach to someone influential has every chance of having a favourable outcome and of being profitable; it will enable you to try something new or to be innovative or creative.

This is not a time to hesitate: you must impose stability on your situation. Take the steps that are necessary and seek the support or advice that you need to make the best possible use of your resources.

5

17

17 6

Thanks to your receptive, calm and resourceful nature, things are going reasonably well. You have complete freedom of choice when it comes to your balance and good health.

Your hopes and plans for finding someone appear to have every chance of being successful. Alternatively, you are in a loving, stable and secure relationship.

You will obtain the agreement you are looking for, which will enable you to achieve something creative or innovative in your family life.

The advent of something new, the realization of an original idea or the fulfilment of a personal aspiration gives rise to a useful agreement, contract or partnership.

Thanks to your healthy and stable financial situation, you can make judicious, rational choices or enter into serious and profitable agreements.

6

17

257

17 7

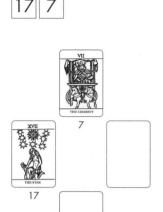

7

17

Your receptive, emotional nature is making you unstable and gullible. Be disciplined and make an effort to overcome your doubts and to assume control of your general well-being.

You are enjoying emotional fulfilment, which allows you to make important, even inspired choices and to overcome any uncertainties in your relationships and realize your emotional hopes and dreams.

You are now free to make new resolutions and informed choices so that you can achieve something new or different in your family life.

Any new enterprise or personal aspiration will be met with the success you have been hoping for as long as it is supported by agreements or some good choices.

Thanks to sensible decisions or agreements, your financial situation is improving slowly but surely, and you are certain to go on to achieve success in this area.

17 8

8

17

You know how to make the best possible use of your receptive nature and natural potential in order to achieve a solid and permanent balance and stability.

Favourable circumstances promise success in your romantic relationships and indicate a well-balanced love life.

Be strict and self-disciplined and you can undertake something totally new to ensure the stability of your family life.

You are going to be successful in anything new you undertake or achieve, bringing about even greater stability if that is necessary.

You can do something new or original to improve your resources and guarantee yourself financial stability.

You have a receptive, sensitive and well-balanced nature. What's more, you are fully aware of its potential to help you achieve personal growth and maturity.

Acutely aware of the depth of your feelings, you will strive calmly for real harmony in your love life.

Harmony and stability within your family are important to you, and you are vigilant and far-sighted enough to make sure it always remains that way.

You discover something new that stabilizes, reinforces or confirms your circumstances or that enables you to make slow but steady progress in your research and investigations.

Be careful with your money to make sure that you enjoy steady and well-deserved financial stability.

17 9

 Focusing on your sensitive, receptive and emotional nature, combined with your great inner strength, will enable you gradually to achieve a lasting maturity.

Thanks to your deep and sincere feelings and the harmony that exists in your romantic relationship, you know exactly what new initiatives are needed to make sure that the relationship continues and develops along solid lines.

Favourable circumstances help you to find original solutions or discover new elements to create a slow, profound and positive transformation in your family situation.

Through an innovation, original new idea or personal discovery, you find an unusual and surprising solution to a problem, which helps to move things forwards in the direction you want.

Being careful and knowing exactly how to value your assets will allow you to improve your financial situation, albeit slowly.

17 10

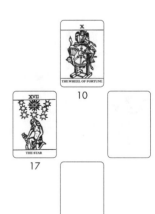

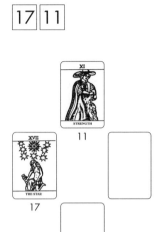

17 11

11

17

You are experiencing a period of change and expansion, which is giving you justified confidence in your talents, abilities and personal qualities. It also allows you to take full advantage of your physical and emotional well-being.

Beneficial circumstances and a harmonious, serene relationship in which you can place your trust are among the key changes taking place in your love life.

Thanks to highly beneficial circumstances, you are able to get what you want and to make your most heart-felt wishes for your family come true.

Beneficial circumstances favour the development and expansion of your plans. As a result, you will be able to achieve the changes for which you have been longing.

This is an excellent time to make full use of your financial resources, thus providing you with considerable opportunities for expansion and progress.

17 12

12

17

Confident of the depth and power of your inner resources, energy and moral strength, you will be able to throw off something that is bothering you and overcome any hardships.

A certain emotional fulfilment or intense harmony in your relationships will encourage you to devote yourself entirely and with confidence to your love life.

You appear to have complete confidence in the external circumstances that maintain the harmony in your family life, but you are, in fact, quietly and benignly in control of it from within.

Have confidence in any new, favourable circumstances that come your way and seize the opportunity to control the situation from within. Make sure that you maintain your prerogatives, even though you may have little choice under the current circumstances.

Strength, courage and persistence are needed if you are to acquire new financial resources, as a result of which you can end an existing stalemate and move things forwards.

➕ Trust your own instincts and natural receptivity when you are trying to find an effective and sensible remedy for anything that might endanger your well-being and health.

❤ In matters of the heart you can now make your dreams, most secret wishes, hopes and aspirations come true and thus reap the benefits of what you have sown.

👪 Take some positive, comprehensive and intelligent steps to bring about something new in your family life, while being aware that it may also provoke radical change.

📋 Something new or an original idea is materializing, and it could well turn out to be highly profitable, bringing about radical but advantageous changes.

💰 You are going to be able to take advantage of new circumstances that will result in major and beneficial changes in your finances.

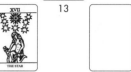

➕ You are strong, confident and healthy and know what to do in practical terms to maintain this state of affairs.

❤ What you are hoping for has every chance of happening as long as you have the flexibility and understanding to adapt yourself to circumstances and to give in to your feelings.

👪 Any hopes relating to your family life may well be fulfilled, as long as you know how to do what is required and when to do it.

📋 Your ambitious plans or original ideas are likely to be realized as long as you remain adaptable to circumstances and open to change.

💰 If you are confident of your resources and certain of the new factors that are likely to improve your finances you can enter into profitable transactions or negotiations.

261

17 15

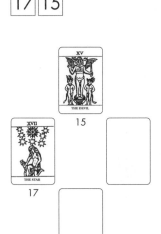

15

17

Even though you are aware of your inner resources, vitality and powers of recovery, you are careful not to exploit them but instead put them to wise and sensible use.

Your hopes and dreams have every chance of being fulfilled in the best possible circumstances. Enjoy your tender and passionate emotions to the full.

Circumstances are very favourable, and you are receiving the right support for a new venture or for the realization of projects for your family or home.

With the support, approval or assistance of an influential person, you can proceed with new projects and advantageous plans.

You can go ahead and make full, but reasonable, use of your material resources; perhaps you need to embark on a new and potentially lucrative project.

17 16

16

17

Although you are currently stable and healthy, your vulnerable and emotional nature will not make you immune to a potential blow to your well-being or to a psychological or physical shock. This may throw your life off balance, but it may also provide you with a form of release.

Your natural sentimentality is making you vulnerable, even though you are searching for harmony in your love life. This will not protect you from a shock or an upset that will force you to make hard choices.

You are well motivated to make wise choices or to embark on new courses of action that may be the catalyst for beneficial and liberating changes to your family life.

Thanks to favourable circumstances, you are able to be innovative and creative or to come to a new form of agreement, thereby finding a way to escape from a current impasse.

Think carefully about your options before you decide to take the opportunity to move on from financial stalemate or to raise some really essential questions.

17 18

✚ Dig deep within yourself to find the discipline, intuition and resources you need to solve any health problems or to overcome any difficulties and troubles. Then you will achieve a calm and balanced state of mind.

♥ Despite your strong but justifiable emotions, you may still experience anxiety, real or imagined, or disappointment if you do not exercise some self-discipline in your love life.

👪 The apparent harmony in your family life does not prevent conflicts or problems from arising. These can be resolved or put right only by means of discipline and fairness.

📋 Delays, problems or concerns will disrupt your current stable situation, but you can overcome all obstacles by being disciplined, perceptive and fair.

💰 Be strict and disciplined in the use of your money because you might well encounter a few financial problems. You will be able to solve these only by behaving in a sensible, careful way.

18

17

17 19

✚ You are acutely aware of your inner resources and their limits and of your cautious nature. As a result you are able to feel in harmony both with yourself and with your environment.

♥ Special, requited feelings reach their height to bring fulfilment and happiness beyond all your expectations.

👪 A new and joyful event in your family life will bring much happiness and satisfaction.

📋 New circumstances or some innovative discoveries will prove beneficial, leading to a clarification of your situation and to the achievement of anticipated goals.

💰 Act calmly and intelligently to take advantage of a favourable financial situation, a fresh solution or new resources that will bring you profitable results.

19

17

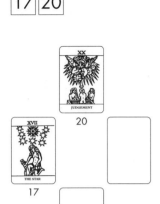

17 **20**

20

17

![health symbol] You are undergoing a period of change and personal development that will result in renewed physical and psychological strength, which will be combined with greater levels of vitality.

![heart symbol] Favourable circumstances and new, happy feelings move your love life forwards in a positive manner. This will lead you to experience emotional renewal and change.

![family symbol] Something unexpected but fortunate may help to improve your family life, putting it on a new, sound footing.

![work symbol] Favourable circumstances may allow you to undertake or achieve something new, so seize on any interesting opportunities and you will make progress.

![money symbol] Things are on an upward curve, and you can rightly expect some beneficial changes or even the complete and fortuitous revival of your financial situation.

17 **21**

21

17

![health symbol] You are resourceful and receptive and have confidence in your mental resources and capabilities, and these qualities bring you radiant health and the promise of real fulfilment.

![heart symbol] Confident, receptive and tender, you know that you can achieve your desires in matters of the heart. You have every chance of obtaining everything you could wish for!

![family symbol] You hold all the trump cards, and the circumstances are just right for you to find something new that will bring contentment to your family, allowing it to flourish.

![work symbol] Some successful new venture or opportunity is likely to open up new horizons for you and to advance your status considerably.

![money symbol] If you take control of the current favourable circumstances, you can be sure that your financial situation will improve considerably.

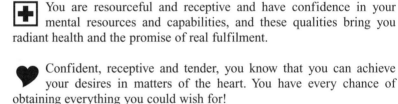

✚ If you are thinking of taking a break or holiday or going on a trip to improve your health and revitalize yourself, do so. It can only do you good.

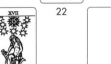

♥ Your emotional relationships are going to bring a change to your life. Alternatively, you may be going on a sentimental journey or will meet the person for whom you have been hoping.

👪 The family journey or holiday or the house move you are hoping for is going to happen very soon. Alternatively, you will hear news of a birth or new developments within your family.

✎ New developments will enable you to change your job or environment suddenly or to embark on a journey to a specific goal.

▣ There is something new in your financial situation – beneficial circumstances or new resources – that gives you the impetus to undertake a project close to your heart.

✚ Despite some minor health problems, you will manage to overcome the worrying symptoms and ward off any risk of serious illness.

♥ Obstacles in your path or feelings of disappointment or anxiety should not prove worrying. Thanks to your good judgement and positive attitude, you should still be able to achieve full satisfaction in your love life.

👪 A brilliant idea or a clever, astute and effective initiative will resolve any problems you are encountering in your family, completely resolving the situation.

✎ A confusing, tricky situation, which is making you feel insecure, spurs you to take the initiative and use all your imagination and ingenuity to overcome the difficulties.

▣ You will manage to overcome the financial problems you are currently experiencing, or you will at least be able to compensate for your financial insecurity by showing initiative and seeking advice.

265

18 2

XVIII 2

18

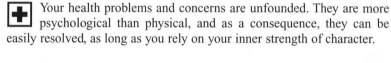 Be patient, cautious and attentive, and you will get back on track. Although it may be a difficult and unspectacular process, it will happen nevertheless.

Disappointment or disillusionment will encourage you to reconsider your feelings and make discreet but serious preparations for the changes needed to put things right.

If you can demonstrate reserve, discretion and patience, the renewal or change awaited in your family life or the resolution of current problems will occur in time.

Be patient and discreet, because the change or renewal you are expecting is going to happen – and without your intervention. Accept that this is the only way things can happen.

Even if you are not yet aware of it, a revival or change is underway that is going to solve your current financial problems.

18 3

XVIII 3

18

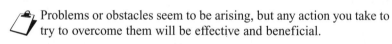 Your health problems and concerns are unfounded. They are more psychological than physical, and as a consequence, they can be easily resolved, as long as you rely on your inner strength of character.

Despite your anxieties, concerns and extreme sensitivity, you have everything you need, including the right qualities, to get what you want out of your love life.

Call on your inner strength and intelligence to solve any problems that are now becoming apparent in your family life.

Problems or obstacles seem to be arising, but any action you take to try to overcome them will be effective and beneficial.

In spite of the financial difficulties you are encountering, or the doubts and concerns you may have, effective and profitable action on your part will resolve your problems.

266

➕ You cannot escape the health-related problems you are currently facing. Seek the assistance, support and advice you need to overcome them and to remedy the condition as quickly as possible.

❤ Premature and irresponsible action will put you at risk of making a mistake. You are going down the wrong road and will only lay yourself open to bitter disappointment.

👪 Face up to the current family-related problems constructively and intelligently. You cannot escape them, so find practical solutions and think carefully before you act.

✍ Seek all the help, support and advice you need but ultimately rely only on yourself to solve current difficulties. Take prompt and practical action to find a way out of this situation.

🎴 Face up to your financial problems constructively and intelligently, resolving them with speed and determination. Try to avoid making the same mistakes in the future.

18 4

➕ If you have health problems or any concerns whatsoever in this area, consult a doctor or have faith in and follow your conscience or sense of duty.

❤ In the event of emotional deception, disillusion or conflict, trust the dictates of your conscience and behave honestly and responsibly when assessing and resolving issues facing you.

👪 Trust your sense of duty and your conscience and perhaps rely on the support of someone who is competent, honest and principled to help you solve family issues.

✍ The problems facing you can be overcome only if you are wholly committed to your duties and obligations.

🎴 You have heavy burdens to bear and need to face up to the constraints that are preventing you from fulfilling your potential; you will succeed to a limited extent.

18 5

18 6

XVIII   6

18

You are having difficulty in finding inner harmony and balance and it is hard to make the right choices about your own health.

The disappointment and disillusion you have felt in the past or the mistakes you have previously made are causing you to be more selective when it comes to affairs of the heart. Don't confuse deliberation with indecision.

Be more determined. The problems you are experiencing in reaching an agreement or in making a decision in your family life are due to a general indecisiveness.

If you are having trouble reaching an agreement or making a decision about your work situation, act with greater determination and more self-confidence.

You are having trouble reaching an agreement, making decisions or identifying the choices that would solve your financial problems. You have no time to lose and must be more resolute!

18 7

XVIII   7

18

By making an effort and fighting against your health problems, worries and any feelings of discomfort you may experience, you will manage to overcome them.

Be resolute and determined in your love life or emotional relationships so that you can conquer any problems, conflicts, deception and fears, whether they are justified or not.

Despite the bad news you receive and the current disillusionment or conflicts in your family life, you are not discouraged from your desire to overcome all your problems.

Don't lose heart. There may be obstacles in your path or serious problems to solve if you are to achieve your objectives, but you must maintain the effort you are making and not allow yourself to be discouraged. You will achieve the success you deserve.

Don't give up or become discouraged. You have everything it takes and the ability to overcome the financial problems you are doubtless currently experiencing.

➕ Be strict and disciplined when you tackle your health problems and you will maintain your equilibrium.

❤️ The problems that are arising in your love life should not be taken lightly. Deal with them in a firm, disciplined manner to make sure you are not thrown off balance.

👪 Do not treat the problems or difficulties that you are currently experiencing in your family life as if they were trivial. Handle them with scrupulous impartiality.

📋 The problems or difficulties at work are not to be taken lightly. Handle them with determination and impartiality. If it should prove necessary and appropriate, take legal advice.

🗓️ Set some strict guidelines and make sure that you observe them very rigorously in order to make up for the mistakes you have made or to balance your financial situation.

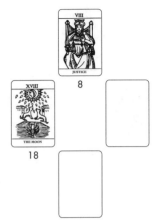

18 | 8

➕ You are facing up to your health problems and are looking at practical, specific and effective solutions that will ensure that you can overcome them slowly but surely, relying on no one but yourself.

❤️ You are aware of what is not right in your love life and are relying on yourself to find solutions to your problems, but this attitude is likely to isolate you to a certain extent.

👪 You are conscious of the problems in your family life and need to be patient, careful and clear-sighted, relying only on yourself to find the solutions.

📋 In the face of the problems that you are currently experiencing and that you are analysing in great detail, be careful, realistic and clear-sighted and rely on yourself alone to find the solutions.

🗓️ You can no longer be fooled by the financial problems you are facing. You need to rely on yourself, and yourself only, to find practical, prudent and realistic solutions.

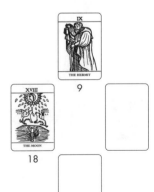

18 | 9

18 10

X

THE WHEEL OF FORTUNE

XVIII   10

THE MOON

18

✚ You will be able to overcome your problems without any difficulty, but your health will remain uncertain. Take positive steps and show determination and you will overcome any future obstacles.

♥ Your love life is confusing and unstable because it is not based on a strong foundation. However, if you are already aware that something is not right, the situation might change and sort itself out quickly.

Your family life is undergoing some ups and downs and is coming up against problems and difficulties that are disrupting or preventing your progress. Do not worry unduly, however, as matters should be settled quickly.

Any problems and difficulties disrupting or impeding your professional situation should soon be resolved, thanks to a fortunate combination of circumstances.

The logical development of your current financial situation indicates an imminent resolution. You will soon be back on the right track.

18 11

XI

STRENGTH

XVIII   11

THE MOON

18

✚ With courage, energy and determination you are managing to tackle and get on top of your health problems, overcoming any difficulties and weaknesses.

♥ No matter what problems, deceptions or conflicts might arise in your emotional life, you will have the courage to face up to them and the willpower to resolve them.

Problems in your family life will not be able to withstand your determination to overcome them. Take firm control of the situation, no matter what else happens.

You have problems to solve and difficulties to overcome, but in doing this you will be able to take charge of the situation and adopt a confident position, achieving success in even the most daunting or bold of undertakings.

You need bold determination and courage to take full control of, and to resolve, your current money problems.

✚ You are not in the best of form, and your current state of health is forcing you to rest and stop all activities. The restoration of complete good health requires serious and careful attention on your part.

♥ You are experiencing deception and difficulties in your love life, and although you have the willpower to resolve this painful situation there is little you can do at present.

👪 Difficulties, problems and conflicts are governing your family life at the moment. Alternatively, you are a victim of your own mistakes. You will no doubt manage to get out of this situation, but it will be a long, hard path.

📋 It seems that you are suffering from the consequences of your own mistakes, that you have reached an impasse or that your current problems are preventing you from taking action that will benefit your professional position.

💰 The problems you are currently experiencing or the mistakes you have previously made are causing a financial stalemate and preventing you from taking advantage of your circumstances.

✚ You need to take decisive and firm action to put an end to your health problems and achieve a complete change.

♥ Following a deception, disillusionment or emotional upset, some radical and irreversible change will take place in your love life.

👪 The problems in your family life or elsewhere will be overcome by the transformation or complete termination of a troubling situation.

📋 A major change is the best way to solve current problems and clear away the obstacles, difficulties and opposition you are experiencing at work or in your professional life.

💰 Take decisive action to end a money problem and bring about a complete change in your financial affairs, or eliminate radically any current difficulties.

18 14

XIV
TEMPERANCE

XVIII   14
THE MOON

18

➕ Consult a doctor and have the appropriate treatment or whatever therapy is necessary to resolve your health concerns. Apply a gentle but effective remedy.

❤ Despite the problems or disappointments currently dogging your emotional life, it is important to be understanding and flexible. Go with the flow and things will sort themselves out.

👪 No matter what problems you are up against at the moment or the difficulties you are encountering within your family, they can be easily resolved as long as you are flexible and know how to reach intelligent decisions.

📋 Despite the delays, obstacles and difficulties you are currently experiencing, solve them by negotiating appropriate settlements.

💰 You are having financial problems but be assured that you will be able to find a way out that will favour your business dealings and may even bring you a merited victory.

18 15

XV
THE DEVIL

XVIII   15
THE MOON

18

➕ You are too indecisive and succumb too easily to temptation, and as a result, you are a victim of your own excesses. When things go wrong, therefore, you need to take them seriously and look after yourself.

❤ You are in an intense, passionate relationship, but you and your partner are not really compatible. As a result, you are likely to be disappointed or deceived.

👪 The problems that are currently besetting your family life might force you to make poor choices. Whatever the case, don't expect to reach an agreement in such circumstances.

📋 It is not always appropriate to try to impose a solution on a problem, come what may. The circumstances are not yet right, and you are in danger of making ambiguous, damaging or downright bad choices.

💰 To solve your financial difficulties and get over your current problems, you will have to make slightly risky, extravagant choices or opt for extreme solutions.

HACHETTE

HACHETTE

HACHETTE

HACHETTE

HACHETTE

HACHETTE

THE MAGICIAN

THE HIGH PRIESTESS

THE EMPRESS

THE EMPEROR

THE HIGH PRIEST

THE LOVERS

THE CHARIOT

JUSTICE

THE HERMIT

THE WHEEL OF FORTUNE

STRENGTH

THE HANGED MAN

➕ It is time to make an effort, shake off your bad habits and bring things to a head. You are perfectly capable of solving your health problems, cleansing your body and correcting any weaknesses you may have.

❤ Bad news or deception on the emotional front will prove a shock or shake up your love life. It will prove disruptive, but nevertheless will also bring with it relief.

👪 The problems and obstacles you are currently experiencing are leading to a crisis or shake-up in the family. However, it could be for the best and will make sure that the same situation does not arise again.

📋 A crisis, upheaval or sudden challenge, which you may yourself have initiated, will enable you to overcome your current work-related difficulties.

⏳ Act with courage and determination. Carry out a thorough check on your financial situation to resolve any money problems and triumph over your difficulties.

16

18

➕ Exert some self-discipline and take your health problems seriously, even if they do not appear to be too bad. Such action will result in a healthier and more harmonious life and increased energy.

❤ The present anguish, deception or problems in your love life must be handled with determination. The world is then your oyster.

👪 If you want to make your family wishes and dreams come true, you must first make up your mind to deal firmly with the problems or conflicts that are currently besetting you.

📋 Despite the existing difficulties, your determination or even successful recourse to the law will turn circumstances to your advantage, helping you to realize your aspirations or instigate the arrival of something new.

⏳ Set some strict rules, adhere to financial norms or exercise self-discipline if you want to overcome your problems and stabilize your resources and expenditure.

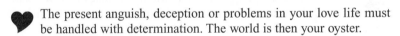

17

18

273

18 19

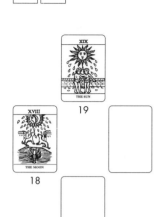

Any health problems are going to disappear, and you will soon feel on top form, in harmony with yourself and with your environment.

Despite the confusion, fears and the problems you are currently experiencing in your love life, things are changing and emotional fulfilment awaits you.

Family problems, difficulties or conflicts can be easily overcome and matters will have a positive resolution.

The problems, difficulties and obstacles you are currently coming up against can be easily overcome. To ensure this, let yourself be carried along by favourable circumstances that will lead to new success.

Despite current obstacles, your financial situation is definitely making positive progress.

18 20

Be courageous and have the confidence to handle your problems properly. Then you will manage to recover and enjoy good health.

If you can focus on your current emotional issues and overcome your fears and anxieties, you will experience a revival, significant change or reconciliation.

You have all the necessary resources and qualities to face up to and resolve the problems you are currently experiencing; matters concerning your family will return to normal as a result of your action.

Show courage and determination in overcoming the obstacles in your path and bring about a change or a renewal in your professional life.

You are in possession of all the necessary resources to control and resolve your problems, overcome your financial difficulties and get back on your feet.

➕ Contrary to what you may think, problems can often be the catalyst for progress. To restore your well-being and achieve fulfilment you need to make a number of sacrifices and acknowledge your difficulties.

18 21

💚 If you are experiencing disappointment, distress or sadness, it is time to acknowledge your feelings of unease. You will then be able to acknowledge what it is you must do to achieve emotional fulfilment without sacrificing too much of yourself.

👪 Your family life is going through a generally difficult and confusing patch, and this is leading to feelings of insecurity. You need to eliminate the cause of these problems if you want to regain harmony and a sense of balance.

📋 Acknowledge your mistakes and accept that loss or sacrifice will be an inevitable stage on your path to a more interesting, healthier life, that is full of potential and new horizons.

🎴 Make sacrifices, acknowledge your errors and honour any debts you might have. If you are prepared to take full responsibility for your financial problems in this way, matters will certainly improve soon.

➕ You cannot avoid your health problems. Do what is necessary to get over them as soon as possible.

18 22

💚 In some circumstances the only possible solution is escape. However, before you succumb to a sudden impulse to tear yourself away from a painful, disappointing or unhealthy situation make sure there is no other possible course of action.

👪 It would appear you have no choice but to go suddenly, leaving behind some difficult, disappointing or distressing family circumstance. But before you act, make sure that there really is no alternative.

📋 The problems, obstacles and difficulties you are currently encountering seem to you so intricate that you would be better to seek help or to abandon the situation altogether.

🎴 The financial delays, constraints and difficulties you are experiencing suggest that you should now seek assistance in escaping from these problems as quickly as possible.

19 1

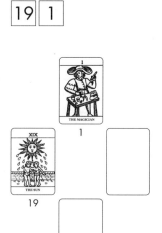

➕ Your current well-being and healthy glow enable you to feel completely rejuvenated and full of dynamic enthusiasm. You should be ready for anything.

❤️ A genuine shared feeling, a sincere union or a real emotional understanding revitalizes your situation, giving you the confidence and inspiration to act as you want and to undertake something new.

👪 The current family harmony brings with it a genuine sense of renewal, allowing you to give free rein to your initiative and your wish to embark on a new and profitable venture.

📝 An unambiguous explanation, a partnership or a timely and positive contract will initiate genuine renewal or a beneficial transformation in your circumstances. You will be ready to attempt the new undertakings you have been considering.

💰 A positive review of your finances or an advantageous event concerning them will revitalize your situation, allowing you to take on all the new projects you want.

19 2

➕ You are in perfect harmony with yourself and your own nature and are in the best of health, even if you are demonstrating a certain reserve, thoughtfulness and moderation in your actions.

❤️ You have come to a perfect understanding or are enjoying a special relationship and a happy, stable emotional life. It may not be apparent yet, but you are heading towards a period of great pleasure in your love life.

👪 Expect to see your family get together, united and happy. This will bring such great joy that you will have trouble restraining yourself despite your inherent reserve and modesty.

📝 Your most secret desires are about to be fulfilled, letting you make ambitious plans or look at different ways to widen your horizons.

💰 Something happy and positive relating to your finances opens up new horizons and allows you to consider serious opportunities for fiscal expansion.

19 3

 You are on top form which enables you to move forwards, to be energetic, to travel or even to indulge in a few extravagances.

The person you will meet or have just met, to whom you are drawn or who is drawn to you, has deep, sincere and happy feelings that mirror your own.

Expect to experience great joy or a happy event relating to your family life. Nothing can now stand in the way of a family trip or a successful house move.

A happy and positive event will clarify your position at work, allowing you to make profitable decisions or to come to an advantageous agreement.

Your financial situation is clear and positive. You can therefore take action to make it even more prosperous.

3

19

19 4

The confirmation of your good health increases your confidence and allows you to behave in a thoughtful, constructive manner.

The special relationship or excellent understanding you have with someone who is dear to you should be consolidated through an imminent meeting.

Your wonderfully happy family environment is underpinning your constructive work and behaviour. You have no problem controlling this stable situation.

An agreement, partnership or successful venture, achieved through the support of, or connection with, an influential person, should bring you complete satisfaction and leave you in control.

A clarification or some positive, happy event in relation to your finances will allow you to stabilize matters.

4

19

19 5

5

19

➕ Although you are enjoying excellent health and feelings of well-being, make sure that you continue to make sensible choices. Do not forget that free will makes you more accountable for your own actions.

❤ All the necessary factors are in place for you to be able to establish a genuine, trustworthy relationship. Alternatively, you will be able to enjoy your special emotional relationship without fear of interruption.

👪 A happy, positive event that takes place in your family helps you to finalize agreements or results in constructive and sound choices.

📝 An agreement, contract or partnership works out well and increases your responsibilities and power.

🎰 Strong positive factors cause you to make good, sensible choices or to reach a profitable agreement.

19 6

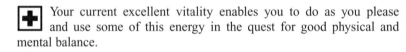

6

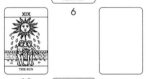

19

➕ Your current excellent vitality enables you to do as you please and use some of this energy in the quest for good physical and mental balance.

❤ There is nothing to stop you getting in touch with your emotions and expressing them to the full. Listen to your heart, reveal your feelings and find that special person very soon.

👪 A happy family event causes great joy and reinforces the current harmony. This gives you the opportunity to make sensible choices and to make progress.

📝 You enjoy success in your undertakings, conflicts or agreements, and this will provide you with all the resources you need to achieve your objectives very soon.

🎰 Thanks to a happy, positive event that has a bearing on your financial situation, you can make the right choices or form the right partnerships. You will make progress towards your goals.

➕ It is time to take appropriate advantage of the stability, vitality and dynamism that you are currently enjoying.

❤️ Genuine, well-balanced emotions and happy, stable relationships allow you to act confidently and achieve the success you are looking for in your love life.

👪 A happy, well-balanced family life allows you to act confidently to obtain what you want or to achieve the goals you have set yourself.

📝 Clear and impartial judgement will allow you to obtain what is rightfully yours. You will be successful in your undertakings, creating for yourself a positive, well-balanced professional environment.

💼 Your secure and soundly based financial situation allows you to attain some interesting objectives or obtain what is rightfully yours.

19 7

➕ Slowly but surely your health and vitality will enable you to establish genuine and long-lasting feelings of stability.

❤️ The happiness you are currently experiencing in your love life causes you to question yourself and reappraise a number of important aspects of your character and to rediscover your inner poise.

👪 Whatever is brought to light concerning your family will be beneficial, helping to make life more stable and secure.

📝 You may enter into an agreement or partnership, but it must be based on a solid, genuine foundation because it will demand discipline and honesty.

💼 In time and as a result of healthy finances, you will find the resources to achieve your specific goals.

19 8

19 9

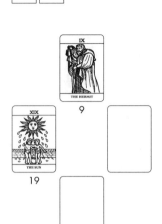

9

19

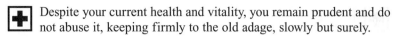

➕ Despite your current health and vitality, you remain prudent and do not abuse it, keeping firmly to the old adage, slowly but surely.

❤ The healthy, happy relationship you currently enjoy is bringing about changes within you and making you question aspects of yourself. This is all for the good.

👪 The happiness and harmony in your family environment help to clarify the way ahead and to emphasize the need for you to do all you can to maintain stable relationships.

📋 An agreement, partnership or positive or fortunate event allows you carefully and realistically to assess its short- or long-term implications and benefits.

A happy, positive event related to your financial situation allows you to evaluate the future consequences or advantages in detail.

19 10

10

19

➕ Your healthy, vibrant energy puts you in control of yourself and of your personal development.

❤ The strong and happy emotional relationship you are enjoying will give you complete confidence in yourself, and you can be sure that you will make progress and enjoy a positive future.

👪 Family harmony and happiness bring you great joy and confidence. You feel in full control, able to move forwards in a positive way.

📋 An agreement, partnership, clarification or happy event at work makes you confident that matters will now progress, allowing you to take control of the situation and exploit it.

Good news about your finances gives you confidence and puts you back at the helm, with the prospect of even more positive developments to come.

➕ You are enjoying great vitality together with excellent discipline and self-control.

19 11

❤️ You are entering a healthy, strong, genuine, deep and rewarding emotional relationship that gives you complete confidence in yourself and in your circumstances.

👪 The harmony and happiness governing your family life and the positive influence you are exerting over it allow you to achieve your goals; this will have a beneficial effect on your situation.

📋 An agreement, a partnership or a positive, happy event currently taking place turns out to be highly profitable, putting you in control of events and operations and thus placing all the available resources at your disposal.

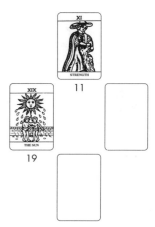

🎰 An agreement or a positive and fortunate event is taking place, bringing with it certain advantages and putting you in full control of your circumstances.

➕ A desire for clear, constructive and intelligent action will have a positive outcome, even if you are aware of your limits and may feel that you do not currently have the resources for such action.

19 12

❤️ A special relationship or a genuine, happy union will encourage you to act in a constructive, intelligent manner. It will release you from existing limitations and put you in control of the situation.

👪 Take advantage of matters being clarified or a fortunate event to remove certain constraints and regain control of your family environment once more.

📋 Some positive news or development or matters being made clear gives you the necessary power and authority to release yourself from the constraints and other factors currently preventing your progress.

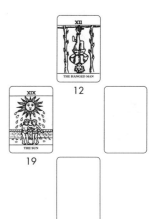

🎰 The clarification of something or a beneficial event allows you to adopt a firm position, escape from your constraints and obligations and regain control.

19 13

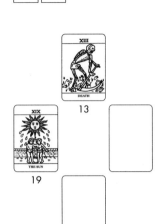

13

19

 Take advantage of your well-being and vital energy to make a radical, essential change in your life. The effects can only be positive.

A happy event in your emotional life or the development of a genuine, deep and trustworthy union brings about a turning point or radical change.

The immediate consequence of a happy event in your family life will be a major, positive change, causing you great happiness and real satisfaction.

An agreement, partnership or positive event, supported by an influential person, is the catalyst for fundamental and beneficial change in your life.

Positive results allow you to bring about a real change in your financial situation and to conclude an extremely profitable deal.

19 14

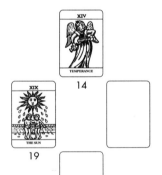

14

19

 You have high levels of vital energy and are maintaining stability by making the right choices, adapting to circumstances and letting things take their natural course.

Relax and enjoy your happy, special relationship, confident in the certainty that your feelings are fully reciprocated.

Thanks to the harmony and happiness that is currently reigning in your family life, you can make timely and wise choices that will be useful for making the best possible agreement.

Everything is ready so that negotiations can now take place under the most positive conditions to enable you to reach the best possible agreement or make the best possible choice.

The clarification of something or a positive event within your financial situation means that your choices, negotiations, transactions or agreements will all meet with success.

You have plenty of vital energy, are in great physical form and feel the need to exert yourself. Do as you see fit, but avoid taking any risks or overdoing things.

Your current, special relationship or union guarantees that, no matter what you undertake in your love life, you will achieve what you want.

Make sure you take this opportunity to enjoy a happy and beneficial family environment and you will achieve all your goals.

Whatever your actions or objectives, you are guaranteed success in your goals and targets and in the fulfilment of your dreams. Enjoy your opportunities – everything is going your way.

Profit from your circumstances and realize your financial goals. Now is the time to relish the opportunities confronting you.

You are full of energy and confidence, but you need to be on your guard. An unexpected physical of psychological shock may upset your balance.

Be alert as far as your love life is concerned, and do not rely too much on appearances at present. There is a risk that an apparently healthy, well-balanced relationship will suddenly be challenged.

Despite the harmonious, serene stability in your family life, do not forget that an upheaval, a challenge or an unexpected, disrupting event can lurk around the corner.

All seems well, giving you a clear view of your circumstances, but be aware that such situations can always be challenged. However, if it comes to a legal decision, expect matters to go your way.

Despite your well-balanced, clear-cut financial situation, do not forget that such situations can always change. Take care and act with thought and moderation.

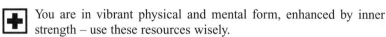

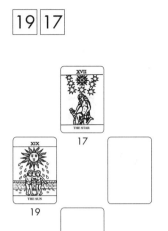

You are in vibrant physical and mental form, enhanced by inner strength – use these resources wisely.

The special relationship you currently enjoy fulfils all your wishes – you are delighted.

A happy event in your family life is exactly what you have long been hoping and praying for, filling you with joy.

Everything is in place for you to achieve something new or unique in your professional life. It is all you could have hoped for or dreamed of.

You learn about or discover by chance a new and positive fact that helps to fulfil your hopes and brings financial benefits.

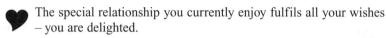

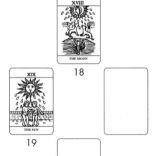

By adopting a positive attitude and looking for clarification in issues of health, you can make progress and bid farewell to your feelings of anxiety or weakness.

There is a risk that shadows will darken the joyful emotions you are currently feeling. Adopt a healthy, positive attitude and shed all possible light on the matters that are disturbing your emotional life and your problems will be solved of their own accord.

Your family life may appear happy or harmonious, but problems still need to be resolved and mistakes put right before it can really move on.

Uncertainty or adverse and disruptive factors are preventing you from making positive progress. However, your work environment throws light on them, allowing them be resolved.

You are sorting out your finances so well that problem areas are highlighted and are thus easier to solve.

➕ The confirmation of your state of health can enable you to make a full recovery, or restore your vitality in a very positive way.

♥ Let yourself be swept along spontaneously by the special relationship you are currently enjoying. Any happy event in your love life will bring with it a positive revival or significant change.

👪 The clarification of something or a happy event helps to restore harmony and normality to your family situation.

📋 A clarification or positive event allows you to put your affairs on a more stable footing, bringing about a renewal or beneficial change and releasing you from a number of constraints.

💰 A positive event or a clarification will help to get your financial situation back on its feet again and bring about a renewal or a beneficial change.

19 20

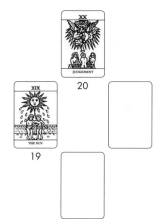

20

19

➕ You are full of energy and positively vibrant good health, and this gives you the opportunity for real self-fulfilment.

♥ Your current, happy relationship and genuinely requited feelings are helping to make your dreams come true.

👪 The current harmony and happiness in your family life, over which you are exercising intelligent and sympathetic control, are bringing you happiness and contentment.

📋 You have the means at your disposal to obtain everything you want, to get your way and to find great satisfaction in activities that encourage the expansion of your work situation.

💰 A healthy, clear-cut and positive financial situation allows you to act as you see fit – to make investments, widen your horizons and enjoy your assets to the full.

19 21

21

19

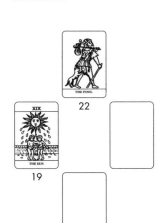

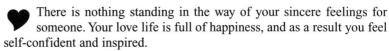 You are on top form and brimming with vitality. You can spread your wings, travel and live life as you see fit.

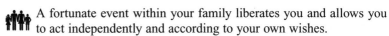 There is nothing standing in the way of your sincere feelings for someone. Your love life is full of happiness, and as a result you feel self-confident and inspired.

A fortunate event within your family liberates you and allows you to act independently and according to your own wishes.

A positive event in your working life frees you from all constraints and may encourage you to take action, to make a sudden departure or to put your own ideas into practice.

Well-ordered and positive finances allow you to undertake whatever you need to make the most of this situation, or to make a journey.

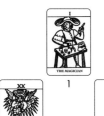

An important change – a rejuvenation or complete recovery – allows you to get off on the right footing. Once again, you now have everything you need to achieve personal fulfilment.

A revival or change in your love life encourages fortuitous and intelligent initiatives, bringing you the wherewithal to achieve your plans and see your dreams come true.

Some significant change or revival in your family circumstances encourages inspired initiatives. There will be an accompanying, natural improvement or the welcome achievement of a child or young person close to you.

A noticeable change or revival favours an improvement in your work situation. However, this depends on the overall action you take, your own professional ability or that of a colleague.

A revival or change allows you to take carefully considered initiatives to expand your financial position. Seize this opportunity.

➕ A revitalization, change or a speedy and much needed recovery is underway, much to your surprise.

❤️ Emotional renewal or change is about to take place. Alternatively, you are going to have an encounter that surprises you. Your feelings will be rekindled and even if you refuse to believe it, it is beyond your power to change things. Accept the facts as they are.

👪 You have reservations about the change occurring within the family, which is rather too sudden for your taste. You have to welcome it, while maintaining stability and keeping your own counsel with your natural caution and clear-sightedness.

📋 You learn about some new development, an interesting proposition or a liberating change. It is just what you were expecting, but you will still look at it carefully before voicing your opinion.

📇 Expect to hear good news about your financial situation in the form of a liberating change or revitalization. No doubt this will be something you have been expecting, and it may be related to calculations you have been making in private.

➕ Thanks to a renewal or evident change, you will be able to benefit more reasonably and more healthily from your overall well-being.

❤️ An emotional renewal or change will ensure that you receive forgiveness or reassurance from someone close to you. This is someone whose feelings are reliable, allowing you to consolidate your love life in the best and most secure way.

👪 Changes in your family life meet with the approval or receive the support of someone close, allowing you to assume a responsible and fuller role.

📋 A proposition, change or new arrangement, coming from an influential person, favours a fruitful business affair.

📇 A necessary but appropriate revival or change in your financial situation allows you to take the right course of action and conclude some interesting business deals.

20 4

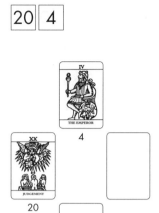

4

20

➕ Reconsider your options and attitudes to your health, or take advantage of a recovery or revitalization of some kind to make decisive choices affecting your stability and well-being.

♥ A change or revival in your love life reinforces your feelings and encourages you to make important choices – even to make peace, if necessary – or to reach the best possible accord.

👪 A change or renewal that takes place in your family life – involving specific, decisive choices – provides an opportunity for you to follow the excellent advice that is offered to you.

📋 A change or revival of some kind allows you to reach a constructive agreement – or to make specific and decisive choices – which will put you in firm control of the situation.

📋 You are back in control of financial matters and confident about any associated choices, decisions and opinions as a result of a change or revival.

20 5

5

20

➕ A prompt recovery or positive change encourages you to be more reasonable and responsible and to show the determination required to overcome health problems for once and for all.

♥ A return to normality or a change or revival is about to take place in your love life. It can have nothing but positive consequences.

👪 Your family situation is undergoing a renewal. Under your influence – or with the support of someone close, whom you can trust implicitly – something positive is developing.

📋 Following some new proposition or change, your circumstances will undergo revitalization or definite progress. This may be the result of your own influence or of the propitious intervention of an important person, with whom you have already had dealings.

📋 Your financial situation is continuing to improve. Go on making the same efforts and you will be able to achieve your objectives.

The current change or revival that you are experiencing should encourage you to make sensible choices that will enable you to be well-balanced and retain your free will.

A change or new development in your love life leads you to make clear, disciplined and impartial decisions.

Changes or a revitalization in your family life will lead to hard choices. Some sort of serious agreement, or impartial resolution, will be involved.

Remain as impartial as you can to any proposed change or revival at work. Take the sensible option and accept any strict, but fair, agreement that is reached.

Your finances are being revitalized or are returning to a more normal state of affairs leading you to make some hard decisions, but also giving you more freedom and making you more responsible for the stabilty of your situation.

 The renewal or change that you are undergoing makes you more mature. It also makes you certain of the direction you are taking and more conscious of what you want to do or achieve.

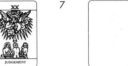

You are learning of a change or revival that is underway in your love life. This allows you to achieve your emotional goals or to find exactly what it is you are looking for.

Thanks to a change or renewal in your family life, you will know exactly what to do to achieve the goals you have set yourself.

You receive a proposal and it is exactly what you have been expecting or hoping for. Alternatively, a change or revitalization of your situation lets you take cautious but effective action to reach your targets.

Thanks to a revival or change in events, you are able to take cautious, realistic and effective action to improve your position and achieve your financial objectives.

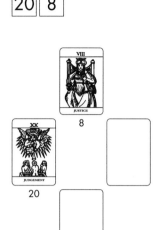

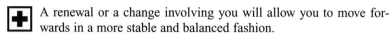 A renewal or a change involving you will allow you to move forwards in a more stable and balanced fashion.

A change or renewal in your love life will allow you to find emotional stability or to submit yourself naturally to some discipline with regard to your behaviour.

A change in or revitalization of your family situation allows it to progress in a stable, well-balanced manner. There may even be a favourable outcome for everyone.

New circumstances or changes at work will lead to stable progress and some deserved rewards for you.

Your financial situation improves considerably as a result of some kind of renwal or change. You need to remain disciplined yet flexible enough to adapt quickly to financial regulations or normal economic practice.

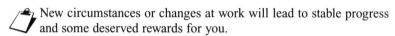 You have the willpower to bring about change, revitalization or recovery and courageously assess your lifestyle. You have good reason to behave cautiously and wisely in this area of your life.

The change or revival you are experiencing in your love life allows you to take control of the situation, demonstrating your wisdom and moral courage.

You tend to view the current change or renewal in matters relating to your family with realism and circumspection. As a result, nothing escapes you, and a successful outcome is guaranteed.

To be sure of complete success, be realistic and cautious when studying suggestions for any changes or renewals at work.

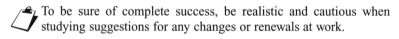 You are taking cautious, moderate and realistic action to bring about a change, improvement or even a revitalization of your financial situation. This astute behaviour will ensure your success.

✚ The recovery or change you have managed to achieve in your health is of great benefit. Now that you enjoy a feeling of well-being, you can go from strength to strength.

♥ Irrespective of the nature or origin of the changes you are currently experiencing, they are helping you in emotional matters. Move forwards and be positive.

A current change is giving you the freedom to take sensible and rewarding steps to help your family life evolve in a positive manner.

Take advantage of the change or renewal of some kind that is currently underway to advance your professional position.

Your finances are improving or undergoing a revival. This should allow you keep money matters on an upward curve.

✚ The current recovery or change in your health allows you to rediscover your self-confidence and to achieve complete freedom.

♥ The renewal or change your are currently experiencing in your love life is restoring your full confidence in the situation and putting you in control of events and circumstances.

A change or renewal of some kind has been imposed on your family life, but by positive circumstances or actions. This is restoring your confidence and guaranteeing success in any family-related venture that you undertake.

A current renewal or change is restoring your self-confidence, putting you in charge of the situation and giving you the freedom to embark on ambitious and constructive projects.

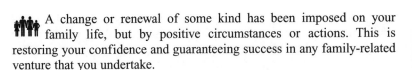

The current renewal or change is allowing you to take things in hand and improve your financial situation.

Despite a change or revitalization, or the recovery you are currently enjoying, you are still plagued by feelings of unease and feel obliged to take precautions. However, this is a sign that the situation will improve.

A change or renewal that is happening in your love life is preventing you from enjoying complete independence or freeing yourself from personal constraints. Don't worry, though, this is a promising start.

Despite the change or revival that is happening in your family life, you are not being released sufficiently from obligations or constraints. Nevertheless, it is possible to identify exactly what is holding you back and preventing necessary moves, which is at least some help.

A change or renewal of some kind is afoot at work but it will not give you the independent or more autonomous role you hoped for in your professional activities. Nevertheless, recognize that this is an improvement of sorts.

Despite the current change or revival in your affairs, you are not yet free from duties or obligations. However, your financial situation is improving sufficiently for you to face up to any remaining problems.

The recovery or revival that is currently underway incites you to make important choices. These will bring about a radical change in your behaviour and solve your health problems once and for all.

A revival of your love life raises difficult yet vital choices concerning matters of the heart as you know that a major change will follow.

The new developments in your current family situation may well encourage you to make hard, but necessary and decisive, choices to bring about a radical change.

The revival currently underway in your work situation could well lead you to conclude some profitable agreement or make an important choice. In turn, this will bring about a radical change.

Your finances are improving and going through a period of renewal. This is a favourable climate for choices, decisions, profitable agreements and radical changes.

Take advantage of the change, revival or even recovery that you are currently experiencing to regenerate yourself still further by recognizing and complying more with your vital needs.

The revival or happy change underway in your love life assures you that ways will be found to allow you to achieve your desires.

The pleasant change in your family life or a renewal of some kind means that everything will now work out for the best.

Thanks to the renewal or welcome change underway in your work, you are able to achieve your objectives and will be sure that the negotiations are successful.

Your financial situation will improve dramatically and you will be able to achieve what you want as a result of a useful change or revival. However, you will only achieve your goals if you remain determined and steadfast.

14

20

The change or revival you are currently experiencing is proving very demanding, or it is prompting you to adopt a very strict regime of self-discipline.

Stronger feelings provoked by a renewal or change are making you take greater control of matters, allowing you to channel any otherwise excesses or passion in the right direction.

Unjustifiable excesses or difficulties are disrupting your family life. However, you can deal with these in a fair and impartial way thanks to the change or renewal that is taking place.

Thanks to a change or revival of some kind that is currently taking place, you are able to contain your impatience and to channel to your advantage all the troubles and disorder that may otherwise have destabilized your position.

A current change or revitalization means that you need to be disciplined if you are to take better advantage of your financial situation.

15

20

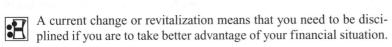

20 16

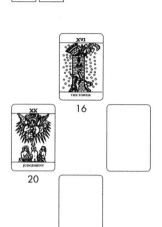

16

20

The renewal or change you are currently experiencing, combined with your awareness of it, will free you of your constraints and allow some beneficial soul-searching to take place.

There is renewal or change in your emotional life, bringing with it a disturbing but healthy awakening and awareness. It is time for some unlooked-for soul searching.

A change or revival in your family situation will lead you to take steps that could disrupt matters still further. However, it will be for the best in the long run.

A change or some kind of renewal is the likely precursor to some disruption or challenge at work; you are intelligent enough to appreciate its importance.

A revival or change that is occurring now should allow you to clarify your financial situation or to raise some useful questions.

20 17

17

20

You are undergoing a period of revival or change in both your physical health and general attitudes. On the whole, this ought to result in favourable personal progress.

Circumstances are right for a complete revival or positive change in your love life, prompting something new, such as a birth, a happy occurrence or some sort of innovation.

The current renewal or change in your family life will result in a period of transformation or innovation, during which a happy event – such as a birth or something new – is sure to happen.

Changes or a revitalization currently taking place should allow you to benefit from exceptional circumstances and to gain enhanced status or to make progress in some way.

You ought now to start to benefit from fortunate circumstances and to take full advantage of your resources thanks to a revitalization or change.

➕ Thanks to a current change or revitalization, your confidence in yourself and your capabilities is experiencing a boost, allowing you to manage your problems and overcome any difficulties more successfully.

❤️ The current renewal or change in your love life is giving you the necessary emotional strength to resolve any problems, difficulties or conflicts.

👪 Due to a change or renewal on the home front you have regained the resources and courage to overcome the difficulties you are encountering and thus to take control of matters relating to your family.

📋 The change or revival that is currently taking place is giving you the necessary resources or means to resolve any problems and difficulties that you will face.

💶 You have restored confidence in yourself and in your situation, giving you the means to overcome all current financial issues thanks to a current change or revitalization.

20 18

18

20

➕ You are going to experience a spectacular recovery or a positive change and feel on top form once again.

❤️ The change or renewal that you are experiencing in your love life is removing all the hindrances to your special relationships and genuine feelings, bringing you joy and happiness.

👪 A liberating change is currently occurring in your family life and justifiably giving rise to joy and happiness

📋 You will obtain satisfaction thanks to a renewal or change that is going to take place and that will remove the obstacles that stand in the way of your success.

💶 The liberating change and the renewal currently taking place bring with them increased clarity or a marked improvement in your financial situation. Complete satisfaction is coming your way.

20 19

19

20

A current revival or change in health matters allows you to see how to achieve fulfilment and regain your strength and inner well-being.

Thanks to the current climate of change or renewal, your love life will achieve complete fulfilment and you are assured of the support and deep feelings of the person closest to you.

With the support of a responsible or reliable person who is close to you, the change or renewal of some kind that is currently underway should favour a fortuitous family gathering.

The change and renewal currently taking place at work should favour the development of your situation, with the support of an influential person. Alternatively, you could be given more responsibility and greater scope at work.

Thanks to the current change or revival, you should be able to expect an improvement in your financial situation.

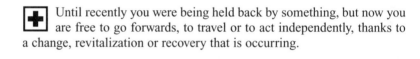

Until recently you were being held back by something, but now you are free to go forwards, to travel or to act independently, thanks to a change, revitalization or recovery that is occurring.

Changed or revitalized circumstances in your emotional life are making you contemplate leaving suddenly to achieve your goals or to join someone you have been thinking about for some time.

The change or renewal in your family situation will lead to a departure, greater mobility, a house move or an important transition in your life.

The proposal you are considering or the renewal of some kind that is currently underway encourages you to leave at short notice to take a new job or to take swift action to improve your professional life.

When it comes to your finances, a current change or revival allows you to act freely and to set out in search of new horizons.

➕ You possess everything that is necessary to be able to act freely, undertake new things, travel and gain total self-fulfilment.

♥ You are full of good intentions. Nonetheless, perhaps you are being slightly clumsy in expressing your feelings. Try to see things from a different point of view and remember that it is not the gift but the way it is given that matters.

👨‍👩‍👧 Thanks to a stable and fulfilled family life, you are able to leave without any difficulty if this is what you need or want to do, or take the initiative in moving house or in introducing an important change.

📋 Now is the time for action or creativity or to seize a work-related opportunity. Be dynamic.

💰 You now have sufficient means to dispose of any financial assets as you see fit. However, don't succumb to too many impulse purchases and extravagances.

1

21

➕ Your mental and physical resources are good and you are showing a reserve, stability and moral strength that do you credit.

♥ You are benefitting from a fulfilling love life with relationships that are genuine, deep and discreet.

👨‍👩‍👧 Your family life seems to be completely fulfilled thanks to the influence of a close couple.

📋 The discreet and helpful influence of an important and supportive person, who has confidence in you, is encouraging you to spread your wings, take on greater responsibilities and gain more influence.

💰 You are disposing of your funds with generosity, but are still aware of your responsibilities and duties, which makes your financial situation privileged but stable.

2

21

21 3

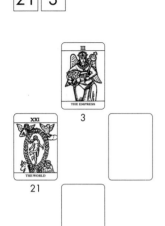

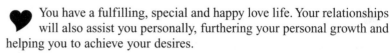 All is well at the moment. Make the most of being in such good health and enjoy your stability and well-being.

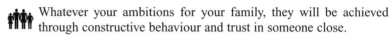 You have a fulfilling, special and happy love life. Your relationships will also assist you personally, furthering your personal growth and helping you to achieve your desires.

Whatever your ambitions for your family, they will be achieved through constructive behaviour and trust in someone close.

You are going to conclude the perfect deal that allows you to act more independently and profitably. New horizons will open up, widening the scope of your job or your responsibilities.

Whatever your current assets or advantages, you can take full advantage of them and genuinely enjoy them. However, you are having trouble resisting temptation.

 21 4

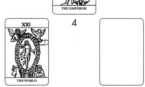

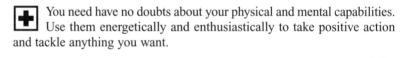 You need have no doubts about your physical and mental capabilities. Use them energetically and enthusiastically to take positive action and tackle anything you want.

All is set for you to obtain or achieve everything you want in your love life and to do so in the way you feel is best.

A fulfilling and happy family such as yours can be built on and developed with guaranteed success.

You now have everything you need to take action to get positive and constructive results as fast as possible. This is the time to achieve your objectives, to carry through any major projects or to improve your situation.

You are in an advantageous situation, with vast financial opportunities. Use these freely and act in a constructive, intelligent way.

➕ You are in good form, fulfilled and well-balanced. When necessary, you know how to maintain a certain discipline in order to sustain your good health and well-being.

❤️ A fulfilled, happy and well-balanced love life promotes your personal development and encourages your innate sense of duty and responsibility.

👪 Your family situation is happy and secure, supported by a responsible person who is close to you and whom you can trust implicitly.

📋 Progress is possible only if you accept a degree of self-discipline and the criticism of your peers or if you obtain the support of an influential person.

🗄️ Although your situation is flourishing, keep your eye on sensible financial practices and adopt a reasonable, responsible and careful attitude to money.

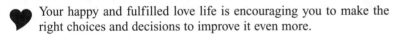

➕ Your mental and physical resources are good and you can thus make some wise choices and resolutions aimed at maintaining your balance and well-being.

❤️ Your happy and fulfilled love life is encouraging you to make the right choices and decisions to improve it even more.

👪 Circumstances are ideal for a decision that will help your family situation to progress or achieve fulfilment.

📋 If your situation at work is to improve, you need to reach an agreement. However, in order to do this you must assemble all the elements that are in your favour so that you have the best possible conditions in which to carry out your plans.

🗄️ The expansion of your financial situation allows you to make realistic, careful and wise choices and avoid being overtaken by events.

21 7

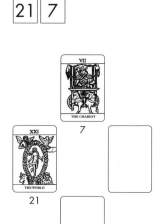

VII
THE CHARIOT

7

XXI
THE WORLD

21

✚ You are in good shape mentally and physically, and are currently enjoying a period of change and fulfilment that brings with it the opportunity for action, travel or dynamic behaviour.

♥ A happy, fulfilled love life has positive surprises in store and is set to develop well. Success in affairs of the heart is assured.

👪 Everything that you undertake is set to help your family make progress and enjoy success.

🗒 The opportunities offered to you encourage rapid development at work. You will find it relatively easy to achieve success in future projects and achieve your objectives.

▦ You are benefiting from a financial situation that is favourable and expanding. As a result, you will rapidly achieve your objectives and be successful in your plans.

21 8

VIII
JUSTICE

8

XXI
THE WORLD

21

✚ You are in good form and will achieve overall stability through your own courage, strong will and strength of character.

♥ You can have complete confidence in the stable progress of your love life. Relax in a happy, fulfilled and secure relationship.

👪 Your family situation is evolving or expanding in a logical, assured and welcome fashion. As a result it will become even more stable, balanced and fulfilling.

🗒 A change or major improvement is happening at work, resulting in a more stable and stronger position for you. However, it does demand a degree of self-discipline on your part.

▦ An expansion or amalgamation will render your financial situation more stable, and better balanced than before.

21 **9**

➕ Take full advantage of your current good health but be calm, cautious and moderate in the use of your energy.

❤️ You are now aware to what extent the person dear to you encourages your attentions. Their positive behaviour and feelings will prove to be sincere and intelligent.

👪 An improved family situation is allowing you to take clear, precise and profitable action on its behalf.

📋 Your working situation is evolving and expanding and new resources or conditions are on offer. It is all very much to your advantage and benefit.

💰 You are going to take full advantage of your financial situation. Significant profits and gains are now within your reach.

9

21

21 **10**

➕ Take full advantage of feeling good to ensure that you can achieve personal growth and fulfilment. Have confidence and make the most of your personal qualities.

❤️ Do not doubt the rapid progress or fulfilment in your love life or the helpful influence of someone who is near you or in your thoughts.

 Your family situation is undergoing a period of rapid, constructive development and expansion, guided by you or under the beneficial influence, authority and protection of someone close to you.

📋 Take advantage of favourable circumstances to demonstrate your authority and determination and you will enjoy rapid and constructive progression on a professional level.

 Make sure you have all possible advantages at your disposal and move your financial situation forwards in a constructive, intelligent and profitable manner.

10

21

21 11

11

21

All your personal qualities, your moral courage and sense of responsibility help you to prove your strength of character. You are on good form and have plenty of energy.

Your happy, fulfilled love life is based on a sound emotional relationship, and you should be able to achieve anything you want in this area.

When it comes to improving your family situation you will succeed in anything you undertake, enabling it to flourish.

Your work situation is progressing remarkably well, bringing with it an increased range of activities as well as significant protection and support. You are guaranteed success in anything you undertake.

You are aware not only of the opportunities and advantages available to you but also of your moral and physical obligations, so you are in perfect control of your financial situation.

21 12

12

21

In order to make good progress in terms of your personal growth you need to make some firm decisions; perhaps even making a few sacrifices wouldn't go amiss.

Enjoy the current peaceful and fulfilled nature of your love life, even if you are finding it a little restrictive or are not feeling completely satisfied by it yet.

In order to help your family situation develop and prosper you are being forced to make some sensible but tricky decisions, and some sacrifices may even prove necessary.

Your work situation is making progress, but, as a result, you are being forced to reach agreements, take important decisions and even to make some concessions and sacrifices. However, the sacrifices should prove useful in the long run and you will be compensated for them.

You may have certain advantages on the financial front or things may be progressing well, but you do still appear to have some important decisions or even sacrifices to make or certain limits that you should set yourself.

You have all the personal resources and qualities you need to make a radical, dynamic change in your life and to make quick progress towards finding complete fulfilment.

♥ Your love life will make rapid and significant progress and undergo some radical but extremely beneficial changes.

Matters on the domestic front are moving along well and quickly. There will be some radical but beneficial changes in this area.

Your work situation is making progress, and this will make it possible for there to be some significant but profitable changes. Any action taken with a view to a reform of some kind will be successful.

Your financial situation is currently improving, and you are guaranteed success in anything you do in connection with making a profit, concluding a deal or moving things forward in general.

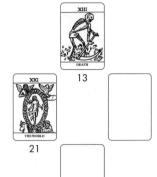

 You are receptive, fulfilled and well-balanced. You are also adaptable, which makes it easier for you to adjust and give yourself a new lease of life.

♥ You have a fulfilled and stable love life, which you should be able to enjoy with confidence.

Take advantage of the fact that your family life is calm and flourishing to make the appropriate arrangements to preserve its peace and stability.

You will find it worth your while to seek rational, well-timed compromises or agreements that are likely to help your work situation progress further or to enable you to obtain what is rightfully yours.

Your financial situation is on an even keel and doing well, and all your efforts should be rewarded.

21 15

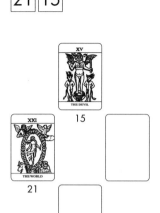

XXI

15

21

➕ You have everything you need to achieve personal growth and fulfilment. You also have plenty of energy and are well aware how lucky you are in this, so take advantage of it.

♥ You are naturally generous and open and act from the best of motives, but don't lose sight of the fact that your feelings are highly charged and have some troubling aspects. Once you are aware of this, nothing will stop you from getting what you want.

👪 You are well placed to achieve what you want for your family in terms of happiness, fulfilment and progress.

📋 The results you are achieving are certainly beyond your wildest expectations and will lead to progress and improvement in your work situation.

💰 You can now fully satisfy your financial ambitions or take advantage of profitable financial circumstances.

21 16

XXI

16

21

➕ You have everything you need to make a liberating change and quickly get rid of anything that is standing in the way of your personal growth. Your sense of well-being will be completely restored.

♥ Everything is ready for you to make rapid progress and achieve complete fulfilment in your love life. This will also involve upheavals that, although unexpected, will prove beneficial.

👪 A significant upheaval is needed in order for your family situation to make some progress, but it should prove liberating and beneficial.

📋 The current progress you are experiencing in work-related matters or the success you are currently enjoying brings with it an inevitable upheaval. However, this will prove liberating and will help you achieve your ambitions.

💰 The rapid progress in your financial situation brings about significant upheaval and some liberating but beneficial challenges.

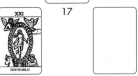

✚ You are not only confident of your personal resources and qualities but are also energetic and receptive. So, make the most of your good health and well-being.

♥ At the moment you are capable of achieving everything you have ever hoped for. Have confidence in the strength of your feelings and enjoy a great love life that will bring you everything you want.

As far as your family life is concerned, you are capable of achieving all your hopes and dreams. Don't think twice about taking constructive, innovative action or about embarking on something new. Success is guaranteed.

At present anything you try to do or achieve is successful. So, take advantage of this useful state of affairs to make some progress in your work situation or even to break new ground.

Current circumstances are extremely beneficial and will help the positive development of your financial circumstances and make it possible for you to make the best use of your resources.

✚ Health problems are hindering your personal development, damaging your well-being and preventing you from achieving fulfilment. You must, therefore, give your health some serious attention.

♥ Problems or conflicts are preventing you from making progress in your love life. You must make some concessions, acknowledge your mistakes and overcome your disappointments.

Problems or conflicts are preventing your family situation from progressing. You may need to make sacrifices or acknowledge your mistakes in order to break the current stalemate.

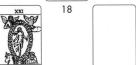

Your work situation has reached an impasse because of adverse circumstances, delays or the need for you to make concessions or even sacrifices.

Your work situation has reached an impasse because of adverse

You can't make any progress in your financial situation because of problems or delays. This is forcing you to make sacrifices and preventing you from making full use of your resources.

21 19

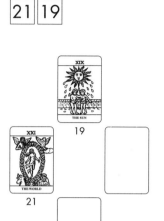

XIX · THE SUN

19

XXI · THE WORLD

21

✚ You are confident of your personal resources and qualities and are in fine shape with plenty of energy.

♥ You are currently doing well in your love life, obtaining everything you want. So, take advantage of it.

👪 Tackle anything you like within your family situation and you will be successful.

📋 You are certain of complete success no matter what your ambitions or achievements are, no matter what partnerships you are considering and no matter what you are currently undertaking. Good progress will be made on the professional front.

🀰 Your financial situation is profitable and you have it well under control. Enjoy it as much as you can.

21 20

XX · JUDGEMENT

20

XXI · THE WORLD

21

✚ The improvement in your well-being will permit you to make a full recovery if you have been experiencing health problems or give you a new lease of life.

♥ You have everything you need to make a significant, beneficial change in your love life or to put it on a new footing.

👪 Your family life is happy and fulfilled. Thanks to the significant support you are receiving, it is undergoing a period of beneficial change or revitalization.

📋 Progress in your work situation leads to a change that will be encouraged or supported by an influential person.

🀰 Conditions are just right for the natural progression of your financial situation and may involve a change that will prove profitable or that will involve renewal of some kind.

➕ You are feeling completely fulfilled and in great shape. Follow your instincts, do as you like and travel as the mood takes you.

❤ You will meet someone who will be the answer to your dreams. Alternatively, you may leave to meet or rejoin someone you love or make a journey with someone you love that will bring you both much joy and happiness.

👪 Success and progress govern everything you do in your family life. No matter what happens, you will not be disappointed.

📋 Thanks to the current developments in your work situation and the success you are experiencing, you can do what you want, confident of your actions and of anything you undertake.

💰 Positive developments in your financial situation allow you to move your money around and do anything you want with the certainty that you will be successful.

21

➕ You are dynamic, impulsive and not lacking in initiative or good intentions. However, take care because you tend to try to do too much too quickly or to be over-enthusiastic.

❤ Your enthusiasm makes you impulsive and irrepressible, and you are often bold and hasty in your love life and intolerant of delays. In other words, you want it all and you want it now – but is this wise?

👪 Either you or, possibly, a young person at the heart of your family circle will leave home suddenly, move house or break away in order to begin a new life.

📋 On a sudden impulse you will either leave or change your job or quickly instigate a new work-related venture. There are a lot of options open to you, but try not to do too many things at once or with too much haste.

💰 You have the resources to make a journey or leave on a whim, or you could take new initiatives relating to your finances. Don't attempt to do too many things at once and avoid extravagance and hasty or impetuous action.

22

With good reason you are curbing your impulsiveness and tendency to be restless and to do too many things at once. Nevertheless, the stability that you achieve by moderating your behaviour doesn't affect your enthusiasm or need for action.

You will receive some news that you have been expecting about your love life. Alternatively, you set off to meet the person you are thinking about and who is expecting you.

Although your actions are probably slightly hasty, they will allow you to get your family situation moving again in the right direction and shake it out of its inertia. You should, however, be able to achieve all this without disrupting its stability.

Don't be over-zealous or too hasty. You need a combination of enthusiasm, wisdom and patience to achieve your goal.

Try to avoid mistakes, extravagance and hasty action in anything you do or during any journeys you make relating to your financial situation. Be restrained and careful with your money.

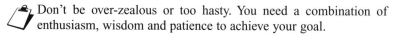

Your actions are being guided by your instincts. They are beneficial to your well-being, even though you do sometimes try to rely too much on your energy.

You decide to leave suddenly in order to meet someone you have been thinking about. Alternatively, you quickly decide to do something that will be beneficial to your love life.

A house move, a journey or an initiative of some kind will enable you to undertake something that proves highly beneficial to your family situation.

Any research, moves or action that you undertake will work well, allowing you either to take further action that is beneficial to your professional life or to succeed with your ideas and projects.

Initiatives, journeys or the movement of money are currently aiding your financial circumstances, enabling you to make the most of your advantages and to meet your financial objectives quickly.

➕ You seem to be sure of yourself, your decisions and your actions. Yet, despite your current dynamism and enthusiasm, you are keen to preserve your inner calm and well-being.

❤️ You have intense and impulsive feelings, but they are tempered by consideration for others because you are keen to behave in a constructive and sensible fashion in your love life.

👪 A journey or a house move allows you to take constructive, sensible action concerning your family situation in order to protect it and put it on an even keel.

📋 The move, trip or change of job you are embarking on at the moment enables you to put your ideas into practice, guarantees your position and brings you unequivocal success.

📠 Initiatives, journeys or the movement of money help your financial situation to become more solid and secure than ever.

$$\boxed{22}\ \boxed{4}$$

4

22

➕ Your impulsive nature, restlessness and tendency to try to do too many things at once are tempered by your sense of duty and conscience. Alternatively, you may have to see a doctor or a specialist for reassurance on health-related matters.

❤️ You will have an important encounter, or will set off to rejoin the person you have been thinking about and for whom you have deep and lasting feelings. Alternatively, you will be able to introduce some stability into your love life or your emotional relationships.

👪 You are duty-bound to make a journey or move or to take action of some sort relating to your family life. Alternatively, a change or house move helps to stabilize things and revives your sense of responsibility.

📋 Any trips or initiatives you take or any research you carry out will have every chance of success. Together with the solid support you receive, this will help to stabilize your work situation.

📠 Whatever you need to do on the financial front, such as moving funds around, taking initiatives or going on a journey, will bring stability to your financial situation and guarantee the support and backing you need.

$$\boxed{22}\ \boxed{5}$$

5

22

22 6

6

22

➕ Despite the fact that you try to do too many things at once and are a little chaotic and excitable, you are also dynamic and enthusiastic and keen to find some stability in your life. You therefore have some important choices to make.

❤️ You have complete freedom in your love life, and your feelings are both spontaneous and reckless. This does not bode well for a stable, clear-cut and balanced situation. You still have some important choices or decisions to make.

👪 You are keen to make some kind of agreement relating to your home life and to make important decisions that will put an end to the generally indecisive atmosphere. Alternatively, you decide to make a sudden departure.

📋 You will succeed in making some important decisions or in quickly reaching the agreement that you have been hoping to make. Alternatively, you will regain your independence in your work situation.

🎲 An initiative, a trip of some kind or a sum of money, received out of the blue, will put an end to your indecision or uncertainties. You will then be free to take the decisions affecting your financial concerns.

22 7

➕ Despite your impatience and slightly over-the-top behaviour, you are capable of overcoming your weak points, solving your problems and achieving your goals.

❤️ Nothing can prevent you from achieving everything you want in your love life, although it may entail a little agitation and upheaval and quite a few changes.

👪 You will move house, travel or achieve a positive outcome with regard to your family situation. As a result of your actions your domestic life will become rather unsettled and eventful, but for all the right reasons.

📋 Act quickly and energetically to change your job, improve your working conditions or achieve your objectives without delay. You are certain of success as long as you do not give up.

🎲 A useful initiative, a journey or a sum of money, received out of the blue, allows you to improve your financial situation and achieve your financial objectives.

➕ As you are able to channel your impulsive and restless feelings in the right direction, you are currently well placed to find stability, health and vitality.

❤️ Fortunately, your self-discipline is controlling your impulsive or rash feelings, obliging you to find a balance in your love life quickly, while submitting to certain rules or principles.

👪 Your vagueness, lack of self-discipline and mistakes are being judged harshly. Nevertheless, on the positive side, the guidelines to which you have subjected yourself are forcing you to try and achieve the balance that your family life needs.

📋 You are changing jobs, considering legal action or are on the verge of leaving in great haste. This suggests that you ought to submit to certain strict limits and principles if you want to see this turn out well.

💰 You will receive a sum of money unexpectedly, but will have to be strict with yourself in order to get matters back on a stable footing. Alternatively, following some reckless and rash spending, you will have to take firm control of your financial situation.

22 8

8

22

➕ You are looking for something that is vital to your well-being and will find it quickly. Alternatively, you will go somewhere on your own to get some rest or find a quiet place in which to rediscover yourself.

❤️ You set off to rejoin someone who is important to you and who is waiting for you. Alternatively, you will hear some news or discover an important fact relating to your love life. This will prompt you to think carefully and act cautiously.

👪 You have a cautious yet realistic attitude towards a house move, a change that is in the offing, some news you have heard or something you have discovered relating to your family situation.

📋 A current change in your work situation, an abrupt departure or an initiative that you take will help you to find realistic and prudent solutions to your problems.

💰 The money you are spending or allocating to something will make you feel the need to be cautious or to find realistic solutions to improve your financial situation.

22 9

9

22

22 10

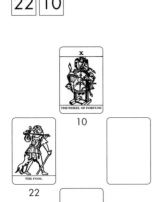

Your enthusiasm and determination ensure you make good progress. Nevertheless, you are a little unsettled and liable to experience some ups and downs.

You make a sudden departure and this, or the decision behind it, prompts some quick developments in your love life.

A house move, a sudden departure or some enthusiastic behaviour on your part causes rapid and positive developments within your family circle.

A journey, an activity or an initiative taken by you will lead to some rapid and positive developments concerning work matters.

A sum of money received out of the blue, a trip or an initiative will improve your financial situation rapidly.

22 11

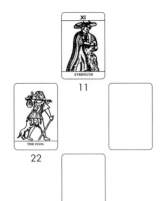

Despite the fact that you may be impulsive or a little unstable and feel the need to change things, you have excellent self-control and a great deal of energy.

Confident in yourself and your environment, you are making progress in your love life and should certainly find fulfilment.

Thanks to a house move, a departure or a change of some sort, you will be successful in any family-related undertakings.

You will soon find what you are looking for or receive a positive response to your demands. Alternatively, a journey or a move may reinforce your current position. Or, finally, you may have made up your mind to change jobs.

Your financial situation is strengthened by an initiative of some kind, a journey or some money received out of the blue. Any of these will assure you of financial success and peace of mind.

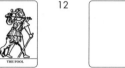

You are being irresponsible and, rather than taking positive steps towards solving your problems and improving your health, you persist in making mistakes and acting wildly. Get a grip on yourself!

You are not managing to express your desires and feelings because you are faced with a stalemate situation that is going nowhere. You would do better to forget about them.

Circumstances are not right for the house move, trip or other change that you are planning or currently undertaking. You will probably have to forget the idea.

You are forced to change jobs. On the other hand, you might need to cancel a journey or abandon a change that you have been planning. Alternatively, it may be that any action you take will be disappointing or unsuccessful.

Try to avoid mistakes and extravagant or reckless spending. If you don't, you might well find yourself in a difficult, financial situation that is going nowhere.

After going through an eventful and unstable period, you will experience a radical change. Alternatively, it may be that you are being forced to make this change because of your impulsive, reckless and badly timed behaviour.

You want to end a particular situation or a relationship suddenly. Alternatively, you leave and this will cause a radical change in your love life.

You feel a sudden desire to leave, to end a family-related situation or even to move house. Any of these will bring a period of your life to an end. Alternatively, you make a journey for family reasons.

You decide to change jobs suddenly, end a particular situation or take some action that proves successful and enables you to make some radical changes.

You can soon take advantage of a profitable situation. Alternatively, as a result of carelessness, extravagance or reckless spending, your funds could dry up.

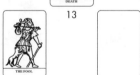

22 14

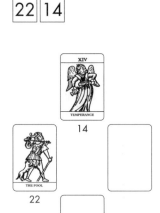

14

22

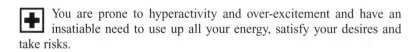 Despite your tendency towards extravagance and your unstable and impulsive behaviour, you nevertheless know when the time is right to be flexible and come to some sort of an agreement, and when you should make an effort.

Supported by the harmony and strength you are experiencing in your love life and with the intention of coming to a sensible agreement, you take a bold and well-timed decision to leave.

You have the opportunity to move house or to make arrangements or compromises that will be useful to your family situation.

You will make some useful arrangements that will soon help your work situation, or instigate an action of some sort or make a trip to negotiate a business deal or contract.

You are trying to negotiate a business deal or contract that may also involve making a journey. Alternatively, you are simply trying to bring your financial situation more into line with current circumstances and requirements.

22 15

15

22

You are prone to hyperactivity and over-excitement and have an insatiable need to use up all your energy, satisfy your desires and take risks.

Your impulses and desires have really taken hold of you and you feel that you must satisfy them at all costs. Nobody, except yourself, of course, can stop you from doing what you have decided to do, regardless of the consequences.

You decide to leave suddenly or to move house. Alternatively, you will not find peace of mind until you have achieved your goals. Make sure you consider the consequences carefully before you act, however.

You feel desperate to achieve something, to leave or to change jobs as soon as possible. The problem is that you are being too impatient or hasty and thus risk becoming the victim of your own irrational impulses and recklessness.

You are determined to get what you want financially as quickly as possible and at all costs. Make sure you consider the consequences that are likely before you act, however.

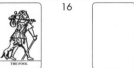

✚ To avoid upheavals or physical and psychological blows to your health, it is essential that you try to avoid feelings of impatience, irrational impulses and reckless action. Take care.

♥ Fired by anger, an emotional blow or a sudden impulse, you decide to leave or to turn everything upside down in your love life. No matter what else you do, avoid irrevocable actions that you might regret.

👪 A hasty departure or house move or a sudden change of some kind disrupts your family situation and raises some essential questions.

📋 Driven by anger, a sudden impulse or a firm decision, you change jobs or leave in a hurry. Alternatively, you raise some important questions or make drastic changes.

🗒 Reckless and extravagant spending is likely to cause you financial problems, unless you do something to break the stalemate you are currently experiencing.

✚ Either you are about to leave or you are planning to make a journey for pleasure or for health reasons. Whichever it is, it will do you the world of good, both psychologically and physically.

♥ You take great pleasure in a romantic stroll or trip. Alternatively, you meet someone who is the answer to your dreams and fills you with hope. Or, finally, you will meet again someone you love and be completely fulfilled and happy.

👪 A house move, a change of some kind, a family journey or a happy event will introduce something new to your domestic life and fulfil your hopes.

📋 You make a journey or trip or bring something new to your work situation that fulfils your aspirations and prompts a revitalization of your affairs.

🗒 A sum of money that you were hoping to obtain improves your financial circumstances. Alternatively, you take steps towards acquiring some new funds.

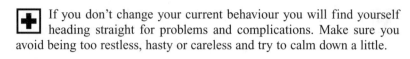

22 18

18

22

If you don't change your current behaviour you will find yourself heading straight for problems and complications. Make sure you avoid being too restless, hasty or careless and try to calm down a little.

You will soon realize the error of your ways. Alternatively, you may be disappointed and disillusioned or feel you are an emotional failure, but a large part of the blame lies with you.

A journey, a departure or a house move is likely to prove disappointing, or it will be cancelled or delayed due to problems or complications on the domestic front.

Anything you seek or undertake or any journeys you make will either fail or be disappointing. If you are planning to change jobs, now is not the right time. Don't be too hasty: you will only regret it.

If you don't change your behaviour you will soon experience financial problems. Alternatively, any action you take or investigations you undertake regarding your financial situation will fail or the results will be poor.

CURRENT SITUATION

22 19

19

22

If you are planning to go away for pleasure, don't hesitate; it will do you the world of good. Otherwise, go ahead and use some of your energy. You have plenty of it.

You will soon meet someone special, make a romantic journey, join someone you love or enter a new and promising relationship.

A family journey, house move or change in your family situation makes you happy and satisfied, bringing with it certain success.

A beneficial change in your work situation brings you a great deal of satisfaction. Alternatively, you reach an agreement, enter a partnership or succeed in your affairs as a result of a business trip or some sort of activity or initiative.

An unexpected windfall proves to be satisfying. Alternatively, an initiative or a journey will not only shed light on but will also improve your financial situation.

You will make a rapid recovery. Alternatively, a trip you make for pleasure or for health reasons will help you to get back on your feet again.

A sudden departure or an encounter puts your emotional life on a new footing. Alternatively, you are determined to correct your mistakes and make amends in order to sort out your love life.

Changes in the family, a house move or a family journey will put your domestic life on an entirely new basis.

A business trip, action taken for professional reasons or a change of job will put your work situation on an entirely new level. Alternatively, you will be in a position to make some interesting propositions or to respond to any proposals you might receive.

You can re-establish your financial situation thanks to a sum of money received unexpectedly or an initiative that you have made.

 As a result of a sudden improvement in your health or a journey you make for pleasure you will feel fulfilled and in great shape.

You will achieve fulfilment in your love life as everything you have hoped for is about to come true.

An important trip, a significant project or a house move is on the cards. This will bring your family the satisfaction it deserves and enable it to make progress.

You are about to make a journey, change jobs or undertake something on the work front that will bring you much satisfaction. It will widen your social and professional horizons and the scope of your business activities.

You will soon be able to achieve great things financially. Alternatively, you can now take full advantage of the privileged situation in which you find yourself, giving you free reign over your money.

PROBABLE
OUTCOME

' The future is just as much a condition of the present as is the past. 'What shall be and must be is the ground of that which is'. '

Friedrich Nietzsche, quoting Zarathustra,
Thus Spoke Zarathustra

✚ Either you will be advised or your own good sense will tell you to be practical and take action to make sure you are healthy and have plenty of energy.

♥ You will find the right way to express your feelings to or establish a relationship with someone who is shy or who is waiting for you. If you are thinking about someone in particular, you should be aware that, even though they are reserved, this person will show real feelings of affection towards you.

👪 You can rely on the encouragement and support of your close family in anything you choose to do. Feel free to embark upon any projects or ventures.

📋 You will be free to carry out a project effectively. It will probably be kept secret, or it may require the unobtrusive support of some competent people to bring it to fruition.

📧 Thanks to your stable financial situation or the money that you have put aside, you will find effective ways of improving your finances.

✚ You have plenty of energy at the moment, which will make it possible for you to concentrate on achieving a specific goal in the most constructive way.

♥ You will find the most effective ways of carrying out your plans or achieving what you want. If you are thinking about someone in particular, you should know that their feelings are genuine and unselfish.

👪 Your family situation is stable and making good progress in both emotional and material terms. This will be a support and encouragement for you in any action you might take, although it should be well thought out and constructive.

📋 A good, steady work situation will be helpful to any carefully considered initiatives you might take. This stability will, in turn, give you the freedom and security to put your professional skills into practice.

📧 Because your financial situation is sound, you will be able to find constructive and astute ways of making practical and skilled use of your resources.

1	4

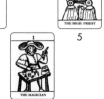

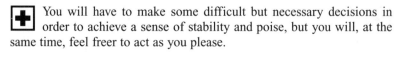 You know how to make the best use of your intelligence and initiative to ensure that, no matter what happens, you will feel full of vitality and energy.

There is no doubt that you will get the approval you need to carry out your projects and make some serious commitments, or to express your feelings. If you are thinking about someone in particular, you should be aware that this person will do whatever is necessary to stabilize their emotional situation.

You will be able to rely on the moral and physical support of your family or of one of its members in particular to carry out your projects successfully.

Thanks to the permission or assistance you receive from an influential person or people in authority, you will be able to take some firm action or make your projects reality.

You will have to find the best ways to cope with your obligations, both moral and financial, acquiring the necessary resources to do so.

1	5

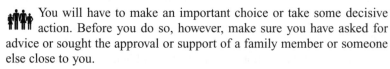 You will have to make some difficult but necessary decisions in order to achieve a sense of stability and poise, but you will, at the same time, feel freer to act as you please.

You will have to make a decisive choice as far as your emotions are concerned, or you will have to take the initiative in your love life.

You will have to make an important choice or take some decisive action. Before you do so, however, make sure you have asked for advice or sought the approval or support of a family member or someone else close to you.

Working with the support or approval of an influential person, you will be able to use your abilities and initiative to reach an agreement or conclude a contract.

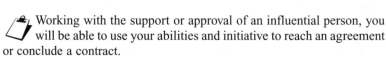 You will have to make an important choice or take decisive action to reach an agreement. Alternatively, you will have to obtain the support you need to make your financial situation more stable.

➕ No matter what choices you have to make or what action you have to take, use your initiative to achieve your objectives and make the best of your vitality and enthusiasm.

❤ The feelings you are currently experiencing or are arousing in someone else give you the freedom to do what you want and make the right choices. At the same time you will be sure of your goal and how best to achieve it.

👪 In order to achieve your family-related goals and end the general atmosphere of uncertainty, use your enthusiasm to make some decisive choices.

📋 A choice you make or an agreement you reach will give you the green light to do what you want, and through skill and hard work you will achieve an objective or carry out a plan.

💰 You will have to take determined steps to resolve an outstanding problem and improve your financial situation.

➕ Your hard work will help you to achieve balance and act in a sensible, disciplined way.

❤ Armed with basic honesty and goodwill, you will behave or express your feelings frankly and freely.

👪 You will be able to impose your will or your plans on people fairly forcefully, but if you want things to work out well you must keep up your efforts and show some initiative.

📋 Through hard work and your will to succeed, you will be able to get your plans and initiatives accepted, making good use of your skills and professional abilities at the same time.

💰 Your current efforts will enable you to achieve a well-balanced financial situation, and this in turn will mean that you can put your plans into action or take some useful initiatives.

1	8

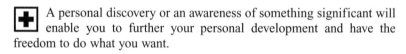

✚ Your well-balanced temperament prompts you to act in a prudent, thoughtful manner, which, in turn, helps you to be dynamic and maintain your sense of well-being.

♥ You will be prompted to act with caution and thoughtfulness to help find a balance in your love life. Alternatively, you will be able to make long-term plans.

👪 The current stability of your family situation will allow you to take cautious and carefully thought-out initiatives and to plan ahead.

📝 You will be encouraged to take prudent and constructive initiatives alone, but in full knowledge of the facts. Alternatively, the stability of your current situation will enable you to make long-term plans.

💰 Thanks to a well-balanced financial situation, you have the opportunity to plan ahead or to take worthwhile, prudent and carefully considered initiatives.

1	9

✚ A personal discovery or an awareness of something significant will enable you to further your personal development and have the freedom to do what you want.

♥ You will be free to do what you want, but a personal discovery or a growing awareness of some particular factor will make you conscious of the changes that this kind of behaviour could bring.

👪 A personal discovery or a new awareness of certain factors will give you the complete freedom to further the development of your family situation.

📝 The disclosure of something that has, until now, remained vague or secret will prompt you to take initiatives that will advance your work situation.

💰 Following a new discovery or the clarification of something that until now has been obscure, you will take an initiative that will help your financial situation develop rapidly.

324

➕ Your personal progress will be such that you will soon be able to gain a degree of control over yourself, improving your mental and physical health.

♥ Thanks to the development of your emotional situation, you will be free to do as you wish and achieve everything you want.

👪 Your current family circumstances or developments within your family circle will help you take bold and constructive action and succeed in everything you do.

📋 The current status of your professional situation and the way it is progressing will help you to make your mark effectively, get your plans approved and be successful in everything you do.

💰 The current circumstances or developments in your financial affairs will enable you to take some daring initiatives that are likely to bear fruit.

➕ Although you are self-disciplined, you don't feel fully in control of your natural resources. You will have to find ways to relax and take better care of yourself.

♥ Although you enjoy strong relationships or have a firm grip on your emotional situation, you won't be able to get what you want from your love life unless you can behave less selfishly.

👪 Although your family circumstances are secure, you still feel as if you don't have much choice in matters and are not free to do as you choose, despite your wish to escape from the situation.

📋 The stability of your current circumstances means that you can work towards achieving more freedom and autonomy in your professional life.

💰 The firm control that you have of your funds will allow you to become financially independent and liberate yourself from certain material constraints.

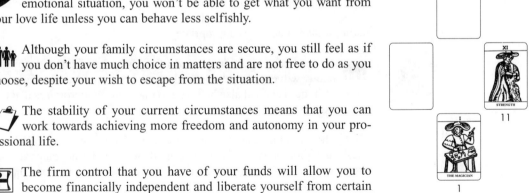

325

1 12

XII
THE HANGED MAN

12

THE MAGICIAN

1

You will be able to take firm action to get yourself back on track, putting an end to your mental and physical weaknesses and re-discovering your dynamism in the process.

You are currently in an unsatisfactory, dead-end relationship and will be prompted to do something radical to bring this to a close or to regain your independence.

You will be forced to take some major initiatives in order to end a difficult situation that is currently going nowhere.

In order to free yourself of certain restrictions and break the stale-mate you will be forced to take drastic action or make some important changes.

Radical action is needed to improve your financial situation, clear any debts you may have or instigate a profitable and important change that will release you from certain constraints.

1 13

XIII
DEATH

13

THE MAGICIAN

1

The end of a health problem or a radical change will encourage you to be a little more prudent, and this, in turn, will help things to become slightly more tranquil on the health front.

A major change or the end of a particular situation will doubtless help you to be more independent. Nevertheless, you will also have to be more flexible when it comes to expressing what you want and in taking whatever action is appropriate.

A significant upset or the end of a particular situation within the family will encourage you to adopt a more compliant and accommo-dating attitude. This will also help you to make any compromises that may be necessary.

The end of a situation, the conclusion of a deal or a radical change will prompt you to make detailed plans and find rational com-promises. This will give you the upper hand in any negotiations that are currently underway.

The conclusion of a business deal or a radical change will prompt you to instigate negotiations, transactions or plans.

Despite your willingness to be flexible and your concern to find the right environment, you still have the tendency to do too much and to over-tax your physical resources. Be a little more moderate in your behaviour and don't spread yourself too thinly.

In spite of the agreements that will have to be reached, your willingness to be flexible and the compromises you are prepared to make, you won't rest until you have achieved your goals. No one will be able to stop you from fulfilling your dreams.

You will always follow your chosen course of action, and nothing will stop you from getting what you want, no matter what agreements or compromises will have to be reached.

Some negotiations or well-timed agreements will enable you to put your plans into action and achieve your objectives.

Various transactions and negotiations will give you the freedom to put some energetic and ambitious plans into action and achieve success on the financial front.

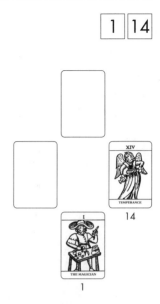

After going through a period of difficulty and upheaval, you may now suffer some form of health crisis. Although it could be quite acute, it should nevertheless be temporary and even turn out to do you some good. Alternatively, you will find ways to find some relief and release from tension.

An uneasy situation or a passionate relationship will almost certainly reach a tumultuous conclusion that will prompt you to make radical but beneficial changes.

You will suddenly decide to bring a situation to an inevitable but useful conclusion. This action will raise many questions within your family but will also have a calming effect and ease tensions.

Something will spur you to take sudden action. It could be either great opportunities or uncertainty and trouble, but it will provoke liberating scrutiny on the work front or an upheaval that could nevertheless prove beneficial.

An awkward or an advantageous situation will prompt you to take disruptive but beneficial action or to question your financial plans.

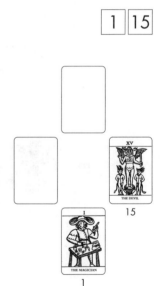

1	16

✚ You will make the best possible use of your natural resources, vitality and enthusiasm following a shock, upheaval or a serious setback to your health.

♥ Following an inevitable but liberating upheaval, the time will be right for you to express some deep and genuine emotions. Alternatively, this upheaval should enable you to take some promising initiatives in your love life.

👪 An upset or a sudden questioning of the situation will mean that you can take some positive action and draw up new plans that go some way towards fulfilling your aspirations. It will be up to you to make them work.

📋 An upset or a sudden challenge will allow you to prove that you are capable of thinking up some original and creative ideas that will help you to achieve your aims.

💰 An upheaval or an unforeseen challenge will prompt you to show your initiative and use your skill to find inventive ways of acquiring new funds.

1	17

✚ Your natural resources are good, but you may find yourself feeling tired or experiencing health problems of some kind.

♥ Despite an apparently harmonious emotional situation or a genuine and meaningful relationship, you will not be able to follow a clear course of action or bring your plans to a successful conclusion.

👪 The circumstances may be favourable or your family situation may be harmonious and congenial, but you will be disappointed or your plans will be thwarted.

📋 Although circumstances are favourable, you will experience some difficulty working out your plans. Unless you knuckle down to the tasks in hand and use your skill and initiative you will have problems concluding matters.

💰 Your financial resources are good, yet you have a tendency to mismanage your money.

328

✚ You will be able to take positive steps towards clarifying health matters and freeing yourself of your problems or concerns.

♥ You will be happy to do what you need in order to clarify matters relating to your love life and to make plans to get together with someone special.

👪 Problems or disappointments will prompt you to take firm action to shed some light on your family situation.

📋 Despite the delays, mistakes or obstacles that must be overcome, you will manage to put your talents to good use sorting out work-related matters and carrying out your plans. Your initiative and skills will be duly acknowledged.

⧗ You will have the aptitude, enthusiasm and initiative to overcome the delays, disappointments or problems you might come up against in financial matters and to carry out your plans.

18

1

✚ Health matters will be clarified and you will gain a new lease of life and will once again feel as if you have a choice in what you do.

♥ An existing, special relationship, or a new one you form, will prompt you to change the way you behave or how you view your love life.

👪 You will be encouraged to change your attitude, the way you act and how you view things by a special family situation or by having your position made clear. This change will also help you work towards putting the family relationship on a new footing.

📋 The clarification of work-related matters or a partnership should prompt you to reconsider your business plans and activities with a great deal of interest. Alternatively, you might decide to instigate a change or put matters on a new footing.

⧗ Clear, positive factors in your financial situation will favour your current plans to get your finances back on a firm footing.

19

1

1 20

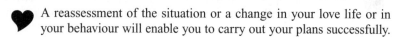 A change in your lifestyle or behaviour or a recovery will put you in a perfect position to find complete fulfilment and make the best use of your natural resources and dynamism.

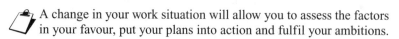 A reassessment of the situation or a change in your love life or in your behaviour will enable you to carry out your plans successfully.

Following a change in, or even the rejuvenation of, your family situation you will be able to start making major plans to assemble all the resources at your disposal.

A change in your work situation will allow you to assess the factors in your favour, put your plans into action and fulfil your ambitions.

Your finances will recover or will be replenished, enabling you to make some significant plans or garner all your resources.

1 21

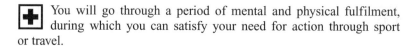 You will go through a period of mental and physical fulfilment, during which you can satisfy your need for action through sport or travel.

You will either have an encounter that will make you feel totally fulfilled or the person currently in your thoughts is about to come back to you. Alternatively, you may decide to leave suddenly.

You will decide to make a sudden departure or move house, or you are expecting the hasty departure or unheralded arrival of a member of your family.

Expect the arrival or departure of someone who has played, or will play, an important part in work-related matters. Alternatively, lured by some interesting and important prospects, you will carry out your plans or make a sudden move to another job.

You may have to assemble all the resources at your disposal to transfer a significant sum of money. Alternatively, your financial circumstances prompt you to make a journey.

You should make an effort to control your impulses and curb your restlessness or more extreme behaviour. A relaxing holiday will do you the world of good.

You will either meet someone or the person in your thoughts is about to rejoin you. Alternatively, you are finally going to make some real plans for your love life.

A sudden event or the arrival or departure of a member of your family will prompt you to act quickly or to make new plans.

The arrival or departure of someone within your work environment should favour your plans, allowing you to make some smart moves and make your mark.

It is likely that you will find what you are looking for and that this will allow you to make some useful plans on the financial front.

You will do what you need to in order to preserve your stability and general well-being on both the mental and physical fronts.

If you are thinking about someone in particular, despite this person's caution and reserve in expressing their feelings, they are sincere and unwavering. Alternatively, you will be able to achieve a cherished ambition that will guarantee stability in your love life.

You will be able to count on the backing or support of a sympathetic person who is close to you. They will help to bring your plans to fruition or give you useful advice.

You will make progress towards achieving a more stable and profitable work situation.

You will plan for and work towards a more advantageous and stable financial situation.

+ You are blessed with plenty of energy and vitality, which will help protect you from health risks and give you an overall stability.

♥ You can place your trust in the discreet, sensible and warm-hearted person you are currently with. Alternatively, you can be confident that your love life will stabilize and your feelings will be long lasting.

👪 You will be able to rely on the protection and moral and physical support of your family or those close to you, even if the support they give you may not always be obvious.

📋 You may not yet be aware of it, but a positive move or decision will clear the way for you to enter into a profitable agreement, getting things back on an even keel or obtaining the backing or support of an influential person.

🗄 You can count on unobtrusive yet reliable support to help you stabilize your financial situation and turn it to your advantage.

+ You will be advised or forced to make an important decision that will help you maintain your health and stability.

♥ If you are thinking about someone in particular, this person will soon reveal feelings they have previously been keeping to themselves. Alternatively, you will be advised or forced to set aside any reservations you may have and make a decisive choice in your love life.

👪 You may not be aware of it yet, but a crucial decision regarding your family, whose importance you will assess but keep secret, will be forced on you by events.

📋 You will have to make an important choice or agreement. Although you might not have received any prior indication of it, it will probably not come as a surprise. You will, however, also have serious reservations about your decision.

🗄 You will be advised or perhaps obliged to make important choices regarding your financial situation, but you will make them extremely cautiously and with a great deal of forethought.

2 5

You know how to take the precautions needed to maintain your well-being and will be reassured about your health.

If you are thinking about someone in particular, this person will soon reveal their feelings to you. Alternatively, you will decide to do something to put your love life on a firmer footing, although you will act with a certain amount of caution.

You will receive some news about your family or reveal some news yourself, albeit cautiously. Alternatively, the approval or support of those around you will enable you to take action to achieve your plans.

Your efforts to make steady progress to stabilize your position at work or to realize your plans will receive the support of someone who is influential.

You will obtain the approval or the support you need to stabilize and gradually improve your financial situation.

5

2

2 6

When you are faced with a choice you will always opt for the most sensible and self-disciplined solution that will benefit your stability and well-being.

You will be selective, self-disciplined and demanding when it comes to making decisions about your love life. As a result, you will have a tendency to put personal stability before your feelings.

Wisdom, self-discipline and prudence will govern your actions when it comes to making decisions. You will reveal what you decide to do only with the utmost caution.

You will be the instigator of a decision or a decision will be made about you. Although discriminating and strict, it will be fair.

The stability of your financial affairs will be guaranteed thanks to a decision that will be made about you or one that you initiate. The decision could be rather strict and severe, but it will be impartial.

6

2

333

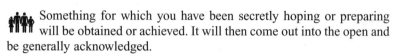

✚ You will finally free yourself of your caution and lethargy and prove to yourself what you are truly capable of.

♥ A particular person you are thinking about will forget their timidity and open up to you. Alternatively, a sudden development will force you to show your true colours and reveal what is on your mind or what you know.

👪 Something for which you have been secretly hoping or preparing will be obtained or achieved. It will then come out into the open and be generally acknowledged.

📋 Things are looking quite positive at the moment. This will help you to understand something that until now has not been clear or will clarify your position at work. As a result, you will be more confident and realistic in the pursuit of your objectives.

📠 Some news or an event will dispel your doubts and confirm your predictions or allow you gradually to improve your financial affairs.

✚ Subjecting yourself to self-discipline and a strict regime will help to ensure that your health will improve slowly but steadily.

♥ You will realize (but will not admit to yourself) that your love life could well be destabilized. However, as this will be for a good reason you have nothing to fear.

👪 You enjoy a harmonious and well-balanced family situation, which will progress and develop in its own natural way.

📋 The self-discipline to which you have the good sense to subject yourself will help to bring about stability and improvement in your professional life.

📠 Because you are wisely exercising some self-control, you will be able to keep a firm grip on the continuous development of your financial situation.

Your self-awareness or your realistic and cautious attitude will help to protect you from health risks and maintain your well-being.

You will find out just how constant and sincere your loved one really is. Alternatively, you will make a personal discovery or become aware of something that will make you more certain than ever of your feelings.

You will discover to what extent you can rely on the backing of your family or on the unconditional support of a person of great integrity who is close to you.

A problem will be solved and something that has hitherto been hazy will be clarified. You will then be able to take firm control of your work situation, although you must act with discretion and caution.

A solution to a problem or a way out of a dilemma will be clarified, making you more cautious and thrifty than ever.

THE HERMIT
9

THE HIGH PRIESTESS
2

Despite changes or upheavals, your health situation will remain the same. You will have no alternative other than to wait for things to start to improve.

Your love life will make some progress, although it will be rather uncertain. You won't be able to do anything but be patient and make sensible preparations for a real change.

Despite changes or upheavals in your family environment, you still won't feel at ease or any freer. You will just have to wait and see what the changes mean for you.

You will need to wait a little longer before revealing what you know or being able to regain a degree of independence, in spite of the changes that will happen.

No matter what changes or upheavals take place, you will still have to be cautious, patient and thrifty.

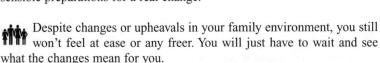

THE WHEEL OF FORTUNE
10

THE HIGH PRIESTESS
2

2	11

+ Courage, moral strength and determination will help you to get rid of anything likely to damage your health or to bring about a radical change in your behaviour or lifestyle.

♥ You will need to act with not a little courage and wisdom to prepare yourself for a fundamental change in your love life, which will be taking an important new direction as a result of your past actions.

👪 By making sure that you have your family situation well under control, you will be able to make a significant and brave change that will help to stabilize and enhance it.

📋 You are not yet aware of the major change that is about to take place, but you should find that it will be to your advantage. In the meantime, maintain your position and remain confident.

💰 By quietly sticking to your guns but at the same time acting with confidence and firmness, you will easily reap the rewards of what you have sown, and the resulting gains will meet your expectations.

2	12

+ You will be forced to take a decision and make arrangements to get some rest in order to restore your vitality and stability.

♥ You will be obliged to reach some tactful compromises to help the stability of your love life. Unfortunately, this does not necessarily mean that these arrangements will be really effective and that wisdom will win the day.

👪 You will be subject to various contradictory influences before you are able to sort yourself out or before you feel compelled to find the compromises needed to solve problems or bring about a change in your family situation.

📋 You will be forced to make some compromises because of various obligations or because circumstances will not change or move forward. You may, however, have to wait some time before seeing the results of your action.

💰 Financial obligations will force you to find appropriate agreements and compromises and to do so as calmly as possible.

A radical change won't disguise your bad habits. They may seem unimportant, but they are damaging your health, so you must make a determined effort to curb them.

A dramatic change or the end of a relationship won't cure your rather excessive and excitable nature, nor will it relieve you of the half-buried desire to achieve something at all costs.

Even if you don't show it, you will derive great satisfaction from a major change on the domestic front or from the end of a situation, even though you have been expecting it.

An important change or the end of a situation at work that you have been quietly predicting will be good for you and may allow you to make some secret acquisitions.

A radical change or significant gains that you have been secretly expecting will improve your financial situation. In turn, this will prompt you to put some money aside or to make profitable investments.

Well-timed agreements or compromises will help you to make some fairly sudden yet useful arrangements to avoid any problems that could be damaging to your health.

Some rather sudden but apt revelations or exchanges of opinion will relieve you of a great burden. This will give you the opportunity to say what has been on your mind for a long time.

Rational and timely agreements or compromises will allow you to contain or minimize the disappointments or upsets that might just be in store for your family.

Any challenges or upheavals you have been expecting will be facilitated by some well-timed agreements and compromises.

You may find that your financial plans are questioned and your forecasts disrupted by transactions and agreements or unforeseen events of some sort.

2 15

+ Although you have a tendency towards excess or find it difficult to resist temptation, you will still be in a position to draw on your energy reserves when it proves necessary and to adopt a healthier, more sensible lifestyle.

♥ Your relationships might be passionate or intense and your love life a little chaotic, but you still have deep feelings, even if you don't show them.

👪 You will find that your wishes will be fulfilled and a joyful event you have been expecting, or secretly longing for, will soon take place.

📋 Thanks to a work situation that is both satisfying and profitable, you will be able to hatch some original plans and ideas.

⊡ Your aspirations on the financial front will be fulfilled well beyond your hopes and expectations.

2 16

+ An upheaval, a blow to your morale or a physical problem might leave you in a serious and unstable condition. Make sure you take precautions to prevent this from happening.

♥ An upheaval or a crisis in your love life might make you ill, prompt you to hold unhealthy grudges in spite of yourself or keep going back over old ground without being able to stop things getting worse.

👪 Some kind of accident, problem or shock or a blow to your morale could leave someone close to you feeling worried and uncertain. Alternatively, you will be disappointed by any upheavals that take place within your family environment.

📋 You will be disappointed by the radical changes that will occur in your work situation. Whatever the outcome, to avoid matters getting any worse or even coming to nothing don't be taken in by appearances or leave anything unfinished.

⊡ Some radical changes or an upheaval will throw your forecasts and calculations into disarray. Expect hard times and disappointments on the financial front.

If you draw on your energy reserves and the resources deep within yourself you will feel on top form and in harmony with yourself and your surroundings.

If you are thinking about someone in particular you need to be aware that, despite this person's reserve, their feelings are deep and sincere. Alternatively, you will soon meet someone or form a really good relationship that will bring stability to you love life.

There is a warm-hearted person in your family whom you can trust and in whom you can confide. Alternatively, something will happen within the family circle that will bring much happiness.

Innovations, inventions or creative ideas will help make things both more productive and stable. Alternatively, favourable circumstances will preside over the founding of a partnership for which you have been able to make intelligent yet unobtrusive preparations.

You will have trouble containing your pleasure when you are faced with favourable circumstances or excellent financial resources that exceed your wildest expectations.

You will need to rest and find some peace and quiet in order to recover from an illness or to overcome some problems that you have encountered.

Problems, disappointments or mistakes in your love life will force you to see that it is necessary to change your attitude and reconsider your situation, although you will do so discreetly.

You will experience problems, conflicts or disappointments that will prompt you to re-examine your family life quietly but seriously and eventually change your attitude.

Any problems or disappointments that you have experienced will make you reconsider your work situation quite seriously. This may cause you to change your attitude, but you will keep your own counsel, not revealing anything unless it is absolutely necessary.

Problems, mistakes, delays or disappointments will lead you to reconsider your financial situation carefully and adopt a different attitude towards it, becoming more thrifty and cautious.

| 2 | 19 |

➕ Thanks to your caution, discretion and calm and stable nature, you will feel completely fulfilled and in perfect harmony with yourself and your surroundings.

♥ If you are thinking about someone special, you should be aware that their feelings are deep and genuine despite an apparent reserve. Alternatively, any hopes and dreams for your love life will be fulfilled. A union or special relationship will bring you much happiness.

👪 You will feel happy, fulfilled and at ease with those around you, prompting you to conceive great plans for your family. Alternatively, you can always rely on the feelings and unobtrusive, yet unconditional, support of someone close to you.

📋 Success in the work place or in a partnership will make it possible for you to conceive major projects, plan how your work situation is likely to develop or put it on a more stable footing.

💰 Thanks to success in financial matters, you will be able make good use of your resources and invest them wisely.

| 2 | 20 |

➕ Following a recovery or a return to normality, you will be off to a good start, but you may still need to go somewhere for a little rest.

♥ You may hesitate before responding to an invitation or proposal that you will receive. Alternatively, you are waiting for the right moment to leave a relationship or to reconsider your present assessment of it.

👪 You will have the opportunity to move house or will receive the offer of a change of some kind, and you will give the matter a lot of thought before replying. Alternatively, the prospect of some kind of renewal will prove to be what you have been waiting for and will give you the go-ahead to do what you have been planning.

📋 You will receive a proposal or a call that you have been expecting. Alternatively, a change or renewal of some kind, or getting a business idea back on its feet will give you the chance to move forwards.

💰 Once your financial situation is back to normal, you will be able to put it on a firm basis and act more cautiously in order not to repeat past mistakes.

You will have many opportunities to help you take on your duties and responsibilities calmly and to enjoy good health and vitality and have plenty of energy.

As you have been predicting, your love life will flourish and be successful, enabling you to stabilize your relationships or form a solid union.

You will be able to rely on the moral and material backing of those close to you. Alternatively, domestic matters will go well and your family life will become stable.

The approval or the quiet yet effective support of an influential person will help work-related matters to develop and be successful, or it will help a situation in which you had justifiably placed much hope to make progress.

Your financial situation will develop naturally and at a reasonable rate. As a result, you will feel more financially secure and better able to shoulder your obligations and responsibilities.

You will obtain the advice and assistance you need to achieve more stability and vitality.

In the face of a rather unsettled situation or confronted by someone who lacks stability, you will keep your cool and would be well advised to remain cautious. Alternatively, you are expecting the arrival or return of someone dear to you.

You are expecting a visit from someone close to you or their arrival or departure. Alternatively, you might have been taking secret action in regard to your family situation.

The arrival or departure of someone in your working environment, a sudden event or an important action will help make your position more stable.

If it proves necessary, you can set out in search of financial backing in order to make your affairs more stable.

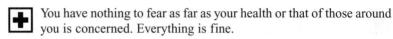

3 1

You have nothing to fear as far as your health or that of those around you is concerned. Everything is fine.

There is no need for you to have any doubts about the special person in your thoughts or to worry about your relationship. You will have the upper hand when the time comes for you to act.

You can have faith in someone close to you and make a necessary decision with certainty.

An initiative or a favourable decision will help to make your situation profitable. You can act with confidence and don't need to doubt the abilities of the person about whom you are thinking.

Get moving and take action: it will only help your circumstances for the better.

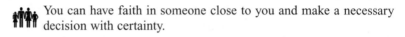

3 2

You are receiving lots of support and are being well advised, so you have nothing to worry about on the health front at the moment.

As long as you continue to be honest and understanding, anything that is being kept hidden from you will become apparent in the natural course of events, and this will enable you to act with a full understanding of the circumstances.

You can rely on the moral, physical and emotional support of those around you.

A wise decision helps you to achieve a productive and profitable outcome at work. You will get all the support you need.

You can count on receiving support or good financial advice from others. Alternatively, you can have confidence in what is a solid and stable financial situation.

You are on good form and have firm control over your vitality and well-being, with nothing to fear.

Someone else's intelligence and determination will support and comfort you in your actions and feelings.

The confirmation of something in particular or the complete support you receive from someone will enable you to take action to get what you want.

Your work situation is being managed with a firmness and intelligence that enable it to progress and move forwards. You have all the assurance or confidence you need to move on.

The confirmation of a certain factor allows you to work towards an improvement in your financial situation.

You need to adopt some self-discipline if you don't want someone else to force it on you.

You have moral obligations and responsibilities that oblige you to be scrupulous in your actions. Alternatively, you can be confident of the honesty and integrity of the person in your thoughts.

If you are finding it hard to impose discipline in your domestic environment at present, try to make your concerns clear to those close to you. Alternatively, your family environment may seem to be rather severe, but it is fair.

A well-established position at work means that everything you do will be more secure from all angles. Be disciplined with yourself and be aware of all the structures and contingencies already in place so that you can make use of them if necessary.

Never lose sight of your obligations if you wish to keep your financial matters on an even keel.

3 6

✚ You may be experiencing feelings of self-doubt. If so, they are making you feel lethargic, despite what are, theoretically, your high levels of energy.

♥ You are plagued by contradictory feelings or you are in an uncertain relationship that requires a choice that you alone can make. Don't be too self-obsessed in all this.

👪 You have a tendency to withdraw into yourself, and this does nothing to further your family relationships. Alternatively, you might be facing two choices and are wondering which way to go. You should trust your instincts.

📋 A particular choice or decision will enable you to do something that is likely to be profitable in the long term. Nevertheless, keep your wits about you, just in case.

🁢 You are facing a choice between two possible courses of action. Think long and hard about them and go for the safer solution.

3 7

✚ You are on fine form, feeling full of vitality and raring to go. Nothing should prevent you from using some of your energy now.

♥ Some good news or a joyful event will allow you to make progress in your love life and act as you think best.

👪 A journey or a house move that you are planning will certainly take place. No matter what happens, the time is right to act and make a positive change.

📋 You are being offered the chance of a good job together with lots of opportunities. What are you waiting for? You will be rewarded for your troubles.

🁢 Don't complain if your money is going out as fast as it is coming in. Make sure you seize the opportunities being offered to you.

3 8

➕ Your equilibrium and well-being cannot be upset. Your self-control is excellent.

❤ Whether a slightly harsh decision has been taken against you or whether you are handling things with some degree of stringency, you should not doubt yourself. You are not to blame.

👪 No matter what problems or difficulties you are currently experiencing or what judgements are being made about you, you have sufficient strength of character to face up to the situation and take control of it with equanimity.

📋 Following a legal decision or judgement, you will be able to take full control of your current circumstances. If, however, the decision or verdict goes against you, stand firm, because you will ultimately be proved right.

🎲 You are perfectly capable of taking control of the situation, regardless of current circumstances.

3 9

➕ Several constraints are making you feel mentally and physically tired. Take some time to be on your own so that you can have a rest, look after yourself and recharge your batteries.

❤ You are doubtless in a situation of dependency that you don't like and that has the effect of isolating you. Don't despair and become fatalistic. Make the best use of these difficulties to give yourself time to think and adopt a more spontaneous and instinctive attitude.

👪 You have reached stalemate. You will have to be patient, find a little solitude and think long and hard about a solution.

📋 You should be able to find the right solution to get your working life moving again. This might well prove to be profitable in the long term.

🎲 The money you are expecting is taking a long time to arrive, but you are able to hold out until the apparent stalemate is broken.

8

3

9

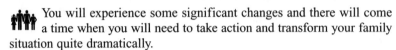

As long as you accept changes and remain responsive, you have nothing to fear. You have good natural defences.

Things are moving forward in such a way that you can move on in your love life or make a change on which you have set your heart.

You will experience some significant changes and there will come a time when you will need to take action and transform your family situation quite dramatically.

The time is right to move forward and make the most of a situation. Don't hesitate to make a significant change if necessary, as you are sure to benefit from it.

You should be able to derive some advantages from a particular situation or to achieve positive financial results and make progress.

10

3

You are doing so well at avoiding any health risks or problems that you have nothing to fear.

Don't doubt the sincerity of the feelings of someone close to you. Alternatively, you will be able to get what you want thanks to your strength of character and your positive, generous nature.

Everything could turn out well for you and everyone involved with your family. Be sure of your rights but remain understanding.

The situation at work is extremely favourable at the moment, and you should be able to achieve what you want.

You are in full control of your financial situation and are, therefore, able to enter into an interesting transaction, make a well-timed agreement or hang on to any rights and privileges that you currently have.

11

3

3 | 12

➕ You have sufficient energy and vitality to act or react as required. Don't be too impatient, however.

♥ You are in a relationship with someone who has a passionate and somewhat over-the-top temperament. Alternatively, you are involved in a passionate relationship that brings you great pleasure.

👪 Getting excited or angry or becoming too self-obsessed won't help solve your problems. Alternatively, someone close to you is in a situation of complete dependence.

🗒 All kinds of restrictions or an unsatisfactory, dead-end situation will prompt you to take firm and quite sudden action to get what you want straightaway.

💰 Be a little more generous and a little less possessive. You have the means to do so. Alternatively, you can be sure of achieving your financial goals.

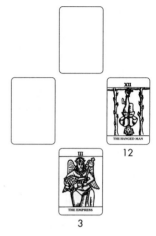

12

3

3 | 13

➕ An important change in your life will leave you in a state of shock. However, you will find yourself in a position to free yourself of all your problems.

♥ You can, and should, do something to release yourself from your constraints. As you have reached a turning point in your life, you can start afresh.

👪 You will come up against a change that will upset or call into question the fundamental basis of your family circumstances.

🗒 You have just undergone a change, or something in your work situation has come to a sudden end. This has knocked you off balance but has also lifted a great burden from your shoulders. You will now have more freedom to do as you want.

💰 Some of your resources have suddenly dried up. Watch out for any destabilizing effects this might have. Alternatively, you will receive a significant sum of money, which will lead to a positive change in your financial situation.

13

3

3 | 14

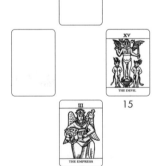

XIV
TEMPERANCE
14

III
THE EMPRESS
3

✚ You are open-minded and are always ready to help people, so you form good relationships, which are an essential element in your general well-being.

♥ Don't doubt the genuine affection of someone close to you. Alternatively, make the compromises or agreements you need to create a situation in which everything is possible.

👪 The current climate and the relationships within your family circle are good and can only help you to fulfil your hopes and dreams.

📋 You can profit from opportunities that will be helpful to any promising projects or ideas.

▨ You should be able to bring off some good financial deals. Use your imagination but at the same time be diplomatic.

3 | 15

XV
THE DEVIL
15

III
THE EMPRESS
3

✚ Don't let yourself get into a serious condition. Be quite radical and do what you need, even if you have to be quite tough on yourself. Take great care to look after yourself and your interests.

♥ You have fallen victim to a passionate relationship and are finding yourself unable to react against it, no doubt because you are feeling vulnerable, anxious and powerless. Alternatively, you are in a relationship with someone who is restless and self-centred, and you never know how they are going to react.

👪 Either you are deluding yourself or you are being too hasty or foolhardy, and this can only lead to disappointment. Alternatively, there is a risk of conflict or illness in your family.

📋 You might experience a disappointment because you have made an error or because of unreliable or demanding external factors. Don't dig in your heels because you need to reconsider your situation.

▨ You are likely to make a mistake or to deal with someone whom you do not trust entirely. Be on your guard and think carefully before committing yourself to anything.

➕ You may currently be experiencing some problems or upsets, but they will be beneficial and have a detoxifying effect, helping to protect you from any risks.

❤️ Don't worry about the changes or disruption in your love life. They have a liberating effect and will allow you to clarify matters and find happiness.

👪 An upheaval or some sudden, unforeseeable changes will create a happy and satisfying situation within the family.

📋 Disruption or sudden changes will help to create a new work-related situation, guaranteeing you success in your business affairs in the process.

🖥️ An unforeseeable event, a breakthrough in a stalemate or some other kind of disruption should bring you joy and success in your financial affairs.

➕ You are in a good position to get back on your feet again and make a fresh start.

❤️ Someone answers your prayers or allows you to view your current circumstances in a happier light. Alternatively, you are faced with a new situation, and your love life gets off to a fresh start.

👪 Something good that happens or favourable circumstances bring about a complete change and allow you to view your family situation in a happier light.

📋 New, extremely advantageous circumstances make it possible for you to carry through your plans or to revive a situation that promises to be profitable.

🖥️ You have been expecting your finances to improve, and this will happen following a change in your situation or after some new, extremely advantageous circumstances arise.

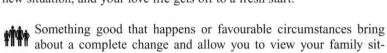
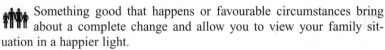
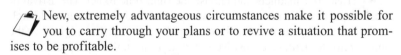

3 | 18

✚ You are more tired and anxious than truly ill. Pull yourself together and call on your natural resources that are more than sufficient to see you through.

❤ You are currently facing a confusing and disappointing situation. Don't lose hope, however, because sooner or later you will find it will bring you what you want.

♙ You are perfectly capable of solving your current problems. You will eventually achieve what you want if you remain confident and rely on your principles and emotional resources.

✎ Your work situation might be difficult or unclear, but you are in a position to make the best of it and achieve results that will surpass your expectations. If you persevere, things will eventually turn out to be to your advantage.

▦ Although you will come up against obstacles, your intelligence and integrity will help you achieve your financial goals.

3 | 19

✚ You are on great form so get going! Be active, try something new or go on a journey. The world is your oyster.

❤ If you have not already done so, you will meet someone special. Alternatively, don't hesitate if you are planning a romantic journey. It will bring a great deal of joy and shared pleasure.

♙ You are keen to be off, depart or move house, and there is absolutely nothing to stop you.

✎ Trust your instincts and choose the right time to act. The arrival or departure of someone you know or somebody you meet could well be the key to achieving personal success. Alternatively, you might have the opportunity to achieve a positive outcome in an undertaking or even to find an advantageous new job. Either way, you should be successful.

▦ Circumstances are currently so propitious that you don't need to worry about what you have decided to do with your money.

✚ Circumstances beyond your control may prompt some serious reconsideration about your health, but you really have nothing to worry about.

♥ You will receive a proposal or be offered an explanation that should confirm your position. However, you should respond only after having carefully considered your moral and physical obligations. Alternatively, you are close to someone entirely trustworthy.

A complete change in your circumstances is on offer. Alternatively, someone does you a favour, makes you a proposal or gives you an invitation. Whichever it is, you would be wise to accept the offer and respond favourably.

Someone will make you an interesting proposition, but before responding you will take material and moral matters into consideration to stabilize your situation. Although you are looking for guarantees, you can have every confidence in this proposal, which seems to be genuine.

Make sure you carefully examine all the financial proposals being made to you as well as all the opportunities currently being offered.

✚ Don't hesitate if you have decisions to make or plans to carry out. You are in a position to enjoy good health, vitality and feelings of satisfaction and well-being.

♥ If you are thinking about someone special, don't doubt the sincerity or generosity of their feelings or that this person can make you feel truly complete. If you are thinking about yourself, happiness is within reach. Grab it with both hands.

You can be confident that someone close to you is sincere and affectionate and that you will experience a certain fulfilment within your family or home life. You should get what you want if you have been hoping for something in particular.

You should find that your prayers are answered and your hard work is rewarded. You are in a good position to enter into one or several profitable associations or business deals and to make some good choices.

If you take care when assessing the alternatives that are on offer, you should be able to make some excellent financial deals and achieve major success in this area.

3	22

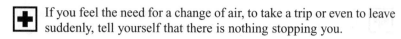

THE FOOL

22

III

THE EMPRESS

3

➕ If you feel the need for a change of air, to take a trip or even to leave suddenly, tell yourself that there is nothing stopping you.

❤ You will almost certainly meet someone new or someone will return to you. If you are intending to leave, it seems that nothing can stop you, but are you sure that your departure is justified?

👪 Expect a visit or the departure or return of someone close to you. You will find out shortly which of these it is to be.

📋 A departure, sudden arrival or an event will allow you to take full advantage of your working situation or to make an interesting business deal.

🗝 If you need help, you will find it. If you have something important to do, you are in a position to do it.

4	1

THE MAGICIAN

1

IV

THE EMPEROR

4

➕ You are self-confident and so do not necessarily listen to the advice you are given. Only you can judge if this is the right way to act.

❤ If you are thinking about someone in particular, bear in mind that you are dealing with an intelligent, determined and reliable person. Alternatively, you are waiting for a decision to be made, or for something to happen that will stabilize your current emotional situation.

👪 You will probably have to give someone a good deal of sensible advice or play the role of protector to someone close to you.

📋 You are waiting for a decision to be made or an initiative to be taken that will allow you to confirm a project or direct some new venture.

🗝 Your financial situation is certain to benefit if you take a realistic view of all the plans and decisions you make.

If you have any doubts whatsoever about your health, you need to be firm with yourself and take the logical step that is now being imposed on you.

You may be involved with someone who is rather shy and reserved and who, although sure of their feelings, is not good at expressing them. Alternatively, if you act firmly, you will be able to achieve all your hopes and dreams.

You are in a position to exert both moral and material influence over your family, and you can rely on the discreet, yet genuine support of someone close to you.

You may be waiting for an important decision to be made with respect to your work or with something you are currently undertaking. If so, you will learn the outcome shortly.

It is possible that you are not yet in possession of all the facts that you need to make a decision. If this is the case, take your time and don't do anything until you are absolutely sure.

You want to stay fit at all costs, and who can blame you? Don't worry, however, because you have both the willpower and ability you need to do this.

If you are thinking about someone in particular, you can be sure that nothing will stand in the way of this person's determination to succeed. Alternatively, the person you are already with is a true soul mate.

You know how you would like things to progress, and this may well happen, although the outcome rests on a couple, probably you and your partner, making a decision or acting together.

Regardless of your current work situation, you are bound to achieve what you want by carrying on and not thinking twice about making your presence felt and establishing your own rules.

You are sure to get what you want financially, thanks to your courage and hard work.

353

4	5

5

4

✚ If you are firm and adopt a realistic attitude, you should be able to free yourself of any uncertainties you might have about your health. This is, no doubt, why you have been feeling tired and lethargic

♥ It is possible that you need time to think, or you may be going through a period of doubt or scepticism, although you are hiding it well. Alternatively, if you are thinking about someone in particular, be aware that they are feeling as you do and are also rather lonely.

👪 When it comes to circumstances beyond your control and when you are faced with moral or material obligations, you seem to have no one to rely on but yourself. Don't worry because you are managing your affairs well.

📋 If you are in a testing situation that demands your full attention, make use of your experience and be firm and authoritative. Senior colleagues will give you any support you need to help carry out your plans or achieve your goals.

🎲 You have a firm grip on your financial situation, and your persistence, precision and sensible attitude will bring you positive results.

4	6

6

4

✚ You know full well that you are set in your ways. You are also sure that, no matter what problems you come up against, you have the resolve and the energy to overcome them.

♥ You are perfectly capable of steering your love life in the direction you want. If you are thinking about someone in particular, be aware that they are determined to act decisively when the time comes.

👪 It is up to you to move things forward in a confident yet realistic way. You will get any help you need from your family and those around you.

📋 A decision, agreement or partnership allows you to take control of a situation and to move it forward in a way that is both profitable and constructive.

🎲 Make up your mind to chance your arm and use your abilities and determination, not to mention a calculated amount of daring. You can turn things to your advantage.

354

 You are determined and not scared of hard work, and you have the will to succeed no matter what happens. There is no need to fear for your health or overall well-being.

You have such a strong will that no one can stand up to it, nor can anything get in your way. Whatever happens, you can be sure of your position. If you are thinking about a particular person, you have no reason to doubt their sincerity, courage or strength of character. You must accept, however, that this person will ultimately make all the decisions.

Your family situation seems to be secure and sufficiently solid to withstand any changes. You have it firmly under control and can rely on the determination and efficiency of someone close to you to take decisive action.

You are determined and immovable. It is always better for others to keep on the right side of you, as you have the situation well under control. If you are thinking about someone with whom you are currently dealing, you can be confident of their competence or desire to succeed.

Be dynamic and firm when you make decisions. You can take full control of any situation.

You are experiencing a problem, but if you face up to it with real determination, you should be able to overcome your weaknesses and concerns.

You are dealing with a person who needs to be firm and unyielding, but whose freedom of action is currently limited. Alternatively, you are the one who will have to act in a resolute way in order to sort out your love life or to stop it from falling apart.

You must take determined, realistic and rational action, setting aside your own weaknesses and illusions, when you are confronted with law and order or when the stability of a situation is under threat.

You don't have a totally free hand, but you still have the power to act and to take account of all eventualities and any principles that are at stake. Stick with your current position. You could well be able to reverse the situation, although you would have to demonstrate your strategic skills to do so.

For the time being you have no choice but to face up to your financial obligations with discipline and determination.

355

4

➕ You are in a position to rid yourself of any doubts or concerns you may have about your health. Go ahead: you'll feel all the better for it.

❤ You have everything you need to start a new chapter in your love life, so go ahead and do it; there is nothing to stop you. If you are thinking about someone in particular, be aware that they are also determined to achieve a radical change in their life.

👪 You have taken all the necessary precautions and know what is involved, so you can now make any decisions that are required. Alternatively, there may be someone close to you who is in the same position. If this is the case, you can be sure that they will make the necessary decisions.

📋 The decision about an important change that affects you directly has been made. You will either hear about this from someone else or find out about it for yourself. You will have to accept it and draw whatever conclusions are necessary.

🏦 You have everything you need to carry out a profitable financial operation or to create a change in your current situation.

4 10

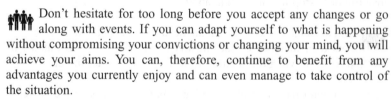

4

➕ If you can be flexible and willing and behave in a moderate way, everything will work out well for you.

❤ Given the current circumstances, you may find that you have to compromise. If you want to remain in control, you must be flexible and understanding but at the same time adopt a firm attitude.

👪 Don't hesitate for too long before you accept any changes or go along with events. If you can adapt yourself to what is happening without compromising your convictions or changing your mind, you will achieve your aims. You can, therefore, continue to benefit from any advantages you currently enjoy and can even manage to take control of the situation.

📋 Thing are going well at work, and you can, therefore, take the lead in your current circumstances by adopting a positive attitude. Be sure of the rights accruing to your position but be flexible enough to reach compromises as and when required.

🏦 You are well placed to carry out some interesting, profitable and well-timed financial transactions.

It is one of those times when you need to be really firm and realistic. If you want to try to avoid risking your health, take steps to ensure that you do not get too excited or become too impatient.

You are facing a clear and unambiguous situation which you may be dominating with a little too much self-assurance and conviction, but you alone can tell if this is the right course of action. If you are thinking about a particular person, be aware that they know what they want and are sure they will get it, which makes them demanding and even intolerant.

Either you or someone close to you wants to succeed at all costs, and only you can tell if what you or this person is aiming at is beyond your resources. No matter what happens, if you can avoid anger and impatience, everything will be all right.

You can be sure that your situation is secure and profitable, but must remain strong and realistic, keeping a firm hold on everything at stake to avoid any disruption. This is the price you have to pay for progress.

You have a firm grip on your current financial situation, allowing you to find ways to improve it even further as long as you are not too impatient. You have all the qualities you need to achieve your objectives.

You are in a position to shake off your physical or mental weaknesses, to put an end to your uncertainty and to recover your health. So don't wait any longer – get going!

Be firm and realistic and you will be able to put an end to a seemingly dead-end situation once and for all. If you are thinking about someone in particular, be aware that they are determined to provoke an upheaval in their life. It is inevitable but should prove to be for the best.

You will be able to break the current stalemate in your situation, free yourself from your obligations or bring about the changes you wish to make. Alternatively, it might be that someone close to you will suddenly force you to change completely.

Assuming you want to take control of the situation once more and regain the freedom to act as you think best, your only realistic option would seem to be to cause an upheaval of some kind or to raise some vital questions.

You need to take some prompt, decisive action if you want to break the current stalemate or free yourself from your obligations.

357

4 | 13

XIII

DEATH

13

IV

THE EMPEROR

4

➕ The difficulties you may have been experiencing are coming to an end. No matter what happens, it is likely that you are about to undergo some notable physical and spiritual changes.

❤ You are in a period of transition following a significant life change. If you are thinking about a particular person, it's almost certain that they also want to make radical changes, to themselves and to their lifestyle.

👪 You will be able to put your family situation on an entirely new footing, as long as a new situation is not forced on you by circumstances or someone close to you. No matter what happens, everything seems to be to your advantage.

📋 Having reaped the rewards of previous actions, you have started a new chapter in your professional life, or a situation has reached its logical conclusion. You are now in a position to make a fresh start, firm up projects or take advantage of these circumstances to achieve your goals.

▦ Your finances are currently going through a period of transformation. It is important to be practical and creative, as circumstances are very encouraging at present.

4 | 14

XIV

TEMPERANCE

14

IV

THE EMPEROR

4

➕ If you keep on making compromises or giving in to yourself, you will be faced with serious, time-consuming problems. Take really good care of your health and behave rationally and moderately.

❤ Your arguments don't hold up in the face of reality. If you want to put things right, you will need to change your attitude. If you are thinking about someone else, you need to know that, despite appearances, they are unsure about things. Behind what seems a realistic and even authoritative exterior, lies a person who is uncertain and easily influenced.

👪 Although compromises have been reached, the situation still seems to be quite complicated. Beware of beliefs that are based on mistaken reasoning. Alternatively, there may be someone close to you who is not getting on well or who wishes you nothing but good.

📋 You are probably facing an awkward, uncertain situation and are having difficulty finding the necessary answers. Alternatively, it might be that delays, complications or serious liabilities are preventing you from seizing an opportunity or from carrying out your plans.

▦ Sometimes you need to let events take their course and accept things as they are. If you can be realistic, you will avoid financial mistakes.

4 15

➕ Although your abundant energy makes you seem slightly chaotic and even highly strung at times, you seem to be at peace with yourself and are fully aware of your capabilities and resources. If you are experiencing any health problems, you have the resolve to overcome them with ease.

❤ Don't be afraid to make your feelings clear. Be constructive and kind, and happiness will be within reach. If you are thinking about someone in particular, you can be sure that their feelings and actions are genuine. This person is looking for truth and harmony and hoping that things will turn out well.

👪 You are in a position to make your feelings and ambitions known and achieve what you want. Alternatively, someone close to you may be imposing their feelings and ambitions on you. Don't complain, however, as it is likely to bring success and happiness to your family environment.

📋 If you are direct, clear and constructive, you should be able to make a profitable business deal. You have the ability to achieve your goals.

💰 You should be able to make a profitable financial transaction or to achieve all your ambitions.

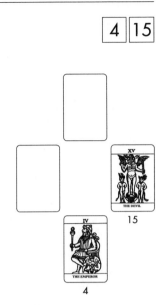

4 16

➕ Your energy and resolve will help you overcome any health problems you may be experiencing. If you have suffered a shock, try to learn from this and change your behaviour for the better.

❤ An upset or personal crisis will force you to reconsider your current situation, although it will also help you to find answers to your problems. If you are thinking about a particular person, they seem to be ready to agree to a reconciliation or to forgive or acknowledge a mistake.

👪 An upset, shock or crisis will prompt you to reconsider your current situation. Alternatively, someone close to you may make you an offer that solves your problems, brings about changes or introduces a breath of fresh air into your family situation.

📋 An upset, sudden change of job or an offer will force you to rethink your situation, to challenge what appeared to be certainties or to reconsider or set up a business deal. Be firm about what you want.

💰 Take a good look at your financial situation so that you can deal with upsetting or unforeseen circumstances. You mistakenly thought your finances were solid, but if you put right what was wrong, you should be able to get them on to a much better footing than is currently possible.

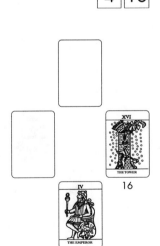

359

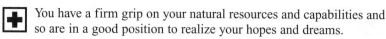

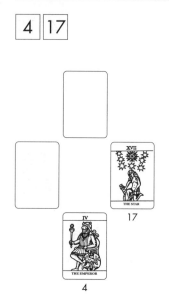

You have a firm grip on your natural resources and capabilities and so are in a good position to realize your hopes and dreams.

If you get the opportunity to achieve what you have been hoping for, don't hold back. Alternatively, if you are thinking about someone in particular, be aware that they have good intentions and high-minded ideals and that their feelings are sound.

A new situation, a joyful event, the success of someone close to you or the chance to broaden your horizons will bring you happiness.

Circumstances are right for you to achieve what you want and have more power to act and make decisions. Your skill and hard work will be fully rewarded.

You should derive a great deal of satisfaction from something new on the financial front, provided you handle your affairs with conviction and firmness.

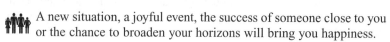

You always think you can avoid health problems but don't really have sufficient resolve to do so. In reality, however, you are well placed to avoid illness or fatigue if you look after yourself properly.

When you are faced with problems you always think that the most logical thing to do is to run away. You may be right, but think long and hard before you make a decision you cannot go back on. If you are thinking about someone special, the situation is such that they have no option but to leave or at least to distance themselves a little.

Either you or someone close to you will have to make a journey to face up to or resolve family-related problems. Alternatively, you may be planning a trip, and despite any doubts and concerns you may have or any problems you are facing, it will definitely take place.

Work matters are unclear at present. You may find that you have to involve someone from outside, make a move or obtain some assurance before acting. If, however, there is no other option open to you, you should abandon the situation, but with no lasting regrets.

If you are disappointed or dissatisfied with your financial situation, think long and hard about what part you may have played in this. It will help you to avoid making similar mistakes in the future.

✚ You seem at peace with yourself and your environment. Any doubts you may have had regarding your health should now disappear.

♥ You are keen to bring some stability into your emotional life, and circumstances are encouraging. If you are thinking about someone in particular, be aware that they want to enter into a long-term relationship or that their intentions are, at least, good.

👪 A successful outcome or the clarification of something makes you feel satisfied, strengthens your current situation and reinforces your convictions. It may be that there is a self-reliant person close to you on whom you can always count.

📝 A personal success, an agreement or a clear-cut situation reinforces your position, enabling you to take more effective and practical action. It also forces you to take on more responsibility, however, although you should not find yourself complaining about this.

💰 By being realistic, practical and aware of your responsibilities, you will be able to put your financial situation on to a firm footing and find it satisfying as well.

✚ It looks as if your problems are about to come to an end. Alternatively, you will be able to enjoy a new lease of life and avoid any difficulties. Whatever the case, the future is in your hands. Make a determined effort to preserve or restore your poise and general well-being

♥ It will be up to you to decide whether to respond to imminent events in your love life. Welcome any new prospects on offer with open arms. If you are thinking about someone in particular, they will be sure of their feelings and confident of their choices.

👪 You can accept the changes that are taking place within your family with confidence and enthusiasm and impose your decisions in a constructive manner, although you will not be oblivious to those around you. Alternatively, someone close to you may assure you of their support and trust and will revitalize your circumstances in the process.

📝 You will have to make an important decision. Alternatively, you might be waiting for an agreement to be reached or a solution to be found. Either way, your position and independence will be strengthened.

💰 A decision will be made that will help you to get your financial situation back on its feet again.

4	21

✚ You are thriving at present, full of energy and resolve, and are determined that nothing will curb your enthusiasm. You are enjoying a period of great personal growth. Don't be afraid of activity, whether it be sport, travel or simply drawing on your plentiful energy supplies in general.

♥ You feel you have everything you want at present. You are convinced that nothing is beyond your reach, and you are absolutely right. So, press on. If you are thinking about a particular person, you need not doubt their determination, confidence or desire to bring you happiness.

👪 The determination and practical decisions made by someone close to you will help you fulfil your aspirations. You can trust this person. Alternatively, if you are sufficiently determined you will get what you want. If you want to make a trip, you only have to put the idea into practice.

📋 The broadening of your social horizons or developments in your professional life put you in an excellent position to make decisions, firm up projects and generally make good progress. Take advantage of this. A journey or a move of some kind should also be beneficial.

🎲 Everything has gone as you planned, but this should not dampen your enterprising spirit. Don't stop when things are going so well. A business trip should be very profitable.

4	22

✚ You are well in control of yourself, and it is this that is giving you the power and freedom to act, travel or make quick decisions.

♥ If you have not already done so, you will soon meet someone new. Alternatively, someone who is important to you may be on their way back to you or may have already returned. Whatever the case, you know exactly what you want and have no intention of changing anything.

👪 You may be awaiting a visit from or the return of someone close to you, or someone in your family may be about to leave. In any case, there are lots of things happening in and around your family, but whatever happens you will remain true to yourself.

📋 Someone's arrival or departure or something new in your work situation should help to confirm your position. It will reinforce your resolve, making you even more determined than ever.

🎲 The intervention of someone or something from outside or an event that takes place suddenly should make your financial situation more secure. Stand firm by any decisions you make.

➕ Circumstances suggest that you should be receptive and dynamic and that you need to be in good health. If necessary, consult a doctor and have a check-up. It is better to be safe than sorry.

❤ If you are thinking about someone in particular, be aware that their feelings are deep and genuine. Alternatively, you are going to form a union with someone and stick to your romantic commitments.

👨‍👩‍👧 The stability of your family life is guaranteed through an initiative or the possibility of something new. Alternatively, someone close to you may force a decision on you that is both useful and beneficial.

📋 Thanks to a project or a new initiative or situation, circumstances should be just right for you to reach an agreement, enter into a contract or form a partnership.

🎴 Someone who is highly resourceful and skilful or a completely new venture should allow you to enter into a partnership or conclude some sort of beneficial contract that will stabilize your financial situation.

➕ Adopt a prudent and restrained attitude and you should be able to stabilize your health and make good use of your energy resources.

❤ Although you are currently experiencing something of a trough or someone close to you is being timid and restrained, you will soon have the capability and resources to move things forward as you would like.

👨‍👩‍👧 No matter what you do, you will enjoy discreet, yet full and effective support from within your family environment. Alternatively, you will receive good news from a family member.

📋 You will be able to take positive action to move things forward or to carry out a project that you have been keeping secret. Alternatively, you may receive a job offer or an opportunity for a business deal that you have not been expecting.

🎴 Even if you don't yet have all the facts or means at your fingertips, you will be able to take action to improve your financial situation and make it more stable.

363

5 3

If you want to remain mentally and physically healthy, it is vital that you take responsibility for your actions. This is the only way you will maintain your state of well-being.

If you are thinking about someone in particular, be aware that this person seems to be concerned with principles and convention, fairness and balance. Alternatively, your emotional life will be subjected to some sort of discipline.

You will be reassured by the generosity, understanding and honesty of someone close to you. Alternatively, you will be able to enjoy a stable and well-balanced family situation.

You will benefit from a legal decision. Alternatively, with the co-operation or support of a lawyer, your situation will develop or become stabilized under strict legal conditions.

A financial problem will require a legal decision before it can be resolved. Alternatively, an important person or a legal adviser will have some influence over developments in your financial situation.

5 4

Some advice that you receive or other factors or developments will help you to find ways of maintaining your good state of health.

It is good that you will keep to all your commitments and responsibilities. However, there won't be much room left for your emotions, which will no doubt make you stop and think.

Constructive factors in your family life will help you to find useful ways to stabilize your family situation.

You will no doubt take time to consider a long-term business venture. Doing this will increase its chances of being successful.

Decisive, constructive factors will prompt you to look for sensible solutions or to undertake a useful re-assessment of your situation.

➕ Confident of your health-related decisions, you will maintain your inner poise and feelings of well-being.

❤ There is no need to doubt yourself or your future relationships. If you have a decision to make about getting together with someone or about bringing stability into your love life, be confident and go ahead.

👪 If you need to make an important decision, you will have sufficient control over events and your family circle to do what is necessary.

📝 No matter what choices, agreements or partnerships are being offered to you, you can be sure that they will help your work situation develop and lead to success.

💰 Regardless of the choices you will have to make and the agreements or contracts you will be offered, you will still have the situation well in hand. You will, therefore, be able to take appropriate action on the financial front.

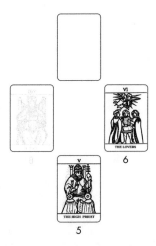

PROBABLE OUTCOME

➕ Thanks to the efforts you have been making, you will be able to accept your mental and physical responsibilities, but you won't be released from them. You should, therefore, expect to feel rather tired.

❤ Despite your best efforts, you won't be able rid yourself of a sense of unease or dependency. Ask yourself if this really matters.

👪 Circumstances beyond your control or some news that you will receive will force you to face up to your responsibilities. If a difficult or unsatisfactory family situation is on the horizon, you will soon have the chance to escape from it.

📝 Some news will force you to act in a responsible manner. Alternatively, as you have already taken care of everything that needs to be done to the best of your ability, you will manage to achieve the objectives you have set yourself, provided you stay on course.

💰 Some news or an event that is currently underway will force you to act reasonably, taking all your financial commitments and responsibilities into consideration.

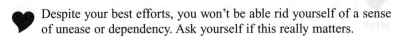

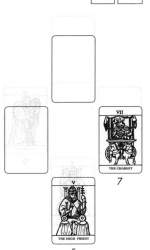

5 8

VIII

JUSTICE

8

THE HIGH PRIEST

5

✚ If you feel that your health and stability are at risk, be strict with yourself and get rid of anything that is not appropriate. Even if something happens that is beyond your control, you will still be able to achieve this.

♥ You will have to bring matters to a close or be ruthless in getting rid of anything that is unnecessary or likely to damage your love life.

👪 You must approve or bring about a radical change in your family situation. You can do this purely and simply by eliminating anything that is unnecessary or superfluous.

If a legal decision is at stake, it will be in your favour, allowing you to instigate some useful and radical changes in your work situation.

A well-balanced state of affairs will allow you to make some profitable, but strictly legal, deals.

5 9

IX

THE HERMIT

9

THE HIGH PRIEST

5

✚ If you feel you have personal limitations, you should, given your natural resources, be able to overcome them or, at least, to push your capabilities to the limit.

♥ After having taken a step back to reflect on your love life, you will be in a position to be more accommodating or to reach a useful arrangement or comprise.

👪 Something important will be clarified. This will allow you to make arrangements or reach well-timed compromises that will be helpful to your family.

Once something important has been pointed out or you have, after much thought, discovered it for yourself, you will be able to make some useful compromises or agreements.

No matter what your material obligations or responsibilities, you will always be able to find the best ways to meet them calmly.

➕ You will always be aware of the part you have to play in everything that happens to you and so will also be able to react energetically to whatever does occur.

❤️ There are going to be some sudden changes and rapid progress in your love life, and you might find them disconcerting. If you are thinking about someone in particular, you will find that this person will be both passionate and demanding.

👪 Current circumstances or developments underway are certain to help you to impose your plans, wishes and ambitions on your family.

📋 Events, changes or opportunities that come your way will enable you to achieve what you want at work.

▦ Thanks to changes, about-turns and the odd stroke of luck, you will be able to fulfil your aspirations on the financial front.

➕ You may have a firm grip on yourself and your resources, but you will still have to be careful or think about some therapy in order to detoxify your body and avoid problems.

❤️ There will be a small, passing crisis in your love life that will, nevertheless, resolve things. Alternatively, you will experience an emotional blow, which may lead to a reassessment of your situation. Deep down, this will bring you some relief.

👪 Although you have your family situation and current circumstances well under control, you cannot avoid some sort of upheaval or reassessment. However, this will relieve you of some of your material and moral responsibilities.

📋 You will have things well under control, which will help you to contain, as best you can, any changes or crises that might arise. If you have an important contract or agreement in mind, this will materialize rather abruptly.

▦ If you can keep tight control of your financial affairs, you will be able to welcome any unexpected changes with confidence. The changes will improve matters and remove some heavy burdens from you. No matter what happens, you will be able to face up to everything.

367

5 | 12

XII
THE HANGED MAN

12

V
THE HIGH PRIEST

5

✚ If you are currently feeling physically or emotionally weak or if you feel you have been letting things slide a little, you will soon know what to do to give yourself a new lease of life. Make sure you get plenty of rest and don't lose hope.

♥ Circumstances may seem a little constrained at the moment, but you will be able to abandon yourself to your feelings and enjoy them or trust that the future will bring something new into your love life.

👪 Although you might feel that your family life is rather too unchanging at the moment, you will soon have the chance to introduce something new to it that is also important to you.

🗒 If you are hoping or expecting something new to happen at work, rest assured that it will certainly come about. You will get all the support and approval you need to set up a new venture or help with an innovation of some kind.

▦ Prompted by your obligations or a financial situation that is currently too restricting, you will look at your resources in a new light or come up with some inventive ways to improve your finances.

5 | 13

XIII
DEATH

13

V
THE HIGH PRIEST

5

✚ If you think you have overcome a health problem, don't forget that appearances cannot always to be trusted. Make sure you are vigilant and strict with yourself in order to keep in good shape.

♥ A major change in your love life will disappoint you or plunge you into some confusion. Find out where you went wrong and make sure you learn any lessons.

👪 A radical change in your family life will force you to take on more responsibilities and draw on all your resources to contain the problems that will then arise.

🗒 A fundamental change in your work situation will mean that you have to take on more responsibility and both material and moral obligations. You should, therefore, expect to encounter some rather significant problems soon.

▦ An interruption in your cash flow or income is likely to put you in a difficult financial situation, all the more so because there will be expenses to be met. Accept your responsibilities and learn a lesson from this rather awkward experience.

➕ Any arrangements or compromises that are made will help you to improve your well-being or clarify your health situation, if this should prove necessary.

❤ Agreements or compromises in your love life will enable you to achieve exactly what you want.

👪 Your family circumstances will make good progress, thanks to various arrangements and agreements.

✎ Negotiations and some well-timed compromises will provide the ideal conditions for you to reach an agreement or enter into an association or partnership and fulfil your ambitions.

💰 You should be pleased with some opportune and profitable transactions that enable you to fulfil your financial ambitions.

5 14

➕ After a period of over-excitement and irritability, your behaviour will become more sensible and better balanced one again.

❤ Having experienced a passionate and rather turbulent phase in your love life, you can rest assured that a full reconciliation is on the horizon or that your current relationship will return to normal.

👪 You will want to reconsider some excessive or unreasonable factors or elements that will arise in your family. Alternatively, you will try to inject some new life into your domestic situation and make a change.

✎ External factors, which are full of potential although rather disruptive and confusing, will enable you to make a change for the better or put your work situation on to a new footing.

💰 You will succeed in achieving your financial goals, and these, in turn, will help bring about some changes or get your finances on a sound footing.

5 15

5 16

5

✚ If you experience a health crisis or problem, put your trust in competent people and you should recover rapidly. Alternatively, make sure you have nothing to do with any hazardous ventures that could jeopardize your stability and well-being.

♥ Things may appear to be at crisis level and in complete turmoil. Nevertheless, you will still be able to get what you want from your love life and even achieve a degree of fulfilment.

A crisis that proves liberating, an upset that proves beneficial or a sudden challenge will help your family situation to make progress or even flourish.

You will experience a sudden but inevitable crisis or upheaval. Alternatively, a sudden and perhaps even shocking event or crisis in your working life could have a salutary and liberating effect. It will result in an increase in your areas of responsibility, giving you more power to act and helping your work situation to develop still further.

A sudden event or an upset will help to improve your financial situation or create some important opportunities for you.

5 17

5

✚ If you have decided to go somewhere for a while or to travel for pleasure, don't delay; it can only do you good. Alternatively, draw on some of your natural resources and keep moving forward.

♥ If you are single at present you will almost certainly meet someone soon. Alternatively, you are sensitive, have genuine feelings and have faith in the future, and this encourages you to be more daring and constructive when it comes to your love life.

Happy times are on the cards for your family, possibly in the form of a birth, a trip or simply something new. Welcome them enthusiastically, but don't lose sight of reality.

Don't delay in making progress and moving forward when you are faced with such favourable circumstances as seem to exist at present. If you are relying on the support of someone important you should easily obtain it. You are on the threshold of a new departure in your professional life.

As long as you keep things moving forward, circumstances are just right for your plans on the financial front. Don't delay any longer.

If you are feeling physically tired and emotionally weak or just generally run down, it would be a good idea to have a thorough examination or take a basic course of treatment.

You are well aware of your duties and responsibilities and will, therefore, be able to contain or overcome any disappointments or problems that you may encounter in your love life.

Accept your responsibilities to the full and draw on your moral strength. You will then be able to resolve any conflicts and tackle any difficulties that arise in your family life.

Circumstances will become uncertain or unsatisfactory, either because you will be confronted by difficult and confusing events or because you will have to face up to problems or delays. You will, nevertheless, find that you have the resources to overcome all these problems.

You will almost certainly experience some delays or disappointments on the financial front, but you will manage to overcome these and meet your obligations, even if it does mean your profits will be reduced.

18

5

Health concerns will be clarified, introducing a degree of stability into this area of your life. This will also enable you to make useful decisions for your well-being, which you can then enjoy to the full.

If you are thinking about someone in particular, you should know that their feelings are genuine and sincere and, if it is not already the case, that they are looking for a full relationship. At any rate, your feelings will be shared, and great emotional satisfaction lies ahead.

A jointly reached decision or a choice about your family circumstances will bring you a great deal of satisfaction. Alternatively, someone close will show you affection and give you their full support.

Achieving a personal success or having a clear, positive way forward should facilitate the favourable outcome of an agreement, partnership or contract. Alternatively, you will be able to make an important and beneficial decision.

The conclusion of an agreement or contract or a decision that you will reach will almost certainly be favourable to the financial arrangements you have entered into, and the choices or decisions made will benefit your financial situation.

19

5

371

5	20

✚ You will enjoy a new lease of life and regain your vitality. However, in order to maintain this state of affairs you will need to follow a strict regime and not stray from it. Your efforts will be rewarded.

♥ If you are thinking about someone special, they will bring you some good news or put your love life on a new footing. Alternatively, a change or a fresh start will enable you to do everything you can to regain some stability.

In a period of change or upheaval or when your family matters have returned to normal, you will be able to do whatever you think necessary to enable you to make progress and become stronger.

Following a proposal or promotion or a shake-up of some sort, you will be able to take some constructive action to improve your work situation and achieve your objectives.

Once you have managed to breathe new life into your circumstances or have received a proposal, you will find your financial situation will make good progress or you will be able to take decisive action to put it on a sounder footing.

5	21

✚ The possibilities for personal growth that are coming your way will help you get into excellent condition, both physically and mentally.

♥ If it is not already doing so, your love life will positively flourish, bringing with it a sense of balance and stability.

Your family life will soon be thriving, if it is not already doing well. It means that you will be able to stabilize the situation and help your family to achieve everything it deserves.

Your work situation will develop in certain directions, becoming more secure and consolidated. Should you have to rely on a legal decision, you can be sure that it will be to your advantage.

If you are expecting a legal decision in your favour or if you are questioning the reliability, efficiency or honesty of someone who is defending your interests, there is no need to worry. You cannot lose in either situation.

5 22

➕ Your life will be a little disturbed or you will find yourself moving around quite often because of professional or social obligations, putting a strain on your energy supplies. To be sure of yourself and your health, rely on the advice of someone who knows what they are doing.

❤ You can expect a visit from someone who has been watching you but whose responsibilities and circumstances mean that they are not entirely free to do as they please. Whatever the case, your love life should soon settle down.

👪 The departure or arrival of someone close to you, a change or a house move will help stabilize your family situation.

📋 You will have to leave suddenly in order to reinforce your position and increase your responsibilities or to find a new job. You will receive any support that you need to achieve your aims.

💱 If you need financial support or advice or if you need to borrow money or find the capital for a financial venture, you should be able to do so in propitious circumstances.

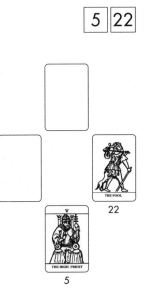

6 1

➕ If you have a choice to make or feel there is something you must do about your health, don't hesitate. You have plenty of energy and vitality, so make use of it.

❤ An encounter, some news or a fortunate event will prompt you to make a choice about your love life. If you are thinking about someone in particular, be aware that they have resolved to make an important decision relating to their own love life.

👪 Someone will show their affection for you or you will make an enjoyable family trip. If you have children, a joyful event concerning them is in store. Alternatively, following a project or an initiative, a decision will be taken that will help your family situation to develop.

📋 An initiative or the need to carry out a project will lead you to make an agreement or join forces with someone. Alternatively, you will make a decision that will help things move forward in your working life.

💱 Following an initiative or a new venture that is still in its infancy, you will have to make a choice that is likely to help improve your financial situation, but you will have your work cut out and will need funds.

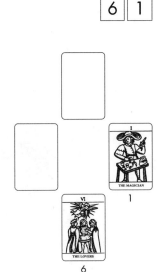

373

6	2

II THE HIGH PRIESTESS
2

VI THE LOVERS
6

✚ If you have any doubts at all about your health, don't prevaricate but start following a regime that will help restore or maintain your well-being. Alternatively, be patient and take note of the shrewd advice that you will be given.

♥ You are waiting for a decision to be made or to find some agreement. For the moment, however, the only assurance that you can have is that the decision will be made with the utmost caution and, whether good or bad, will be final but fair.

👪 A strict but fair decision has been made that will affect your family situation, but you are not yet aware of the result. However, you have been expecting this for some time now and are well prepared.

🗒 Although you have not as yet been told about it, a difficult yet fair decision about your position at work is going to be forced on you. Alternatively, be patient and you will find the agreement or stability for which you have been waiting.

▦ You will be forced to make a decision about your finances. You will probably have to meet someone halfway or reach a reasonable agreement with them.

6	3

III THE EMPRESS
3

VI THE LOVERS
6

✚ If you have a decision to make about your health, trust your instincts and go for the safest, most sensible option.

♥ If you are thinking about someone special, be aware that this person is waking up to their feelings and the important choice they have to make. Alternatively, it may be you who has to make a serious, rational choice about your love life.

👪 You will have to make a decision or do something that will be extremely beneficial to your family situation. Alternatively, you might be about to appreciate the genuine feelings your loved-ones have for you.

🗒 Although your current situation is satisfactory from a material point of view, you will realize that you still have important decisions to make. Take some time to reflect on the best course of action, unless a work colleague presents you with other options.

▦ If an apparently profitable financial deal is offered to you, think long and hard and assess the true value of the situation before you make any choices or commit yourself.

You seem to be experiencing some ups and downs as far as your well-being is concerned. Make the right choices and follow the path that allows you to exert the same influence over your health as you do in other areas of your life.

A fact or event will force you to make a sudden and rapid choice that will result in immediate changes in your current situation. If you are thinking about someone special, rest assured they will make a prompt and practical choice as far as their love life is concerned.

You will be faced with a decision that will prove favourable to the progress of your family situation and the relationships you have with those around you. Don't feel that you are under duress, especially if you often feel uncertain and have difficulty making decisions.

Thanks to someone close to you, you can make a decision about your work situation, and this will prove to be beneficial. Alternatively, you are sure to come up against new options in your professional life. Have faith in the relationships you have with your colleagues.

You will have to make a choice or even several choices about the likely progress of your financial matters, but be specific.

Even when faced with circumstances beyond your control, firm choices and resolute action should help you gradually overcome any problems. Alternatively, listen to useful advice and recommendations.

If you are thinking about someone in particular, bear in mind that their feelings are genuine. As a result, they are confident and hope to maintain the current state of affairs or to find a happy relationship. Alternatively, you have a stable love life with solid emotional relationships.

Someone close to you is assuring you of their genuine feelings and integrity. This is leading to good relationships between family members. If there is a choice or decision to be made, it will be a positive one.

Someone important or influential will help to finalize a significant professional agreement. You will be free to make the choices you want and initiate new ventures.

You will be advised to make some constructive choices and pick the sensible option or to promote an agreement or contract with regard to your financial situation. You can trust the people around you and should not doubt the usefulness of your decisions.

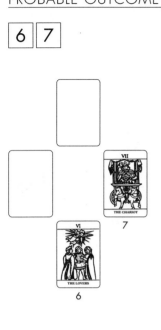

6	7

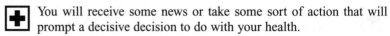 You will receive some news or take some sort of action that will prompt a decisive decision to do with your health.

If you are thinking about someone in particular, they will make an important decision that will cause a radical change in their private life. Alternatively, you may have reached a turning point and will have to make an important choice about your love life.

You will receive some news or discover that some action has been taken, and this will cause you to make a change or an important choice about your family situation, Otherwise, a change or decision might be imposed on you by those around you or as a result of circumstances.

A trip, some news or the progress that has been made thanks to your hard work will lead to a radical decision that will enable you to make a profitable agreement or carry out the projects you want.

A sound and advantageous decision, made in the wake of some news, a trip or your own efforts, will enable you to reach an agreement that will help your financial situation to develop further.

6	8

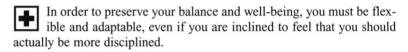 In order to preserve your balance and well-being, you must be flexible and adaptable, even if you are inclined to feel that you should actually be more disciplined.

If you are thinking about a particular person, you should know that in spite of their well-balanced attitude, they lack flexibility and understanding where their feelings are involved. Alternatively, as far as you are concerned, you appear indecisive and uncertain but open to all possibilities.

 A stable family situation makes communication and relationships easy for you. If you are forced to make a decision, be adaptable and try to find solutions that satisfy those around you.

 A well-balanced work situation has definitely tipped circumstances in your favour. You can form good working relationships, make shrewd decisions, negotiate advantageous agreements and contracts that will benefit everyone, and are more than capable of adapting to circumstances by being flexible and understanding as well.

Although your financial situation is well-balanced, you seem to be letting yourself be guided by events and circumstances. If you have some decisions to take, make sure you assess your chances carefully and take your resources into account.

➕ Your conscience has been pricking you or you may have been told to be careful, but you just can't curb your rather excessive tendencies. You are free to do as you choose, but be aware of the consequences.

❤ If you are thinking about someone in particular, be aware that their feelings are fiery and uncompromising. Alternatively, even though you are fully aware of the situation and are trying to be careful and sensible, you won't be able to control your passionate impulses.

👪 Despite the caution, vigilance and clear-sightedness shown by you or someone close to you, it will be difficult to control turbulent domestic relationships or to prevent wrong choices being made.

📝 Having looked into the situation in depth, you will have to make a shrewd choice that could turn out to be profitable in the long run.

💰 You have thought long and hard about your financial situation, and now you need to make some important choices that could turn out to further the long-term development of your finances. Make sure you keep your wits about you all the same.

➕ If you are going through a health crisis at the moment, don't worry, because it should only be temporary and could even prove beneficial in the end by helping to restore your equilibrium. Alternatively, don't think twice about rejecting any dangerous enterprises.

❤ Your love life is currently going well, and you will make a choice that will prove decisive or you will meet someone who will turn your life upside down. Alternatively, the person you are thinking about is undergoing an emotional crisis and may be feeling disturbed.

👪 Following a complete about-turn in your circumstances, you will have to make some fairly radical or uncompromising decisions. If there are relationship problems within your family, tell yourself that they are necessary and inevitable but that they will be only temporary and, ultimately, will help to lighten the atmosphere.

📝 After a sharp reversal of events or rapid developments in your work situation, you will reach an agreement or free yourself from a restrictive contract. Alternatively, you may make decisions that speed up events.

💰 Following a number of decisions that you have made, your financial situation is developing fairly rapidly. This could be good or bad, so you need to be cautious and determined, no matter what the circumstances.

| 6 | 11 |

➕ You have good self-control and seem to have a firm but calm hold over your current situation. Despite this, you have an emotional nature, are receptive to circumstances and sensitive to your surroundings.

❤️ If you are thinking about someone in particular, be aware that they are confident in their feelings and decisions and are looking for a special relationship that is based on real empathy. Alternatively, you are in control of circumstances and sure of your future decisions.

👪 You are in control of your family circle, and this allows you to take advantage of the favourable circumstances and special relationships that are likely to help you achieve what you want.

📋 You have a firm grip on events, and, what is more, the circumstances are right for the introduction of new trends. This will also help with any agreements or decisions you are hoping to make and will also contribute constructively to your new ideas.

📠 You have a firm grasp of events, and circumstances are now right for you to make some inspired choices and innovative decisions as far as your financial situation is concerned.

| 6 | 12 |

➕ Your decisions are being hampered by your anxiety and confusion, so you are finding it extremely difficult to free yourself of constraints and health problems. Try to be more focussed.

❤️ If you are thinking about someone special, they feel incapable of responding and may be too easily influenced to assert their independence. Alternatively, it may be you who is not free to act. If your attitude does not change, you may become disillusioned.

👪 You face all sorts of constraints in your family life. As a result, satisfaction is giving way to insecurity and disappointment. Eliminate any confusion that is surrounding you and be more decisive.

📋 The constraints, conflicts and confusing relationships that seem to be dominating things are making your working life unsatisfactory, to say the least, and you can no doubt add a feeling of disillusionment. Try to be firmer and more clear-sighted when making decisions.

📠 You will be forced to make a difficult, painful and even disappointing decision about your finances. You are finding it hard to make up your mind to be firm about this, but what choice do you have?

You have managed to get rid of anything that could have harmed your health or well-being. Having done so, you are now happily about to embark on a harmonious period of your life.

Having undergone a change or eliminated any potentially harmful factors, you will start a new chapter in your life and enjoy a new relationship or find real harmony on the romantic front. If you are thinking about someone in particular, they will find the happiness they seek after putting an end to certain matters once and for all.

Following a radical change, you will be able to make some positive decisions and enjoy good relationships.

Once a current situation has gone as far as it can or a radical change has occurred, circumstances will be ideal for you to enter a partnership or make a profitable agreement or decision. This should help you to carry out a successful business venture or make progress at work.

Following changes or financial gains, you will be able to make profitable decisions. Alternatively, on a more basic level, you will be able to carry out your plans or achieve something that is important to you.

Once you have carefully weighed up the pros and the cons and thought about everything that is at stake, you should decide to revert to the kind of stable behaviour that best suits your temperament.

You will be able to make all the practical agreements and compromises you need in order to get your love life on to a new footing. If you are thinking about someone in particular, be aware that they are determined to make the right concessions, to correct their mistakes and to start afresh when it comes to their own emotional affairs.

The discussions that are taking place or the opportunities that you are being offered could help to shed some light on any resolutions or decisions that you have to make. They will also enable you to review your family situation and make some progress towards a fresh start, from both an emotional and a relationship point of view.

Following some well-timed discussions or a necessary exchange of opinions, you will be able to take a decision or make an agreement that will put your working life on a new footing.

Following a timely transaction or a worthwhile discussion, you'll be able to make the right choices to get your finances back on their feet.

6 15

You will be in great shape physically and full of energy. As a result, you will be raring to go, making far-reaching decisions and good resolutions for the future and generally enjoying yourself to the full.

You will meet someone new or have a passionate relationship. Don't let yourself be carried away by the heat of the moment, however, and make sure you still have room for relationships that are deep, lasting and fulfilling as well as those that are intense but not enduring.

You will achieve your most cherished ambitions. Alternatively, a decision taken by those close to you will make you happy.

Thanks to extremely beneficial circumstances, you will be able to achieve your ambitions by reaching an agreement, entering into a partnership or taking some decisions that will further your business deals and professional life.

You will have to make a decision or establish an agreement or partnership that will help the development of your financial situation and satisfy your ambitions.

6 16

Following an upheaval or an unforeseeable, yet inevitable, event, you will have to make a sudden decision about your health, which will raise some concerns about your overall well-being.

Your love life will be turned upside down after a new encounter or a broken relationship. As a result, you may take the sudden decision to make a new start. Alternatively, you will achieve your goals.

An upset, an abrupt reconsideration of your family situation or an outburst of temper will lead you, or someone close to you, to decide to leave. Alternatively, you will be able to take the decisions that you have been wanting to make.

Following an upheaval or the resolution of a stalemate or after questions are raised about your situation, you will be able to start afresh and put things on a new footing, free from constraints. This will involve making some new choices, creating new partnerships and taking the decisions you want to make.

As a result of an upset, you will be forced to find new support and make a new start. Alternatively, you will finally be free to take the decisions that you want to make about your finances. Whatever the case, if you have made any mistakes, be careful not to repeat them.

You are undoubtedly receptive to your circumstances and in tune with your environment, and this will help you to find stability and achieve a sense of well-being. This is your way of protecting your health.

Circumstances are right for a new relationship; take decisions with the stabilization of your love life or the start of something new in mind. If you are thinking about someone special, their feelings are genuine and any decisions they make will be constructive.

Following a birth or something new entering or occurring within your family life, you will find your relationships are stronger and will be able to make any decisions that your duty or family feeling dictate.

Favourable circumstances will enable you to reach an agreement, set up a partnership or make some serious resolutions with a view to putting an original idea into practice or creating a new situation at work. Incidentally, your professional relationships remain excellent.

Your financial resources are extremely healthy. Coupled with favourable circumstances, this means that you can make some progressive decisions or shrewd choices to make the best use of your funds.

No matter what health problems, anxieties or concerns you may have at present, don't let things slide. Make firm decisions and be resolute and determined to regain your health and stability.

You will experience a disappointment in your love life, or you will be tempted to make a choice, fall into a trap or be deceived about something. Be careful about your relationships. They are not as simple as they might appear. If you are thinking about someone in particular, despite some underlying problems, their feelings are genuine.

Although problems, delays or conflicts could arise within your family, you will still be able to make the decisions you need to sort matters out or to help you reach an agreement.

After coming through a difficult period or being faced with a confusing and complicated situation, you will take the decisions you need to find an agreement or make a tricky, but necessary, choice. Don't let yourself be influenced by circumstances or by those around you.

You will experience financial disappointments or disillusionment. If you have made mistakes, take these into account and be more careful when making choices or playing the stock market in the future.

381

6 | 19

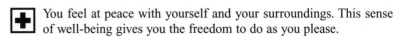

 You feel at peace with yourself and your surroundings. This sense of well-being gives you the freedom to do as you please.

You will find complete satisfaction on the romantic front, irrespective of your intentions or desires. If you are thinking of someone in particular, they are looking for a genuine relationship.

Harmony rules at home and in your family relationships. This will make it easier for you to make some progress and to make bold choices and decisions, which will, in turn, help your situation to develop well or simply give you a great deal of satisfaction and pleasure.

Once you have reached an agreement, set up a partnership, achieved real success or managed to clarify a situation, you will be able to take some wide-ranging and progressive decisions or resolutions.

A clear-cut financial situation is a contributory factor to success, particularly if you have important decisions, tricky choices or agreements that you want to reach amicably. This is likely to improve your financial affairs or simply give you good control over your resources.

6 | 20

 Once you have emerged from a difficult period, reviewed your health and returned to a degree of normality, you will have to embrace logic and discipline to restore your general good health.

Because, or in spite, of a fresh start or renewal of your love life you will make some sound and rational decisions. Your aim will be either to find harmony and establish stable romantic relationships or to break off a relationship once and for all. Try to be fair in your decisions, however.

Having reconsidered or made changes in your family circumstances, put them on a new footing or received a proposal of some sort, you will have to make some difficult but clear-cut decisions, taking into account the stability and good relationships that exist within your family.

 A business venture or a proposal will enable you to reach some sensible, well-balanced agreements, but you may also have to make some harsh but fair decisions or uncompromising choices. You will want to sort out anything that is unclear once and for all.

Despite the proposals that may be offered to you and the prospect of a revival in your affairs, stand firm when making decisions and make sure you remain within the letter of the law. This will enable you to achieve a stable financial position.

You are currently in a period of personal growth and are broadening your horizons. You would be well advised to think carefully about your choices and decisions, however. Don't let opportunities get in the way of your search for balance and well-being.

You will realize that emotional fulfilment is well within your reach. If you are thinking about a particular person, be aware that any choices they have made will focus on their own goals.

You seem to be completely satisfied with your family situation. This is encouraging for long-term choices and relationships.

Circumstances are just right for positive developments in your working life and for broadening the possibilities open to you. Alternatively, contacts in far-off places will prompt you to make some realistic decisions or to reach some agreements. You will then realize to what extent your resolutions will prove to be the deciding factor.

There are interesting prospects within your reach, but be careful, precise and realistic about the decisions you will have to make or when you are embarking on any agreements.

A journey or an initiative will enable you to make some decisions that will help you find stability. If by any chance you have not yet made up your mind to make this trip or take this action, don't delay.

Following a journey or an encounter, you will make a decision about your love life. If, however, you have not yet made up your mind to make a journey or take some action on the romantic front, don't hesitate any longer. If you are thinking about someone in particular, be aware that their arrival in your life will prompt you to make more of a romantic commitment than you had anticipated.

Your family relationships will be strengthened as the result of a trip, initiative, visit, departure or return.

Following an initiative, a journey or someone's arrival or departure, you will be able to reach an agreement, make some important choices or set up a partnership that will be useful to your work.

An action or the arrival or departure of someone will leave you in a position to make some important decisions or reach agreements that will help you manage your finances efficiently. Alternatively, it might simply be that you are saving for a journey that is important to you.

383

7 1

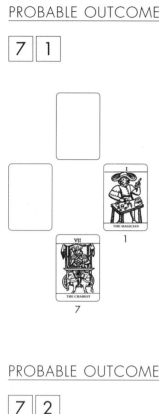

✚ If you want to feel balanced and assert your will, you will have to be brave and submit yourself to some sort of regime or discipline.

❤ A decision or a new, but uncertain situation in your love life will lead you to take action to impose your will, but you should bear in mind the need to be fair. If you are thinking about someone special, consider the possibility that they may be involved in this situation.

👪 You will have to take positive action and submit yourself to some sort of regime or discipline in order to carry out a project or initiative relating to constructive developments in your family life.

📋 Following an initiative or during your quest to carry out your plans or create a new situation, which is still unclear, you will act decisively to take the matter completely in hand. You will make sure you leave nothing to chance so that you can achieve what you want.

▦ After completing a particular initiative or emerging from financial uncertainty, you will have to submit yourself to certain rules or disciplines, which will, nevertheless, prove profitable.

7 2

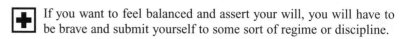
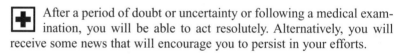
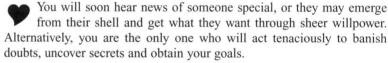

✚ After a period of doubt or uncertainty or following a medical examination, you will be able to act resolutely. Alternatively, you will receive some news that will encourage you to persist in your efforts.

❤ You will soon hear news of someone special, or they may emerge from their shell and get what they want through sheer willpower. Alternatively, you are the only one who will act tenaciously to banish doubts, uncover secrets and obtain your goals.

👪 You will hear some news soon from someone within your family circle. Alternatively, after careful thought, you will decide to do something about putting an end to doubts or carrying out some plans for your family that you have kept secret until now.

📋 You will soon receive the news you have been expecting about someone or something that will dispel your doubts. This will give you the go-ahead to take some positive action, and you will be certain that you can achieve what you want because you will have taken the trouble to study the matter in advance.

▦ You will receive some long-awaited news, which will give you the green light to move your financial affairs forward, albeit cautiously. It will give you more assurance that you will be able to achieve your aims.

➕ Trust your instincts. and you will obtain what you want through your own efforts and willpower.

❤️ It will be up to you to take the initiative and arrange matters so that they are in your favour. If you act with courage and determination, you will achieve your emotional goals.

👪 You can be confident of progress on the domestic front. Your courage and generosity of spirit mean that your plans will bear fruit and you will overcome any obstacles in your path. No matter what takes place, you will be in control.

📋 A productive and promising situation will enable you to make real progress. Be bold and act now to take advantage of circumstances, control events and achieve your aims.

💹 Advantageous circumstances will help you make financial progress. Be proactive but stay in control.

➕ You will have the confidence to do whatever you want, reaping the rewards of your own efforts and willpower.

❤️ You will be so confident emotionally that nothing will come between you and what you want. If someone special is in your thoughts, rest assured that you are both on the same wavelength.

👪 With the support of a strong, stable domestic situation, you will be able to help your family circumstances to develop naturally and freely while remaining happily in control.

📋 You will receive the assurance you need to be proactive and make progress at work. Alternatively, you will take slow but sure control and effect significant developments on the professional front.

💹 You will be able to act independently, remaining in control of your finances and having a free rein to expand.

385

7 5

+ You will need initiative, self-discipline and a healthy lifestyle if you really want to overcome any problems and recharge your batteries.

♥ You need to get a grip on yourself and release your emotions from their current constraints. If a special someone is in your thoughts, you should be aware that they also wish to overcome their difficulties but that they may forced to leave.

You will be obliged to leave, either by moving house or by going on a journey, to escape from an awkward and frustrating situation. Only then will you be able to tackle difficulties or problems for which you feel responsible or silence concerns over your dependency or weakness.

Bold and determined action is needed if you are to make progress on a professional level or free yourself from the limitations and responsibilities currently hampering your development.

Material and moral commitments will force you to develop matters on the financial front, leaving you free to take on new commitments.

7 6

+ You will need to be proactive or to make an important choice before you can eliminate any potential health risk.

♥ You will have to make a choice, bring to an end an emotional issue, overcome your indecision and institute important change. You need to be aware that the person in your thoughts wants to implement radical change in their life and will succeed in doing so.

A joint agreement or choice will lead to decisive action on the domestic front. Change, progress and control lie ahead.

Following a mutual agreement, choice or decision, you must act positively and with determination to ensure that you make progress and exert control in your current professional environment.

An agreement or resolution will soon enable you to achieve your financial objectives, reap the rewards of your endeavours or transform your current fiscal situation.

7 8

If you are striving for independence and a sense of fulfilment, you need to accept the rules, adopt a regime of self-discipline and make an effort to stay on the right track, no matter what temptations come your way. You can be certain that you have the energy to succeed.

You will be tempted to respond aggressively or even violently to an intractable or frustrating situation, and you should ask yourself if this is reasonable behaviour. If a particular person is in your thoughts, you should know that they are thinking along the same lines as you.

An inflexible situation will encourage you to impose your will, make an effort to get what you want or engage in concerted, even feverish action to reach your targets without delay.

If you think the law is on your side, you should push for a strict but fair judgement that supports your situation. Alternatively, you should avoid being too quick to impose your will on any problem in need of resolution.

Strictly controlled and well-balanced finances may help you to assert yourself, impose your own wishes or achieve your established targets.

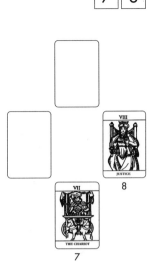

7 9

Someone will let you know, or you will discover for yourself, what action you need to take to cast off current health concerns. You would also do well to avoid embarking on a major journey or undertaking anything too hazardous.

You will realize that you need to move on and bid farewell to obstacles along the path to your emotional goals. If your mind is on someone special, be aware that, after thinking about it carefully, they may leave suddenly or seriously question their position.

After careful consideration, you will abruptly embark on a course of action to implement change. Alternatively, some astonishing news will come your way, which you may have been secretly half-expecting.

News arrives that may prompt you to question your situation or provide it with some answers. Any subsequent upheaval will lead to steady personal progress, as long as you stick to your intended course.

You will hear some surprising news, but if you know how to take the necessary precautions and learn from this sudden challenge, you will stay on track and keep pace with events.

387

7	10

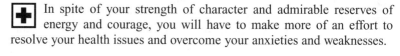

No matter what the outcome of your current circumstances, you will always manage to revitalize yourself by drawing on your resources and remaining open to what is going on around you.

A situation destined to be to your advantage will assist you in your efforts to introduce something new into your love life and will help you achieve your emotional goals. Alternatively, expect some good news.

Domestic issues are developing quickly and positively, giving you the chance to introduce something new and fulfilling to your family.

Steady progress in your profession will help you act independently to move things forward quickly and introduce something new, unique or creative. Alternatively, you should expect to hear news that relates to one of your own ambitions.

A lucky situation will encourage you to assert yourself in a particular direction and you will gain the upper hand. As a result, you will make positive progress on the financial front.

7	11

In spite of your strength of character and admirable reserves of energy and courage, you will have to make more of an effort to resolve your health issues and overcome your anxieties and weaknesses.

You may feel in calm control of your emotional life, but you still have difficulties, disappointments and concerns to overcome. Alternatively, you should expect to hear bad news, but you have enough courage and willpower to overcome any challenges that result.

Even though you feel in control of domestic issues, you are not quite at the end of the road and need to make more progress before reaching your target. Expect to receive disappointing or frustrating news, but remember that it will not constitute a permanent setback.

You may feel in full control at work but there are still some issues and obstacles in your path. Keep your target in your sights and don't give up the struggle.

No matter what your financial difficulties or disappointments, you will still manage to keep control of your situation. Your efforts will pay off in the end.

7 | 12

➕ Don't confuse letting go with giving up. No matter what happens, you will always have enough willpower and courage to act or react in a positive manner.

❤ Although you feel you lack autonomy or independence, you will find greatest satisfaction by being clear about your motives. You will soon hear some good news that brings both happiness and relief.

👪 Allow events to carry you with them and things will develop positively and satisfactorily on the domestic front. You should also expect some wonderful news.

📋 Things have become somewhat stale at work, but you have the resources, both internal and external, to move on, and you will reach agreements and succeed in your initiatives. Alternatively, no matter what situation you find yourself in, don't rest on your laurels and you will see your efforts richly rewarded.

⏳ You will achieve a certain financial autonomy and release yourself from the constraints of a stagnant situation or impasse or you may be able to pay off your debts. Alternatively, you should expect to receive a piece of good news associated with your finances.

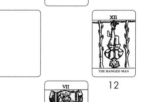

12

7

7 | 13

➕ After eliminating any potentially harmful factors and introducing radical change or bringing a situation to a conclusion, you will feel revitalized and ready to make further progress through sheer willpower.

❤ Following a major change or the conclusion to a domestic matter, you will be able to work towards reconciliation, rehabilitation or renewal in your emotional life.

👪 Some important transformation or inevitable conclusion will enable you to rectify your position and encourage admiration and respect from your peers through a willingness to change.

📋 After the conclusion of something or a change on the professional front, you will be able to act with a renewed vigour or take advantage of the possibilities for change that you will be offered.

⏳ Following the receipt of profits or the termination of a particular source of income, you must work hard to kick-start your business or re-float your finances.

13

7

7	14

✚ Following an understanding or compromise or because of your own flexibility and adaptability, you will manage to achieve your full potential, expand your horizons or embark on a beneficial journey.

♥ A positive compromise, intelligent arrangement or exchange of views will enable you to make uninterrupted progress towards your targets. You will move forward in your emotional life.

👪 Following some timely agreement, sensible compromise or useful opportunity, you will be able to embark on a long journey or work towards your goals. You will witness improvements in your domestic situation and lifestyle.

📋 An opportunity, settlement or successful negotiation will enable you to widen the scope of your activities and broaden your horizons. Your efforts will be generously rewarded.

▣ Take advantage of opportunities that encourage improved finances by being flexible and open to change. Your efforts will be duly repaid.

7	15

✚ Action is an end in itself for you, and you have an insatiable desire to get what you want and to be continually on the move. Try to avoid over-excitement, which can often involve unnecessary risks or lead to serious mistakes.

♥ Overwhelming desire, intense passions or general excitability will prompt a sudden reaction or an abrupt departure in search of satisfaction. Be aware that the person preoccupying your thoughts may tend to overreact and become uncontrollable.

👪 You will probably have the opportunity to make a swift departure or take sudden action to satisfy your desires on the domestic front. Alternatively, an upsetting or emotionally fraught situation will cause you to overreact, aggressively and thoughtlessly.

📋 A highly beneficial set of circumstances will prompt you to leave or take swift action to achieve your ambitions. You will also be able to make immediate progress, and you should expect events to take off on a professional level.

▣ Nothing will get in the way of your financial dreams. Only you can decide if your behaviour is beneficial or harmful.

➕ An accident or blow to your health will require an effort on your part to overcome your challenges and restore your inner harmony.

❤️ Following an upheaval, unavoidable crisis or sudden challenge in your emotional life, you will have the inner strength to pursue any course of action dictated by your sense of commitment and duty.

👪 Some upset, sudden challenge or crisis will not be enough to make you lose control. You will carry on at your own pace, oblivious to all except your sense of duty. Your efforts and willpower will enable you to overcome your difficulties.

✍️ No matter what upheavals, crises or sudden challenges you may experience, you will continue to work towards progress, bolstered by your keen awareness of your responsibilities or by the support of an influential and proactive person.

🗝️ Following a shock or a sudden challenge you will be able to improve your finances and make them increasingly dependable.

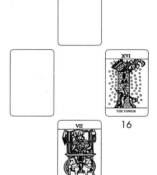

➕ After a chance to reappraise your health or recover your inner strength, you will be able to make positive moves towards your established or newly set goals. You will be able to maintain a healthy stability in your life.

❤️ You will succeed in forging relationships and emotional links that will match your hopes. Alternatively, you will meet someone who provides the answers to your most intimate questions. If you are planning to embark on a journey in pursuit of love, you will be more than satisfied.

👪 Following a fortunate combination of events or in the hope of achieving something new and original, you will assert yourself and your desires. Those who love you will follow your lead.

✍️ Excellent professional circumstances will present choices, decisions, agreements and a need for positive action. You will make excellent progress at work and come up with something entirely new.

🗝️ New circumstances will encourage negotiations, resolutions and choices relating to the management of your funds. You will make progress in your financial affairs.

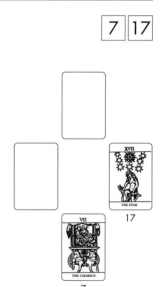

| 7 | 18 |

✚ You will have to make a huge and courageous effort if you are to overcome your fatigue or health concerns. You cannot afford to shrink from the hard work involved.

♥ Against a background of turmoil, challenge or disappointment, you will have to prove your sincerity. Only then can you resolve your emotional issues.

Despite, or perhaps because of, a confused and disappointing situation, you will embark on a journey. Alternatively, your efforts to solve your problems and overcome your difficulties will succeed.

Your willpower has probably helped you to escape trouble. From now on, you will be able to take the initiative and make progress, but only on the condition that you always stay in control.

When you have overcome current financial difficulties, the world really will be your oyster. Choose any course of action that takes your fancy.

| 7 | 19 |

✚ If you act clearly and calmly, you will have the inner resources to improve your fitness and energy levels. You will gain sufficient strength to tackle anything that comes your way.

♥ A sincere union or a new transparency in your relationship will put you back on course or prompt you to do what is necessary to restore matters to normal in your emotional life.

Your harmonious and happy domestic life will give you the support you need to make progress and reach your targets.

New light shed on professional issues will help you impose your own structure, introduce improvements at work and achieve your objectives – all with determination and efficiency.

An explanation or positive situation will support you in your purposeful and efficient efforts to remain on course for financial progress and success.

Expect to receive some good news about your health. Alternatively, after things return to normal, you will need to be more careful about how you expend your energy. You will finally achieve your goals.

News will come your way, prompting you to review or seriously rethink your emotional situation. Alternatively, a suggestion, reconciliation or return will encourage you to take a sensible course of action and make matters both clear and positive.

You will receive a proposal or invitation. Alternatively, as the result of a changing situation or its radical reappraisal, you will find all the facts at your disposal to achieve your goals.

Following a proposal or change, you will make cautious, pragmatic but efficient moves to meet the new professional goals you have set yourself or to implement the desired changes.

A proposal or positive change will help you put more serious, long-term moves in place to meet your financial objectives.

A promising and rewarding development will help you in your struggle to achieve your full potential. If you are planning a trip, it will bring positive benefits.

A reassuring and satisfying situation will help you express your feelings and emotions, but, better still, it will improve your love life. A journey will bring emotional fulfilment.

Security in your home will encourage you in your efforts to introduce positive direction to the family environment, helping it to expand and mature.

A situation that promises to widen your horizons and expand your power base will encourage you to keep going at work. You will make rapid progress and steer your activities in your chosen direction.

There will be great potential for you to expand financially and make positive progress towards the goals you have set yourself.

7 22

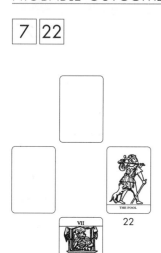

VII

22

THE CHARIOT

7

➕ Feel free to embark on any actions, journeys or moves you may choose. Continue along the path you have carved out for yourself.

❤ You will have to make a sudden, hasty departure if you want to get your own way. Alternatively, someone else's departure will lead to developments in your love life.

👪 You will be able to leave, and through your resolve, follow the path to true progress. Alternatively, the arrival or departure of someone in your immediate circle will soon improve matters. A further option is that you will soon move house.

📝 Someone's arrival or departure, a move or journey or, indeed, a period of transition will determine how your professional situation evolves. In any case, you have the strength of character to make things work out the way you want and achieve great success.

🏠 If you make the right moves and play your cards correctly, your efforts will be rewarded and you will achieve the financial success you deserve.

8 1

I

THE MAGICIAN

1

VIII

JUSTICE

8

➕ You know the right decisions or correct moves to make in your cautious but determined search for stability on the health front. Slowly and surely, well-being will come your way.

❤ Faced with what is still a vague desire, you will need to be tough and demanding and show some forethought. Given the circumstances, only you can tell if this attitude is the right one.

👪 You will to have to come to a decision alone. Alternatively, you will need to assess an idea or project concerning someone within your family circle, but this will not upset the apple cart or threaten the order and stability of your domestic situation. No matter what happens, you will be resolute in your decision.

📝 Projects and plans or new horizons will help you in your search for stability. Have faith, but bear in mind that whatever your talent and expertise, you will have to play by the rules.

🏠 Moves, initiatives or the expertise of a third party will encourage stability in your financial situation. Even though you are sceptical, place your trust in the proposals made to you.

Something you hear or read will urge you to be cautious. You will adopt a healthy and self-disciplined lifestyle, which will help your personal development.

A conclusion reached but yet to be revealed will improve your love life. You can do nothing until all the facts are known. If a special someone is in your thoughts, be aware that an apparent reserve or indifference conceals a reliable, stable nature that is able to develop emotionally.

You are no doubt waiting for a decision or judgement in your favour or for things to return to normal. You won't have to wait long for your own stability and balance to win through.

It may sometimes be necessary to wait patiently and quietly for things to return to normal before you can move on. Alternatively, an anticipated legal decision, about which you can do nothing, will be given in your favour, prompting a development at work.

The time will come when there is nothing you can do but wait for things to fall into place. If this does not happen, the stability of your position will prompt its own development.

Your instincts and intelligence will help you find the right balance. You will never lose your self-assurance or control.

You should be aware that the feelings of someone who is in your thoughts are sincere and their behaviour is honest and balanced, and you can have complete confidence in them. On the other hand, no matter what happens, you can rely on a strong and balanced emotional life.

You will always be able to rely on a solid, harmonious domestic situation or count on the impartial, if rather harsh, judgement of the person who controls the stability of your home environment.

You are involved in a stable and solid professional environment and can count on it to last. Alternatively, you will be able to take thoughtful, constructive steps to further ensure its stability and durability.

You will be able to embark on productive, intelligent steps to put your finances on a stable, solid and reliable footing, bringing you increased security.

395

8 4

+ You need to adopt a regime of self-discipline and a lifestyle that both limits your actions and maintains your sense of balance.

♥ The constraints in your emotional life are evident. You may have to confront authority, misunderstanding, prejudice and strict judgement without being able to do much about them.

👪 You will be the object or victim of a harsh legal judgement, to which you cannot respond. Alternatively, you will be able to establish some sort of domestic balance simply by virtue of the constraints imposed on you by a personal choice or impulsive decision.

📋 You are in danger of coming up against harsh, uncompromising judgements that lead to an intractable situation. Alternatively, you will face an authoritarian person, who refuses to give way on even the smallest point and sticks to their guns obstinately.

📇 You will be faced with tough, uncompromising circumstances, against which you will be almost powerless. You may obtain confirmation of the precarious stability of your financial situation.

8 5

+ You will come to see how important it is to eliminate any potentially harmful factors on the health front. It is time for some serious self-discipline.

♥ You must make a decision that will bring a relationship to an end. This change or turning point in your life will help you regain balance in your relationships.

👪 A decision will be reached after due consideration and there will be no going back on it. Your integrity and sense of justice will be rewarded, unless, of course, you were in the wrong, in which case the ruling will go against you.

📋 A radical and inflexible ruling will be pronounced, resulting in a turnaround, conclusion or rejection of a previously held position. Alternatively, a strictly worded legal contract could turn out to be highly profitable for you.

📇 You will reach an agreement, sign a contract or be involved in a profitable and entirely lawful business.

8 6

➕ You will have no trouble making choices, taking necessary decisions or accommodating events that will promote your general health.

❤ You will be fair-minded in your decisions and choices and enjoy a more balanced and flexible emotional life as a result.

👪 Certain key relationships will encourage positive agreements, useful compromises and fair solutions. These will please everybody, promote stability and make it easier for the right choices to be made.

📋 You will have to reach agreements or conclude reasonable deals that will help bring stability to your professional situation. This will, in turn, be reinforced by your own flexible and adaptable response to external trends and events.

▦ If you have to make choices and decisions, apply self-discipline, clear thinking and pragmatism. Try to take advantage of any opportunities on offer that could encourage greater flexibility on your part.

8 7

➕ You will have to make an effort to be more self-disciplined if you hope to keep your heightened emotions under control and make proper, balanced use of your energy.

❤ You may need to be rather harsh and inflexible in order to rein in the chaos and upheaval that could occur in your love life. If you do this, order will be restored and your efforts will be rewarded.

👪 You will not make progress unless you stick rigorously to the rules, come what may.

📋 An item of news or the results of a past action will help you establish the solid foundation for a highly profitable situation, which will also require self-discipline. Any ruling made will be to your advantage.

▦ Past efforts will help you assert yourself without delay, and you will be able to rely on a profitable situation that is to your advantage, with a reassuringly solid foundation.

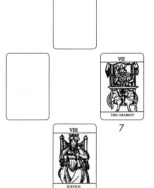

8 9

IX
THE HERMIT
9

VIII
JUSTICE
8

➕ A sudden enlightenment, a word of caution from someone close or a personal discovery will prompt you to be self-disciplined and put in place a much more balanced regime.

❤ A realization or discovery will prompt you to make a decision that is in line with your instincts. Alternatively, you may need to be more self-disciplined and less open in your search for true love.

👪 In time, you will succeed in stabilizing matters, thanks to profound, creative and innovative resources and favourable circumstances. Be patient and do not give up.

📋 You will continue to demonstrate vigilance and determination and will make your situation stable but dependent on something new. It could be an original idea, a new product or another innovation.

🗄 You are going to realize how urgent and necessary it will be to re-establish your financial basis.

8 10

X
THE WHEEL OF FORTUNE
10

VIII
JUSTICE
8

➕ In spite of your fears or health concerns, your self-discipline and natural stability will steadily increase.

❤ No matter what problems you may encounter, you should be strict, tough and unbending in your judgements. This is the only attitude to adopt in the face of a situation that is fraught with potential confusion and conflict, and it will lead to the restoration of order.

👪 Any problems you may experience in your family life will resolve themselves of their own accord, simply fading away in the face of your emotional stability.

📋 If there are problems or conflicts in your situation, you need only show stability and inflexibility at every hurdle and the problems and difficulties will vanish as if by magic.

🗄 Your situation is going to evolve in a way that will allow you to put your finances in order and sort out all your problems.

➕ You will remain in control of your circumstances and maintain a healthy balance.

8 11

❤️ The ease with which you maintain control of your situation combined with your complete faith in yourself and your circumstances will help you to make clear, positive judgements. Alternatively, you will achieve a level of happiness and balance in your emotional relationships with others.

👪 The assurance with which you deal with events will make it possible for you to pass clear judgements on your situation and achieve a degree of emotional balance and progress.

📋 The natural development of your position together with your control over your circumstances will enable you to conclude a strictly legal agreement, which will represent a real achievement and bring you great success.

💼 Natural expansion of your professional horizons will combine with your calm, assured control of your circumstances to bring about an important, strictly legal and highly successful deal.

11

8

➕ Following a return to normality, you will realize that from now on your stability will depend on a strict regime of self-discipline.

8 12

❤️ A harsh, impartial and logical judgement will be passed, allowing you to start afresh and no longer feel constrained or trapped.

👪 A strict, logical and unbiased judgement will bring both relief and a release from certain emotional constraints.

📋 If you wish to free your situation from current constraints or put an end to the stalemate, you will be obliged to go back on your judgement or question the stability of your position. Alternatively, a ruling to this effect will be enforced.

💼 You will be subject to a harsh, impartial but logical judgement, which will prove vital to the renewed stability of your situation.

12

8

8 | 13

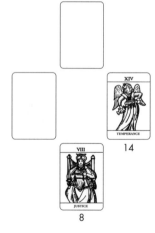

XIII

DEATH

13

VIII

JUSTICE

8

➕ When you bring a particular set of circumstances to an end or change something in your way of life, you will find a rewarding balance and stability.

❤️ Your relationship will undergo significant changes or even a radical transformation, and you will find the emotional and psychological stability for which you have been hoping.

👨‍👩‍👧 A change or transformation will enable you to make your situation more balanced and fulfilling.

📋 Following a change or transformation, the development of an advantageous situation or the conclusion to a project, you will be able to make your situation more balanced or help it develop, which will also assist its stability.

🂠 A profitable situation, in which you were involved and which may now be at its conclusion, or a change in circumstances will help you put your financial affairs on a more stable basis.

8 | 14

XIV

TEMPERANCE

14

VIII

JUSTICE

8

➕ Following a significant event or after evaluating the pros and cons of your situation, you will feel sufficiently strong mentally either to leave or to accept an imminent change.

❤️ Careful consideration, an extended period of indecision over how best to respond to a situation or a lengthy discussion will be followed by an abrupt but fair decision to conclude something, taken in a spirit of compromise.

👨‍👩‍👧 Exchanges of opinion, discussions or personal observations will enable you to reach the right compromises to maintain stability at home. You will be able to pass on or enforce a tough decision.

📋 You will be in a position to increase your professional stability. Alternatively, negotiations will end in agreements and compromises, with a just and fair decision taken about your work situation.

🂠 Following an opportunity, agreement or transaction, you will be tempted to question or adjust the basis of your financial situation.

✚ You risk the imposition of a strict course of treatment or rigorous diet. If you have been diagnosed with a serious illness, you will be forced to take rapid and extreme measures.

♥ A passionate situation or reckless relationship or indulgence in emotional excesses will be judged harshly, and unfortunately there will be nothing you can do about it.

👪 A harsh, inflexible judgement is going to be made against you, your family circle or a member of your family. Alternatively, you will come to a strictly legal agreement or make a contract relating to your domestic situation.

📋 A tough, restrictive legal decision will be passed against or in favour of you at work. If it is the former, you need do nothing about it; if the latter, it will lead to greater financial stability.

💰 A judgement will be passed in your favour and to your benefit. Alternatively, the prospect of carrying out a profitable operation will enable you to conclude an agreement or sign a contract that will improve the stability of your financial position.

✚ Following an upheaval, blow to your health or accident, you will have to adopt a regime of self-discipline. Alternatively, you will manage to avoid potential harm to your health. Whatever happens, take care.

♥ An upheaval, crisis or serious challenge to your emotional situation will mean that your equilibrium will be somewhat upset. You will, however, still have to make some harsh, but ultimately fair and positive resolutions or decisions.

👪 An upheaval, crisis or breach will ultimately turn out to be beneficial and to your distinct advantage when you are making difficult but fair decisions.

📋 Following an upheaval or sudden challenge, you will to have to adopt a rather rigorous albeit fair regime and implement tough but equitable decisions to make progress on the professional front.

💰 A salutary upheaval, or a sudden challenge or crisis, will prompt harsh but justifiable decisions that will ultimately prove indispensable to your financial situation.

8 | 17

XVII
THE STAR
17

VIII
JUSTICE
8

➕ Your dynamic and reliable state of health will be reinforced by positive events, and you will be able to impose your will, both firmly and fairly.

♥ Wholly beneficial circumstances and genuine feelings will help you remain emotionally balanced.

👪 Positive events will make it easier for your circumstances to develop once you have put in place a framework of stable, balanced or equitable values.

✍ Fortuitous events, innovative developments, new products or innovative ideas will create a firm basis for your professional progress.

📇 New and positive circumstances will help your finances to develop in a steady and balanced way.

8 | 18

XVIII
THE MOON
18

VIII
JUSTICE
8

➕ Don't worry about your health or lose sleep over problems, irritations or anxieties as these can be easily solved by a strict regime of self-discipline.

♥ Conflicts, problems, disappointments or mistakes will prompt you to be highly self-disciplined. You will manage to eliminate anything potentially harmful or upsetting in your emotional life.

👪 A confused, confidential and disappointing situation will lead you to adopt a strict regime, both physically and mentally. This is the only way that order can be re-imposed on the domestic front.

✍ Problems, conflicts and arguments will encourage you to resort to the law to establish your case. Expect to be judged accordingly.

📇 If you have made a mistake, you will have to accept the consequences. Otherwise, a conflict or awkward situation is going to force you to adopt a scrupulous attitude or strong measures to decide matters.

➕ Light will be shed on your health concerns, allowing you to find or slowly but surely restore your balance and stability.

♥ Your sincere and reciprocated feelings will lead to the emotional stability you have been searching for.

👪 A degree of harmony in your family relationships and emotional life, or new light shed on these, will reinforce stability at home. You will act more wisely, naturally and logically.

📋 Following a fresh insight into your professional situation or as a result of a fair and positive agreement or well-deserved success, you will feel satisfied that everything that could be accomplished has been. Your situation will then become more stable and consistent.

💰 Following a clarification of your finances and a positive agreement, you will be able to achieve the balance and stability for which you have been searching.

8

➕ A recovery or renewal will bring feelings of rejuvenation. You will see your general health improve, thanks to your new-found balance and stability.

♥ Everything will fall into place naturally and spontaneously in your emotional life. You could experience a renewal that leads to positive and stable developments.

👪 You will make progress on the domestic front, resulting in a more stable and rewarding home environment.

📋 Following a proposal or change of some sort, your professional situation will develop in a stable, balanced way.

💰 A proposal will make it possible for your finances to develop in a balanced, fair and profitable way.

8

| 8 | 21 |

XXI
THE WORLD
21

VIII
JUSTICE
8

➕ Your natural horizons will expand and your health will flourish, leaving you feeling more confident and secure.

❤️ Emotional fulfilment or the realization of your wishes will make your love life both stable and well-balanced.

👪 A happy and contented family environment will be combined with an opportunity to realize your deepest desires, and this will help you make your domestic life stronger and more permanent.

📋 A situation full of potential or the natural progression of your professional life will enable you to assert yourself and become established on a more secure basis at work.

🗳️ Your finances will develop profitably, enabling you to enjoy a more stable and unchallenged situation.

| 8 | 22 |

THE FOOL
22

VIII
JUSTICE
8

➕ Following a journey, a trip or some other activity, you will return full of good intentions and able to take tough, wise decisions. In short, you will feel much more level-headed.

❤️ Someone's arrival or departure, a journey or a course of action will encourage you to be more sensible, wiser, tougher and, importantly, more stable in your emotional life.

👪 The arrival or departure of someone else, a journey, a house move or a move for other reasons will reinforce or affect the stability of your situation.

📋 The stability of your professional status will be confirmed following the departure or arrival of a third party or after a journey or other course of action. You will then feel fully within your rights and at ease in your work environment.

🗳️ If you have been extravagant with your money, you will suffer the consequences. Alternatively, you should continue the search for anything that could help you to establish financial equilibrium.

9 1

An initiative or decision that has been carefully considered will encourage you to take precautions, including cutting yourself off for a while, to bring about gradual but effective changes in your health.

If you are thinking of someone special, you should be aware that they are wondering what they too can do to advance their own position. Alternatively, you may have to demonstrate patience, wisdom and determination to bring about change.

You will be faced with an initiative concerning progress on the domestic front. Behave sensibly but pragmatically. Alternatively, you may have to advise a young person to follow this same advice if they are to succeed.

In order to be successful in your plans or initiatives, you will behave sensibly, seeking the wisest and most certain way of advancing your professional status.

You need to remain aware that slow but sure progress will be made through your own efforts, skills, work or other enterprises.

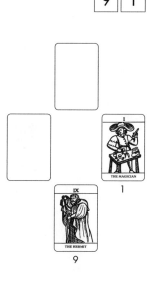

9 2

You will come to realize what topics interest and worry you most and gain control of your physical and mental well-being.

You will discover something new about yourself. If you want to be in control of your life and not at the beck and call of others, you will have to show patience, vigilance and determination.

When you have considered the question closely and waited for the right moment, you will gradually move in the direction that your experience, good sense and maturity will suggest.

Before you can make a move or any real if slow progress, you will go through a period of reflection, withdrawal and scepticism, from which you will draw the conclusions that will give you the assurance you need to see the way ahead clearly.

Only after you have really thought about your financial situation will you be able to take the necessary sensible steps relating to it.

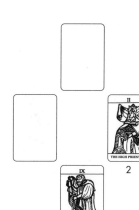

405

9	3

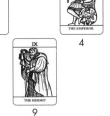

➕ In spite of yourself, your instinct for self-preservation will force you to take an honest look at yourself. You will then be more sensible, stronger and see the way ahead more clearly.

❤ You will see the extent to which you are attached to, and dependent on, someone you love. Alternatively, you will be forced to seek a way out of a situation that is limiting your activities.

👪 You will feel somewhat isolated and restricted at home or in your family life, but you will look for ways to emerge from this situation.

📋 A materially advantageous and profitable situation will encourage you to study, consider and patiently, if painfully, research a long-term objective.

🗒 A profitable, if somewhat restricting, situation will lead you to painstaking, careful consideration of better and wiser methods of dealing with it.

9	4

➕ You will soon be convinced that you should implement change and act cautiously but with determination to eliminate factors or tendencies that could prove harmful.

❤ You will discover that it is safer and wiser to bring a certain situation to an end. It is time for you to make radical changes on the emotional front.

👪 Working alone or with the help of someone close, you will reach the conclusion that a major change or the cessation of a situation is required in domestic matters.

📋 After serious consideration or discussions with those able to shed light on your circumstances, you will become convinced of the need for rewarding and profitable change.

🗒 Despite your scepticism and stubborn realism, you will soon be convinced of the need to implement profitable change.

➕ You may need to have a medical check-up, but there should be no need for major concern.

9 5

❤️ Commitments and responsibilities will prompt you to implement the most profitable agreements and accept necessary compromises and concessions in order to make slow but sure progress in your love life.

👪 You will probably be persuaded by your commitments or your sense of what is right and wrong to try to reach the agreements or make the compromises needed to adapt more easily to your circumstances. Do not be fooled and stay in control of the situation.

✏️ Compromises and concessions will be required if you are to find favour with an important decision-maker or influential person and if you are ultimately to achieve your long-term objectives.

💰 You will have to find better ways of using or managing your money and discover the solutions best suited to your current circumstances.

5

9

➕ Take your time and stand back a little before resolving anything. Concentrate all your mental and physical energy on making choices about your state of health.

9 6

❤️ Although you are cautious and are determined not to be fooled no matter what happens, you will find it hard not to act or react in an emotional and egoistic way.

👪 Do not be fooled by the intense or extreme behaviour that will dominate your domestic life or by the selfish choices or arbitrary decisions taken by others. Unfortunately, simply avoiding being duped does not achieve that much.

✏️ You will have to make an important decision, concentrating all your efforts and mental and physical energy. It does not matter how long this takes nor how you go about it – the important thing is that you do achieve your objective.

💰 You will be able to get down to the business of making critical choices and taking extremely important decisions in order to avoid the temptations of chaos and ensure long-term stability.

6

9

9 7

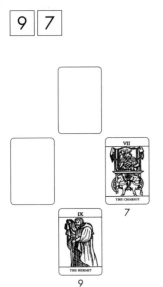

➕ Caution and foresight will enable you to avoid risks but will also help to speed up your steady personal development.

♥ You will hear disturbing news or discover something that could well present a challenge in your love life. Be aware that the person in your thoughts is coming to a difficult but positive awareness of their own situation and may decide, after careful consideration, to make a sudden departure.

👪 Despite considerable effort, you will come to see that a crisis, upheaval or challenge is inevitable. The sooner it happens, the better it will be for you and your situation. Alternatively, after careful consideration, you may decide that it would be best if you were to leave suddenly, thereby initiating useful change.

📋 After making every effort to achieve your objectives, you will come to appreciate the best way in which to speed up progress towards your ultimate goal.

📋 You will receive disturbing news or perhaps discover something that will take a huge weight off your shoulders, mirror the results of your own research or solve your problems.

9 8

➕ If you wish to maintain or regain stability on the health front, you will have to adopt a strict regime of self-discipline, a positive lifestyle or a tough stance towards your own psychological health.

♥ You can rely on your inner strengths and discipline to support your search for new emotional experiences and feelings.

👪 A balanced situation will help you to fulfil your hopes or desires for new experiences and horizons or for personal discovery.

📋 You will be able to count on a reliable professional background to pursue your quest for original ideas and discover new factors to help your long-term projects.

📋 A difficult situation will enable you to identify new possibilities and will inspire you to improve your finances.

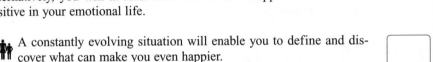

➕ You will be in a strong position to identify and clear up health problems and do all that is required to stay balanced, fit and well.

❤ A sudden change or development or even unexpected circumstances will enable you to find the love you have long been searching for. Alternatively, you will at least have the means to appreciate all that is positive in your emotional life.

👪 A constantly evolving situation will enable you to define and discover what can make you even happier.

🖉 Positive professional developments will help you see things more clearly, leaving nothing to chance. Alternatively, you will be able to act cautiously to achieve your aims and hopes of long-term success.

💹 Changes in your circumstances will help you to clear up your financial affairs and show you the way forward.

➕ Your self-restraint and physical and mental control will enable you to concentrate on personal quests, research or investigations. Important changes in your behaviour and way of life will result.

❤ Trust in your relationship or the person in your thoughts to help you find the answers you are looking for. You will know precisely what you need to say and do in order to implement positive change.

👪 A stable, solid family background or related situation will help you find answers to problems and introduce significant, new and positive changes or proposals.

🖉 You appear to be in control of your business affairs and professional situation. Despite, or perhaps because of, this, you will look for new perspectives and answers that could bring long-term gain.

💹 Trust your experience and you will implement useful and intelligent moves aimed at improving your financial situation.

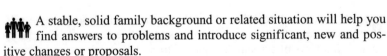

9 | 12

12

9

✚ A stalemate or a certain amount of physical and mental frailty may prompt you to take yourself in hand so that you can recover your energy levels.

♥ You will eventually succeed in finding your ideal love. However, you will still have to make a few sacrifices and realize some key facts about yourself.

👨‍👩‍👦 You will find ideal ways to widen your current horizons and to solve potential problems that could undermine or even halt your projects. Your desires will be fulfilled.

📋 You may be forced to give up or sacrifice something. This may seem hard, but it will probably mean that you exchange evil for good. In the longer term, it will enable you to widen the scope of your business and your objectives and ambitions.

📠 A rather stagnant situation may provide you with an opportunity to speculate or entertain other financial possibilities and enable you to find both temporary and long-term answers.

9 | 13

13

9

✚ Radical change will bring with it a real awareness of your state of health. You may be prompted to adopt a degree of detachment, which may even take the form of a departure.

♥ You will need time to take stock of the radical change that has occurred in your love life. In response, you will dispense with your apparent stoicism and make a final decision to cut yourself off, move away or even leave for good.

👨‍👩‍👦 A major, and doubtless inevitable, change will lead to some self-revelations. Say what you have to say, realize exactly what is going on and find ways of extricating yourself from the situation.

📋 You will not have to wait long for a radical change or for a situation to reach its logical and inevitable conclusion. You will then have to rely on yourself, bolstered by your own experiences, to search quickly for other solutions or a new position.

📠 You are in danger of finding yourself without money and forced to look for help. Alternatively, a radical and profitable change in your situation will bring you greater financial freedom.

➕ After a positive assessment of your possibilities or a medical check-up, you will adopt a wiser, more considered and more responsible attitude. You will then gain or regain full control of yourself.

❤ Honest explanations and timely compromises will help you see exactly what is going on. You will then understand your position and find the sensible solutions that are necessary.

👪 If discussions, agreements and compromises are proposed, make sure you give them due consideration. No matter what happens, you will not be fooled but will remain cautious and fully aware of your duties and responsibilities.

✍ Frank and open discussions and exchanges of opinions will allow you to find the solutions or agreements you need to create a solid foundation for your long-term schemes.

▦ You will be able to study your financial situation in depth and find solutions to any current problems. Before you do this, you may well have to accept compromises or carry out a few well-timed transactions.

➕ Temptations will be placed in your way and you may not be able to resist them. You alone must decide what attitude to adopt. Alternatively, after a period of upheaval and turmoil, you will see the need to make some hard choices.

❤ You are in danger of being plunged into a troubled, passionate situation. You will come to realize that it is not always enough to be cautious and sensible when choosing and making up your mind.

👪 You will not be prey to the troubled, excitable or over-heated atmosphere at home nor to the way things have spun out of control in your family life. You will have to make concentrated, sensible efforts to see through it and make the necessary, intelligent decisions.

✍ A rewarding possibility will lead you to take sound decisions and make key, precise choices, perhaps with the aim of reaching an interesting agreement or finding a profitable solution in both the short and long term.

▦ You will make thoughtful and correct decisions about your finances. Indeed, in the circumstances, you would be wise not to overestimate your resources and look to the long term.

411

| 9 | 16 |

➕ A blow to your health, an accident or an upheaval in your life has put you in a state of shock. You are determined to learn from this difficult experience and show more caution in future.

💚 You will draw the obvious conclusions from a sudden challenge, unavoidable shock or a necessary crisis in your emotional life. Bolstered by this experience, you will turn to face the future with real determination.

👨‍👩‍👧 A crisis, shock or sudden challenge will make you weigh up your situation calmly and firmly. You will then be able to impose your will and achieve your ends.

📋 A shock or sudden upheaval will enable you eventually to achieve your objectives. You can work towards your long-term goals without fear of the effort involved.

📇 Following a shock or sudden challenge, you will need to weigh up your situation seriously and find effective, long-term solutions.

| 9 | 17 |

➕ You are as open and attentive as ever to what is happening within and around you. Consequently, without resorting to extremes, you will find it easy to establish stability and draw on your inner resources.

💚 Positive circumstances will fulfil your expectations, or deep feelings will create an emotional stability. Love is not always a battle and it may be in your interest to let go a little more.

👨‍👩‍👧 New and positive circumstances will create the domestic stability you are seeking and leave the way open for you to be your usual accessible and highly receptive self, albeit to a more moderate, sensible and subtle degree.

📋 Positive change will encourage original but tough solutions at work. You need to weigh up all the elements involved first, however, and give the matter serious and due consideration.

📇 Your efforts to find long-term financial stability will be helped by new and positive circumstances.

412

9 18

➕ The health problems you have experienced will make you more aware of the need to adopt a more sensible and serious attitude all round, even if this requires cutting yourself off for a while or being supremely patient.

♥ It may not be what you want, but you will at last stop being taken in by what is going wrong in your emotional life. Your anxieties or weaknesses will have no effect. If it is what you want, this will be the moment for you to pull through, to become aware of your mistakes and to learn lessons for the future.

👨‍👩‍👧 You will realize what is going wrong at home, but you will feel too isolated or too alone to act or respond appropriately. It is, however, time you found practical answers to your problems.

📋 You will experience professional disappointment or realize that you have made a mistake. No matter what happens, you are going to find yourself on your own, with no one to rely on but yourself when you are solving your problems and seeing matters through to their conclusion.

⏳ Monetary problems are on the cards, or you will realize that you have made financial mistakes. No matter what happens, don't count on anyone else to find a way out of your current situation.

9 19

➕ Fortuitous events will shed light on your health and help you work out what you need to do to ensure slow but steady progress.

♥ A genuine union, special relationship or happy love life will give you the answers you need on the emotional front.

👨‍👩‍👧 An apparently happy domestic situation or a positive environment will encourage you to be cautious, considerate and also take care to preserve what you will come to see is a precious treasure.

📋 A personal success, notable achievement or excellent agreement will enable you to define your short- and long-term objectives clearly and make appropriate changes.

⏳ A clear and generally positive situation will supply the answers to your financial questions or help you take steps to develop your finances slowly but surely.

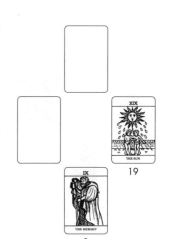

413

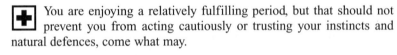

➕ Following a change or revival or the recovery from illness, you will do what you think is necessary to achieve self-control.

❤️ A renewal or major change in your emotional life will help you assume control of your love life in a happy, harmonious and long-lasting way.

👪 Following changes on the domestic front, you will be able to take the steps needed to control the situation or make positive moves. You will reveal just how strong and self-disciplined you are.

📋 A revival, change or proposal will present itself. Take time to think about it before giving a definitive answer, and you will be able to secure your position, expand your role and pursue your personal goals.

🗄️ A change of opinion or situation will enable you to find ways of managing your funds, investments and capital more sensibly and with a view to long-term growth.

---

9 21

➕ You are enjoying a relatively fulfilling period, but that should not prevent you from acting cautiously or trusting your instincts and natural defences, come what may.

❤️ You will come to appreciate that someone has sincere and genuine feelings for you, and this will be a revelation. Alternatively, a real feeling of emotional fulfilment will give you more time in which to realize your full potential.

👪 A fulfilling family environment will present opportunities for you to meet your domestic goals.

📋 The broadening of your powers to investigate and take action, or the natural progression of your professional situation will help you take prudent, realistic steps to achieve your objectives.

🗄️ Show caution, pragmatism and determination and you will be able to assess and control your financial situation and reap its rewards.

➕ You will appreciate the significance of a key factor in your psycho-logical and physical well-being.

9 22

❤️ Someone else's arrival or departure will make you aware of an important fact or factor that only you can discover and understand, even if you have to be alone to appreciate this to the full.

👪 The arrival or departure of someone in your immediate circle will make you think more seriously about things. Alternatively, after a somewhat troubled transitional period, you will find exactly what you were looking for, or you will leave to be alone.

📋 You will need to travel to find what you are looking for. Alternatively, a developing situation will force you to be somewhat isolated and to rely on your own experience to find realistic solutions.

💰 After taking a particular action or moving funds, you will appreciate the current state of your finances and find the practical answers to the questions that have been raised.

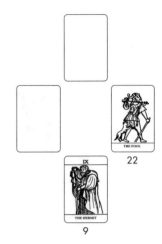

22

9

➕ Take the initiative or make moves to profit fully from your inner energy and sense of dynamism.

10 1

❤️ If someone special is in your thoughts, be aware that although they are young and untried, they know what they want and where they are going. Alternatively, you will be able to control your emotional life and, as a result, achieve your goals.

👪 An initiative or decision will allow circumstances to develop in a positive and expansive way.

📋 Your initiatives, decisions and expertise at work will advance your position both rapidly and positively, while allowing you to retain complete control.

💰 Your ability to take the initiative together with your skills and expertise will help you improve your financial situation without delay. You will channel your resources more efficiently and create a solid, long-term foundation.

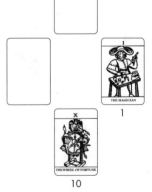

1

10

415

10	2

II
THE HIGH PRIESTESS
2

x
THE WHEEL OF FORTUNE
10

✚ Sensible precautions, great patience and natural reserve will not be enough to stem the tide. You are in danger of seeing your health deteriorate if you do not react more firmly.

♥ If someone special is in your thoughts, be aware that their reserve, poor communication skills or general inertia will hinder progress on the emotional front. Alternatively, your patience will not be rewarded and your development will be hampered.

👪 Your family situation has been limited by a lack of communication or commitment. You risk becoming weak or vulnerable on the domestic front and may be caught in a trap you had not envisaged.

📋 You will be restricted at work by the excessive reserve or 'wait-and-see' policy of others, which threatens to block your professional development and progress.

🏠 There may be something hidden or undisclosed that will have the effect of halting growth in your financial situation.

10	3

III
THE EMPRESS
3

x
THE WHEEL OF FORTUNE
10

✚ Trust your instincts and eliminate from your lifestyle anything that is potentially harmful so that you will be able to enjoy your health and well-being.

♥ You should expect radical change on the emotional front. If you are thinking of someone special, tell yourself that they are probably the cause of this change or that they themselves are experiencing a significant sense of upheaval.

👪 Someone in your family circle may trigger a positive development, or your own understanding, intelligent and generous attitude will act as the catalyst for change.

📋 Following a profitable and favourable result, things will develop at work, and you should expect radical and positive change.

🏠 The time is right to profit from advantageous circumstances, which will bring about positive progress on the financial front.

Practical advice about your health and lifestyle will help you behave in a more flexible and beneficial way.

In spite of your own convictions or those of someone who is in your thoughts, developments on the emotional front will require you to be more adaptable to circumstances and to accept what is happening around you.

No matter what you believe about the progress of your family circumstances, you will still have to reach agreements or make some compromises in order to adapt better to events and derive benefit from the current state of affairs.

You will receive helpful advice or support that will enable you to reach the necessary agreements or make the required compromises.

Your financial situation depends on a structure that is imposed on it or on practical advice given by others.

10

You will have to take some urgent and extreme measures to put a stop to your present decline. Alternatively, take care that your responsibilities do not lead you to excess and over-indulgence, which may endanger your health.

In spite of the advice you have received, it may be best to let things move along at their own pace and to stop worrying about the possible consequences.

Despite the rules or restrictions that will have been put in place, your situation is in danger of taking a backwards step or becoming disorganized, though this could be advantageous.

An important person or an official agreement will promote significant progress or even promotion.

Important and official financial transactions and agreements will soon prove very profitable.

10

417

10	6

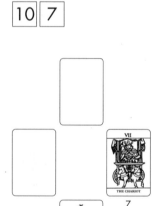

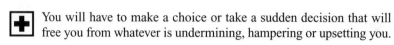 You will have to make a choice or take a sudden decision that will free you from whatever is undermining, hampering or upsetting you.

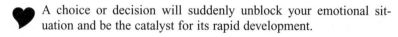 A choice or decision will suddenly unblock your emotional situation and be the catalyst for its rapid development.

A choice or decision will lead to a sudden change, which will be positive and liberating but also difficult because of its disconcerting nature and the challenges it presents.

An agreement, choice or decision will cause a sudden upheaval, which will be both liberating and positive in its final outcome.

Financial decisions or choices will promote a rapid improvement in your affairs, provided that they are put into practice quickly.

10	7

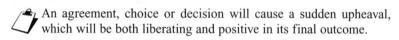 Your efforts will be fully repaid, and you can to go back to basics, with your batteries completely recharged. If you are planning a journey, rest assured that it will do you a great deal of good.

A journey could prove beneficial. Alternatively, all your efforts will bring a degree of emotional fulfilment and lay the foundations for something new and happy.

You will have to be tenacious and hard-working if you are to improve your domestic situation. Events around you will encourage the improvement and herald something new and welcome.

Go your own way and achieve your goals with ease. Events will help you on your path, and your efforts will be rewarded.

You may receive excellent news concerning your resources or finances. Alternatively, work on your financial affairs will reward all your efforts and advance matters considerably.

➕ In spite of the self-discipline you were advised to embrace or willingly adopted, you will not be able to avoid the turbulence and instability caused by your physical and mental fatigue.

♥ A strict regime will not help prevent things from degenerating into turmoil and confusion. You will be disappointed emotionally and unable to solve all the issues on this front, contrary to appeareances.

👪 If you were expecting a legal decision, you will be disappointed, because it will probably not be as you hoped. Alternatively, in spite of the strictures imposed on your situation, it will head towards disorder and confusion.

📋 Any legal decision will disappoint you. Although you have imposed strict rules, your situation is likely to be beset by problems, errors and deception.

⏳ You will be unable to rely entirely on your financial stability. It will prove precarious or deceptive, and you should expect difficulties or annoying problems.

➕ You will be encouraged to be cautious or a new discovery will prove positive on the health front.

♥ You are in search of a genuine relationship with someone who feels as you do. You will find your partner and experience real happiness.

👪 You will suddenly find the harmony and domestic happiness you were looking for. Indeed, things are already moving in this direction. Alternatively, following some sort of revelation or personal discovery, you will experience great joy.

📋 A personal discovery will help matters progress in a positive way or be a crucial factor in your personal success and happiness. Alternatively, after carefully considering and analysing a particular factor, you will reach an agreement or create the working partnership you sought.

⏳ After demonstrating caution and an ability to weigh things up fairly and thoroughly, you will let your finances follow their natural, positive course, in both the short and long term.

10 11

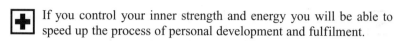

If you control your inner strength and energy you will be able to speed up the process of personal development and fulfilment.

Your faith in your current situation will help it to develop. It will also enable you to enjoy its progress and lead to a degree of emotional fulfilment.

Your domestic situation may well develop and bring short- and long-term happiness and fulfilment, leading to an expansion of its social and geographical horizons.

Hold your ground calmly but firmly. If you keep control of your circumstances and on-going events you will succeed in making considerable advances.

Make sure that you can depend on your financial situation. Stay in full control of circumstances, and you will have no trouble directing its growth.

10 12

Past experiences of frailty and immobility will be replaced with an opportunity to start afresh. It could now be time to rest, relax and regain your health.

You will do everything you can to extricate yourself with all speed from a limiting relationship. If you are thinking of someone special, be aware that events may force that person to leave or to return in a hurry.

Someone in your family circle will probably be forced to leave or return suddenly. Alternatively, the way out of a static situation will unexpectedly present itself. Take care not to make the same mistakes again in the future.

Your only possible means of escape from stalemate or constraints is to leave, tearing yourself away without looking back. Alternatively, the arrival of someone or a journey will probably make you freer in your professional life.

Take care not to repeat mistakes you have made in the past and your finances will improve rapidly.

Following a radical change or the elimination of what was troubling you or damaging your equilibrium, you will behave more sensibly, both mentally and physically.

 After a major change, disappointment or break-up, matters will develop in a more sensible way.

A fundamental change will help circumstances to evolve and guide you towards greater stability.

Significant change, a delay or rejection or, indeed, the profitable outcome of negotiations will help you make more assured progress at work.

You may well profit from a change or delay or the conclusion of a situation. In order to make progress, you need to be aware of all your obligations and responsibilities.

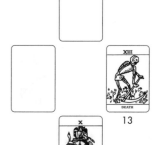

10 13

13

10

 You will always know how to adapt to circumstances and give yourself a new lease of life with ease and flexibility, but your negligence will leave you feeling both unstable and vulnerable.

Positive arrangements and compromises will help matters develop on the domestic front. Doubts will remain, however, because sooner or later you will have to make an important choice or significant decision. Alternatively, your emotional relationships will remain unstable and unsettling.

Thanks to certain relationships and your own adaptability to even the most varied circumstances, your family life will go well.

Compromises and agreements will come easily, bringing with them helpful choices and decisions at work.

Compromises, agreements or positive transactions will help your finances to grow. This will ease doubts and bring a period of uncertainty to an end.

10 14

14

10

421

| 10 | 15 |

XV

THE DEVIL

15

X

THE WHEEL OF FORTUNE

10

✚ Come what may, your hard work and willpower will enable you to channel your vitality and energy. You may be slightly reckless or excessive in your behaviour, but your control will remain effective and have a positive effect on your development.

♥ Although your heart may be ruling your head, you will continue to make every effort to satisfy your desires as soon as possible.

👪 You will be able to realize your domestic goals and positive progress will be made within the family.

📋 You will manage to achieve your wishes quickly and easily. The benefits you reap from this will enable you to make substantial professional progress. Do not relax your efforts, however, and make sure that you remain in control of events.

💰 Financial progress will be made once you have nudged matters in the right direction.

| 10 | 16 |

XVI

THE TOWER

16

X

THE WHEEL OF FORTUNE

10

✚ Following a physical or psychological shock or sudden health problem, you will have to adopt a regime of self-discipline if you are to restore your equilibrium.

♥ You will experience an emotional shock or rupture, which will be judged accordingly.

👪 You will experience an upheaval in, or sudden challenge to, your domestic situation, but in time stability will be restored.

📋 Despite upheavals or challenges that may occur at work, you should expect a swift reversal that will ultimately result in improved stability and greater self-discipline.

💰 After a troubling and unsettling period, your financial situation will return to normal, even if some sort of stringency must limit its progress for a while.

10 17

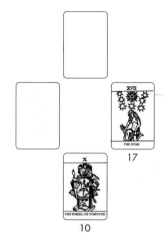

17

10

➕ Positive circumstances will encourage your psychological and physical development.

♥ New emotions or a burgeoning, highly promising relationship will bring your hopes and wishes nearer to fulfilment.

👪 New and positive circumstances will help matters on the domestic front to progress in a sure, positive direction.

📝 New and very positive circumstances will allow you to make sure and long-lasting progress at work.

🖥 You know exactly how to introduce new and beneficial elements to improve matters on the financial front in both the longer and shorter terms, and why you must do so.

10 18

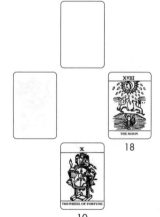

18

10

➕ Despite your health difficulties and anxieties or your physical and mental concerns, you should manage to overcome your problems with ease.

♥ You will be confronted by a difficult situation. For better or worse, things are in danger of developing along unsettling lines.

👪 Delays, twists and turns or conflicts will not stop your domestic situation from making spontaneous progress, even if the outcome is not wholly stable or reassuring.

📝 A disastrous atmosphere will prevail at work, or you will be confronted with conundrums and disappointments. In either case, your professional progress will slow down and may well change course.

🖥 Problems, delays and disappointments are going to restrict progress on the financial front. However, things will follow their natural, if not entirely reliable, path.

10 19

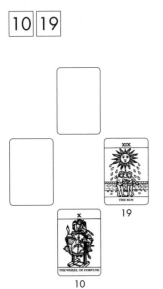

✚ Some happy and positive circumstances will allow you to exercise calm, sound and intelligent control over your own physical and psychological development.

❤ You will experience great joy and satisfaction in your love life, confident that your feelings are reciprocated.

👪 You will experience happiness within your family circle, and you will be able to follow your own plans in total confidence.

📋 An agreement, partnership or successful project will help you make positive and lasting progress at work.

An agreement or successful agreement will result in an improvement in your finances in both the short and long term.

10 20

✚ If you have been ill, you may well recover soon. Alternatively, following a return to normal, you will adjust your behaviour and adopt a more natural and healthy lifestyle.

❤ You will experience an up-turn in your love life, triggered by a reconciliation or an encounter. Whichever is the case, it will lead to happy developments.

👪 A proposition, change or renewal will soon occur within your family situation and help it make excellent progress.

📋 As long as you are able to make intelligent use of the opportunity, a proposal, change or revitalization of some sort will soon occur and boost your professional status.

A change of some kind is essential if there is to be progress in your financial affairs.

Your open, receptive and generous nature guarantees constant progress and development, and you will enjoy the benefits of your own self-control.

You will achieve all your emotional goals. Your love life will be marked by constant and positive development.

New horizons will present themselves, or your family will gather together to guarantee their support and protection.

You will soon receive confirmation of concrete success at work, and you will be able to expand in your chosen direction.

Significant achievements or your potential will enable you to maintain intelligent and positive control over your finances.

 A sudden departure or a journey that you will undertake will prove to be beneficial.

A meeting, departure or the arrival of someone dear to you will enhance your love life.

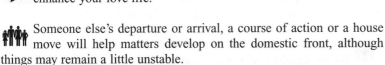 Someone else's departure or arrival, a course of action or a house move will help matters develop on the domestic front, although things may remain a little unstable.

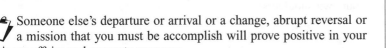 Someone else's departure or arrival or a change, abrupt reversal or a mission that you must be accomplish will prove positive in your business affairs and promote progress.

Following a movement of funds and capital, you will make rapid, if somewhat precarious, financial progress.

11 1

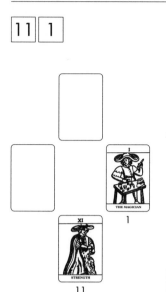

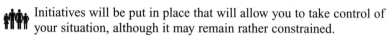

✚ Your excellent health may be jeopardized if you continue to feel restricted or constrained when you express your natural dynamism and vitality.

♥ Someone in your thoughts is perfectly willing to be independent, but their situation is still not letting them be so. Alternatively, despite all the efforts made to release you from a certain situation, you will realize that you will have to take control in order to be totally free.

👪 Initiatives will be put in place that will allow you to take control of your situation, although it may remain rather constrained.

📋 Although plans have been laid, steps taken and skill demonstrated in their execution, your professional situation will remain rather static. All you can do is stay in control.

▦ Your efforts, skills and initiative will give you control of your finances, although their growth may still seem rather limited.

11 2

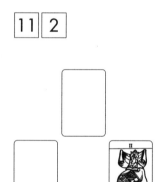

✚ Show caution, discretion and wisdom when you are deciding on and adopting positive change that will benefit you.

♥ Although you want to preserve a relationship and will use all your experience and strength of character to do so, it is by no means certain that you will succeed. A dramatic change may take place.

👪 You will take your time and act with discretion and caution before finally deciding on a major change, taking all the responsibility on your own shoulders.

📋 After a period of inertia, patient waiting or painstaking analysis of a matter, you will implement useful, positive change, which may appear somewhat unsettling at first.

▦ You will have to study a financial issue sensibly and in great detail. In return, as long as you are prepared to take charge of any potentially profitable changes in your situation, you will make progress.

You will have no difficulty adapting to circumstances and maintaining gentle, subtle control. You will enjoy consistent energy levels.

If you are thinking of someone special, be aware that their feelings are genuine and that their sympathetic, instinctive intelligence and strength of mind will bring a sense of real fulfilment. Alternatively, your emotional state is excellent, and your relationships are harmonious.

You will have no trouble getting what you want if you reach agreements, make useful compromises and demonstrate understanding, strength of mind and sincerity.

You can be confident of the reliability of your professional situation. Work towards reaching agreements and compromises that will help it progress.

You will be in control of your finances and able to carry out timely transactions, implement profitable operations and achieve a degree of financial success.

11 3

You will be in complete control of your dynamic nature, and there will be no danger of over-indulgence or excess.

If you are thinking of someone special, be aware that little seems capable of countering their elitist, authoritarian behaviour. Alternatively, your gentle and intelligent nature will help you to curb your own excesses and keep your emotions under control.

You will receive assurances that your wishes will be fulfilled. Alternatively, if you are dealing with an authoritarian and inflexible person, you should make good use of your gentle nature to make them your ally.

You will probably have to face people who are rigid and determined and who refuse to budge an inch. However, your own self-belief will help you take control successfully and turn opposition into support, acquisition and expansion.

Matters are proving generally advantageous, and you will have no trouble controlling events. Alternatively, you will find the means to improve your finances significantly.

11 4

11 5

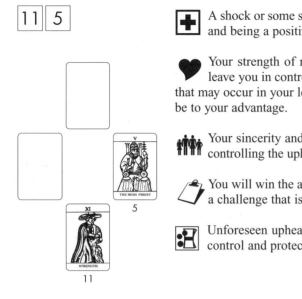

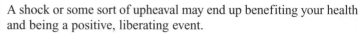 A shock or some sort of upheaval may end up benefiting your health and being a positive, liberating event.

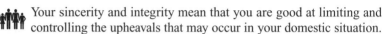 Your strength of mind, integrity and loyalty to your commitments leave you in control and able to learn from any shocks or upheavals that may occur in your love life. Ultimately, you will find that events will be to your advantage.

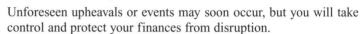 Your sincerity and integrity mean that you are good at limiting and controlling the upheavals that may occur in your domestic situation.

You will win the approval or authorization needed to be able to face a challenge that is, in the end, part of your natural progress.

Unforeseen upheavals or events may soon occur, but you will take control and protect your finances from disruption.

11 6

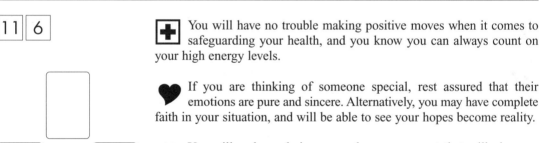

You will have no trouble making positive moves when it comes to safeguarding your health, and you know you can always count on your high energy levels.

If you are thinking of someone special, rest assured that their emotions are pure and sincere. Alternatively, you may have complete faith in your situation, and will be able to see your hopes become reality.

You will make a choice or reach an agreement that will give you greater control over your circumstances and, as a result, bring you complete confidence.

An agreement will leave you in control of your professional environment and challenges. You will also be able to take innovative steps to improve your status at work.

An agreement will bring stability to your finances and give you control over external events.

You will overcome your anxieties with ease and be able to resolve any health issues. You should not be shy of hard work, so keep a firm grip on your health.

You may have to be ready for a struggle and have to make an effort if you want to overcome the problems and challenges that lie on your path to emotional balance and control. You have all the resources that you need.

You may meet with delays, obstacles or difficulties, but nothing will stop you from achieving your aims, provided you keep up your efforts and are genuinely willing to see things through.

Challenges and obstacles may restrict your professional promotion. Keep up your efforts come what may and do not let go of your control over external factors. You will manage to assert yourself.

You are certain to overcome all your difficulties, and you will be able to follow your chosen path to financial progress.

Even if a certain degree of discipline is imposed on you, it will be a positive factor in maintaining your balance and self-control.

You will enjoy a new, sincere and harmonious relationship. If this is already in progress, rest assured that it will be a solid and successful partnership.

Although you have to submit to a degree of self-discipline and a rather strict regime, these are the factors that will help you develop and that will guarantee domestic harmony and happiness in the future.

You will reach an agreement or form an advantageous partnership that will encourage professional progress and, ultimately, success. If you are relying on a legal decision, it will be in your favour.

Although your situation is subject to a measure of self-discipline or must conform to strict rules, you are sure to achieve significant financial success.

11	9

➕ Advice to be cautious, a new awareness or personal discovery will help you rejuvenate yourself and take control of any changes that may occur in your life.

❤ A factor will come to your attention that will be key in prompting a review of your situation. You may decide to implement change or renew something, secure in the knowledge that this is the best move. What's more, you will be proved right.

👪 You will come to see how sensible and necessary a review of your domestic situation really is. You will reconsider certain factors and implement some changes, while not letting go of control.

📋 You are probably going to be faced with the likelihood of changing or renewing your situation, but you will take positive action only when you are sure of yourself and of the firm proposals on offer.

🔳 You will come to see for yourself or you will be advised by others that a change in your situation or, at least, its renewal or review is necessary. You will take control of events.

11	10

➕ You will enjoy positive progress on the health front that will assist your personal development.

❤ Your love life will develop positively and your wishes will be granted. Emotional fulfilment is coming your way.

👪 You will be responsible for all the positive opportunities and favourable changes occurring in your family life and the great potential it shows.

📋 You will be able to push back the boundaries, while remaining in control. Alternatively, you will be able to choose among the various possibilities on offer and, as a result, widen your horizons and accomplish all you desire.

🔳 Your finances will improve and you will have many more options among which to choose.

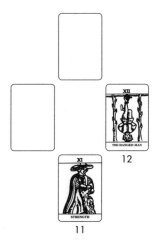

✚ You have the energy and physical strength required to deal with moral and material constraints and responsibilities.

♥ Your relationship will prove to be both reliable and solid, and you can have total confidence in it.

👪 You will be dependent on limiting circumstances or situations, but you will be able to shoulder your responsibilities and take control of your obligations.

✎ In order to free yourself from the constraints imposed by your situation, you will have to show just how reliable and full of integrity you are. You will be in control of events and in a position to consolidate your professional status.

💰 Although you may have to cope with rather taxing obligations, you will be able to face them and build a strong if somewhat limited foundation for your finances.

✚ After a key change in a situation or its conclusion, you will overcome your problems and maintain a strong sense of well-being.

♥ A radical change in your emotional life will occur, making you more confident of your choices, decisions and relationships. You will overcome all your ordeals.

👪 As a result of significant changes or the conclusion of a matter, you will feel better placed to make important decisions and tackle any obstacles in your path.

✎ Your professional situation will improve after some significant intervention. You will be more confident and better placed to form partnerships or renew contracts.

💰 Your finances will benefit positively from change or finality. You will be in charge of decisions and agreements.

431

11 14

XIV
TEMPERANCE

XI
STRENGTH

14

11

➕ Your adaptable, flexible and open nature enables you to exercise real self-control and channel your energies so that you achieve success in all your undertakings.

❤ Following appropriate agreements and intelligent compromises, you will be in a position to make your views clear, gently but firmly, thereby achieving your aims. No matter what happens and no matter how flexible you may be, you won't give in before achieving your goals.

👪 Agreements and compromises will give you greater control over family issues. Matters will progress well on the domestic front and you should achieve your aims.

📋 You will make the compromises needed to bring your plans to fruition and make progress at work. You will achieve your aims slowly but surely.

🗄 Well-timed deals or skilful compromises will help steer your finances in the right direction and bring your target closer.

11 15

XV
THE DEVIL

XI
STRENGTH

15

11

➕ Although you do occasionally give in to temptation or excess, you will maintain your balance in the end. Most importantly, you will become more self-disciplined if this should prove necessary.

❤ When faced with a highly charged or passionate relationship, you will adopt a firm stance that soothes both hearts and minds. Your strength of character will win through.

👪 An element of confusion is invading or prevailing on the domestic front, and you may have to take firm, tough action to bring about balance at home.

📋 You will achieve your professional ambitions and strengthen your position at work. No matter what happens, you will have to abide by the rules and regulations.

🗄 Strict rules will have to be enforced if you are to maintain your current financial situation or achieve financial growth.

DEATH

TEMPERANCE

THE DEVIL

THE TOWER

THE STAR

THE MOON

THE SUN

JUDGEMENT

THE WORLD

THE FOOL

11 16

➕ Disruptive, upsetting and unforeseen events will force you to behave sensibly and cautiously. This is the only way you can overcome the difficulties facing you.

♥ You will have to draw on all your inner strength and experience if you are to ride the storm brewing in your emotional life.

👪 You will have to face an upsetting and disconcerting situation, but your experience and clear-sighted approach will help you keep your footing and remain in control.

📋 A positive crisis, challenge or upheaval will finally allow you to exercise greater control over your business affairs.

⏳ Despite the unforeseen, inevitable upheaval that may take place in relation to your finances, you will stay in the driving seat.

16

11

11 17

➕ Your receptive and resourceful nature leaves you feeling fulfilled. You will achieve personal growth just as you had hoped.

♥ Things are progressing on the emotional front, and your hopes and dreams are within reach. Feel free to enjoy this positive phase.

👪 Fortuitous events will help domestic matters develop according to your wishes.

📋 A happy combination of circumstances will give you a firm grip on the way your professional status develops. You will then be ideally placed to profit from any potential for new or innovative ideas and put them into practice.

⏳ Favourable circumstances will allow you to direct and control the progress of your money and achieve your fiscal goals.

17

11

433

11 18

XVIII THE MOON
18

XI STRENGTH
11

✚ You will go through a period of fatigue, lethargy and turmoil or, indeed, suffer from more serious health problems. You should, however, easily recover, thanks to your own considerable physical and mental energy.

♥ You will solve your emotional issues and overcome obstacles in your love life by staying in calm control of events and showing your strength of character and self-confidence.

After undergoing a degree of turmoil and anxiety, experiencing a false sense of security or being beset by conflicts, problems and disappointments, you will take matters fully in hand and exercise a positive influence over both events and those close to you.

After a period of confusion and uncertainty or in spite of delays, obstacles or misunderstandings, you will be at the helm and making good progress.

After a difficult, testing and uncertain period, you will be able to steer your finances towards success.

11 19

XIX THE SUN
19

XI STRENGTH
11

✚ Your sparkling energy and natural resources will help you maintain your self-control gently but firmly. You can then enjoy your well-being to the full.

♥ You will experience great joy in your love life. You will be able to act in total confidence with the freedom to achieve what you want on the emotional front.

No matter what you have to do to consolidate and enrich your family life or to help its natural growth, you will get there in the end.

A profitable partnership, a perfect, positive agreement or a total professional success will give you more your freedom and enhance your immediate and long-term projects.

Your financial situation will be reassuring and enable you to act freely, enjoying your resources to the full.

434

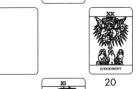

You will review or reconsider your position and be surer of yourself and more confident of your abilities as a result. You will feel more robust in general.

A change or renewal will bring greater certainty to your emotional situation. You will be more flexible in the face of events while respecting their integrity.

Your domestic situation will become more soundly based and reliable thanks to a change or fresh start. You will be able to act freely and practically.

A significant change, fresh start or practical suggestion will bring with it protection and freedom, consolidating both your position and your rights. Positive action will result.

Your financial situation will be made more secure and more reliable as a result of a major change or a new opportunity.

You will enter a fulfilling phase, during which you will enjoy increased stability and greater self-assurance.

Emotional fulfilment will come your way. You will feel confident about the genuine nature of your relationships and the stability of your position.

Things will be much more stable on the domestic front, and you can be assured of both its integrity and its potential for expansion.

Your social and professional horizons will widen. Your professional future will be confirmed when an agreement or contract is concluded, consolidating your status and bringing increased responsibilities and greater decision-making powers.

Great financial possibilities will come your way. You will need to demonstrate your strength of character and sense of responsibility in order to reap the full rewards of their potential. You can then introduce greater stability to your fiscal affairs.

11 22

XI

22

STRENGTH

11

➕ You will be able to travel and act freely to revive and rejuvenate your energy levels. You can then take full advantage of your new sense of well-being.

♥ Following a meeting, a journey or a period of transition and uncertainty, your emotional life will become more stable.

👪 A journey or house move or the arrival or departure of someone within your family circle will strengthen the foundations of your domestic situation.

📋 Someone else's arrival or departure, a course of action or a journey undertaken will strengthen your position, consolidate your status at work and lead to professional success.

🗄 The arrival, departure, actions or travel plans of others or yourself will strengthen and secure the basis of your finances.

12 1

I

THE MAGICIAN

1

XII

THE HANGED MAN

12

➕ You will have to use all your skill, willpower and energy to combat potential physical or psychological frailty.

♥ Despite, or perhaps as a result of, your initiatives, an emotional impasse or a moribund relationship will come to a logical, inescapable conclusion.

👪 An initiative within your domestic circle is certain to fail. Alternatively, an apparent impasse will come to its destined and logical end or will force you to make a sacrifice.

📋 You will have to make sacrifices if your initiatives or plans are to come to fruition. They will ultimately prove positive, however, because they will bring matters to their proper conclusion.

🗄 Restricting circumstances may well act in your favour if, through your own initiative and understanding, you are prepared to make the necessary sacrifices.

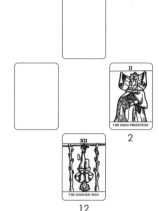

12 2

➕ If you do or say nothing or if you wait too long, you risk succumbing to rather overwhelming mental and physical frailty.

❤️ If you don't act soon or emerge from your shell you will have to make concessions or sacrifices that may well not be appropriate for you, or you may find yourself in a relationship that is distinctly unsatisfactory emotionally.

👪 If you don't express your thoughts or say what you know, you will be forced to make compromises or agree to actions that you don't particularly enjoy but can do little to refuse.

📋 Someone, possibly you, has been patient for too long and should perhaps have acted more promptly. Whatever the case, you will end up in a situation with limited potential, and you will have no choice but to adapt to events around you and let matters take their course.

📇 You will have to act with caution and make use of both your reticence and your ability to be economical in order to maintain the precarious stability of your finances.

12 3

➕ You have an annoying tendency to satisfy your desires and ambitions at all costs. In the process, you waste energy and become over-excited. Take care because you may find that you can do little to change this.

❤️ You are in danger of becoming a slave to your feelings, a victim of your desires and trapped in a dependent relationship that will only lead to emotional frustration.

👪 Despite your understanding and the intelligence and the generosity of someone in your family, you will be unable to avoid angry scenes or the confusion, division or dissension prevailing in your domestic life.

📋 Intelligent, skilful moves and profitable negotiations will help you make an abrupt exit from a somewhat limiting situation and turn its negative constraints into a positive professional achievement.

📇 You may be able to make far-sighted moves to improve your finances, but you will never really be satisfied with what you gain.

437

12 4

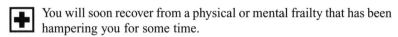

IV
THE EMPEROR

4

XII
THE HANGED MAN

12

➕ You will soon recover from a physical or mental frailty that has been hampering you for some time.

❤ You will suddenly be able to regain your autonomy and freedom, but this may come as something of a shock because you will have no say in how this event comes about.

👪 A shock or upheaval will occur in your domestic situation, freeing it from current constraints and limitations. Be aware that the effects may be somewhat disconcerting, if not actually devastating.

📋 If there is conflict or some dissatisfaction at work, take care because uncompromising opposition could put you in danger of losing your job. Alternatively, you can be confident that a particular professional stalemate will suddenly be overcome and you will be free of its limitations.

💼 You will eliminate all the limiting factors in your financial situation, doing so in a determined and transparent way. To do this, however, you must prove that you are not afraid to make some crucial sacrifices or meet some positive challenges.

12 5

V
THE HIGH PRIEST

5

XII
THE HANGED MAN

12

➕ You will have to rest, relax and draw on your resources before you can restore your self-confidence and get yourself back into shape.

❤ Things will get back on track of their own accord and develop in a natural, positive way. You can revive relationships and enjoy them in total confidence.

👪 You will have the opportunity to be involved in new and happy circumstances at home, or in a new domestic achievement.

📋 You need to accept change or a development at work, and this will help you get back on course, develop and make progress.

💼 If you want to realize your dreams, achieve something new or simply get matters back on course, you will be forced to make a sacrifice or at least proceed with caution.

➕ You risk exposure to a contagious disease, or your health will make you temporarily inactive. Take steps to guard against this danger.

❤️ Your feelings may not be reciprocated, and you will be the victim of betrayals and disappointments. Sadly, there will be little you can do about this.

👪 You are in danger of returning to an awkward situation. You may fall victim to potentially damaging relationships around you or you may be disappointed and forced to recognize your mistakes. Sadly, there is little you can do about this.

✍️ You will either fail to reach an agreement or be advised against making it. In either case, you will be disappointed and will find yourself facing challenging and uncertain events and various constraints, obstacles and delays. As a result, you will not reach your professional goals or agreements.

📠 You risk making unfortunate choices, incorrect decisions or futile agreements, all or any of which bring matters to a financial stand-still. If there is still time, try to avoid such steps.

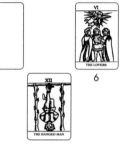

12 6

6

12

➕ It is time to enjoy a period of relaxation and rest, to take a trip for pleasure or simply to have some time to yourself to help you get back into shape.

❤️ Expect to receive some excellent news about your love life. You may find that your emotional position has been completely changed, leaving you able to enjoy a genuine relationship based on sincere and mutual feelings.

👪 A period of waiting, denial or devotion has not been in vain, and your efforts will be rewarded. Despite constraints and challenges, you will eventually be able make matters on the domestic front clear, positive and rewarding.

✍️ Challenges and obstacles may appear in your path, but you will overcome them if you make the right concessions, keep constant tabs on your situation and do not give up trying.

📠 You will overcome financial difficulties that hamper your progress and, despite everything, will achieve your goals in the end.

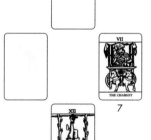

12 7

7

12

12 8

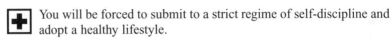

+ You will be forced to submit to a strict regime of self-discipline and adopt a healthy lifestyle.

♥ In order to regain a measure of emotional equilibrium, you will be forced to make amends or to accept changes or a return to the status quo in your love life.

So that your domestic situation can return to normal, you need to repair any harm you might have caused and accept a potentially important change.

A legal decision will authorize you to find the solution to, or a way out from, a situation that has been stagnant for some time and unable to develop naturally.

Laws or rules imposed on you will oblige you to review your finances and return to some sort of normality. Only then can you get back on track.

---

12 9

+ You will come to understand that the most sensible course of action is to be aware of your own limitations and to assess them carefully in the light of your natural resources. You might then be able to go beyond even your own boundaries.

♥ You will realize that you must make sacrifices in your emotional life and accept events that will turn out to be rewarding. Relax and let matters take their course.

You will soon come to understand the need to make sacrifices, give something up or allow things to take their course. You will then get exactly what you want.

You will come to see the benefits of letting things happen of their own accord. This will allow you to overcome your current limitations and find exactly what you are looking for.

Either working on your own or under the direction of others you will soon discover the ideal solutions for financial recovery and even expansion.

440

➕ You will soon be able to rid yourself of a health problem, but you should avoid ill-considered actions or ill-timed departures.

❤ Developments on the emotional front will make you feel that you really must depart. If you do go, make sure that your move is just-ifiable, and if you are really determined to turn a page in your life, take care that you do not fall back into the same trap later on.

👪 Although there has been progress on the domestic front, leaving will be the only way of freeing yourself from constraints and a state of dependency.

📝 Despite hopes of professional progress and freedom, you will ultimately be forced to abandon your dreams, go off in search of adventure and begin a new chapter in your professional life.

📋 To be free of constraints and limitations on the financial front, you will have to seek help or alternative ways to escape from your situation and make a new start.

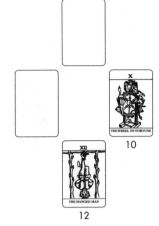

➕ You have great strength of character and physical energy, but you will need time to accept the constraints imposed by your obli-gations. They will become vital to the maintenance of your well-being.

❤ If your thoughts are of someone special, be assured of their total devotion. Alternatively, you will probably find yourself in a rather constraining situation. Paradoxically, by shouldering your responsibilities and honouring your commitments, you will win your independence.

👪 You will handle family matters with subtlety, showing loyalty to your commitments, obligations and domestic responsibilities.

📝 Professional rules, commitments and responsibilities will leave you little room for manoeuvre. Nevertheless, you will gain the upper hand by virtue of your forceful character and psychological strength.

📋 You will be able to honour your commitments and take on your responsibilities and professional obligations.

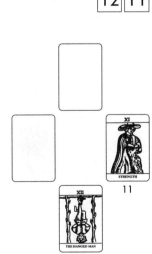

441

12	13

➕ A radical change in your lifestyle or the end of a current phase in your life will allow you to overcome difficulties and challenges and make a full recovery.

♥ A relationship, revelation or radical change will come to an end in your emotional life, allowing you to overcome current constraints and to take steps to regain your independence.

👪 A major change or the inevitable conclusion to something will present you with the opportunity to put matters back on course or to become independent.

🗒 To get things back on course or to overcome the obstacles in your path, you will have to bring about or undergo a radical change. You can then reach your professional goal.

💰 A source of income will dry up and force you to get things back on course. Alternatively, a sudden profit will help you make moves towards renewed financial independence.

13 — DEATH
12 — THE HANGED MAN

12	14

➕ You will have no choice but to adapt to and accommodate changes, although your health may remain precarious for some time to come.

♥ The agreements and compromises that will be reached will not enable you to relax fully, and your love life will remain precarious and restricting.

👪 You will have to reach agreements or make compromises to preserve domestic equilibrium. It will still not give you much satisfaction, however, because the process will also involve a frustrating regime of self-discipline.

🗒 Current negotiations, compromises or agreements will not bring you professional freedom. Unfortunately, your position will continue to be precarious, restricted and constrained.

💰 Deals and current negotiations or agreements will enable you to maintain your current financial status, but, it will continue to be precarious and restricted.

14 — TEMPERANCE
12 — THE HANGED MAN

Your excessive behaviour, over-indulgence and excitability will put both your mental and physical health at risk. It is time to ease up and rest.

A passionate and intense relationship will probably plunge you into an emotional cul-de-sac or a period of isolation, but realizing this is insufficient in itself to extricate you. You will also have to learn from the experience and take a step back when appropriate.

Apart from being patient and sensible, there is little you can do to prevent a confused and somewhat reckless situation from developing.

Pursuing your goals at all costs will mean that you risk being professionally immobilized or isolated, and you have no choice but to be patient or to give up.

Your intense ambition or excessive desire to increase your finances will result in disappointment. You will then be forced to take a step back and find more sensible, practical solutions.

Following an accident or mental or physical shock, you will need to rest to recover your health and get over this troubling event.

You will experience a crisis, challenge or break-up in your love life, from which it will take some time to recover.

There will be a disruption, crisis or sudden challenge to your home and family circumstances. You may well have to suffer the consequences while you are waiting for the storm to abate.

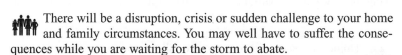

Upheavals or sudden challenges and reassessments of your professional situation will have their inevitable consequences, but they will also enable you to establish, or re-establish, your autonomy at work. Good may, therefore, come from bad.

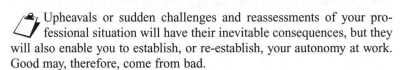

You will suffer the consequences of a financial crisis, and it will not be easy to escape. To get things back on course, you will have to accept a number of constraints and surrender some of your rights.

443

12	17

XVII — THE STAR

17

XII — THE HANGED MAN

12

➕ No matter what your difficulties or what health concerns may arise, your resourcefulness and strength of mind will help you resolve them with ease. You will be able to enjoy your subsequent well-being to the full.

❤️ You will be able to relax and devote yourself to your feelings with total confidence, enjoying a stable love life.

👪 New and positive events will give you unprecedented confidence in your domestic situation. You will be persuaded to commit yourself wholly to your family life and exercise subtle but firm control.

📋 You will get everything back on course, thanks to new and encouraging circumstances. You might be able to inject your professional standing with a renewed and unprecedented energy and potential for success that to date it has doubtless never had.

⏳ Beneficial circumstances or fresh resources will help you get your finances back on track. You will regain your freedom to act.

12	18

XVIII — THE MOON

18

XII — THE HANGED MAN

12

➕ You may fall ill and be forced to rest completely. You will have to take positive action to make a speedy recovery.

❤️ If you are thinking of someone special, you should understand that they may be hurt and disappointed or in an emotional impasse. Alternatively, you will suffer an emotional disappointment that leaves you no option but to accept the inevitable.

👪 Domestic issues will force you to take wise action; otherwise, you risk falling prey to jealousy, hypocrisy or the slander of a member of your family.

📋 Problems, delays or mistakes will force you to give up a futile professional situation or one that falls short of its original promise.

⏳ Mistakes, delays, debts or lack of revenue will force you to establish order and impose certain limits on your financial options.

444

12 19

✚ You will be able to enjoy a sense of well-being with full confidence and no disruption.

♥ You may feel dependent in an otherwise happy relationship, but you remain in full control of it, albeit subtly and quietly.

Although your domestic position is happy and fortunate from many points of view, it must always bow to your authority or that of the person who acts on your behalf in your family.

Despite the success of a partnership, a professional achievement or the new light that is shed on your job, you will have to work hard to make sure it comes to fruition.

Although you have sorted out your finances or achieved a degree of monetary success, you will still have to establish proper order to keep the situation stable.

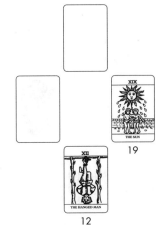

19

12

12 20

✚ Despite a recovery or partial return to normal, you will have to have regular check-ups or a course of treatment before you can make a complete recovery.

♥ A renewal or change in your emotional life will force you to accept responsibilities and sacrifices.

A change on the domestic front will probably fail to bring the renewed challenges you had anticipated. You will still have to shoulder obligations and responsibilities that won't leave you much freedom of choice.

 Your professional situation will undergo a revival or change that will bring with it more responsibilities and constraints. You won't have much room for manoeuvre.

Despite a change or probable improvement you won't manage to free yourself from your financial and moral obligations, but you will have to take on yet more responsibilities.

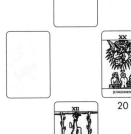

20

12

12 21

XXI
THE WORLD

21

XII
THE HANGED MAN

12

✚ Although you want to feel fulfilled and able to achieve your potential, you will still have trouble deciding on the choices or resolutions that lie ahead. You will, therefore, remain vulnerable and easily influenced by others.

♥ Your emotional situation may seem rewarding and full of potential, but you will still have to make concessions, take difficult decisions and even give up some of your relationships.

♦ The potential for the success of your domestic situation depends on a decision you reach alone or one that is imposed on you.

✎ The vast and positive potential in your professional situation will force you to research and agree key contracts and make essential choices and resolutions.

▣ The expansion of your financial situation will involve vital and decisive choices or require key agreements.

12 22

THE FOOL

22

XII
THE HANGED MAN

12

✚ You will be forced to take a complete rest and undergo a course of treatment. Consequently, all you can do is be patient.

♥ The departure or arrival of someone will have no effect other than to leave you on your own, powerless to act. Alternatively, you will not be able to leave because to do so would be merely an escape, rather than a solution.

♦ An anticipated journey or the arrival or departure of someone in your circle will not now take place, or a change or departure will force you to stay at home alone. Alternatively, you can expect nothing from your domestic situation for the moment.

✎ Despite your endeavours, you will not manage to make progress or free yourself from current constraints. Read the writing on the wall, but do not let it discourage you.

▣ No matter what you try to do it may prove pointless in the end. You will have to content yourself with a limited and precarious financial situation. Resign yourself to this, but do not give up hope of finding a favourable way out.

446

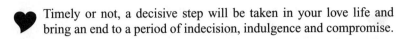 Your accommodating nature and spirit of initiative will help you recover your health and well-being and take advantage of your natural adaptability.

Timely or not, a decisive step will be taken in your love life and bring an end to a period of indecision, indulgence and compromise.

A decision or initiative will probably make all discussion and arrangements seem in vain because it will result in the conclusion of a matter or a dramatic change.

An initiative or decision will allow you to profit from agreements or compromises and bring your target closer. This may involve a major change that will significantly advance your situation.

An initiative, decision or plan of action that is currently in hand will help you benefit from various deals and play an important part in your financial situation.

You may well be forced to take measures to eliminate anything potentially harmful or prejudicial to your physical well-being. Although you may not admit it to yourself or even be fully aware of the fact, this is the key to your health.

In spite of your reserve and apparent inertia, you know full well in your heart that a major change is inevitable. You will then have to bring an end to a troublesome situation.

You may not actually be saying or doing anything, but you are certainly thinking about putting an end to a situation. You would be wise to do so or accept an anticipated and radical change.

A predicted change or one that was not yet common knowledge and for which you were secretly preparing will inevitably take place and bring matters to a logical end.

Although it may not yet be public knowledge, you will profit from the conclusion of some business affair. Alternatively, you will not be able to avoid fundamental changes in your finances.

13	3

+ Maintaining or recovering your well-being will probably require a sudden and important intervention to eliminate something that is potentially harmful to your physical and mental health.

♥ A major and definitive change will occur in your emotional life, but there will be nothing you can do except understand that things have to be this way.

👪 Your domestic situation will undergo a radical or sudden change, allowing you to remove potential dangers and embark on a new chapter in your life.

A major change will inevitably occur in your professional life. Expect it to be both sudden and violent and for it to challenge a number of existing factors.

There will be a major upheaval in your financial situation. If it is for the better, it will be liberating and helpful; if it is for the worse, expect a serious downturn in your affairs.

13	4

+ Any lifestyle changes that you judge to be necessary can be made both firmly and with confidence. They will enable you to benefit fully from your open nature and sense of well-being.

♥ You will probably be obliged to bring a relationship to an end or cut yourself off somewhat from your feelings. Although this may seem harsh and difficult, if you do not take the initiative, it is possible that this fundamental change will be imposed on you – as if by fate.

👪 You will probably have to give up your desires to implement something new, because members of your family are opposed to them or circumstances are unfavourable.

Your constructive and intelligent work will enable you to profit from a new product, an original idea or certain innovations. This may require major change and a number of investments, however.

Unless you can invest in, and profit from, a new product or original idea, difficult circumstances mean that you may risk losing some of your assets.

➕ You will probably have to see a doctor or specialist, who will give you everything you need to put an end to your health problems and ease your worries.

❤ You will have no option but to eliminate problems, disappointments, conflicts, unspoken thoughts and misunderstandings – in other words, everything that is wrong or harmful in your emotional life.

👪 You must put an end to the conflicts, disharmony and problems in your domestic situation and sort out this area of your life as thoroughly as you can.

✍ A decision will be taken above your head to eradicate potentially negative factors at work. You will be forced to admit that this was the only viable solution in the circumstances.

▦ You will be ordered or recommended to sort out your financial situation or to carry out radical changes so that you can eliminate anything that is liable to damage or challenge its stability.

5

13

➕ You will make a judicious choice that will necessitate a major change to your lifestyle. As a result, you will feel at one with yourself and your environment.

❤ An emotional choice, agreement or new relationship is certain to occur in the best possible circumstances and will involve a fundamental and favourable change in your love life.

👪 An agreement or relationship will cause a significant and beneficial change in your domestic life.

✍ A wise choice, agreement or partnership will reach its logical conclusion and bring about major changes in your situation, proving profitable from many points of view.

▦ You will profit from a decision or agreement that will bring about a significant and important change in your finances.

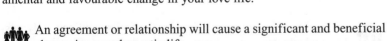
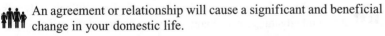
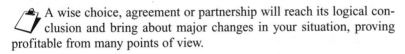

13 6

6

13

13 7

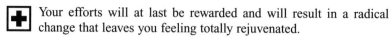

The Chariot VII — 7

Death XIII — 13

➕ Your efforts will at last be rewarded and will result in a radical change that leaves you feeling totally rejuvenated.

♥ You will be able to take the necessary steps and implement the changes required for your love life to take off again.

👪 Your domestic situation is certain to develop steadily, finally bringing about renewal and major change.

📝 You will profit from an interesting suggestion that is made to you with your professional development in mind. Alternatively, you will be able to make moves to generate important changes and progress.

💰 A financial achievement that resulted from a real struggle or the profit gained from a positive transaction will help you renew your financial situation or bring about a major change.

13 8

Justice VIII — 8

Death XIII — 13

➕ The stability of your mental and physical health will help you take full advantage of all the possibilities on offer or even enable you to bring about a significant change in your general lifestyle.

♥ You will experience a complete change in your love life, a change that appears as the inevitable and logical conclusion to events.

👪 You will benefit from the right to make major, and generally positive and advantageous, changes to your domestic situation.

📝 You will be strictly within your rights if you decide to make major and extensive changes to your position at work. Alternatively, a legal decision will put an end to a particular concern and create new potential for your professional situation.

💰 The financial stability you have managed to achieve will allow you to invest with a certain amount of liberalness or make significant profits and changes.

450

➕ A personal discovery or a word of caution from someone else will help you curb your tendency to indulge in excessive and impulsive behaviour. You may then decide against the idea of a sudden departure or a premature, ill-timed journey.

❤️ A realization or personal discovery will urge you to rein in your impulses and put an end to your ill-considered actions. It may also prompt you to abandon totally any decision to leave or to make unjustified or pointless, sudden moves.

👪 After carefully considering a question or discovering something important, you will give up the prospect of leaving or moving house. Nevertheless, you will still implement a key change in your home and family circumstances.

📋 You will make a personal discovery or find a solution. This will allow you to make the changes you have been secretly planning for some time.

📇 You will find a solution or a logical, realistic way out that heralds the end to your search. It will prompt you to abandon what you see to be extravagant or risky enterprises.

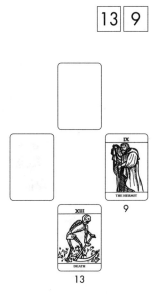

13 9

➕ Matters are developing in such a way that you will have to make a necessary change in your lifestyle or behaviour. This will involve adopting a more reasonable and well-balanced attitude.

❤️ Your love life will develop in a way that makes you understand the need to accept major changes, which will be prompted by your sense of duty and conscience.

👪 Domestic developments will make a necessary change inevitable. It will then be your responsibility to adopt this change or to help to bring it about. You can then proceed along the path to progress.

📋 Your professional situation will develop in such a way that it embraces major change or reaches its logical conclusion, but all this is certain to be to your advantage.

📇 You will be able to benefit from the development of circumstances to help your finances progress and become more stable, although you may need to implement significant changes to bring this about.

13 10

13 11

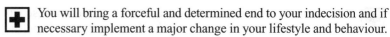

➕ You will bring a forceful and determined end to your indecision and if necessary implement a major change in your lifestyle and behaviour.

❤️ In spite of your strength of mind and emotional control, you must resolve to make important decisions and bring about a significant change in your love life.

👪 The positive control you exert over your domestic circumstances will lead you to make definitive choices and essential decisions, put an end to indecision and implement a fundamental change.

📋 The hold you currently have over your professional situation will help you reach agreements, resolve matters and, at last, bring about essential and carefully considered changes.

💰 You have complete control over your financial situation at present and are, therefore, in a position to bring an end to indecision, to conclude advantageous deals and to implement both far-reaching and profitable changes.

13 12

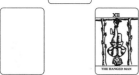

➕ An important change is taking place, and it will enable you to regain your free will and revive your energy levels. You can then press ahead.

❤️ A major change will offer you a way out of your current stalemate and away from your sense of powerlessness and dependency. It will also free you from the constraints and shackles that have caused your emotional inertia.

👪 You will be powerless to stand in the way of fundamental change. It should, however, provide you with the way out you have been expecting and offer you freedom from your domestic constraints. You will make progress at home.

📋 You can no longer prevent a major change from taking place. Ultimately, however, it will help you overcome obstacles, remove constraints and make a valuable professional transformation.

💰 A fundamental change will make you feel freer with your money, more enterprising and more confident about progress.

➕ If you demonstrate flexibility, adaptability and understanding, you will manage to eliminate doubts and anxieties and identify the changes you were seeking.

❤️ Being flexible and adaptable to events, debate or compromise will help you find the way out of an emotional situation. This will serve to banish your doubts and anxieties and institute major changes in your emotional life.

👪 Intelligent compromises and carefully timed agreements will help you find the most appropriate answers. You can then throw off your doubts and anxieties and make changes that are both useful and correct.

📋 In the current circumstances, negotiations, intelligent compromises and timely agreements will lead you to the right solutions. A thorough and far-reaching transformation of your position will result.

💼 Negotiations or deals will bring you the appropriate and necessary solutions, leading to changes in your finances and ending your doubts and concerns.

14

13

➕ Despite your excessive, hyperactive behaviour or your use of extreme measures, abrupt and radical changes in your lifestyle are on the cards.

❤️ Passionate relationships or overwhelming desires will inevitably entail a radical, rapid but uncertain change in your emotional life, and it may not necessarily involve the person you think.

👪 Your wishes and hopes will soon reach their logical and inevitable conclusion. Progress, although real, will remain uncertain, however.

📋 You will not rest until you have achieved your aims. Everything will, however, soon come to its inevitable, logical conclusion, and although this will probably be to your ultimate benefit and advantage, it will involve a radical change.

💼 You will achieve your aims and profit from a change or transaction that will make your situation more advantageous.

15

13

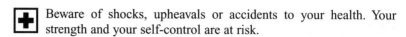

`13` `16`

Beware of shocks, upheavals or accidents to your health. Your strength and your self-control are at risk.

You are in danger of experiencing an upheaval or fundamental challenge in your love life, and you will have neither the desire nor the courage to resist it. Do not lose your self-assurance or self-control in the face of these disconcerting events.

There is a danger that an upheaval, profound challenge or inevitable, significant change will discourage you or make you lose the control you thought you had over your domestic situation.

Expect upheavals, major changes and serious challenges to your situation. There is a danger that all your gains will collapse and disappear abruptly, but don't let go – face things bravely.

Expect abrupt and serious challenges to your financial situation or even monetary losses. Nevertheless, try to maintain control over events and yourself.

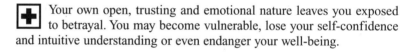

`13` `17`

Your own open, trusting and emotional nature leaves you exposed to betrayal. You may become vulnerable, lose your self-confidence and intuitive understanding or even endanger your well-being.

You risk losing the affection of someone dear to you. Alternatively, you may experience a fundamental, genuine and profitable change in your emotional life.

New, positive circumstances and innovations will bring about a major change and serious but profitable moves at home.

You will be able to profit professionally from changes or from the development of an original idea, innovation or new product.

You will benefit from favourable circumstances that prompt a positive change that will help your finances.

13 | 18

➕ You will be in a position to resolve your health problems completely or to eliminate anything that could harm your physical well-being.

♥ A negative, confused or disappointing emotional situation will come to its inevitable, logical conclusion. You will then without doubt enjoy a complete change in your emotional life.

👪 Obstacles, conflicts and worries will resolve themselves in a logical and inevitable fashion. You can then bring about a fundamental change in your domestic situation.

📋 Problems, errors or disappointments that have come to light at work will inevitably reach a logical resolution. You can then implement key, constructive and intelligent changes.

🎛 You will eventually succeed in sorting out your financial problems and regain control over the constructive and profitable changes that are involved.

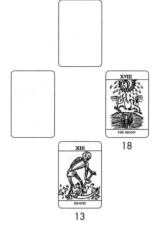

13 | 19

➕ Once you have learned more about your own health, you will be able to assume responsibility for it with greater confidence and introduce an important change into your lifestyle.

♥ You will enjoy great emotional joy or begin a relationship that will bring many developments into your life.

👪 Your domestic situation will undergo a serious but fundamentally positive transformation.

📋 The support of an influential person, a positive agreement or a favourable partnership will give you the assurance you need to make important and profitable changes in your situation.

🎛 You will enjoy great satisfaction on the financial front that will clarify matters, enabling you to implement important changes that will help things develop even further.

455

13 20

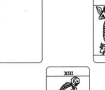

➕ A recovery or partial return to normality will require a radical change in your lifestyle. This signifies an end to your indecision and prompts some essential choices.

❤️ A request, suggestion or renewal of some kind in your love life will involve decisions and key choices and will mark the end of an indecisive period and the start of an important and radical change in your relationship.

👪 You will face choices, change or renewal in your domestic situation. You will then have to make important decisions and take radical steps to implement the changes.

📋 Other people will make suggestions and offer options for change and revitalization, and you will then have to make key choices, take important decisions and bring about a thorough transformation.

🎴 Suggestions or important changes will force you to make decisions that are the catalyst for a major deal or the revival of your finances.

13 21

➕ A radical change currently underway will give you the freedom to enjoy your vitality to the full and to benefit from your enterprising and generous nature.

❤️ A major change that is currently happening will leave you free to act as you choose in your search for emotional fulfilment.

👪 You can be certain that a major change currently taking place will go according to your wishes, marking a turning point in your domestic arrangements. Things will develop healthily on this front.

📋 You will enjoy both progress and success, thanks to a key change currently taking place. You should, however, keep up your efforts if you want to see matters develop and come to a speedy conclusion.

🎴 Your efforts are sure to pay off, allowing you to reap significant profits from a business deal or transaction or bring about astonishing growth in your financial assets.

Following a departure, journey or endeavour of some sort, you will have to make a radical and significant change in your life. Nevertheless, you should be careful not to make mistakes, behave carelessly or take pointless risks.

You will depart, leave your past behind and make a new start, thereby reaching a significant turning point in your emotional life.

You will depart, move house, turn over a new leaf or even perhaps leave your home and your family. This will represent a real turning point for you.

You will suddenly go in search of new possibilities, give up your job and, most certainly, undergo a radical change and transformation in your professional life.

You will soon be able to bring your endeavours to fruition, and this will result in a greatly changed financial situation.

Your spirit of initiative and dynamic nature will help you to adapt to extreme circumstances. It is important not to confuse flexibility with negligence, however.

You will reach compromises, come to agreements or take steps, all with a view to keeping the peace or achieving your aims at all costs and by whatever means.

If you wish to put your plans into action on the domestic front, you will have to present your arguments carefully, bring to bear all your powers of conviction and agree to difficult but necessary compromises.

Heated negotiations, well-timed agreements and difficult but necessary compromises will help you bring projects to fruition and achieve your goals.

You will be in a position to conclude profitable deals and negotiate hard for business or come to tough but vital compromises on the financial front.

PROBABLE OUTCOME

14 2

✚ Don't confuse stability and reserve with pointless patience or indecision. Alternatively, you risk either being drawn into a situation that is dangerous to your general sense of well-being or falling prey to an accident or blow to your health.

♥ It would be wise for you to come to an agreement or sensible compromise that will release your emotional situation. Matters have reached a delicate stage and you risk veering off course towards a crisis.

👪 You will eventually break your silence and say what you think. This will ease the atmosphere, remove constraints and help you reach helpful and profitable compromises or agreements.

📋 After a period during which you have held back and been patient or after a hiatus, negotiations, compromises or well-timed agreements will make your professional environment more relaxed.

▦ After time spent economizing and showing excellent financial sense, you will suddenly shake things up dramatically by concluding new and well-timed deals.

PROBABLE OUTCOME

14 3

✚ Your healthy lifestyle and high energy levels leave you ideally placed to reach the compromises needed for peace of mind. You will discover how best to behave in order to turn over a new leaf.

♥ Relax and enjoy your own feelings and those that others have for you. Enjoy the happy, lucky times that come your way and look forward to more in the future.

👪 Your instinctive intelligence and generous nature or those of someone close to you give you greater flexibility. You will adapt easily to the new and fortunate events that will occur on the domestic front.

📋 You will put positive agreements in place, and these will help improve productivity levels and enable you to realize your professional ambitions.

▦ A healthy and advantageous situation will enable you to carry out new transactions and enjoy your assets to the full, as well as to increase them.

➕ You have been given plenty of practical advice and a number of warnings, but you will still tend to let things take their course, passively putting up with everything that is wrong with your health rather than being proactive about improving it.

❤ You will fail to reach the necessary compromises or you will accept an awkward situation rather than taking steps to change it. As a result, your emotional life will not be a happy one in the near future. You will feel that accounts have yet to be settled.

👪 You will face prejudice and lack of understanding or be forced to come to terms with a mistaken and difficult situation that is full of conflict. You will try to reach agreements or find compromises, but it will not be easy.

📋 You will face hostile elements or stubborn opposition, which will force you to deal with a difficult situation or make awkward and frustrating concessions.

🗄 You will encounter problems, delays or unyielding opposition in your attempts to find a compromise or reach an agreement. You will be forced to accept financial concessions that will not necessarily prove to be advantageous to you.

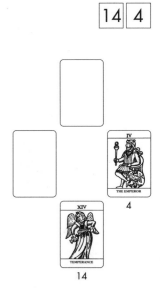

➕ You will have no difficulty in finding a way to adopt a lifestyle that allows you to use and express your energy and inner harmony more fully and overtly.

❤ Events and arrangements will shed light on your emotional situation, enabling you to begin a genuine relationship that is based on sincere and mutual feelings.

👪 The support or approval of someone influential in your family circle will help you come to a clear and appropriate agreement, enabling you to make progress on the domestic front.

📋 An important person will profit from the positive agreements you are about to negotiate. These will lead to real success and satisfaction in your professional life.

🗄 You will be advised to accept agreements that will be instrumental in shedding light on your financial affairs. You will then be able to take advantage of offers and opportunities that could come your way.

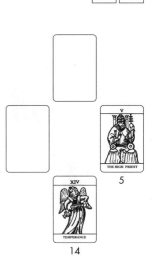

459

14 6

VI
THE LOVERS

6

XIV
TEMPERANCE

14

✚ Your own choices and decisions will prompt you to review your lifestyle and encourage you to adopt a more flexible approach to your health.

❤ You will feel that the time has come to reconsider your choices and develop a suitable environment in which your emotional life can really take off.

👪 Choices, decisions or harmonious relationships currently ruling your domestic circle will prompt you to reach an agreement. Things will then return to normal, or you will be encouraged to see matters in an entirely new light.

📋 You will reach decisions that prompt a review of your professional situation at a key moment. You will then put in place the structure needed to help it take off once more or return to normal.

💹 Agreements, choices or decisions will enable you to negotiate a possible and timely revitalization to encourage your finances to flourish once more.

14 7

VII
THE CHARIOT

7

XIV
TEMPERANCE

14

✚ A journey or holiday away that you may be planning will do you nothing but good. Alternatively, your current efforts will result in excellent health that will give you even greater potential.

❤ Your efforts will be rewarded and your wishes on the emotional front will be granted, leaving you free to enjoy the results in complete confidence. Alternatively, you will make appropriate arrangements for relationships to turn out for the best.

👪 Thanks to your hard work and keen desire to succeed, you will put in place all the agreements and compromises that are needed for domestic matters to reach their full potential. Your hopes for your family will be more than satisfied.

📋 You will do all you possibly can to negotiate the ideal environment in which to succeed on a professional level.

💹 You will finally put in place the structure required for you to negotiate a successful expansion of your finances.

If you are prepared to accept certain guidelines, circumstances will enable you to leave, travel (if you wish) or be more flexible in the face of events.

A sense of justice and normality will reign once more. You will put in place a framework that allows you to depart freely, act instinctively or witness the arrival or return of someone special.

No matter what harsh judgements or strict rules govern your home life, you will put in place a fruitful, positive arrangement that gives you greater freedom.

Order and self-discipline will bring about a useful compromise. If you are awaiting a legal decision, tell yourself that it will be something of a compromise and will prompt either you or someone in your professional environment to leave.

The stability of your finances and asset base will help you carry out well-timed deals, make a journey or transfer funds.

14 8

8

14

You will come to see that it is actually more reasonable and sensible to put up with a number of restrictions if you want to maintain your stability and well-being. Once you have come to this decision, you will know how to proceed.

When you have thought the matter over and taken appropriate and sensible precautions, you will make the compromises needed for your own emotional stability. Other people will give you the support you need to achieve your aims.

When you have taken a step back and had time to consider the issue, you will see what action or compromise is needed to keep things stable on the domestic front.

After a period of uncertainty, during which you reflect on professional matters, you will come to useful compromises and agreements. You may be lucky enough to find an influential person who will lend you their support.

After thinking long and hard, you will put the structures in place to reinforce the stability and reliability of your financial situation.

14 9

9

14

14 10

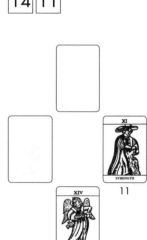

➕ Circumstances and the way your situation develops will prompt you to be as adaptable as possible in order to cope with your somewhat precarious balance, but you will manage it quite successfully.

❤️ You will tend to let your emotions guide or influence you. As your love life develops, however, you will appreciate what actions or compromises are needed to maintain and preserve its tranquillity.

👪 Despite developments on the domestic front, you remain undecided and largely influenced by the choices of your family. You will, however, find you have no difficulty in agreeing to these.

📋 Matters will develop at work, making compromises and flexibility vital. Take heart, not all compromises are for the worse.

🗐 Encouraging events and circumstances will help you to make positive compromises or choices with both ease and success.

14 11

➕ Your easy and natural control over both yourself and events around you means you are able to embark on fruitful, useful endeavours or to be sufficiently flexible to come out on top.

❤️ Keep a grip on events and you will succeed. You will find it easy to make the necessary compromises, and your emotional life will develop accordingly.

👪 If you are flexible and prepared to let events take their course, you will be able to influence things subtly but confidently, giving you control over your domestic situation.

📋 You will remain in control at work and bring about appropriate compromises and agreements. Your negotiations will succeed, and you will hold your ground while demonstrating great flexibility and adaptability, according to circumstances.

🗐 Your efforts will be rewarded and you can be totally confident of reaching important compromises and making appropriate deals. Rest assured of the success of your negotiations.

462

➕ If you are prepared to adopt a degree of self-discipline, a serious course of treatment or a strict regime or diet, you will regain your balance and well-being.

♥ You will be forced to reach compromises and fair agreements. Your flexibility will help you to maintain your emotional balance and peace of mind.

👪 Impartial, just compromises and agreements will surface to help things return to normal on the domestic front. You will have to put up with the changes that result.

📋 Fair compromises and agreements will help return things to normal. You will have to demonstrate your professional flexibility and accept any judgements that are made or decisions that are taken.

🏠 A fair and just compromise will help you regain a measure of financial equilibrium. You will, however, have to agree to make economies and limit your expenditure.

14 12

12

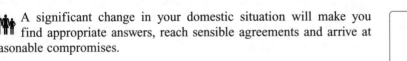
14

➕ You will be forced to accept a compromise or radical change. Alternatively, you may have to adapt to the major changes in behaviour and lifestyle that will become necessary.

♥ A major change in your emotional life will force you to reach sensible compromises and find appropriate answers. It may also oblige you to accept things as they are and agree to take a step back.

👪 A significant change in your domestic situation will make you find appropriate answers, reach sensible agreements and arrive at reasonable compromises.

📋 Significant changes are inevitable at work. You will have no trouble adapting, as long as you reach reasonable compromises or find the appropriate answers.

🏠 A radical change or the conclusion of a business transaction will make you reach sensible and fair agreements or reasonable compromises. You need to identify exactly what is required to resolve your financial problems.

14 13

13

14

14 15

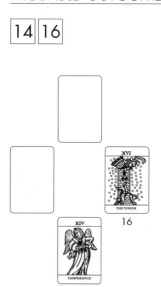

+ Despite a tendency to over-indulge, you will manage to keep a firm but flexible grip on yourself at a key moment.

♥ You will probably instigate compromises and agreements that will help you channel and control whatever passions, influences or unwarranted feelings arise in your emotional life.

♦♦♦ You will reach agreements to achieve what you want or influence events sufficiently for everything to fall into place and work out as you would wish.

✎ You will, ultimately, get what you want. You will reach compromises that will help you satisfy your ambitions and control negotiations that are useful to this end.

⊞ You will be able to control negotiations, agreements and compromises that have the potential to benefit the growth of your finances and help you satisfy your desires or ambitions.

---

14 16

+ A mental or physical shock or upheaval will encourage you to take appropriate steps to adopt a healthier lifestyle.

♥ Following an emotional shock or challenge, your natural instincts and intuition will prompt you to make intelligent moves to establish order in your emotional life.

♦♦♦ Your family life will face an upsetting challenge but one that will probably turn out to be helpful and beneficial in the long run. You will demonstrate appropriate behaviour and re-introduce normality to your domestic situation.

✎ A confrontation or inevitable upheaval will occur at work, and you will take the necessary steps to make sure that professional order is established once more.

⊞ A strong challenge or inevitable upheaval will cause you to take appropriate, thoughtful steps to get your finances back in order.

464

14 17

You will have no trouble adapting both firmly and flexibly to the most varied of circumstances. No matter what happens, you will remain calm, safeguard your independence and protect your health.

You will be assured that someone's feelings for you are sincere. You may well be enjoying a wonderful love life.

New and favourable circumstances will prompt you to take certain action or reach the intelligent and constructive compromises that are required.

Your negotiations will be entirely successful, thanks to new and encouraging circumstances. You will then come to compromises or arrangements that prove useful to your situation.

Your healthy, regular income will enable you to use your money as you intend and make you sure of your opportunities and rights.

17

14

14 18

You will probably have to seek the advice of a doctor, act sensibly and not overdo things for a time and agree to be looked after.

Your sense of responsibility and duty will prompt you to come to agreements and compromises or to put up with a situation that is far from satisfactory.

You will reach sensible compromises and agreements and gain the upper hand in domestic conflicts or difficulties, through your strength of character.

To resolve or limit your problems at work, you have no choice but to take sensible steps or to reach agreements and compromises dictated by your sense of duty and moral resolve.

You will be obliged to resolve or limit your financial difficulties and reach intelligent compromises, dictated by your sense of duty.

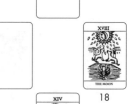

18

14

14 19

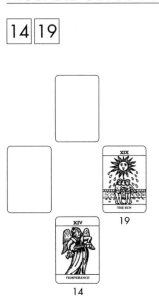

14

19

The Sun (XIX), Temperance (XIV)

✚ You will do everything in your power to be at one with yourself and those around you, maintaining your essential equilibrium and enjoying life's pleasures to the full.

♥ The success of a love affair or a union allows you to let yourself go and enjoy it to the full. Be sure to take advantage of the happy times that come your way.

👪 You will do all you can to maintain happiness and harmony in your domestic situation. You can then enjoy the good times you will have with your family with an easy mind.

📋 Events will conspire to help you come to positive and beneficial agreements and compromises at work.

💼 Once you have come to a clearer understanding of your situation, you will realize what action is required for agreements and choices to be made and an effective financial strategy to be enforced.

14 20

14

20

✚ After a partial return to normality or a recovery, you will still need to make an effort and avoid letting things slide if you really want to regain your energy and sense of dynamism.

♥ A change of situation or the way your emotional life is viewed will prompt you to reach agreements or compromises that help you to take things in hand and move forwards.

👪 Your domestic situation will experience a change or new start, which will help you to come to positive, dynamic agreements. Use this opportunity as a springboard to attain your objectives.

📋 An appreciable change or a fresh start at work will bring about dynamic and well-timed new agreements that help you negotiate your way ahead successfully and progress.

💼 A change in your situation or a marked improvement in your finances will encourage the movement of funds or an important transaction. Your hard work will pay off.

14 21

✚ Auspicious events or a period of calm, rest, peace and mental fulfilment will rejuvenate you and help you do everything you need to maintain your well-being.

❤ You will enjoy a period of emotional fulfilment, which will help you to stay calm, healthy and balanced.

👪 A rewarding domestic situation will encourage you to reach agreements and compromises that guarantee family peace and harmony.

📋 Things will come together to impose order on professional negotiations. They will bring about positive changes and compromises and help you push back the boundaries at work.

▦ Great financial potential is on the horizon, but you will have to embrace strict agreements and tough compromises to keep expenditure within your means.

21

14

14 22

✚ If a journey or move fails to bring you peace of mind, it will at least provide the relaxation and tranquillity for which you were looking.

❤ A rendezvous or hasty encounter will prompt you to review matters. You will be tempted to let things take their course and not intervene.

👪 Whether you expected it or not, you will be forced to tolerate the comings and goings (departures, arrivals, travel plans or house moves) that will dominate your family life.

📋 The departure or arrival of another person will help you conclude negotiations. Alternatively, a move of some kind will increase your own flexibility and adaptability.

▦ Take care that you are not too passive in the face of events and that you do not give in to whims or irrational impulses on the money front, even if your books appear to balance at the moment.

22

14

467

15	1

Think hard before taking any action or initiatives that might involve you in any untoward or potentially dangerous risks. If you fall ill, do everything you can to recover as soon as possible.

If you are thinking of someone special, you should know that they are not to be trusted. Sadly, their main aim is to achieve their own goals. Alternatively, be wary of impulsive, even violent responses that could lead to irreparable mistakes.

Sudden, even aggressive action will upset your domestic life and cause damage in the process. It may be, however, that you just have to go through this in order for the problems to come to an end.

Premature, over-ambitious and inappropriate action, or indeed reckless or illegal business, may put your job at risk.

You are at risk of losing everything through premature, badly timed, ill-considered, illicit actions.

15	2

Despite your reserve and stability, you will draw on all your resources if necessary and use your energy to fulfil your desires or begin a new chapter.

After keeping your counsel and being patient, you will give in to your strong feelings and do all in your power to get what you want. If you are thinking of someone special, be aware that they have a passionate nature, despite their apparent reserve.

Your unspoken desires or secret hopes will soon be fulfilled and the results will surpass your expectations.

When you have held your peace for a while and thought things over, you will finally be able to introduce original ideas and profit from a new, innovative product or business enterprise. The results will surpass even your expectations.

After a period of patience, reserve or economizing, you will be in a position to enjoy your profits and satisfy your desires.

➕ Although you possess both excellent health and a generous nature, you could easily be subject to a sudden health crisis, caused most probably by your own excesses, general fatigue and accumulated tensions.

❤️ Despite your own feelings, you will not be able to avoid a crisis of passion in your love life, leaving you vulnerable both to bitter disenchantment and to a violent response. You need to take great care.

👪 You will have trouble coping with the shock caused by imminent domestic problems, which bring with them disappointment and a troubled, unhealthy atmosphere.

📋 You risk spoiling an imminent and possibly useful professional situation by trying to take from it what it cannot offer, exhausting its potential and exposing it to chaos and confusion.

🏠 Your material situation would appear more positive if you were not jeopardizing it through unreasonable and excessive expenditure. Your behaviour is putting your finances at great risk.

➕ Your strong sense of self-protection and self-control allow you to enjoy high levels of energy and excellent health without making you hyperactive or over-excited.

❤️ No matter what temptation or resistance you face, nothing can apparently control your desire to satisfy your wishes or restrain your emotional life.

👪 You will soon be able to impose your authority and protective framework on your domestic situation. Alternatively, you will have to take into account the support and advice of an intelligent and positive person in your circle, who could well help you achieve your goals.

📋 Assurance and support will come your way at work, helping you to reach your targets, come to a profitable agreement or form an advantageous partnership. Your initiatives will succeed.

🏠 You will receive the assurance, support or advice you need to achieve financial success.

15 5

V
THE HIGH PRIEST

5

XV
THE DEVIL

15

➕ Quite justifiably, you will be instructed or advised to employ whatever means you can to make a complete recovery and return to normal health.

❤ You will be obliged to do everything possible to change a situation or an opinion someone holds concerning your emotional life, even if it means taking apparently disproportionate measures.

👪 Extreme measures will be needed to bring about a review of your domestic situation, to implement change or to restore order.

✍ You will achieve your ambitions, implement profitable change at work or make a fresh start, but you must remain legally irreproachable, especially if you employ extreme measures.

🎲 You will profit from the re-floatation of a business or from a thorough review of your financial situation. It must be done within a strictly legal framework.

15 6

VI
THE LOVERS

6

XV
THE DEVIL

15

➕ Decisions and determination will be necessary if you are to enjoy your health to the full without letting things drift and risking a deterioration in your mental and physical energy.

❤ A choice or special relationship will enable you to fulfil your desires and give way completely to your passions.

👪 You will have to make important choices on the domestic front, but they will help it expand and develop in the end.

✍ A major choice, profitable partnership or positive agreement will bring professional targets closer and push back boundaries at work.

🎲 Positive agreements or sensible choices will bring important benefits. You will witness a general and significant growth in your financial situation.

470

➕ Although you clearly want to maintain your self-control, a degree of carelessness, impatience and impulsive, if not reckless, behaviour may well lead you to make mistakes or take pointless risks.

❤️ You will have no rest until you achieve your aims and get your own way. It is up to you to decide if your desires are justified or if your demands are futile.

👪 You will soon be able to achieve what you want on the domestic front or leave or move house, but the departure or change involved may happen sooner than expected or in a somewhat brutal, chaotic way.

📝 Keep a firm grip on your situation and follow your own path if you want to achieve your set targets. You will soon get what you want, but be prepared for events to happen quickly.

 You should be able to take steps to help your financial position develop quickly or even hurriedly. This will benefit or speed up the movement of funds.

➕ You may be forced to resort to stern measures to rid yourself of your weaknesses, control your anxiety or tendency to become over-excited and increase your awareness of your high, if sometimes chaotic and even wasted, levels of energy.

❤️ Difficult or stringent circumstances will force you to overcome your weaknesses and act in a more sensible, responsible way in your emotional relationships.

 👪 Harsh and difficult circumstances will encourage you to channel any domestic problems and passions that appear or carry out ambitious projects that could help achieve family balance and harmony.

📝 If you have recourse to the law, you may fall prey to someone who is prepared to use any means to achieve their aims. Alternatively, you will gain the support of someone influential. It could be that through self-discipline and sensible behaviour you will reach your professional targets.

 A difficult situation will urge you to manage your funds more sensibly or to organize your financial situation better, so that you can satisfy your ambitions.

471

15 9

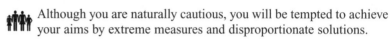 Despite your relative caution and the discoveries you have made yourself or through others, you will probably take radical decisions, make serious choices or be tempted by adventures or dubious proposals.

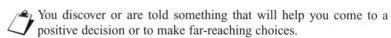 You will come to see that you are arousing passionate and intense emotions, either despite or conversely because of yourself. Alternatively, you will appreciate how shallow, self-centred and without motivation your emotional life really is.

Although you are naturally cautious, you will be tempted to achieve your aims by extreme measures and disproportionate solutions.

You discover or are told something that will help you come to a positive decision or to make far-reaching choices.

You will need time to think before understanding or learning what is necessary for you to profit from an agreement, choice or decision concerning your finances.

15 10

Your physical and emotional development is on a distinctly upward curve. You will probably be bursting with energy and will need to take active steps to burn it off.

Nothing will prevent you from satisfying your emotional desires. You will get what you want in your love life.

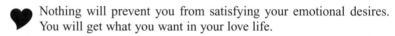 You will soon be in a position to achieve all your goals on the domestic front. Things are looking positive and set to improve.

Conditions are so positive and dynamic that you can expect to move forwards quickly and dramatically, making your presence felt and reaching all your targets.

Circumstances are encouraging your spirit of enterprise. You will fight to achieve your financial goals.

➕ Your self-control will protect you from over-indulgence or dangerous temptation. You will adopt a regime that may be strict but that will help you maintain your well-being.

❤️ Your strength of mind will give you confidence and allow you to tame your passions, control your impulses and bring some stability to your love life.

👪 If you demonstrate strength of mind and self-discipline in the face of every obstacle, you will have no trouble overcoming your problems, introducing moderation and countering dissension in your family circle.

🖋️ As long as you can be self-disciplined and tough, you will have such a strong will to succeed and exercise such control over your professional environment that nothing and no one can stand between you and your goals.

💲 You will achieve your financial goals if you make sure the law is on your side and if you are able to be extremely self-disciplined.

➕ You will look for all possible ways out of a difficult situation or a state of mental and physical weakness. You may be tempted to do too much, go too fast or make extreme choices.

❤️ To get out of a difficult, stagnant situation, you will tend to resort to excessive behaviour or extreme measures. Unfortunately, these will do nothing to help you achieve your goals. Be on your guard.

👪 You will find all sorts of extreme and questionable solutions or measures to extricate yourself from a tricky and even ambiguous stalemate. None of these will solve your problem, however, so calm down and be sensible.

🖋️ You will do everything you can to extricate yourself from an impasse. If you eventually resort to extreme measures, it will only be after you have given serious consideration to all the factors involved.

💲 Although a situation appears to be difficult, stagnant or restricting, you will be tempted to try disproportionate solutions or embark on financial ventures beyond your means. You would do well to be cautious.

473

15 13

➕ Even after a major change or the recovery from a health problem, you will still feel troubled and vulnerable to your own weaknesses and excesses. Your future state of health is somewhat uncertain.

❤ Following a radical change, a break-up or the end of a relationship, your emotional life will develop uncertainly and you will tend to live from day to day.

👪 An important change, transformation or the end of a situation will tend to make your domestic life develop in turbulent, rocky and uncertain ways.

📝 A significant change or serious transformation in your situation will enable you to achieve all your goals, even if events may be disconcerting, uncertain or confusing.

🔲 You will soon profit from a fundamental change or the conclusion of an agreement. Alternatively, a source of income could come to an end and lead to financial uncertainty or cause you to panic.

---

15 14

➕ If you demonstrate flexibility and adaptability, discover a happy medium and reach the right decisions on the health front, you will be able to moderate your intense levels of energy and tendency towards excess and become more self-assured and in control.

❤ You will reach an understanding, compromise or degree of harmony in your love life that will give you greater control over your feelings and desires and enable you to remain calmer.

👪 Agreements, compromises and concessions will introduce moderation into your domestic circle and protect it from potential excesses, confusion or difficulties.

📝 Heated negotiations and agreements without concession will help you find exactly what you are looking for and enable you to keep potentially awkward situations under control.

🔲 You will make compromises or transactions that will bring greater profits from your finances.

15 16

A crisis or accident affecting your health may force you to make important changes and demonstrate your toughness and strength in order to correct excesses and weaknesses.

You may react in an extreme and angry way to the challenge of a crisis or break-up, and you will be faced with stubborn opposition. Make sure you guard against this sort of emotional turbulence in future.

A crisis or sudden upheaval will plunge your domestic situation into turmoil. You will then have to reckon with stubborn opposition, division, dissent and fierce disagreements.

An upheaval, crisis or sudden and inevitable challenge at work may discredit you and your position. You will be faced with unyielding opposition and be plunged into a troubled, confused situation.

An upheaval or sudden and inevitable challenge to your financial situation may cause a great deal of trouble or force you to face stubborn opposition. Alternatively, it could bring considerable profits.

16

15

15 17

If you remain open and attentive to people and events around you, you will be able to avoid abuses and excesses or resist potentially harmful temptation.

The emotional fulfilment you appear to be enjoying at present or a state of high excitability may tempt you to behave passionately or recklessly. You need to stay emotionally grounded.

The support of your family or of someone in your immediate circle will help your wishes come true. Alternatively, it may herald the advent of something new that is much hoped for and close to your heart.

Propitious circumstances or strong support will help you achieve what you want professionally or bring about something new and greatly to your advantage at work.

Your personal resources or financial support will help you bring your projects and ambitions to fruition and with significant profit.

17

15

475

15 18

XVIII
THE MOON

18

XV
THE DEVIL

15

✚ In order to recover from illness or weakness for good, you may make extreme, difficult or even brutal choices. Be prepared to feel the backlash soon.

♥ A disappointment in love, a difficult situation or disillusion of an emotional kind will lead you to live rather recklessly and follow the dictates of your desires rather than your good sense.

👪 Disappointments, disenchantment, mistakes or difficulties on the domestic front will lead you to respond violently to satisfy your own desires, without any thought for the consequences.

📋 In spite of the delays, disappointments and difficulties you will experience, your burning desire and overwhelming determination to reach an agreement or make decisive resolutions will remain undiminished. As a result, you will, one way or another, achieve your aims.

💰 Your financial ambitions or decisions will gain strength from the delays, disappointments or difficulties that lie in your path.

15 19

XIX
THE SUN

19

XV
THE DEVIL

15

✚ Nothing will stand in the way of your desire to exert authority or your inclination to express your intense feelings and dynamism in any activity, struggle or effort.

♥ Great emotional joy, gained through a happy, genuine relationship, will make you more impatient and determined to achieve what you really want in your love life. Nothing will stand in your way.

👪 Happiness in your domestic life will enable you to press ahead and achieve your hopes and wishes for everyone.

📋 A positive partnership or a new light that is shed on your professional environment will encourage your entrepreneurial spirit and help you make concrete progress.

💰 The support of a partnership or renewed clarity in your financial affairs leaves the field open for you to reach your targets and make obvious and profitable progress.

15 20

Your recovery from illness or a review of your health will make you moderate your behaviour, and you will do everything to secure a more certain and healthy balance.

Following a renewal or change in your emotional life, you will be forced to adopt a fairer, more conventional and balanced attitude, and this will lead you to curb your passionate, excessive and sometimes unstable behaviour.

A revival or change in your domestic situation or a partial return to normal will enable you to impose a disciplined and strict regime, controlling any turmoil and disorder with precision and care.

In the wake of an upturn or readjustment of your work situation, any divisions and disagreements will be judged impartially or will have to subjected to discipline and strict, tough regulations.

A change in your finances – even the re-flotation of your business – will force you to curb your spending and exercise some sort of financial restraint.

20

15

15 21

You will experience a sense of both intellectual and physical fulfil-ment and, as a result, will enjoy excellent health and well-being but at the same time demonstrate your inherent self-restraint and caution.

This will be a rich and fulfilling time in your emotional life, but you will not succumb to the temptation to be too passionate, reckless or uncontrolled in your relationships.

Your domestic situation appears to offer wonderful prospects, but you must be vigilant and moderate in your behaviour if you are to hold everything together and avoid instability.

Encouraging prospects for development at work will depend on caution, self-restraint and circumspection. Otherwise, there is a real danger that you will ruin your chances through impatient, foolish or greedy behaviour.

Excellent financial prospects are within reach, but you will have to demonstrate vigilance and caution if you are to resist the temptation to overspend or squander your money.

21

15

15 22

15 — THE DEVIL

22 — THE FOOL

➕ Nothing will prevent you from ignoring the most basic of precautions to satisfy your desires and follow your current path, even though you are putting your well-being at considerable risk.

❤ Departures, arrivals, meetings, impulsive actions, desire, emotional excess, seduction and overindulgence – all these will feature in your emotional life, leaving little room for real love.

👪 A departure, house move or unexpected event may well tip the balance in your domestic circumstances, resulting in a period of turbulence and chaos that will be hard to control.

📋 A departure, journey or a sudden event involving your work could be followed by a period of turmoil in which you may experience both intense excitement and extreme impatience.

💰 A sudden event or journey will allow you to satisfy your financial ambitions, but you will be tempted to make mistakes or overspend.

16 1

16 — THE TOWER

1 — THE MAGICIAN

➕ You could well be the victim of a crisis or suffer a blow to your health. This will disrupt your overall well-being for a while, but it will force you to turn over a new leaf, which will prove beneficial in the long term.

❤ You are going to experience an upheaval, crisis or sudden change in your emotional life. This will probably be the result of your own initiative, though its ramifications will extend beyond anything you can imagine.

👪 You are likely to be able to bring your plans to rapid fruition and to take some initiatives that will completely change your situation in a positive way.

📋 Your projects will suddenly come up against some stimulating challenges. Alternatively, exceptional and momentous circumstances may enable you to do something new and unprecedented.

💰 An upheaval or crisis will force you to reappraise your financial plans or resources. Paradoxically, events will be to your advantage.

➕ You will have to exhibit great self-discipline and endurance to survive an inevitable but ultimately positive crisis. In the long run it will free you from illness or a chronic health concern.

❤️ An anticipated but sudden change or crisis will soon occur in your emotional life. Like a summer thunderstorm, it will clear the air, ease the atmosphere and take a weight off your shoulders.

👪 You, or someone in your immediate circle, will act as the catalyst for an abrupt change or crisis or will bring a difficult matter to a conclusion, freeing your domestic life of its current problems and concerns.

📋 Either you are anticipating or you will instigate a sudden change or reversal in your professional life. This will allow you to remedy the situation and start to make progress, having eliminated the troublesome, pointless or damaging elements.

🁣 An expected but sudden change or a dilemma of your own making will give you an opportunity to benefit by allowing you to sort out your accounts, bring order to your finances, rectify your mistakes and focus on what is really important.

➕ You will take thoughtful and positive steps to shed light on and bring stability to your state of health. You will eliminate anything that is potentially harmful.

❤️ You will resolve your emotional life intelligently and positively, giving you the freedom to start a new relationship. If you have someone in mind, this person will suddenly make their feelings clear.

👪 An intelligent, understanding person in your circle will probably cause a sudden reversal or upheaval. This will actually bring your family both happiness and satisfaction.

📋 Intelligent, constructive and profitable measures will clarify your professional situation and trigger a change that will be positive from everyone's points of view.

🁣 Things will become clear on the financial front, and constructive, sensible and profitable decisions will bring positive results.

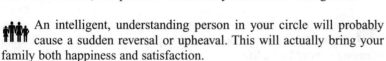

479

16 4

IV
THE EMPEROR

4

XVI
THE TOWER

16

➕ You will be advised or instructed to undertake a radical review of your health and lifestyle. Should you fall ill, you may well make a spectacular recovery.

❤ Someone will advise or instruct you to rethink your attitude, to accept the importance of evaluating or reappraising your emotional life, to make amends and to offer forgiveness.

👪 You will encounter an imminent crisis or sudden change in your domestic life. Be aware that it is both necessary and constructive, however, and that it will bring with it positive renewal.

📋 A major upheaval will take place in your work, but it will result in the improvements required to kick-start business and implement positive change or reassessment.

💷 You need to look carefully at your finances, review them or be obliged to consider an entirely new fiscal strategy.

16 5

V
THE HIGH PRIEST

5

XVI
THE TOWER

16

➕ If you follow the dictates of your conscience or sense of duty, you will come to a sudden and dramatic realization that could help you assess your potential resources and profit from them accordingly.

❤ You are going to experience major upheavals and positive changes in your emotional life. They are sure to reflect your wishes, however, and will more than satisfy your hopes and desires.

👪 You will have the support or approval of someone close or perhaps of your family when you come to implement changes that will bring harmony to your home life.

📋 Someone influential will give you their support or approval to carry out major changes that lead to success in your work.

💷 You will suddenly achieve great things on the financial front, but only after winning the approval or support of someone influential and competent in this field.

✚ A crisis or blow to your health could force you to change your travel plans. Alternatively, you will have to make a sudden departure for health reasons.

♥ You may suddenly leave to join someone special or you may have an upsetting, unexpected encounter. Alternatively, you may be the cause of an emotional crisis or even its victim. Whichever is the case, your life is about to go through a turbulent period.

♦ Major transformations, upheavals and sudden changes will affect your domestic situation. They will, however, have the support of the whole family.

✎ An agreement or difficult choice will bring major transformations or upheavals to your working life. Alternatively, you will feel free to pursue your own course from now on.

▣ An agreement or disagreement will trigger upheavals in, or sudden changes to, your financial situation. They will be unsettling but ultimately beneficial.

✚ Assistance, advice or support will make it possible for you to act in your own best interests and free yourself from your problems quite radically and suddenly.

♥ Your efforts will now bear fruit, and a beneficial upheaval or an abrupt challenge in your emotional life will leave you free of worry and conflict.

♦ Current measures or efforts will cause major changes that will certainly be good for your domestic situation, bringing with them mental and physical relief from a series of obligations.

✎ Struggles or on-going events will result in a sudden change to your situation, freeing you from certain responsibilities and allowing you to move on with all the support you need.

▣ If you decide to reassess your finances and free them of some of the restrictive burdens placed on them, you will be able to instigate positive, profitable change.

16

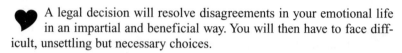
An accident or blow to your health may threaten your current well-being, forcing you to make some major, salutary decisions.

A legal decision will resolve disagreements in your emotional life in an impartial and beneficial way. You will then have to face difficult, unsettling but necessary choices.

Sudden changes, disagreements or conflicts may well upset the balance of your domestic situation. It is time to reach a radical and impartial but strict decision.

A legal decision taken with regard to disputes, conflicts or sudden challenges or reappraisal in your working situation will doubtless prove both impartial and beneficial.

You will probably be forced to question choices, decisions and options affecting your finances. You need to act quickly to avoid risking their stability.

16 9

16

Your caution, vigilance and experience will help you to respond in an appropriate and timely manner, so that you avoid an accident or health problem and steer well clear of danger.

You will come to see the need for an immediate reappraisal or even a brusque change in your emotional life.

When you have considered the matter carefully, you will see that a rapid upheaval or change in your domestic situation will be to your advantage.

After careful consideration, you will appreciate that a major change in your financial situation is both necessary and beneficial. It is the only way you will be able to overcome problems and make real progress.

When you have thought the matter over, you will see that it is both useful and necessary, to reassess and resolve your financial situation before real progress can be made.

You are at risk of being involved in a moral crisis or upheaval that will seriously unsettle you and threaten your stability, but will not undermine you fundamentally.

♥ Your emotional life needs a major shake-up. Only then can conflicts or lingering issues be addressed, assessed or resolved.

Disruption or a reappraisal is vital if order and balance are to be restored to your family life.

A reappraisal or upheaval must take place at work to enable you to assert your rights and make clear decisions about problems, conflicts or disputes.

If you are to be sure of your rights and assets, a review or disruption and change on the financial front is essential; only then can things return to normal.

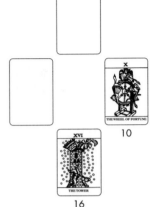

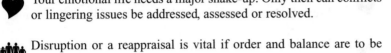 Showing both courage and determination, you implement lifestyle or behaviour changes or act as the catalyst for a positive crisis, which brings with it increased self-awareness and realism.

♥ Despite your strength of mind and serious desire to control the situation, you will be unable to prevent a dramatic and essential change in your love life. However, this will prove to be both beneficial and to your advantage.

You will finally realize that the upheavals or changes that are sure to occur in your domestic situation will, ultimately, prove useful, salutary and positive.

Stay calm, lucid, focused and pragmatic, keeping a firm grip on your rights and privileges, and you will succeed in benefiting from imminent and positive changes.

Take in your stride all the upheavals that may occur in your financial situation; you can learn short-term and long-term lessons from them.

483

16 | 12

✚ If you fall ill, you are likely to make a spectacular recovery. Alternatively, a mental or physical shock will be the catalyst for a new sense of self-awareness and speedy development.

♥ A situation provoking excessive dependence or great annoyance will soon undergo a spectacular, beneficial and liberating change.

👪 Sudden changes to, or a reappraisal of, your family life will bring about rapid progress and freedom from current restraints.

📋 A stalemate will be resolved in a spectacular, challenging but positive manner. You will be able to throw off any constraints and obstacles, moving on quickly and positively as a result.

💷 Beneficial changes will get things moving again and free your financial situation in an extraordinary way. You can then make speedy and positive progress.

16 | 13

✚ A major change will make you face potential upheaval with both courage and strength. You will be able to solve your problems once and for all.

♥ Your emotional life will undergo a radical and far-reaching change. However, you will remain strong enough to face further inevitable but positive upheavals.

👪 Although fundamental and radical change will occur in your domestic life, you will still find the strength and courage to tackle inevitable but ultimately fruitful challenges.

📋 Major change, significant profits or the conclusion of a concern will bring important and advantageous challenges at work. You will regain an element of professional freedom.

💷 Following radical change, significant profits or the logical conclusion to a business deal, your financial situation will change for the better and allow you to act with greater freedom in the future.

You will be appropriately flexible and submissive when accepting challenges or disruptions to your health. As a result, you will enjoy a greater sense of freedom and well-being.

You will succeed in reaching the understandings and compromises that you had planned, leaving you at liberty to follow your desires.

Timely and useful compromises or concessions will provoke disruption that should nevertheless help you in your family life and give you the opportunity to congratulate yourself.

Useful and profitable negotiations will inevitably result in changes and disruption, but you will be able to profit from these to conclude an excellent deal.

Successful negotiations or profitable transactions will enable you to bring a financial stalemate to an end in an advantageous manner.

If you fail to exert rigorous self-discipline from now on you may well suffer emotional and physical consequences. Put an end to over-indulgence and excess.

The only possible outcome of your excessive and troubled relationships is an abrupt, if not violent, conclusion that will cause great upheaval in your emotional life.

You will suddenly become acutely aware of your real desires and ambitions. Alternatively, the problems and divisions at the heart of your domestic situation will suddenly resolve themselves, after a stormy but liberating period.

Someone with authority or ambition will soon open doors for you, enabling you to achieve your objectives, although their action will, of course, serve their purposes and desires rather more than your own.

Confident of your own strength and ambitions, you will do everything possible to disencumber your finances with all haste. Be careful not to abuse your money or authority, however, and be sure to stay within the law.

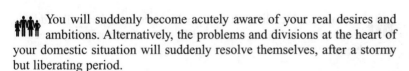

16 17

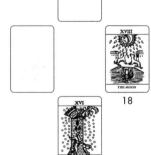

Your open, receptive and naturally resourceful nature puts you in the perfect position to make decisive and positive choices about your balance and well-being.

Inevitable disruptions will cause your hopes to be disappointed, and you will have to reassess your emotional choices. However, new developments will help you see that good can come from bad.

Your hopes will probably be disappointed and your choices and decisions interrupted by unpredictable and inevitable challenges in your domestic life. Things will turn out for the best, however.

Your hopes of finding an agreement or of achieving something new will probably be modified, or even dashed, by an unpredictable but inevitable chain of events.

Unpredictable upheavals or new developments, possibly positive ones, may nevertheless make your hopes and agreements seem pointless and ineffectual.

16 18

You will be able to emerge from and disregard chronic or temporary health issues, perhaps by triggering a crisis that will prove beneficial, or by being hard on yourself.

A turbulent, disappointing or illusory relationship will suddenly work out for the best, ending with a break-up, departure or a painful but necessary crisis.

An inextricable, difficult and troublesome situation will suddenly come to an end. Your domestic life will be overturned but freed of its problems.

You face a welcome, liberating change at work, which will enable you to overcome the obstacles and problems in your path.

Beneficial disruption is on the cards, bringing with it the opportunity to overcome the financial problems you have encountered of late.

Although your balance may have been undermined by an illness or even by a sudden, temporary condition, its detoxifying effect will ultimately prove beneficial.

It would be both useful and beneficial to clear up matters in your love life. You can then question certain aspects and carry out any necessary but ultimately useful changes.

Challenges on the domestic front will cause you to review certain matters and bring about more harmonious relationships or even a happy event.

Forming a partnership, coming to an agreement or shedding new light on professional issues will create positive challenges in your work environment.

A positive and profitable agreement, change or event will bring about alterations in your financial position and restore its equilibrium.

16 19

19

16

You may be able to make a recovery on your own using patience, caution and careful consideration.

A review, reassessment or renewal of your love life will bring with it challenges and disruption. Any lingering doubts and worries will be banished.

After a change or renewal in your domestic situation, your family life will probably undergo some useful and beneficial disruption, as you had expected.

The beneficial results you had envisaged will follow in the wake of a change of job or opinion ,or a suggestion or renewal of some kind, or even a useful and positive upheaval.

Your financial situation will change for the better following a review, a suggestion or renewal of some kind, or useful and beneficial disruption – your doubts and worries will vanish.

16 20

20

16

487

16 21

21

16

➕ Your open, receptive and welcoming nature will allow you to move things along speedily in the direction you have chosen.

❤️ Your happy, flourishing emotional relationships will cause sudden, but ultimately positive, change, and some rapid developments which will add to your current happiness.

👪 Your domestic situation is likely to be fulfilling and satisfying, but only after it is has undergone major disruption.

📋 Your professional life will expand significantly, enabling you to deal easily and successfully with any disruptions that might result.

🗄️ Great potential is within reach, or the opportunity to expand and release your finances, ensuring rapid growth.

16 22

22

16

➕ Your unstable, excessive behaviour could well lead you to make mistakes, take pointless risks or act dangerously. Take extra care and remain calm.

❤️ Someone's departure or arrival is going to trigger an upheaval or sudden change in your emotional situation. Your own departure may well follow.

👪 After spending time in uncertainty, on a quest, or following an abrupt decision made on a whim, you will experience major upheavals on the domestic front.

📋 Another person's departure or arrival, a journey or an event will result in major disruptions in your professional situation. You will then be free of current restrictions and able to travel in your turn.

🗄️ Some sudden expenditure will have a destabilizing effect on your finances, or, conversely, a sudden in-flow of revenue will have a liberating effect on them.

➕ A useful idea or appropriate and effective course of treatment will help you feel revitalized and renewed in some way, although there may also be suffering involved.

❤️ Circumstances may appear satisfactory, but you are in danger of being bitterly disillusioned or of taking a wrong turn in your love life by being too sensitive or sentimental.

👪 Initiatives on the domestic front will take the form of an innovation or a birth. However, it will be difficult for events to come to fruition without total devotion or dedication on your part.

✍️ It will be difficult for an original idea, novel initiative or new product – even the start of a job, new business or company – to get off the ground and become concrete.

🎛️ You will have difficulty in finding new resources unless you demonstrate great ability or a capacity for hard work.

| 17 | 1 |

1

17

➕ Your patience and insight will pay off, and you will be able to enjoy your natural resources and radiant health to the full.

❤️ Your patience and wishes will be fully rewarded, and you will experience genuine emotional happiness.

👪 Your patience and deepest desires on the domestic front will be rewarded, and you will enjoy a period of great happiness in your family life.

✍️ Although some of the aspects involved in your projects have yet to be revealed, you can be confident that the creative, innovative plans you have for a partnership or new company will be fully realized.

🎛️ Your shrewd, economical behaviour will allow you to enjoy everything that is now at your disposal, and you will profit from the financial advantages on offer.

| 17 | 2 |

2

17

3

17

➕ You are healthy, robust and generous of spirit, and you will enjoy a wealth of natural resources and achieve all your goals.

♥ If someone special is preoccupying your thoughts, you can be sure of both their sincere feelings and their honest intentions to implement changes in their life. Alternatively, your hopes and desires will be satisfied, bringing renewed emotional energy.

👪 Something new, pleasant and fortunate will occur in your domestic life, bringing with it changes and a real sense of renewal.

📋 Conditions are now right to launch a new product or innovation, to re-float a business or to expand a budding company. You will profit significantly from the results.

🎲 You hold all the trump cards needed for productive, intelligent moves to revitalize your resources, and you will enjoy and profit from the results with confidence.

17 4

4

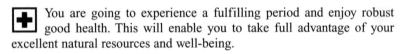

17

➕ You are going to experience a fulfilling period and enjoy robust good health. This will enable you to take full advantage of your excellent natural resources and well-being.

♥ You will be able to take sensible steps to achieve your heartfelt desires and enjoy a fulfilled emotional life.

👪 You will be in a position to take intelligent, constructive steps to achieve what you want for your family and allow your domestic life to reach its full potential.

📋 Solid support or constructive, intelligent measures will help put in place plans for expansion or innovation. Your professional horizons will open up.

🎲 You will be in a position to bring about significant financial growth that will be favoured by circumstances and solid support.

You will probably be advised or recommended to take a holiday or travel and take the opportunity to relax and review your lifestyle. Recharge your batteries and you can then move on.

You may be about to go on holiday or take a sentimental journey. Alternatively, the person who is on your mind is probably on their way to see you.

You will win the support or approval you need to accomplish a new project, personal goal or house move quickly. Alternatively, a happy event may occur in your domestic life.

You are going to win the support or approval you need to launch something innovative, a new product, an original idea or achieve a personal goal.

The support, approval or advice that you need will be forthcoming and will help you find new funds with all speed to make your financial situation more stable.

You are going to make judicious and delicate choices that will help you make the most of your natural resources in both a calm and confident manner.

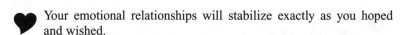

Your emotional relationships will stabilize exactly as you hoped and wished.

As a result of either a positive agreement or difficult but decisive discussions, you will put in place a new plan or achieve something creative or innovative on the domestic front to universal approval.

An agreement, contract or partnership will be the catalyst for something new, such as an innovative product, fresh idea, new company or personal goal.

A judicious choice, profitable agreement or beneficial contract will enable you to profit from increased stability and security on the financial front.

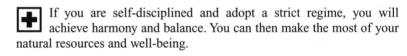

17	7

➕ Don't relax your efforts or resolve. You will slowly but surely succeed in finding inner harmony as long as you make sensible choices and intelligent decisions that will benefit your health.

♥ You will eventually achieve your aims and experience a degree of emotional fulfilment that leads to positive choices and perfect harmony in your love life.

👪 You will receive some good news to do with your domestic life. Alternatively, you will come to some thoughtful conclusions and make imaginative choices or new resolutions, or something new will develop on the home front.

📋 Hoped-for success that comes your way or anticipated good news that you receive will produce something new at work. This will in turn be confirmed by some inspired choices or agreements.

🎲 You will achieve hoped-for success or hear news on the financial front that you have been expecting. You will benefit from the choices or agreements you make.

17	8

➕ If you are self-disciplined and adopt a strict regime, you will achieve harmony and balance. You can then make the most of your natural resources and well-being.

♥ The balance governing your emotional life will ensure the depth of your feelings and allow you to achieve all you hold dear.

👪 Your home life is so stable that you can confidently and freely put into practice a number of initiatives that will bring about a new venture or ensure that your personal ideas or ambitions are achieved.

📋 A stable situation or the regime and self-discipline you impose on yourself will mean that your undertakings or new and original ventures meet with success.

🎲 Your financial stability or the self-discipline to which you willingly submit will result in increased resources or welcome reward for your efforts.

+ An awareness or personal discovery will prompt you to review your lifestyle and draw on your inner strength. You will enjoy a sense of security or harmony.

♥ Your patience, good sense and foresight will enable you to experience emotional balance in your relationship. This is what you need in your love life.

👪 Vigilance, determination and foresight will bring you the harmony and equilibrium that you seek and which must form the basis of your family life.

📋 You will discover a new factor that will help to bring balance to your work situation. Alternatively, an investigation or careful review will result in the creation of something new or innovative, strictly within a legal framework.

⚖ You will discover a new factor or come by the means of acquiring new resources, which will restore balance to your finances.

9

17

+ Your personal development or that of events around you will help you to assess your levels of inner energy in a clear and precise way. A new sense of tranquillity will be yours.

♥ Progress in external events or your emotional life will continue, enabling you to assess the depth and potential of your feelings. You will become more emotionally mature and realistic and cherished wishes will be realized.

👪 Your domestic situation will develop advantageously, enabling you to make slow but meaningful changes, find original solutions or achieve new targets, albeit slowly but surely.

📋 Circumstances will develop favourably, or your professional situation will allow you to find unexpected solutions or accomplish something new and original in line with your ambitions.

⚖ Developments in your finances will allow you to make an accurate assessment of your current funds and potential gains.

10

17

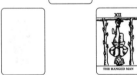

11

17

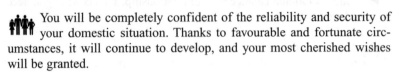 Maintain calm, confident but energetic control over current issues, and you will make the progress you want and deserve.

As long as you keep calm, remain confident and exert energetic control over your emotions, your wishes will come true.

You will be completely confident of the reliability and security of your domestic situation. Thanks to favourable and fortunate circumstances, it will continue to develop, and your most cherished wishes will be granted.

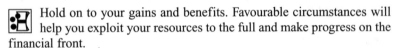 Keep a firm and confident grip on your position, and positive, advantageous circumstances will help you put in place new and original ideas and make progress.

Hold on to your gains and benefits. Favourable circumstances will help you exploit your resources to the full and make progress on the financial front.

17

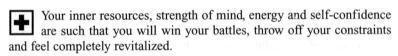 Your inner resources, strength of mind, energy and self-confidence are such that you will win your battles, throw off your constraints and feel completely revitalized.

Although you feel rather dependent and passive, you will later be pleased that you decided to place your trust in your feelings and events. Your desires will be fulfilled.

Allow events to take their course, accept that your circumstances are advantageous if somewhat restrictive and maintain control by exercising your subtle inner strength. You will then achieve your desires and bring about something new and beneficial in your domestic situation.

You have no choice but to trust the new and positive events that will come your way. Through them you will find success.

You will succeed in throwing off constraints and establishing a renewed financial independence by showing courage and strength of character and by creating new resources.

12

➕ A radical change in your life or attitude or the end to a problem or illness will encourage you to adopt a healthier lifestyle and have more faith in your natural instincts.

♥ A major change or real turning point will bring you genuine fulfilment in your love life, and you will be able to achieve your most cherished wishes.

👪 A dramatic change, the conclusion of a situation or the start of a new chapter will bring about initiatives that will ultimately create something new and happy in your domestic life.

📝 Following a significant change or the logical, inevitable conclusion of some aspect of business, you will have the time to create or achieve something new, productive and profitable.

🗄 An important change or the logical, beneficial end to a transaction will enable you to profit from new circumstances, improve your finances or achieve something new.

| 17 | 13 |

13

17

➕ You will have no difficulty making the right arrangements to protect your inner strength. Flexibility will bring calmness and serenity, and will give you a new lease of life.

♥ You will reach agreements and understanding with ease, helping to bring the realization of your emotional aspirations closer. You will feel free to give into your feelings and to achieve what you want in your love life.

👪 You will have no problem in initiating compromises or making concessions that could help you to achieve something new on the domestic front. You will then feel relieved and happy.

📝 Negotiations will give you complete power to realize your dreams or put in place a creation or innovation in your professional life.

🗄 Timely negotiations or skilful transactions will guarantee that you acquire new funds or achieve financial security or success.

| 17 | 14 |

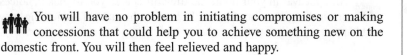

14

17

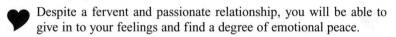

17	15

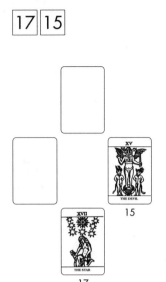

➕ You may be obliged to take serious measures to restore your health. Alternatively, after a period of over-indulging and misusing your energy, you will need to rest and relax.

❤️ Despite a fervent and passionate relationship, you will be able to give in to your feelings and find a degree of emotional peace.

👪 Positive circumstances and wonderful support enable you to realize your hopes and aspirations in your home and your domestic life.

📋 Someone influential will act in conjunction with fortunate circumstances to help you fulfil your plans and hopes for a new job, unique product or original idea.

💰 Lucrative transactions or a significant improvement in your financial situation will give you the freedom to enjoy your resources to the full and with an easy conscience.

17	16

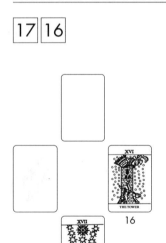

➕ Following an emotional or physical shock or a sudden but transient risk to your health, you will be encouraged to make some healthy resolutions and sensible lifestyle choices to regain a measure of peace.

❤️ You will have an emotional upheaval or fall madly in love, which will encourage you to listen to your feelings and make some sensible choices for the future.

👪 An upheaval in your domestic life will enable you to make choices or reach agreements that could lead to the start of something new and happy.

📋 A sudden change will help you reach the agreement you hoped for. It may encourage you to make inspired, innovative choices or start afresh in a new situation.

💰 An upheaval or sudden change may well put an end to your financial deadlock, bringing new agreements within reach or giving you greater freedom to exploit all the resources at your disposal.

✚ After experiencing health problems and emerging from a difficult, unsettling phase, you will find a deeper sense of calm and balance, which will allow you to draw on your natural resources.

♥ After a confused, turbulent, worrying, disappointing or disconcerting period, you will go through a calmer phase in your emotional life and experience deep, sincere feelings.

👪 Firmness, fairness and affection will win through over the turmoil, trouble or conflict that may cloud the atmosphere of your domestic life. In this way, everything will return to normal.

📝 Any judgement due to be made will probably be in your favour. It will, therefore, resolve problems in your situation and also provide you with new circumstances and prospects.

📋 You will meet with a few financial difficulties but will succeed in balancing the books and making sure your financial situation is healthier and more stable.

17 19

✚ A welcome light will be shed on your psychological and physical health. This will allow you to enjoy and make the most of your natural resources.

♥ Reciprocated feelings, a happy relationship or a genuine meeting of minds will emerge, providing just what you have sought and wanted for a long time.

👪 Great happiness in your family or a new slant on domestic affairs will offer you the chance to learn or reveal new facts, or favourable circumstances will lead to the birth of a new situation.

📝 A partnership, success or revelation will help you to discover or uncover a new fact or aspect at work. You will be able to continue your research and investigations into new areas.

📋 Light shed on your finances or your achievement in this area will help you discover new solutions or monetary resources of obvious benefit to you.

17 20

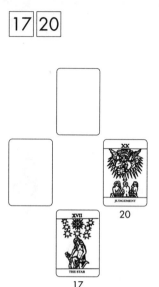

+ Following a change, renewal or recovery you will feel healthier or emotionally and physically calmer. You will have the chance to see your health progress positively.

♥ Following change or renewal in your emotional life, you will be able to make considerable progress.

👪 A change or renewal will occur in your domestic life and bring with it new and propitious circumstances for your family.

📋 Changes, proposals or renewed professional opportunities will enable you to undertake and achieve something new and original at work. You will profit from improving circumstances.

🎲 A proposal will be made to you or an opportunity for change or renewal will come your way, which will help you to develop your financial resources and offer you the chance to make the most of the currently encouraging circumstances.

17 21

+ You have enormous physical and intellectual potential and will doubtless manage and take full advantage of your natural resources to achieve the personal growth you desire.

♥ Your most cherished wishes will be more than satisfied. You will then be able to realize your hopes and feel happy and fulfilled, confident of your feelings and your ability both to trust your environment and control your emotions.

👪 The prospect of expansion or new possibilities within your domestic situation will help you benefit from positive circumstances to achieve something new and beneficial.

📋 Your circumstances will develop and open up to different possibilities and new horizons. You will then be in a position to gain or accomplish something new, unprecedented and original, which will have every chance of success.

🎲 Improved finances or the fruitful use of capital will enable you to acquire new monetary resources or to profit from positive and favourable conditions.

➕ You will probably have the chance to go away on holiday or leave to accomplish something new in your life. This will do you enormous good, both emotionally and physically.

❤️ Following the travels, meeting, departure or arrival of another person, you will be in a position to make a sudden journey or to leave, and this will lead to something new and happy in your love life.

👪 Following the departure or arrival of someone in your family or as the result of your own actions, you will soon be able to move house or achieve something new on the domestic front.

📝 The departure or arrival of someone in your professional circle or a venture undertaken by you yourself will soon enable you to accomplish new things.

💰 Your actions or moves will bear fruit, and you will then benefit from new funds, which will allow you to tackle something different or to realize your financial hopes.

➕ Expert suggestions, effective treatment or a healthy determination to deal with things will resolve your health issues.

❤️ Useful expert advice will shed a beneficial light on your emotional life. Despite delays or difficulties on the way, your plans will finally come to fruition and bring you great happiness.

👪 Proposals and plans concerning your domestic situation will be delayed, but you will succeed in overcoming these difficulties and achieve your goals.

📝 Original and astute proposals together with interesting plans will finally see the light of day. They will overcome the obstacles and disappointments that are put in your way and prevail against the doubts, concerns and difficulties expressed by others.

💰 Despite delays or obstacles, your initiative and perceptive nature will win through, overcoming financial difficulties and enabling you to carry out your plans.

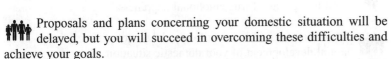
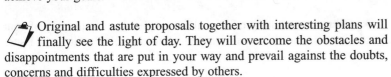

18 2

2

18

➕ You will need to be patient, careful and calm in order to make a slow but sure recovery and enjoy a complete return to good health.

❤ Although you do not reveal it or perhaps want to admit it, feelings of disappointment or disenchantment in your love life will cause you to review your emotions and introduce changes.

👪 The difficulties and problems you will encounter in your domestic life will, as expected, resolve themselves as a result of new circumstances or logical changes that are also necessary.

📋 Even if you are not fully aware of all the facts, rest assured that a change is going to occur in your situation without requiring your intervention. Things will happen just as you envisaged.

Although you may not yet be aware of it, the changes that you have expected will soon occur and will solve your problems and financial difficulties.

18 3

3

18

➕ Trust your intelligence and your instinct to solve your problems or curb any anxieties about your health. If you feel depressed, try to use your depression as a springboard to fulfilment and well-being.

❤ The difficulties, anxieties and worries you will experience will not stand in the way of true emotional happiness.

👪 Difficulties or problems will only delay, not prevent, the positive, natural development of your domestic situation.

📋 Obstacles in your professional path will not get in the way of your success, and the expansion you need to resolve your work issues will result.

The obstacles you are due to encounter cannot prevent your efforts from succeeding. As a result, you will experience financial growth and resolve current difficulties.

If you have been trying to avoid health issues by failing to take them seriously, you could well suffer the consequences. Seek the help, support and advice you need to get over them.

Practical and intelligent advice will be offered to you, but you will still be tempted to make the same mistakes, take the wrong turning or run from your problems rather than confront them. Look before you leap and do not be stubborn.

If you disregard the practical and considered advice that has been forthcoming you will leave and take your problems with you. Nothing can then be resolved. Think hard before you do anything and leave only if there is no alternative.

Despite the practical advice on offer, you will try to escape from your problems without attempting to solve them. Alternatively, you will meet with such opposition that you will have no choice but to remove yourself instantly from the situation.

Have faith in the advice you will be given and absent yourself from the current troublesome and unhealthy financial situation. Avoid making the same errors in the future.

Your material and emotional obligations will probably be at the root of feelings of turmoil and fatigue to come. Keep an eye on your health and consult a doctor if necessary.

Although your emotional life looks secure, you cannot prevent problems from arising. You will be the victim of bitter disappointment and will be forced to assess this event with honesty and integrity.

You will be able to rely or draw on the judgement, support and advice of someone close, who is both honest and irreproachable. They will help you sort out the problems within your family.

You will have to shoulder heavy responsibilities and probably take on additional obligations. However, this will help you succeed in overcoming obstacles, limiting difficulties and resolving problems.

You will probably have heavy financial burdens and additional obligations to shoulder, but given your sense of responsibility and duty, you will assume them (and not without a certain amount of pleasure).

501

| 18 | 6 |

✚ Although you exercise freedom of choice in matters of health, you will be tempted to make questionable decisions, take wrong turnings and make yourself unnecessarily ill.

♥ You will experience some difficulties in finding the emotional harmony you are looking for. However, if you fail to take care and allow yourself to be indecisive or gullible, you may end up disappointed.

👪 You might believe you have come to an agreement or made the right choice, but you will realize that this is an illusion or error on your part. You have taken the wrong turning and nothing has been resolved.

✎ If you are hoping to reach an agreement, you will be disappointed. Alternatively, if it still remains a possibility, take extra care because you may take a wrong turning or trip up.

⊞ Agreements reached or choices made will still fail to resolve your financial problems. You will need more determination to overcome the current difficulty.

THE LOVERS — VI
6

THE MOON — XVIII
18

| 18 | 7 |

✚ Don't relax your efforts and, despite the obstacles or difficulties you will face, you will eventually succeed in conquering all your health problems.

♥ Do not despair. You will succeed in conquering all your problems, despite the challenges in your emotional life, conflicts that may arise or disappointments you may experience.

👪 Although difficulties, bad news or disappointments are imminent, you will manage to overcome all the issues in your domestic life. No matter what you do, don't give in or give up.

✎ It will be a long, difficult, laborious, often discouraging and sometimes apparently insuperable task. In the end, however, you are bound to succeed in overcoming all obstacles that appear and then enjoy well-deserved success.

⊞ Although you may meet with difficulties and receive disappointing news, at the end of the day you will overcome the obstacles and solve the financial problems facing you.

THE CHARIOT — VII
7

THE MOON — XVIII
18

502

➕ Your balance and stability will probably be disturbed by mild health problems, but you will still have to maintain self-discipline to prevent the situation from getting worse.

❤ The stability of your emotional life will probably be disturbed by imagined problems, unfair conflicts and misunderstandings. You will have to exercise considerable self-discipline to prevent circumstances from deteriorating.

👪 Problems and conflicts are liable to disrupt your domestic life. You will have to deal with them strictly but fairly in order to prevent a worsening of the situation or the occurrence of injustices.

📋 Only through the strict application of the law and accepted rules will you be able to curb or resolve the problems, difficulties and conflicts in your path.

💰 You will have to submit your financial situation to the rule of law, strict regulations and self-discipline in order to solve your money problems and find a better way of handling things.

18 8

VIII
JUSTICE

8

XVIII
THE MOON

18

➕ You will probably discover that your health problems are more intractable or take longer to resolve than you originally imagined.

❤ Sadly, simply being aware of problems is not enough to solve them. You are going to experience disappointment or disillusionment.

👪 Good sense, caution and insight will probably not be enough to solve the problems you will come across in your domestic life. You will need to find practical, down-to-earth solutions.

📋 All the problems that could arise in your work situation will soon make themselves apparent, and practical, realistic solutions will be needed to sort them out.

💰 You will be obliged to understand and admit what is going wrong financially. Only if you implement down-to-earth solutions will matters gradually change for the better.

18 9

IX
THE HERMIT

9

XVIII
THE MOON

18

18 10

X

THE WHEEL OF FORTUNE

10

XVIII

THE MOON

18

✚ You will experience real highs and lows before finally understanding your true health issues. Do not let your health deteriorate and take energetic measures to look after yourself properly.

♥ There are still points of disagreement, problems to solve as well as complications and troubles to clear up in your love life, but everything should work out.

👪 Your family life will soon be in turmoil, or difficulties or conflict will curtail domestic progress. As a result, a change is needed as soon as possible.

📋 Although you have made progress, problems will still need solving. Do not delude yourself, because you will still have to be proactive if you are to emerge from this unstable and ambiguous situation.

💼 Problems, obstacles or mistakes from the past will interrupt the logical development of your financial matters. You will still have to take action to get out of this insecure situation.

18 11

XI

STRENGTH

11

XVIII

THE MOON

18

✚ You will successfully confront the health problems you may face, thanks to your courage, high levels of energy and uncommon strength of character.

♥ You will succeed in conquering problems, overcoming difficulties and weathering disappointments with courage, strength and determination. You will then feel surer of yourself, your love life and your emotions in general.

👪 The problems or difficulties that are bound to arise in your domestic life will be no match for your determination. You will solve or conquer them with courage, strength and generosity of spirit.

📋 You will have serious problems to solve and major difficulties to overcome in order to achieve success. However, you will manage to deal with the situation with strength, courage and determination.

💼 Your assurance and determination will enable you to overcome your financial problems and difficulties.

✚ It will be a long, frustrating and hard road to travel before you can throw off your health concerns or a long-standing problem. However, you can make it.

❤ You could be the victim of disappointment or disillusionment. You will then have trouble extricating yourself from the situation and recovering from it. You will be forced to admit that you were wrong.

👪 You could be the victim of a disappointment or conflict, of an error you have made, of slander or of an insecure home environment. You will need time to get over it and disentangle yourself.

✎ There will not be much you can do to escape from your current problems until you have admitted your own mistakes and understood that you are in a confused, insecure position.

▦ You will be unable to do much to escape from your financial difficulties until you have admitted your mistakes and appreciated that your true position is problematic.

✚ Despite a complete change, you will still have health concerns to confront and resolve. Serious problems could result from the failure of an important function, and you should take immediate measures against such risks.

❤ The end of a relationship or a radical change in your emotional life will probably let you down, plunge you into grief and leave you in a position of little hope.

👪 Some major change is unlikely to have the positive effect you were hoping for. It will leave you with problems to solve, material difficulties to overcome and opposition to confront.

✎ A situation coming to a temporary or even permanent end, or a fundamental change in your situation will cause problems, difficulties and opposition. You must face matters with authority.

▦ Funds drying up, an expiry date or the end of a situation could well cause problems and difficulties and plunge you into financial insecurity. Take immediate steps to counter such risks.

18 14

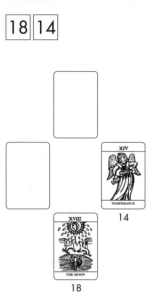

XIV

TEMPERANCE

14

XVIII

THE MOON

18

➕ Don't confuse flexibility and co-operation with negligence. You could risk the deterioration of your health and a potential worsening of your problems.

❤️ Distinguish between intelligent compromises and damaging concessions and between accommodating others and giving into them without thinking. If you do not, you could well experience disappointments, difficulties and bitter disillusionment or make serious mistakes in your emotional life.

👪 Compromise and appeasement will not be enough to solve the problems and difficulties in your domestic life. Avoid making pointless and damaging concessions in exchange for a quiet life.

📋 The compromises and concessions you could be tempted to make will serve no purpose, and your negotiations will come to nothing. You must simply shoulder your responsibilities and own up to any mistakes.

🔲 You will not gain the payback you were expecting, nor will you succeed in reaching the settlements or compromises that would have enabled you to overcome your financial difficulties. You need to reconsider the issue using different criteria.

18 15

XV

THE DEVIL

15

XVIII

THE MOON

18

➕ If you continue to give in to your predilection for excess and over-indulgence and fail to resist dangerous temptations, you will most certainly face a serious health problem.

❤️ A turbulent and passionate relationship will lead only to disagreement, disenchantment, treacherous behaviour or very unsatisfactory emotional responses. It will all end in disappointment.

👪 The turmoil, over-excitement or differences prevailing in your domestic life will lead to conflicts, indecision and insecurity.

📋 The upheavals and chaos to come and the resulting divisions will prevent you from reaching or carrying through an agreement, although they will make you realize that you have taken a wrong turning.

🔲 The desire to fulfil your needs and ambitions at all costs could well lead you to make dangerous choices or put in place dubious agreements, but you will ultimately experience disappointments and serious difficulties on the financial front.

➕ An accident or blow to your health is likely to give you trouble for some time, but you will emerge from it well.

♥ A crisis, upheaval or break-up in your emotional life is certainly going to upset you physically and emotionally and let you down badly. You will, however, still manage to extricate yourself and recover.

👪 A crisis or upsetting change in your domestic life will leave you with problems and conflicts to resolve and obstacles and difficulties to overcome. You will manage to cope well.

✍ Following a shake-up, crisis or sudden change, you will have to be brave and determined in your battle to resolve the resulting problems and conquer the obstacles you will face.

▣ A disruption, emergency or sudden change will cause you problems and financial worries. There will be subsequent financial obstacles and difficulties to overcome, but you can rest assured that you will resolve them successfully.

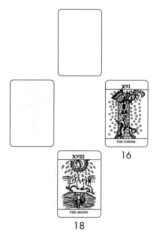

16

18

➕ Your inner energy and strength will be disrupted by minor health problems, but you will still have to approach matters seriously and treat them with determination in order to prevent imbalance.

♥ You will probably be disappointed in your love life, but you will show discipline and strength in overcoming anxiety, forgetting disillusion and solving the problems that will confront you.

👪 You will have trouble achieving your domestic hopes and aspirations. Nevertheless, if you exert self-discipline you will overcome these difficulties.

✍ You will encounter problems in achieving a new venture or realizing your hopes or aspirations. The instability of your work situation may mean you have to face the stringency of the law or exert a measure of self-discipline.

▣ You will have trouble realizing your financial hopes unless you resolve current difficulties with determination and self-discipline

17

18

Shedding light on health issues will help you to overcome your problems with ease and gradually regain your energy.

A happy relationship, committed union or reciprocated affection will assist you in overcoming problems and making positive progress in your love life.

The act of making things clear or a sense of happiness will enable you to sort out problems and overcome the difficulties facing you in your domestic life.

An explanation or the realisation of a partnership will enable you to make positive progress at work and overcome any problems or obstacles you encounter.

Fortunate circumstances or sudden clarity on the financial front will help you to resolve issues and move things forward, despite potential difficulties, obstacles and delays.

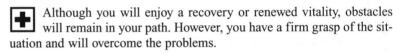

Although you will enjoy a recovery or renewed vitality, obstacles will remain in your path. However, you have a firm grasp of the situation and will overcome the problems.

Despite a significant change in your emotional life, there will still be difficulties to overcome and anxieties or fears to control, but you are likely to succeed.

A change in your domestic life will disappoint you or it will enable you to take a difficult situation in hand and resolve it.

You may be disappointed by a proposal, but you will recover. Alternatively, you may be able to solve problems as a result of change or renewed energy.

Although your financial situation will undergo a partial recovery, you will still have difficulties to overcome and problems to solve. You will, however, easily succeed.

➕ Although you have great potential, you will face certain challenges in health-related matters. If you want things to improve or to eliminate problems entirely, you will have to suffer for a while.

❤ When you have seriously considered your overall situation, you will have no choice but to accept the fact that not all is well in your emotional life and you need to recognize where you went wrong.

👪 Unless you accept that sacrifices need to be made within your family life, you will feel constrained by problems and unable to make progress.

📋 The opportunities for growth on the work front will not be completely satisfying, despite its considerable potential, and you will be forced to make sacrifices or lose out in a disappointing situation.

🗒 Despite the possibilities that are within reach and your dreams of improving your finances, you will still have difficulties to face, responsibilities to shoulder, obligations to assume and sacrifices to make.

18 21

➕ Self-indulgent or irresponsible behaviour could well lead to foolish mistakes being made concerning your health. Listen to advice and take your health seriously.

❤ You cannot escape your problems, mistakes or reckless behaviour, and despite your good intentions, you will suffer disappointments. Alternatively, someone's departure will cause you grief.

👪 The departure or arrival of someone will probably cause you problems. Alternatively, a move or change of residence could unsettle your family situation and disappoint you.

📋 The steps you have taken will not lead to success. It could be that another person's departure or arrival will cause you problems or that you will be unable to escape from imminent difficulties and conflicts. Do not make the same mistakes and avoid foolish, unthinking behaviour.

🗒 Past efforts will not bear fruit. If you continue to make the same mistakes, your financial situation will not improve. It's time to be more realistic.

18 22

➕ Thanks to the sensible steps you have taken, you will feel radiant, refreshed, dynamic and ready for action.

❤️ Changes made in your emotional life will prove positive and prompt a real revitalization, great happiness or the advent of something new and meaningful.

👪 Your efforts will result in great happiness in your domestic environment. At the same time, new light will be shed on your situation and a renewed sense of joy will prevail.

📋 Recent professional or work activity has every chance of bearing fruit and engendering a positive and profitable change.

🗄️ Initiatives taken on the financial front will have beneficial and positive results. Renewal and change are on the cards.

➕ Your reserve, stability and moderation will enable you to enjoy excellent health and to feel completely at one with the world.

❤️ Your patience will not have been in vain. Indeed, you are going to experience emotional fulfilment, have a rewarding relationship and enjoy a profound, stable and sincere union.

👪 Someone in your domestic circle will give their total support. This will lead to great happiness, allowing you to enjoy all the good things you could wish for in your family life.

📋 Financial success at work will come your way. You may have been half-expecting or making preparation for this change, without really believing that it would happen.

🗄️ You will enjoy real success on the financial front, which you may have been expecting or working towards without being completely convinced that it would materialize.

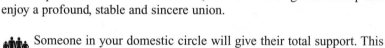

19 3

✚ Your healthy levels of energy and sense of well-being will enable you to tackle the activities, journeys or undertakings that you anticipated. You will enjoy your good health to the full and make the most of this happy time.

♥ An imminent and important encounter will affect your emotional life. Alternatively, the person in your thoughts is on their way to find you or you are on your way to them. Whichever is the case, your love life is on the move.

👪 Your efforts will prove so effective that you will be able to make that hoped-for journey, move house under excellent circumstances or accomplish something important and positive on the domestic front.

📝 Profitable moves will enable you to form a partnership, reach an agreement, shed important light on a situation or feel free to live and control your life as you wish.

▤ The steps taken to clarify your financial situation or make it more prosperous will prove successful. You will then be able to enjoy your capital as you wish.

3

19

19 4

✚ Any advice offered and followed will make health issues clear to you, leaving you alone responsible for your well-being.

♥ You will get the agreement or support you need to start a relationship, stabilize your emotional situation and experience happiness in your love life.

👪 You will be able to make constructive, intelligent moves and work towards a positive outcome for your family.

📝 The guarantee and support needed to reach agreement, form a partnership or achieve something positive and very satisfying will be forthcoming.

▤ You will be able to operate constructively and intelligently and to enjoy the satisfying and positive financial consequences.

4

19

PROBABLE OUTCOME

19	5

+ You may be enjoying excellent health, but you will have important choices to make to ensure it remains on a stable basis in the future.

♥ The accord and support you may need will come your way, helping you to establish a sincere and solid relationship. Alternatively, you will enjoy the emotional relationships to which you quietly aspire.

👪 You may need to make some effort in your domestic situation to bring out the best in various relationships and to make choices and decisions that will please everyone.

📋 You will have the support and approval you need to initiate a profitable agreement, establish an excellent partnership or make some opportune decisions.

🗄 An agreement, contract or accord will improve your finances a great deal and offer you the opportunity to make some excellent choices at the same time.

PROBABLE OUTCOME

19	6

+ The decisions and measures you have taken will prove beneficial to your well-being. They will allow you to enjoy good health, dynamism and energy, all of which you will use wisely.

♥ Choices made and actions undertaken in your emotional life will be positive from every point of view. You will be able to achieve satisfying and happy results.

👪 Any choices made, measures taken and agreements reached will prove to be positive, leading to happiness and success in your domestic life.

📋 Agreements and decisions will aid your progress and allow you to be successful in all your undertakings. Through your own efforts you will enjoy total unmitigated success in your projects.

🗄 Choices, agreements and decisions will bring new clarity to your finances and allow you to achieve your goals with ease and speed.

Your efforts will be rewarded, and you will enjoy excellent health, a sense of dynamism and high levels of energy, all of which will have a firm, well-balanced foundation.

Keep up your efforts and see things through to the end. You will experience happy and stable relationships that are based on sincere and wholly reciprocated feelings.

The efforts made and actions undertaken will have the required effect of shedding new light on the domestic front and enabling you to achieve happiness and balance at home.

Your efforts will help to bring the clarity you both seek and deserve, enabling you to attain the aims you have set yourself.

Your action and efforts will enable you to clarify and make a fair assessment of your situation and reap your just rewards.

Unless you exert a certain amount of self-discipline you won't be in a position to assess your state of health or to appreciate exactly how things stand.

The resilience and self-discipline demanded of you will help you to understand the true nature of your feelings and relationship.

You will make some difficult decisions and subject yourself to a degree of self-discipline in order to benefit from new and useful insights into your family situation. A greater sense of calm and harmony will result.

Tough decisions and strict self-discipline will produce positive results and lead you to a more precise assessment of your professional prospects.

You will have to subject yourself to some hard questions and answers, but they will make your financial situation clearer and show the exact state of your current funds.

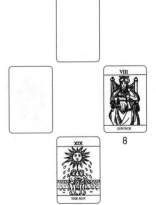

19	9

IX

THE HERMIT

9

XIX

THE SUN

19

➕ A new clarity and self-awareness or your own caution and moderation will enable you to make clear and positive progress, both physically and psychologically.

♥ You will discover something important and beneficial, leading to a happy and positive change in your love life.

👪 You will become aware of a new and important factor that is certain to benefit the calm progress of your domestic life.

📋 Your long-term vision and wise, thoughtful assessments will prove to be correct. Your circumstances at work will develop positively, just as you envisaged and planned.

▦ Your proposals and assessments for the long term will prove to be accurate and, as a result, your financial situation will improve as you had planned.

19	10

X

THE WHEEL OF FORTUNE

10

XIX

THE SUN

19

➕ You will benefit from the steady progress made towards achieving strong, healthy levels of energy and total self-control.

♥ Your emotional life will progress in a positive way. You will then maintain strong, deep and calm relationships or find a stable and genuine bond.

👪 As a result of your efforts, your domestic life will develop positively, and you will maintain the stability and harmony at home, bringing happiness, joy and fulfilment.

📋 Changed circumstances will be the catalyst for partnerships, agreements and positive moves at work. The progress you desire will be made through positive action, flexibility and determination.

▦ Circumstances will develop well and bring you happy and positive results. You will find yourself able to take both control and advantage of your financial situation.

Your excellent self-control will guarantee high energy levels and a strong, healthy disposition.

You are self-confident, emotionally sincere and able to exert subtle but firm control over your feelings. As a result, you will enjoy deep and meaningful relationships.

Your subtle but firm control over your domestic situation will give you the opportunity to enjoy sincere and warm-hearted relationships with those close to you. You will be able to achieve all you want on the home front.

You will succeed in getting what you want, and you will be able to control events and arrangements and enjoy a profitable contract, partnership or new business.

Financial success is in store for you, and you will also be able to control your own circumstances and have an opportunity to enjoy your profits and resources.

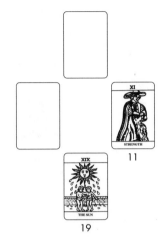

Remain aware of your own limitations and be suitably flexible about the advice you are given. You will then be able to take full advantage of the excellent health and high energy levels you will enjoy.

Despite the constraints, obligations and obstacles you will have to face, you will succeed in sorting out your emotional life, forming a new and happy relationship or consolidating an already established union.

There may be restrictions and obligations or difficulties along the way, but you will eventually succeed in putting into action all your domestic plans.

You will succeed in freeing yourself from constraints and anything that threatens to block your progress. The results will be turn out to be very positive.

Despite the constraints, duties and obligations that may limit your financial progress, you will see positive results.

19 13

+ A radical change brought about by a number of factors will bring you great vitality and energy. You will be able to make sound and sensible use of this.

♥ A major change will bring about a happy event, or you will embark on a new and honest relationship.

A complete change will trigger an opportune and positive event in your home life. It will bring your family much joy and contentment.

A fundamental change will enable you to reap what you have sown and achieve positive results, such as a partnership or agreement with someone influential.

A radical change, the logical outcome to a situation or some profitable business will guarantee excellent financial results.

---

19 14

+ Flexibility and adaptability are the keys to good health and will help you to make clear, sensible and appropriate choices about your health and further your search for balance and harmony.

♥ You will have no trouble reaching the understandings or compromises required for a new relationship or genuine love affair. This will be based on mutual attraction and will bring you real joy.

Understandings and compromises will bring about a positive event in your domestic life. Great joy will ensue.

Your negotiations will trigger a positive and beneficial change, with success for you in any choices, agreements, contracts or partnerships you form.

Timely settlements and compromises will bring success to your agreements or help you make clear and wise financial decisions.

➕ You are going to benefit from high levels of energy and will be on top form, enabling you to do anything you wish.

❤️ You will get the green light to press ahead and achieve exactly what you want in your love life.

👪 You will be in a position to take effective, positive steps to clear up matters in your home life. Domestic goals will be met.

📋 An advantageous situation will help you achieve your objectives and successfully realize your ambitions.

🔲 You will be able to benefit from propitious circumstances that will bring monetary reward and enable you to realize your financial ambitions successfully.

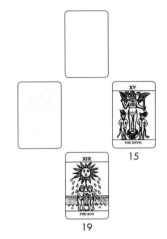

➕ Following an upheaval, a physical or emotional shock or a sudden change to your health, you will embark on a reappraisal of your lifestyle and behave in a healthier, more balanced way. Things will only get better.

❤️ An upheaval or change will make things clearer in your emotional life, bringing you welcome relief and giving you a more balanced and sincere relationship.

👪 Matters will be cleared up on the domestic front by a challenge or change, enabling you to ensure its clear, uninterrupted stability in the future.

📋 An upheaval or change will lead to a tough and rigorous reassessment of your professional situation. However, it is for the best and is perhaps the catalyst for a positive and satisfying outcome.

🔲 Changes or challenges will shed light on your finances, making them healthier, better balanced and more secure.

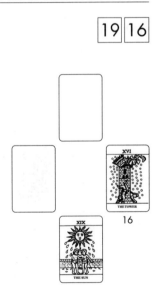

517

19 17

XVII
THE STAR
17

XIX
THE SUN
19

➕ Your wealth of natural resources will enable you to take stock of your state of health and regain your sparkling physical and emotional form.

❤ You are going to see your most heartfelt wishes and secret desires fulfilled. As a result, you will experience sincere, mutual feelings and great happiness in your emotional life.

👪 A happy event in your domestic life will soon be revealed to you or will occur and may be the answer to some long-held wishes, filling you with great joy and happiness.

📋 A new product or original idea, something unprecedented or the start of a new situation will be profitable and successful for you.

📠 You will soon find out that your financial situation has a happy and imminent surprise in store for you.

19 18

XVIII
THE MOON
18

XIX
THE SUN
19

➕ No matter what symptoms or health problems you may experience, you will have no cause for concern. They will not be serious and will be easily contained by your strength and vitality.

❤ Despite the delays, difficulties and problems that will beset you and the disappointments you will feel or the conflicts you will have to face, your emotional life will progress positively and happily.

👪 Any difficulties that arise or any conflicts or obstacles that come your way will not prevent your domestic situation from ultimately becoming positive and happy.

📋 Despite the problems, obstacles and difficulties that you will have to overcome, your position will progress in a clear, positive and favourable way.

📠 The difficulties you will encounter will not disrupt the progress and growth of your finances.

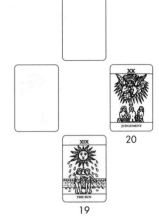

➕ No matter what your health problems or weaknesses, you will be able to take stock of your condition and make a good recovery.

❤️ A change or renewal will help to re-establish a happy situation and bring about a return to normal relations and deep, reciprocated feelings. You will then be able to enjoy your emotional life to the full.

👪 A change or revival will effect a return to normality within your family and will lead to healthier, more harmonious relationships.

📝 A proposal or beneficial change will make your professional situation clearer or, indeed, re-establish it. A beneficial event will give you cause for pleasure.

💰 Your financial situation will benefit from an upturn or positive change that will free you from various constraints or obligations currently restricting its development.

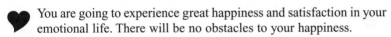

➕ The possibilities that you will be offered or the resources that will be at your disposal will ensure that you have healthy levels of energy. You will be able to use this vitality in an intelligent and positive manner.

❤️ You are going to experience great happiness and satisfaction in your emotional life. There will be no obstacles to your happiness.

👪 You will experience happiness at home and find yourself in a position to accomplish great things in your domestic life. You will then be guaranteed success in achieving your goals.

📝 Professional development and growth will enable you to establish yourself and guarantee positive results.

💰 The possibilities for growth at your disposal will guarantee you a very positive financial situation. You will then be able to take full advantage of this.

19 22

THE FOOL

22

XIX
THE SUN

19

➕ Your activities, journeys or moves will help you to make positive use of your vitality and enjoy it to the full.

❤️ Nothing will get in the way of your feelings and enthusiasm, which will, in turn, lead to great happiness in your emotional life.

👪 The journeys, trips or upheavals that could occur in your domestic life will bring you nothing but contentment.

📋 Your endeavours will bear fruit and bring you great personal and professional success.

▣ Following a business trip or a profitable step you have taken, you will have cause to feel pleased with yourself about the advantageous consequences. You will then enjoy the benefits of a very positive financial situation.

20 1

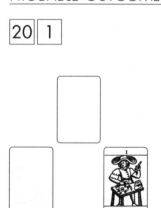

THE MAGICIAN

1

XX
JUDGEMENT

20

➕ A clever and timely initiative will enable you to recover fully or enjoy a sense of complete renewal. You will then feel fulfilled and able to enjoy your considerable potential.

❤️ Positive and intelligent moves will trigger an important renewal in your emotional life or significant changes that will help it blossom.

👪 Useful and positive initiatives will bring about important changes or developments in your family life. Alternatively, a child or young person will be able to make their mark and flourish.

📋 Skilful initiatives will help you make progress at work and put things on a new footing. New horizons will open up as a result.

▣ Your finances will be revitalized and will improve as a result of skilful, timely initiatives that open up great possibilities.

Common sense, stability and patience will enable you to recover or to revive yourself, both physically and emotionally, more quickly than you thought.

Having waited patiently, quietly and sensibly, you will finally enjoy invigorating changes in your emotional life.

The liberating change or renewal you anticipated or have been secretly working towards will probably happen more quickly than you expected.

The uplifting change, new proposal or return to normal you were expecting or relying on will probably come about more quickly than you thought.

What you were expecting or relying on, without daring to discuss or really believe in, may well take place sooner than you anticipated.

20 2

II THE HIGH PRIESTESS

2

XX JUDGEMENT

20

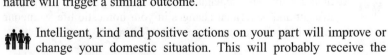 You will forced to re-establish or modify your lifestyle and adopt a more sensible and responsible attitude if you want to maintain your health and enjoy life to the full.

If a particular person is currently in your thoughts, you can be confident that they will be the catalyst for a renewal or significant change in your emotional life. Alternatively, your intelligent, generous nature will trigger a similar outcome.

Intelligent, kind and positive actions on your part will improve or change your domestic situation. This will probably receive the approval or support of a family member.

Intelligent and profitable moves will instigate progress, change or interesting suggestions at work. These will come from someone influential and will benefit from their support or meet with their approval.

Sensible and productive moves will result in a much-needed revival of your financial situation.

20 3

III THE EMPRESS

3

XX JUDGEMENT

20

20	4

The Emperor — IV

20 — JUDGEMENT

4

✚ Following the constructive advice that is offered to you or thanks to the external factors that are imposed on you, you will be able to re-establish yourself, reappraise your choices and revive your balance and inner harmony.

♥ The object of your thoughts will be the catalyst for emotional changes. Alternatively, you will be able to move ahead and prompt a happy change in your love life.

👪 Either someone in your circle or positive external elements will trigger beneficial change. You will then be able to reconsider your choices and decisions in a clear and constructive light.

🗒 Positive moves and circumstances will help you take another look at the choices and decisions you have made. You will then be able to make positive progress.

🗄 The good advice that will be given to you or other positive and material factors will enable you to reappraise your decisions and agreements and revitalize your financial situation.

20	5

The High Priest — V

20 — JUDGEMENT

5

✚ You have at your disposal all that you could need to effect a speedy recovery, a dynamic resolution of your problems or a noticeable improvement in your health.

♥ Important and reliable factors will help your love life to develop positively. It will be transformed or, at least, changed for the better.

👪 Against a stable and dependable background, you will experience significant and beneficial changes in your domestic life. Someone in your circle will give you their support or blessing.

🗒 Someone who has influence or stable and dependable factors will bring about dynamic developments and change at work. Professional matters will take a positive turn.

🗄 As long as you keep up your efforts, reliable and dependable factors will improve your financial situation and should enable you to achieve your objectives.

The choices and decisions you will be encouraged to make will help re-establish or renew your equilibrium.

The choice that you will be led to make or the free hand that you have as far as your emotions are concerned, will prompt a serious but impartial reappraisal of, or a change in, your current situation.

If you wish to re-establish order and stability you will have to make choices or reach decisions that could bring about changes or renewal in your domestic life.

You will embark on a course of action or reach an agreement that will renew or improve your situation, restoring the stability and durability it currently lacks.

Decisions or agreements will be reached that will stabilize, revive or improve your financial situation.

6

20

The efforts you have so far made will help you implement an expected change, achieve recovery or give you a new lease of life. You will draw important lessons from these.

Future efforts or on-going events will help to revitalize or change your love life, just as you wanted or expected.

You will soon discover or appreciate the significance of an improvement or change in your domestic life, which will be brought about by your own efforts or by on-going, external events.

Your own hard work or achievements will bring about change at work. You will receive the proposals or witness the improvements you wanted while achieving the goals you set yourself.

Forthcoming news of some improvement or development in your circumstances will be both propitious and instrumental in helping revive your finances.

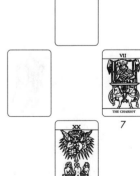

7

20

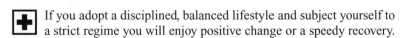

20	8

➕ If you adopt a disciplined, balanced lifestyle and subject yourself to a strict regime you will enjoy positive change or a speedy recovery.

♥ A tough but fair and impartial decision or a stable, balanced relationship will help your love life to develop positively and put it on a new footing.

👪 Balance, stability and an acute sense of what is right or wrong, fair and just, will help your domestic situation gain a new lease of life and move forward positively.

📋 Professional harmony or strict but just factors with which you will deal will help your work situation become revitalized, change for the better and flourish.

💰 You maintain a balance in your finances or impose some strict self-discipline that will bring about change and speedy and positive improvement in your fiscal situation.

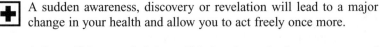

20	9

➕ A sudden awareness, discovery or revelation will lead to a major change in your health and allow you to act freely once more.

♥ A fact will be revealed that will bring dramatic change or renewed vitality to your love life. You will remain in calm control and handle the transition successfully.

👪 Caution and good sense or even newly discovered factors will help you bring about concrete and beneficial change or a revitalization of your domestic situation.

📋 Your own caution and pragmatism or, indeed, facts that you discover will trigger tangible, positive changes or an improvement in your situation.

💰 You can remain confident that as a result of either your own good sense or even recently discovered facts your finances will undergo a renewal or receive the boost they require.

Current developments will lead quite naturally to a change that will enable you to find or profit from a renewed sense of well-being.

Developments, reversals or on-going events will trigger positive and fruitful changes in your love life.

Changes or events now taking place will lead to an alteration in your domestic situation that will benefit all concerned.

Current developments will lead to a significant revitalization of your professional circumstances and a profitable change.

Events now taking place will result in an interesting improvement or very profitable developments on the financial front.

10

20

 Your self-confidence and ability to control events around you will guarantee a change leading to improved health and well-being.

Necessary changes in your love life will come about if you are self-confident and sure of your feelings, your status and the events going on around you.

Your courage, strength of character, self-belief and control over your circumstances will enable you to implement the changes or revival required in your domestic life.

Have confidence in yourself, in your status and rights and trust in the events and circumstances over which you will exercise control. You can then instigate the developments needed for further success.

You have a firm grip on your financial situation, and you can be confident of an imminent improvement on this front.

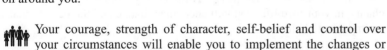
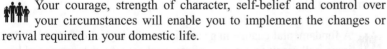

11

20

20 12

XII

THE HANGED MAN

12

XX

JUDGEMENT

20

➕ If you secure the expert advice or support of a doctor or specialist, you should be able to make a full recovery.

❤ No matter what the constraints or opposition in your love life, you may be sure that a liberating change is imminent.

👪 Obstacles or restrictions on the domestic front will crumble when imminent changes or developments become reality.

📋 No matter what delays or restrictions affect your professional progress, you will be able to sweep them aside with the help of an influential person, whose support or approval will facilitate your progress.

🗂 The restrictions and duties you face stand in the way of the opportunity to enjoy your financial resources. Change or renewal will soon alter this.

20 13

XIII

DEATH

13

XX

JUDGEMENT

20

➕ A radical change or the final resolution of your health concerns may allow you to experience a real sense of renewed vitality and enjoy a gradual return to harmony and balance.

❤ The resolution of an emotional problem or conflict will bring with it a sense of inner peace. Alternatively, following a significant change in your love life, you will encounter change and the need to make an important choice.

👪 A fundamental change in a situation or the logical conclusion of an issue will result in a period of renewed activity, autonomy and harmony in your domestic life.

📋 A major change or the logical outcome of a situation or business deal will lead to further positive progress.

🗂 Following a radical change or the logical conclusion to a transaction, you will be free to renew your decisions and agreements, re-float your business and improve your finances.

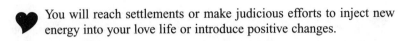 Reaching compromises or making intelligent changes will enable you to recover from an illness or enjoy a renewed feeling of dynamism and energy.

You will reach settlements or make judicious efforts to inject new energy into your love life or introduce positive changes.

Timely settlements and skilful moves will be put in place, triggering imminent and beneficial changes in your family life.

Successful negotiations, well-timed efforts and skilful settlements will bring dynamic revitalization and change to your circumstances in the near future.

Profitable negotiations and transactions, astute efforts and timely settlements will probably prove to be the right catalyst for an improvement in your finances.

14

20

After a period of excitability, reckless misuse of your energy or over-indulgence, you will experience a change in your health and recover your balance.

A change will follow a period of excess, disruption and passionate behaviour, thanks to which you will recover a measure of balance in your love life.

After a period of frenetic activity, order will be restored and your domestic situation will return to its customary peace and equilibrium.

The current unsettling disruptions or excesses in your professional life will soon be attended to and judged appropriately. Order will be restored, but you may have to have recourse to the law to bring it about.

The advantages from which you may benefit mark the start of a period of financial renewal and a return to stability.

15

20

527

20 16

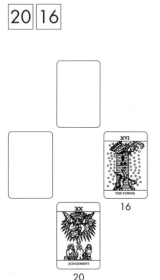

+ In the end, the effects of a salutary upheaval or a tough reappraisal will bring about a revitalizing, liberating change and a sense of real freedom on both an emotional and a physical level.

♥ An upheaval or transformation in your love life will result in a liberating change or a new and positive revival of emotions. You will realize just how important these are.

♛ Following an upheaval or sudden reappraisal of the situation, there will be a genuine and liberating change, the significance of which will not escape you.

✐ Upheavals or sudden challenges will be followed by a period of change in your situation, the true value of which you will eventually come to appreciate.

⊞ After a period of upheaval and unsettling but beneficial reviewing of your situation, your finances will undergo significant improvement.

20 17

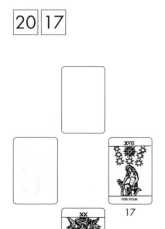

+ You will benefit from strong inner resources and favourable circumstances that should trigger a genuine revival on both a physical and an emotional level.

♥ A new or happy event, or favourable circumstances will provoke positive change and renewal on the emotional front.

♛ Encouraging circumstances and fortunate events will bring revitalization, change and positive and significant developments in your domestic situation.

✐ A happy combination of circumstances or an innovative idea or original creation may lead to real and positive changes at work.

⊞ New resources or fortunate circumstances are likely to help you refloat your affairs and instigate a positive change in your finances.

No matter what your health concerns, you will deal with them effectively, regaining self-control and restoring your physical and mental energies.

The problems, conflicts or disappointments you are experiencing in your love life will finally be resolved, leaving you in full control of subsequent developments.

Drawing on your own courage and strength, you will overcome obstacles or difficulties in your path, giving your domestic situation a new lease of life and opening the way for positive developments.

Delays, obstacles and difficulties will not prevent a revitalization or progress being made. You will then be in control of your own working life once again.

Despite the delays, difficulties and disillusion you will experience, a fortunate change will occur in your financial situation, putting you back in control.

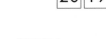

18

20

Positive and fortunate circumstances will bring with them a sense of renewal and freedom. Alternatively, should you fall ill, you will make an excellent recovery.

The happy and fortunate relationship you are enjoying represents a liberating change in your love life.

Positive elements and sincere relationships will revitalize your home life or bring a new sense of freedom.

A partnership, matters becoming clearer or personal success will bring about a liberating change, revival or rehabilitation at work.

A clarification or positive event concerning your finances will prompt a liberating change or re-establish your situation fully.

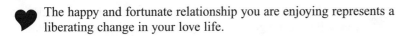

19

20

20 21

THE WORLD

21

JUDGEMENT

20

✚ The great potential you have will combine with your open and accessible nature to help you regenerate and revive yourself.

♥ Something or someone is going to be the answer to your wishes in the best possible way and make a genuine change in your love life. This will take place under excellent circumstances.

Progress in your home life should encourage positive developments, which will benefit from favourable circumstances and the support of a close contact, who is both responsible and morally irreproachable.

A genuine improvement in your professional life will have the approval and support of someone influential, and both your status and potential will be enhanced.

Excellent conditions will encourage a revival of your finances, but you will remain fully aware of the possibilities offered to you and the responsibilities they bring with them.

20 22

THE FOOL

22

JUDGEMENT

20

✚ After a period of indecision, upheaval and uncertainty or following a journey, you will experience either genuinely renewed levels of energy or a complete return to stability and well-being.

♥ A meeting or journey or the departure or arrival of someone dear to you will trigger a genuine change or renewal in your love life.

Someone in your circle will move house, go on a journey, depart or return, thereby instigating a revitalization of your domestic situation.

An act, journey or departure will trigger a key development or restore a situation to its customary order and balance.

Your efforts and research will bear fruit and give your financial affairs a new lease of life.

If you are planning to go on a long journey or undertake great things, you will be universally encouraged to do so and will really benefit as a result.

If it has not already taken place, you will experience great joy or fulfilment in your love life. You may meet someone during a journey or move or encounter a new person from distant shores.

Skilful initiatives will be the catalyst for a major change, house move or long journey or, possibly, the departure of someone close.

Thoughtful changes will help bring major plans to fruition and push back the boundaries at work. You may change your job under ideal circumstances.

Your financial situation is sure to develop rapidly and dynamically with the help of wise moves on your part. However, there will also be a few unavoidable upheavals.

The reserve or discretion you have shown will not stop you enjoying your sense of well-being or diminish your awareness of your physical and emotional potential and enjoy personal growth.

Despite the reserve, discretion or modesty demonstrated by you or the person who is close to your heart, your love life will still be able to blossom.

The discretion and wisdom demonstrated by you or by someone in your circle are sure to encourage your family situation to develop and flourish.

You have not waited in vain. Indeed, the support of someone who is influential will enable you to widen the scope of your activities, take on greater responsibilities or get a new job in a company or group.

Past self-discipline and responsible actions will place you in a stable and prosperous financial situation, of which you can take full and responsible advantage.

21 3

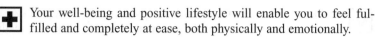

Your well-being and positive lifestyle will enable you to feel fulfilled and completely at ease, both physically and emotionally.

The feelings of the person of whom you are thinking are deep, sincere and constant. Alternatively, definite moves on your part will bring success in your love life.

Your ventures will succeed and help your domestic situation to grow and become more harmonious.

Positive and profitable changes will bring about an important agreement or contract and open up new professional horizons for you.

Your financial situation will prosper, and you will see excellent results, from which you will reap the significant rewards.

THE EMPRESS

3

THE WORLD

21

21 4

You will be in a position to enjoy personal growth and use your energy positively and enthusiastically.

Events will turn out according to your own wishes or those of someone dear to you. Everything will come together in your love life, enabling it to blossom.

No matter what intentions or objectives you have set yourself in your domestic life, you will achieve them all and enjoy happiness and contentment as a result.

You can feel assured of success in your goals and will make significant progress at work.

You can now meet your financial objectives and take full advantage of your considerable achievements.

THE EMPEROR

4

THE WORLD

21

21 5

✚ Positive, encouraging circumstances will favour your well-being which relies upon balance and harmony.

♥ A solid and reliable background will help your love life become stable and balanced and allow it to achieve its full potential.

👪 Dependable and stable factors will help your domestic situation to develop, bringing you both happiness and harmony.

📝 If you have to resort to the law, you will obtain what is rightfully yours. Alternatively, someone influential will help your situation to develop according to well-defined rules, which you would be well advised to adopt.

📊 The logical, balanced growth of your financial situation will profit from a solid and reliable background. You will be able to obtain what is rightfully yours.

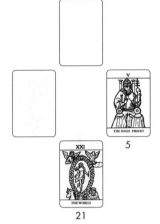

5

21

21 6

✚ The choices you make and independence you enjoy will help you in your quest for fulfilment and an untroubled sense of well-being.

♥ Important choices will help your love life to flourish, and you will become aware of the great potential on offer.

👪 Choices made, decisions taken or agreements reached will help your domestic situation make progress and bring you fulfilment.

📝 Future choices or agreements will help your professional prospects expand and your ventures succeed, possibly well beyond your hopes or expectations.

📊 You may be encouraged to make choices or reach agreements that result in significant profits, possibly outstripping your expectations.

6

21

21 7

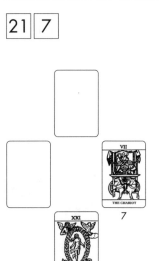

VII

THE CHARIOT

7

XXI

THE WORLD

21

➕ Your dynamic nature will play a key role in your health and its improvement. If you are planning a holiday away, rest assured that it will do you the utmost good.

♥ Future efforts and current events will favour the rapid and dynamic development of your emotional life, helping it to expand and become completely fulfilling.

👪 Steps taken or changes currently being implemented will help your domestic situation to develop and flourish.

📋 Future efforts or changes that are underway will encourage your professional position to develop quickly.

💰 You will make moves and achieve goals that bring financial gain, with more to come.

21 8

VIII

JUSTICE

8

XXI

THE WORLD

21

➕ As long as you are tough and self-disciplined, you will remain in calm and complete control of your balance and well-being.

♥ Your personal and emotional development will flourish against a steadfast, secure background. Your love life will be equally stable, and your wishes will be granted.

👪 The stability of your domestic situation or the strict regime and discipline that will be imposed on it will help it to become even stronger and reach its full potential.

📋 A sound if strict infrastructure will encourage professional progress. Based on reliable and firm foundations, your ventures will succeed.

💰 The balance and stability of your finances or the discipline with which you handle them will help your affairs to do well. You will exercise complete control over your financial situation.

You will demonstrate caution and wisdom and as a result your health will flourish. You can take advantage of your increased sense of well-being.

You are going to appreciate the intelligence and honesty of someone close to you. Their positive attitude and generosity of spirit will bring you real emotional fulfilment.

You will find ways to help your home life develop. Alternatively, you will realize how the actions and influence of a generous person in your circle will help your family situation to develop.

Factors that are revealed or that you discover will give vital support to your ambitious projects, positive moves and general expansion of your professional status.

A discovery you make or something that is revealed to you will exceed all your plans and expectations and bring some pleasant and profitable surprises.

Your general health will make significant and speedy progress. Take advantage of this to pursue the fulfilment that you desire.

Your love life will blossom under the constructive and positive influence of someone who is in your thoughts or is close to you.

The rapid, constructive progress that lies ahead in your domestic situation will owe much to the support, influence and protection of someone you know or, indeed, to your own positive actions.

Rapid changes currently taking place will enable you to extend your present boundaries, guaranteeing you greater power and widening the scope of your activities.

Developments will take place that put at your fingertips every conceivable advantage or benefit, leaving you in confident control of an increasingly healthy financial situation.

21 11

XI

STRENGTH

11

XXI

THE WORLD

21

➕ Calm control of your circumstances and your physical and intellectual qualities will allow you to achieve well-being and personal growth.

♥ Remaining in control of circumstances should ensure that you achieve all your emotional goals and your love life flourishes.

👪 Steady and uninterrupted control of circumstances will enable you to achieve everything you want for your home life. It will be totally fulfilling.

📋 Having confidence in your status and rights should help you broaden your professional horizons or bring additional, significant support for your ventures. Your projects will succeed.

🏦 Have faith in your prerogatives and resources and you can be confident that your finances will improve.

21 12

XII

THE HANGED MAN

12

XXI

THE WORLD

21

➕ Important decisions and some appropriate sacrifices are the keys to recovery from delicate health or to overcoming a tendency towards inactivity.

♥ Although you may be feeling restricted or dissatisfied, you will still find happiness in your love life.

👪 You may experience restrictions, limitations and obstacles in your domestic life, but you will still have all you need to help it expand and reach its full potential.

📋 Constraints or limitations that will be imposed on your actions or an apparent stalemate will not prevent you from coming to an important, much-anticipated agreement. You will make key decisions and reap the rewards of all your efforts.

🏦 You may be at the mercy of restrictions or limitations or you may find that you are compelled to make sacrifices, but in time you will expand your finances and make the right choices.

536

Following a radical change or important development on a physical and emotional level, your health will finally flourish.

A radical change or an important development will help you find total fulfilment in your love life.

An essential change, major development or transformation in your domestic situation will bring harmony to your family and success to all your initiatives.

As a result of a fundamental change, important expansion or the logical conclusion of a business deal, your bold initiatives and ambitious ventures should prove successful.

You will see your finances grow considerably as a result of some fundamental change, an important development or the logical and profitable conclusion of a transaction.

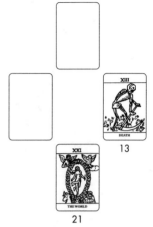

21 13

13

21

 If you are able to demonstrate flexibility and adaptability you will thrive and enjoy satisfaction and balance on both a physical and emotional level.

With the help of compromises and agreements, you will enjoy a love life that is based on solid and reliable foundations.

Compromises, agreements and understandings will assist the logical and steady development of your home life. You will help your family reach its true potential.

Current negotiations combined with future agreements and compromises will help your professional life to expand or will allow you to obtain what is rightfully yours.

Negotiations or transactions are underway, changes will occur and compromises will be reached. Your funds and resources will increase, and you will enjoy what is due to you.

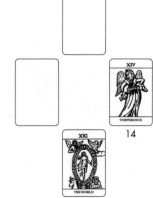

21 14

14

21

21 15

XV
THE DEVIL

15

XXI
THE WORLD

21

➕ In spite of possible excesses or your state of over-excitement, you will finally succeed in taking advantage of all your positive qualities and flourish.

♥ You will succeed in obtaining everything that you desire and hope for in your love life.

👪 Positive factors will soon help your domestic life to develop and expand, and you will feel more fulfilled than you could have hoped.

📋 The results you obtain will exceed even your most optimistic predictions. You will be able to satisfy all your ambitions and witness significant developments at home.

📋 You will achieve positive results that will surpass any previous predictions or hopes and, as a result, will be able to enjoy a very advantageous financial situation.

21 16

XVI
THE TOWER

16

XXI
THE WORLD

21

➕ A shock or upheaval may well prove liberating, and you will be able to take advantage of this freedom to enjoy your sense of well-being and successfully pursue personal goals.

♥ A major upheaval will help you find total fulfilment in your love life and allow you to make rapid, positive progress on the emotional front, just as you had hoped.

👪 Your domestic situation will develop quickly and favourably with the help of a major upheaval or sudden change. Everything will then work out as you wish.

📋 An important, sudden change or reappraisal will assist speedy developments at work, helping you to realize your ambitions with remarkable success.

📋 A key development or reappraisal will help your finances improve, and you will then be able to profit from the significant benefits that will accrue.

You are in full control of your potential and rightly confident of your excellent natural resources. It's time to take advantage of this vitality with an easy mind.

Your most cherished hopes and desires for your love life will be granted. You will obtain everything you hope for.

Every conceivable new and positive development you could wish for your family will happen. Make sure you take advantage of these beneficial circumstances.

You will profit from the constructive and positive results of all your efforts and undertakings. Make sure you take advantage of your happy and successful professional life.

Positive circumstances will encourage your finances to expand and make it possible for you to enjoy all the advantages this brings.

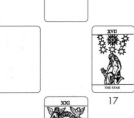

17

21

Chronic health issues or temporary conditions will prevent you from achieving your goals. You must agree to make sacrifices or concessions in order to regain your health.

Problems, upheavals and conflicts will stand in the way of a happy love life, forcing you to make difficult and frustrating concessions before you can resolve the issues.

Problems, challenges and conflicts will restrict developments on the domestic front and compel you to make sacrifices and difficult but inevitable concessions so that order can be restored.

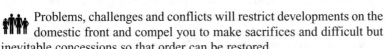

Delays, difficulties and disruptions will hamper your success at work. You will have to make concessions or sacrifices if everything is to return to normal.

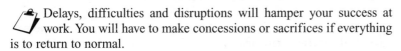

Difficulties, delays, mistakes or disappointments will restrict the expansion of your financial situation and force you to make sacrifices in order to achieve a positive outcome.

18

21

21 19

XIX

THE SUN

19

XXI

THE WORLD

21

✚ It may be necessary for you to look carefully at your health issues before you can be confident of your well-being. You will then enjoy high levels of energy and glowing health.

♥ Your emotional hopes and desires will all work out, and either you or someone close to you will guarantee this outcome.

Things augur well on the domestic front, where natural progress and development will be helped by obviously positive circumstances and by the harmony and happy atmosphere in your family.

You will achieve positive results and will enjoy success at work in partnerships, goals or new ventures and in anything you undertake on the professional front.

Your financial situation will become clearer and expand, guaranteeing profits and contentment for you.

21 20

XX

JUDGEMENT

20

XXI

THE WORLD

21

✚ After recovery or major change, you will find that you hold all the trump cards needed to enjoy your well-being and achieve fulfilment.

♥ Following a change or the revival of a situation, your love life will reach its full potential and settle down happily and harmoniously.

A change of some sort will benefit the growth or happy development of your domestic circumstances, which will occur with the support or protection of a responsible family member.

Any changes that take place will be to your advantage, and you will be supported or helped by someone influential.

Your financial situation will be improved as a result of some new and beneficial circumstances.

✚ If you are planning a recreational journey, it will more than meet all your hopes and wishes and allow you to take full advantage of your health and well-being.

♥ Following a visit, the arrival or return of the person in your thoughts or even your own journey to join that person, your love life will reach its full potential.

👪 Someone close to you will go on a journey, move house or return home. This will give rise to a period of growth and contentment.

📋 Following a business trip, an initiative or a period of transition, you will enjoy great progress at work and achieve complete success.

💰 A journey, initiative or significant movement of funds will help your financial situation develop to your advantage.

✚ Following a personal initiative or an impulsive action, you will suddenly decide to leave. Take care that you do not misuse your energy or precipitate action. If, on the other hand, you want to go away for health reasons, nothing is really stopping you.

♥ The special someone in your thoughts is on their way to see you or is impatient to reveal their feelings. Alternatively, you are going to decide to leave suddenly or to declare your own feelings.

👪 A personal initiative will make you decide to leave home suddenly, move house or change your lifestyle. It may be that all this heralds the departure or return of a young person close to you.

📋 Either following some personal initiative or in response to a desire for change, you will decide to leave suddenly or change your workplace or your role. You may become more open to new possibilities.

💰 You will take new initiatives concerning your financial situation, but you will probably have trouble resisting the temptation to spend your money recklessly or impulsively.

+ You will bide your time, think things over and remain calm in order to preserve your balance and stability. You will then feel at liberty to behave just as you wish.

♥ You will soon receive news about your love life or a new fact will be revealed. In either case, it will prompt you to leave suddenly or decide to travel to the person in your thoughts.

♟ Something you are expecting and secretly working towards is going to work out suddenly. Alternatively, something new will emerge to make changes to your domestic situation. Imminent news could prompt you to leave.

✎ You will be cautious and make all the necessary preparations before you feel ready to leave. Alternatively, you will work quickly and efficiently to achieve your aims or bring about a major change in your professional situation.

⬛ After a period of patient caution, you will be able to act more freely within your financial limits but without disrupting their foundations.

+ Your actions will be dictated by your instinct and should prove helpful to your well-being and enable you to enjoy it to the full.

♥ An open and generous attitude will be rewarded by rapid progress in your love life. Alternatively, someone special is coming to join you or you will suddenly decide to go off and meet them.

♟ Positive actions, probably undertaken by someone close, will help your domestic situation to develop, introducing change or a profitable house move.

✎ New, positive circumstances will help you make quick and profitable progress. Your plans and ideas can now take shape, although you will have to be proactive and willing to travel.

⬛ Financial success will give you the freedom to undertake some profitable ventures or initiate the successful movement of funds. You will be able to use your money as you originally intended.

✚ Armed with self-confidence and a belief in the correctness of your decisions, you can enjoy the opportunity to travel and use your energy as you wish, without fear of impairing your general state of health.

♥ Confident that your decisions and intentions are right, you can make progress in your love life. Someone you are thinking of is coming to join you, and their feelings and intentions are obvious.

♟ A positive and encouraging set of circumstances or the shrewd advice and support of someone close to you will help your domestic situation change or develop smoothly, including moving house.

✎ A secure background or the significant support of someone else will help you succeed in your actions, proposals and enterprises.

⊞ Positive factors or shrewd advice will bring about a change in your financial affairs or in any plans involving travel and the movement of your funds.

✚ You have the right or duty to travel, probably for health reasons. Alternatively, the intervention of a doctor or specialist will put your mind completely at rest about health matters.

♥ A special someone will soon join you, and you will find that their feelings and intentions are serious and trustworthy. Alternatively, you are going to have to leave to join the person you love and stabilize your relationship.

♟ You may have to travel or take serious steps concerning your domestic situation. Alternatively, following a major change, you will soon manage to stabilize matters.

✎ You will probably have to travel, take a business trip, undertake some research or take some other productive steps. The results should enable you to benefit from the major support that will result and help you to stabilize your situation.

⊞ Sincere support is a reliable and positive factor in your efforts to stabilize your financial situation. It will facilitate your actions or travel plans or the important movement of funds.

22 6

✚ After a period of indecision and instability, you will make some important choices and key decisions abruptly. When things ease up somewhat, you will focus on achieving balance and stability.

♥ A period of uncertainty and instability and the lack of responsibility in your love life will precede important and imminent choices.

👪 Vacillation and ambiguity will be followed by a rapid decision or agreement to leave or move house or to make a sudden change of some kind.

📋 A journey, business trip, move of office or the arrival of a third person will follow a period of indecision and uncertainty. This will enable you to come to a speedy agreement or make choices about your situation, all of which will enable you to regain some freedom of action.

⊞ Your uncertainty and indecision will come to an end when you undertake a journey or take an initiative that will allow you to resume your financial independence and freedom of choice.

---

22 7

✚ If you are thinking of making a recreational trip or journey for health reasons, bear in mind that it will do you the utmost good. Alternatively, you will feel free now to make the efforts needed to sort out your problems and overcome your weaknesses.

♥ You will achieve your aims enthusiastically and passionately, or you will bring about what you want in your love life. It may prove to be turbulent and exciting, but nonetheless it will be positive.

👪 Your domestic situation is going to experience a turbulent, exciting period that will enable you to improve your family's standard of living, move house or rapidly achieve some domestic objectives.

📋 Past efforts or events that are currently happening will soon enable you to achieve your objectives, improve your situation or help you forge ahead. You can be certain of success no matter what you do.

⊞ A request, house move, business trip or sudden windfall will soon enable you to achieve your financial objectives.

22 | 8

Doubtless you will be obliged to submit yourself to some self-discipline, forcing you to seek balance rapidly and to assure yourself of your stability and vitality.

A strict regime will soon force you to curb your reckless, volatile and thoughtless behaviour and to seek stability in your love life.

You will have to face difficult and tough demands in order to establish domestic stability. Control your impulsive nature, impose self-discipline and adopt the rules and principles governing your domestic life.

Serious constraints will make it necessary for you to involve the law to maintain your position or obtain what is rightfully yours.

Tough restrictions will force you to limit your reckless expenditure and regain financial stability as soon as possible by adopting a regime of self-discipline and restraint.

8

22

22 | 9

You will soon realize or caution will dictate that you need to take a break. Relax and make time to ask yourself some useful questions.

You are going to discover something that will prompt you to leave suddenly, declare your true feelings or reveal what you now know. Correct your mistakes and avoid repeating them.

You will hear news or become aware of something that will initiate a potential change of situation or a house move. Approach all change cautiously, pragmatically and with circumspection.

News or fresh information will come your way and will provoke pragmatic, cautious and thoughtful behaviour, which will enable you to achieve your targets or results at work.

You are going to hear news that will urge caution on your actions or expenditure. It will also prompt you to find answers that are practical and useful for improving your finances.

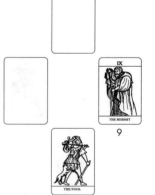

9

22

22 10

➕ You are going to enjoy a rapid improvement in your general health but you will still feel somewhat unstable and excitable and experience significant mood swings.

❤ Prevailing circumstances or events will affect the rapid progress of your love life, involving a change of situation, a departure or return or, alternatively, fresh discoveries.

👪 Circumstances or current events prompt a rapid development or change on the domestic front, or a house move or journey.

📋 Current changes or events will quickly help your situation improve, facilitating your initiatives and prompting impressive solutions and rapid results.

💰 Your financial situation will soon improve, thanks to new circumstances or events, which will smooth the progress of initiatives or any journey to do with your money.

22 11

➕ Control exerted over both current circumstances and yourself will enable you to make the right use of your natural energy and avoid any mistakes, over-indulgence or reckless behaviour.

❤ Remaining in control of circumstances and your emotions will soon allow you to achieve what you want in your love life.

👪 Combining a firm control over events with strong, reliable domestic foundations will help bring about positive change, a house move or potential journey.

📋 Self-confidence and an awareness of your rights at work will help you to change your situation or to strengthen your position through the success of your ventures and initiatives.

💰 You feel secure in your stable financial situation and are confident of the success of all you undertake.

✚ You tend to be too impatient and impulsive in the face of the health problems you encounter, and you are in danger of making the same mistakes again, so be on your guard.

♥ You are trying to extricate yourself from a relationship that is going nowhere. For the time being, all you can do is curb your impatience, impulsiveness and thoughtlessness.

👪 You will try to change your domestic situation quickly or leave or move house. However, obstacles will hinder you, and you will have to give up your plan or come to the conclusion that it is pointless.

📋 You will be forced to make a change in your work, or obstacles will prevent you from implementing this change and hamper your initiatives or travel plans.

💷 You are constrained by current financial regulations and obligations. All you can do is to put up with them rather than try to escape from them. Alternatively, avoid irresponsible expenditure in the future.

12

22

✚ A radical change in your behaviour or a sudden event connected with your health will prompt you to leave abruptly, turn over a new leaf or perhaps change your lifestyle.

♥ A situation or relationship will come to an end and force you to leave suddenly, with no hope of return, but also with no regrets. This will mark the start of a new chapter in your love life.

👪 The end of a situation or a period of your life will urge you to leave abruptly or change your lifestyle altogether. Alternatively, a loss in the family will cause you to make a journey.

📋 The end of a situation is forcing you to leave or to change tack or your place of work. It could be that, following a dramatic change or the end of a business deal, you will take positive steps at work.

💷 A considerable windfall will accrue to you after the logical conclusion of a profitable transaction. Alternatively, your resources will dry up, prompting you to seek immediate help, support or financial aid.

13

22

22 14

XIV

TEMPERANCE

14

THE FOOL

22

➕ The compromises or agreements you have reached will probably give you the chance to travel for health or leisure. This will both relax and invigorate you.

❤ Agreements or compromises will leave you free to depart or return or help you to adapt more flexibly to current circumstances and events in your love life.

👪 Agreements and compromises will help you move house or enable you to depart and return in the best of circumstances.

📋 Negotiations will soon enable you to reach profitable agreements and adapt your position so that it is more appropriate to your current circumstances and requirements.

📠 Agreements or compromises will enable you to adapt your financial situation to new circumstances and demands, facilitating transactions or the timely movement of funds.

22 15

XV

THE DEVIL

15

THE FOOL

22

➕ Your current state of hyperactivity and your lack of concern about the problems involved could well lead you to commit thoughtless and negligent acts and take pointless, impulsive risks.

❤ You will probably be in the grip of a passionate relationship, which will be more a question of satisfying impulses and assuaging desires than feeling any true emotions. You should think seriously about the consequences of what you are doing.

👪 The general chaos or intense emotional climate prevailing in your domestic life may prompt a sudden departure, move or exaggerated response. You would do well to think about the consequences.

📋 You will not rest until you have achieved your aims, obtained some longed-for results or satisfied your ambitions and desires. Stay calm, even if everything around you seems to be happening too quickly.

📠 You will not rest until you have succeeded in achieving your financial goals and satisfying your ambitions and need for money. However, you will have to take into account the imminent consequences of any actions.

A shock, impulse or whim will provoke your sudden departure. You could then make regrettable mistakes or commit thoughtless acts. Be very cautious.

Following an upheaval, shock, break-up or change in your love life, you will leave suddenly or the other person involved will leave you, impulsively or in a fit of anger.

A material or emotional upheaval will lead to a rushed departure, rapid house move or an abrupt change of circumstances.

An inevitable but salutary upheaval will cause an abrupt reappraisal, a sudden departure or rapid alteration in your situation.

A surprise or change will prompt you to leave abruptly, take immediate action or travel in order to release your finances. However, thoughtless financial moves could result in the loss of your money.

16

22

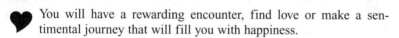

Fortunate circumstances will allow you to travel for health or leisure reasons, leaving you feeling invigorated both emotionally and physically.

You will have a rewarding encounter, find love or make a sentimental journey that will fill you with happiness.

After a period of patient anticipation, fortune will smile on you and you will enjoy a house move, change of situation, family visit or something new and pleasant in your domestic circumstances.

Beneficial circumstances favour the success of your actions or any innovation and will be the answer to your professional aspirations.

You will be able to make progress or embark on a journey to acquire new resources or realize your financial hopes.

17

22

22 18

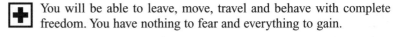

No matter what your health problems, you are soon going to be able to throw them off. If you are convalescing, avoid any premature departures and think before you act.

No matter what problems you confront, disappointments you experience or mistakes you make, you will manage to extricate yourself from them by an abrupt departure. Alternatively, your partner will leave suddenly and for the better.

Conflicts, difficulties and worries will force you to make a sudden departure or prompt you to leave home or your domestic circle abruptly. It might be more sensible to ask yourself how this situation has come about.

All sorts of problems, conflicts and difficulties will force you to leave abruptly and seek immediate, positive solutions or urge you to change your job as soon as possible.

You will have to seek aid and support quickly or go in search of new resources in order to solve your problems and extricate yourself from your financial difficulties.

22 19

You will be able to leave, move, travel and behave with complete freedom. You have nothing to fear and everything to gain.

The person you love is travelling to see you, or you will soon embark on a romantic journey. Alternatively, a happy event will allow you to leave or settle down with the person you love.

A happy event or the harmony of your domestic situation will benefit from a change in your circumstances, a house move or from a happy family journey.

An agreement, partnership or revelation will bring about speedy change and enable you to make the necessary moves or embark on a journey to further the progress and success of your initiatives and affairs.

Fortunate developments or an increased understanding on the financial front will enable you to use your advantages, take profitable action or travel.

✚ After recovering your health and returning to normal, you will be able to travel for leisure or to convalesce. Alternatively, you will be able to set off again on the right foot.

♥ Following a return to normal, or having got your situation back on the right footing, the person you love will soon be able to come to you. Alternatively, you will leave suddenly to join your partner.

👪 A revitalization of some sort, a change in your circumstances or a return to normal in your home life will mean that you can travel freely, move house or take a journey with your family.

📋 You will be able to give speedy answers to any proposals made to you. Alternatively, a renewal will make it possible for you to change your situation, take action or travel for business reasons.

💰 Following the revival, re-floating or recovery of your financial situation, you will be able to make a business trip or initiate a useful movement of funds.

22 20

20

22

✚ You will enjoy excellent health, and this will allow you to embark on a long journey, make plans for the future and fulfil your potential.

♥ Everything will come together to enable you to achieve your desires. You will find the person you love or enjoy an important encounter and a fulfilled love life.

👪 Your domestic situation will fulfil its potential under ideal conditions, making it possible for you to implement plans to move house, widen your horizons or undertake some long journeys.

📋 Great possibilities become available to you or positive, effective plans are already underway to help you forge ahead, widen the scope of your business or change your work situation in a positive way.

💰 Excellent financial prospects are within reach. Alternatively, you will benefit from fortunate circumstances that will enable you to use your resources freely and enjoy them to the full.

22 21

21

22

Bibliography

Beni, L., *Votre destinée par les tarots* (De Vecchi 1989)

Bevilaqua, M., *Les tarots à votre porteé* (Artefact 1986)

Court de Gebelin, A., *Le tarot* (Berg International 1983)

Dicta, F., *Le tarot de Marseille* (Mercure de France 1981)

De Veer, O., *Les secrets du tarot divinatoire* (Solar 1986)

Hadar, K., *Le livre du tarot: la clef de votre évolution* (Courteau, L. 1985)

Kaplan, *La grande encyclopédie du tarot* (Sand)

Lind, F., *Le tarot* (Garancière 1985)

Lionel, F., *Le tarot magique* (Rocher 1980)

Simon, S., Picard M., *Le langage secret du tarot* (Sand)

Simon, S., *Le tarot: l'avenir dans les cartes* (Nathan 1986)

Turpaud, M.F., *La maîtrise du tarot divinatoire* (Solar 1987)

Ugerin, G., *Les tarots de Marseille* (De Vecchi 1989)

Victor, J.L., *Le tarot chinois* (Peyret, Y. 1987)

Virgne, P., *Le tarot: connaître son destin* (Encre 1985)

Wirth, O., *Le tarot des imagiers du Moyen-Age* (Sand)

Amber, K. and Azrael Arynn, K., *Heart of Tarot: an Intuitive Approach* (Llewellyn Publications 2002)

Bunning, Joan, *Learning the Tarot* (Samuel Weiser 1998)

Campbell, Joseph, *Tarot Revelations* (Vernal Equinox Press 1987)

Decker, Ronald and Dummett, Michael *The History of Occult Tarot* (Gerald Duckworth 2002)

Fiorini, Jeanne, *Invitation to Wonder* (Suite One Design Group 2002)

Giles, Cynthia, *The Tarot: History, Mystery and Lore* (Fireside Books 1994)

Gordon, Richard and Taylor, Dixie, *The Intuitive Tarot* (Blue Dolphin 1994)

Gray, Eden, *A Complete Guide to the Tarot* (Bantam Books 1979)

Greer, Mary K., *Tarot for Your Self: A Workbook for Personal Transformation* (New Page Books 2002)

Kaplan, Stuart R., *Encyclopedia of Tarot* (United States Games Systems 1988)

Jayanti, Amber, *Living the Tarot* (Wordsworth Editions 2000)

Jette, Christine, *Tarot Shadow Work* (Llewelleyn 2000)

Ouspensky, P.D., *The Symbolism of the Tarot* (Dover Publications 1976)

Pollack, Rachel, *Seventy Eight Degrees of Wisdom* (Harper Collins 1997)

Porter, Tracy. *The Tarot Companion* (Llewellyn 2000)

Sharman-Burke, Juliet, *The Complete Book of Tarot: A Step-by-Step Guide to Reading the Cards* (St Martin's Press 1996)

Card illustrations on the cover and inside the book:
Bibliothèque nationale, *Tarot de Vergnano*, 16th century, Italy and *Henry Dreyfuss Book of Symbols*, McGraw-Hill (1972) D.R.

YOUR
PERSONAL
NOTES